The Politics of Taxation

COMPARATIVE POLITICS

Edited by Gillian Peele

Lady Margaret Hall, Oxford

Books in the Series:

Colin Campbell, SJ *Bureaucracies*

John Francis *Regulation*

Bruce Graham *Representation and Party Politics*

Philip Norton *Legislatures*

Graham K. Wilson *Interest Groups*

Figure

The Politics of Taxation

A Comparative Perspective

B. Guy Peters

BLACKWELL
Cambridge MA & Oxford UK

First published 1991

Basil Blackwell, Inc.
3 Cambridge Center
Cambridge, Massachusetts 02142, USA

Basil Blackwell Ltd
108 Cowley Road, Oxford, OX4 1JF, UK

Library of Congress Cataloging in Publication Data
Peters, B. Guy.
The Politics of Taxation: A Comparative Perspective / B. Guy Peters.
p. cm. – (Comparative politics)
Includes bibliographical references and index.
ISBN 1–55786–210–9 (alk. paper) – ISBN 1–55786–211–7 (alk. paper)
1. Taxation. 2. Comparative government. I. Title. II. Series: Comparative politics (Oxford, England)
HJ2305.P46 1991
336.2—dc20 91–25264
CIP

British Library Cataloguing in Publication Data
A CIP catalogue record for this book is available from the British Library.

Typeset in 10½ on 12½ pt Sabon
by Photo·graphics, Honiton, Devon
Printed in Great Britain by T.J. Press Ltd, Padstow

This book is printed on acid-free paper.

Contents

Tables and Figure

Tables

Preface to the Series

This new series in comparative politics has been designed with three broad objectives in mind. In the first instance it is hoped that, by focusing on a number of contemporary themes and issues in comparative politics, the individual studies may cumulatively make a contribution to the subject. Comparative politics has never been an easy discipline; and the subject has become more difficult as conceptual approaches have proliferated and the weight of material available to scholars has increased. As a result there has been a certain fragmentation as the task of refining the conceptualization has become separated from the detailed studies of institutions and political processes across political systems.

This tendency for discussions of the framework of comparative politics to become divorced from the subject's empirical research agenda has certainly been debilitating for the discipline. But it has also been misleading for the student. A second aim of the series is therefore to fill a gap in the literature by providing volumes which will combine empirical and theoretical material in easily accessible form. Each study will introduce the student to the current debates between political scientists about the major issues involved in the comparative study of a particular subject. However, each study will also deploy sufficient information drawn from a range of political systems to enable the reader to evaluate those debates for himself.

A third goal of the series is to take account of recent political developments which make it necessary to look at governmental systems in new ways. The enhanced importance of supra-national institutions (such as the European Community) and the resurgence of free market doctrines are but two examples of changes in the political landscape which have major implications for the organization of government in a number of states. Thus in addition to the familiar canon of topics in comparative politics, the series will contain studies which explore themes which are perhaps less frequently handled in a comparative manner. The series will contain volumes on such central subjects as legislatures and pressure groups; but studies which examine taxation, regulation and the politicization of bureaucracies have also been commissioned.

Although this series has been designed with clear goals in mind, the individual authors have been allowed to exercise their judgement about which countries they include in their discussions. The only requirement is that they should provide an introduction both to the theoretical debates about their chosen theme and to the way the issue presents itself in the context of modern government.

Guy Peters' study of taxation – which is the second volume in the series to be published – tackles a subject which has too often been neglected by students of comparative government, despite the centrality of the topic to politics and public administration. As Professor Peters shows, taxation is not simply a technical exercise designed to raise enough money to allow government to fund their programmes and their debts. It involves a range of choices which will be politically driven by such factors as the values of a society and the preferences of political actors such as parties and pressure groups. Moreover, a country's adminstrative structure will exercise a powerful influence over the mix of taxes which is adopted. A country's taxation structure is thus a useful prism through which to examine other key political issues such as its public philosophy and its capacity to implement public policy. However, as Professor Peters' discussion underlines, there is much to be gained from looking at the problems of taxation policy in comparative perspective rather than simply from the standpoint of a single political system. Many advanced industrial countries in the recent past have engaged in similar kinds of programmes of tax reform; and many have encountered similar difficulties in relation to funding extensive programmes in democracies where the citizenry has become increasingly averse to paying taxes and has given organized expression to that aversion in a variety of ways, including the passage of Proposition 13 in California and the continuing opposition to the community charge (or poll tax) in Great Britain.

Professor Peters brings to this study a wealth of relevant expertise. He is familiar with the structure of government and public administration in a range of political systems but he is especially knowledgeable about the United States, Great Britain and Scandinavia. It is important also that he is sensitive to the theoretical literature on the many intersecting areas of public administration covered by his study. I am therefore extremely pleased to be able to include this volume in the series and hope that it will shed new light on an issue which has occasioned many western governments no little amount of concern in recent years.

Gillian Peele
Lady Margaret Hall
Oxford

Preface

This book represents the culmination of a long (probably too long) period of thinking and research about tax policy. The good news is that the subject has become no less interesting during the time that I have been working on it. Indeed, some of the delay in completing the project is a function of the numerous changes in national policies, and the consequent need to rewrite, and then rewrite some more. Even with that, events may outpace the words recorded here between completing the manuscript and its publication. If that does not occur prior to publication, it is almost certain to occur thereafter, although the basic themes and patterns will persist. The increased visibility of, and interest in, tax policy has been sparked in part by the numerous tax reforms adopted in the 1980s and 1990s. A number of countries have seen fundamental changes in their tax policies, and citizens have found new tax regimes to complain about, and to avoid. Further, especially in the United States, the crisis over the budget deficit and the discussion of taxes which might help solve the problem have increased awareness of tax policies and their impacts. Most citizens have been vaguely aware of the taxes they have paid, but it is now difficult for any thinking citizen not to think about the "contributions" that he or she is making to the continuing revenue needs of the public sector.

It seems especially important to examine tax policy comparatively. Most citizens are aware of their present contributions to the public sector, but they may think of only a very limited range of possibilities for financing government. That limited range may be the same even for reasonably sophisticated citizens and policymakers who might have been expected to think more broadly about their revenue options. A great deal of tax policy therefore appears to be conditioned by the collective experiences and cultures of countries. By examining the opportunities for public finance comparatively, therefore, we can illuminate the options available to governments and perhaps point to mixes of taxes and other means of finance that would be viable. There is the danger of learning too much too fast, and not understanding adequately the cultural and institutional foundations of particular tax mixes, but at least the opportunity for learning is presented.

In addition to the potential practical benefits of studying tax policy comparatively, there are significant intellectual benefits for the advancement of political science and policy studies. As I discuss tax policy in this book, I will be making two types of comparison. One will be an explicit comparison of tax policies across the industrialized democracies, pointing to the similarities and differences in their policy choices. The other, generally more implicit, will be between tax policy and other types of public policy. There have been a number of assumptions in the literature that tax policy and the process by which it is made differ significantly from other policy areas. I have not tested those assumptions systematically in this book, but point to a number of instances in which they do appear supported. In fact, in some instances tax policies and the tax policy process appear to correspond more closely across countries than they do with other policy areas within a single country. These similarities are likely to increase as the internationalization of economies forces greater uniformity in the treatment of financial affairs in the industrialized world.

This book will be somewhat unusual in that it is a political science book about tax policy. Public finance and tax policy traditionally have been the domain of economists, lawyers, and accountants who have been able to dominate the discussion with narrow technical expertise. The question of how government will raise its raxes, and the associated question of how it will spend money, are central political issues and should therefore be addressed politically. My belief, supported by the evidence I have collected, is that although economic and legal considerations may be used to initiate a discussion of tax policy, it is politics that will decide the outcome of the discussion and the final shape of the laws. This may not be the best finding for the economic well-being of the society, but it is still the nature of the process of making public policy. In this way at least tax policy is little different from other policies.

As mentioned above, this is very much a book about tax policies in the industrialized democracies. This choice of locale was made for a variety of reasons. One was the simple practical matter that the Organization for Economic Operation and Development (OECD) produces excellent comparable data on the governments of its member countries so that the presentation and analysis of data was greatly facilitated. In addition, my own interest and expertise lies with the developed democracies rather than other political systems. On a more intellectual level, comparisons of revenue collection across the whole range of countries in the world might produce such extreme differences that extensive description and discussion of exceptional cases would dominate the discussion. This description might be interesting, but also would make advancing the more analytical concerns in this enterprise that much more difficult.

I should express my gratitude to a number of people who have made this book possible. First, Richard Rose initially got me to think about tax policy as a viable subject for political scientists and has continued to provide useful insights into the issues through his own work and our conversations. Gillian Peele has been a helpful and constructive critic of earlier drafts, and has been effective at prodding me to finish the manuscript even when yet another tax reform looms on the horizon. First Sean Magee and then later Simon Prosser at Blackwell's also have been encouraging and helpful. The Hochschule St Gallen, and especially Professor Ernst Buschor, provided a very congenial locale in which to write a draft of much of the mansucript while looking out at the Säntis. A number of graduate students at the University of Pittsburgh, most notably Julio Carrion, Raylene Boots, and Anthony Zito, provided substantial research assistance. Finally, as ever, my family has borne the brunt of obsession.

1
Understanding Tax Policy

This will be a book about tax policy in industrialized democracies. Any government must find the means to pay for its own existence and for the services it provides to citizens. Taxation, therefore, is an essential activity if there is to be a government, but their necessity does not make the taxes any more popular. Citizens generally dislike paying taxes, and therefore politicians dislike passing laws calling for new or increased taxes. George Bush made a great deal of political mileage in the 1988 presidential campaign in the United States by telling people to "Read my lips – No new taxes." His reneging on that promise in 1990 may present several political difficulties for him in a try for reelection. The trick for government is to find ways to pay for themselves and their services while escaping the wrath, or perhaps even the notice, of their citizens.

Achieving the political balance between needed revenue and popular reactions involves not only decisions about the amount of tax money being extracted from citizens, but also how that money is raised. Some taxes (especially the income tax) are very visible to citizens and are more likely to produce political repercussions than are less visible taxes such as the value-added tax. Also, a large number of taxes charged at lower rates usually will generate less political opposition for a government than will a few taxes charged at higher rates, although the administrative costs for government will be much greater with the number of smaller taxes. Thus, governments have a number of important and delicate decisions to make when they choose their tax policies.

I will concentrate my attention on the political issues involved in tax policy, but there are a number of other issues involved as well. Many of these are economic, and the discipline of economics has tended to dominate the study of taxation. The principal question which economics raises is what effect will the tax policies have on economic growth, and on the efficient use of resources in the national economy (Musgrave and Musgrave, 1984). The economics literature tends to place substantial emphasis on the distortions which taxation may create within economies, and therefore attempts to develop optimal systems of taxation that can generate needed public revenues without any serious distortions. This approach generally argues for low levels of taxation, and for broadly-based tax systems that collect some revenues from a variety of sources. It also tends to argue for granting very few special treatments for different types of income or expenditures – tax loopholes.

These desires by economists for simplicity and uniformity are often in conflict with political pressures, which tend to create numerous specialized benefits for groups, and even individuals, through the tax system. For example, governments have found it more convenient to subsidize middle-class housing by offering tax relief on mortgage payments than to provide a direct subsidy. Because tax policy is perceived to be extremely technical by politicians and citizens, it is often easier for political entrepreneurs to create benefits by taxation than through expenditures (Manley, 1970; Witte, 1985). The same amount of benefit that would be obvious in an expenditure bill can be easily hidden in tax legislation.

Another of the concerns expressed by economists over tax policy is its potential effects on the distribution of wealth and income in a society. This again is often motivated by a concern with economic efficiency, and with the continuing maximum participation of citizens in the labor market (Hausman, 1981; Blomquist and Hansson-Brusewitz, 1990). The practical concern can, however, coincide with a more deeply ethical and social policy concern with the effects of tax policy on people, and especially on the poor (Page, 1983, 22–41). The more wealthy and powerful in a society generally have greater political influence than do the poor, and have been able to shape most tax systems to suit themselves. This influence may have produced perceived (and real) inequities, and yet another set of criteria comes into play when we consider tax policy. These are the criteria of justice and fairness, and the possibilities of achieving those goals through the tax system – and through the expenditures funded by that taxation. These more philosophical criteria may be interpreted very differently by different people (Rawls, 1972; Nozick, 1974) but still constitute important factors in evaluating the impacts of tax policies on society.

Taxes are enacted by law, but the money they attempt to raise does not roll in automatically. Taxes must be administered, and people in government must devise means to collect the money that government is owed. Some taxes are easier to collect than are others. Sales tax in American states and cities, for example, is collected for government by merchants and is a simple percentage of their sales. On the other hand, income tax in most countries may be charged at a number of different rates with a number of possible exemptions and deductions; deciding who owes how much income tax is a very difficult task. Not only are different taxes more or less difficult to administer, but governments can make choices that can minimize those difficulties. For example, in the United States, Canada, Sweden, and several other countries citizens are required to assess themselves for the income tax, while in most countries government itself does the assessment. The Internal Revenue Service in the United States, and its counterparts elsewhere, must still check to be sure that citizens have been honest and accurate when they have computed their taxes, but the amount of work and personnel required by government itself is still much less (See chapter 9). Therefore, another set of criteria to consider when making tax policy choices is how difficult the tax is to implement, and what revenue yield can be had at what cost.

We now have at least four sets of criteria to utilize when talking about tax policy – politics, economics, ethics, and administration. In this policymaking game, however, politics is trumps. None of the other criteria will carry much weight unless government is willing to accept it and enact it into law through the political process. Therefore, this chapter will concentrate on possible political explanations for tax policy choices, and it will be a review of the existing literature in the field. Although tax policy has been somewhat neglected by political scientists relative to other policy fields, there is still a substantial and interesting literature upon which to draw (Hansen, 1983; Steinmo, 1989; Robinson and Sandford, 1983; Hadenius, 1986; Good, 1980; Wilkes, 1980). This chapter therefore will set the stage for the remainder of the book, and its concerns with the politics of taxation. In addition, some of the themes introduced here will be returned to in subsequent chapters, as an attempt is made to provide explanations for the tax choices made by industrialized democracies, as well as for their differing levels of budget deficit.

The Political Roots of Tax Policy

Although often made to appear very technical and difficult to understand, tax policy is in many ways just another type of public policy. It is made in approximately the same manner and the process of adoption can be conceptualized through much the same process model as used for other types of policy (Jones, 1986). In addition, tax policy has the same types of effects on citizens as do other policies; it advantages some and disadvantages others. Tax policies, however, provoke stronger reactions from citizens than do many other policies, and may have to be adjusted frequently to meet changing political and economic circumstances (Hogwood and Peters, 1983). With these similarities to other types of policies, tax policy should be explicable through many of the same models and concepts.

At the same time, however, tax policy is also somewhat different. All policies have their own peculiarities, but tax policy is somewhat more distinctive than are others. First, although all citizens must pay taxes, few claim to understand tax policy (unlike policy domains such as education or transportation). It is perceived as sufficiently technical and complex that most citizens simply grumble and pay their taxes. Second, more than most other policies, the formulation of tax policy tends to be dominated by economists and lawyers. Lawyers are concerned with writing tax laws that are sufficiently watertight for government to collect the revenue it should. Economists are concerned with the potential negative economic effects of taxes and ways to prevent them (Aaron and Pechman, 1981). Again, both groups must accede to political concerns if there are conflicts, but these experts are heavily involved in giving advice during the formulation stage of tax policy. Politics in this arena may involve mustering experts as well as mustering interest groups.

A third distinctive feature of taxation is that politicians can rarely use this policy area for their advantage in electoral politics. They are able to gain a great deal of power within the institutions of government by a thorough knowledge of tax policy, but citizens may not really appreciate the politicians responsible for tax laws. Even tax legislation which benefits many people, such as the tax reforms of the 1980s, may have harmful consequences politically. Those who are harmed by the legislation are more likely to remember who was involved than those who benefit, and any tax legislation simply places the issue of taxation before an unappreciative public. Only a relatively few politicians, such as Russell Long of Louisiana, have been able to achieve political popularity through their control of tax policy.

Finally, a great deal of tax policy is made while it is being implemented. Try as they might, the lawyers and politicians drafting tax legislation can think of only a small portion of the individual circumstances that can arise, and therefore a great deal of tax policy must be made as the collecting agencies confront individual taxpayers and the complex cases they present. Implementation is important in defining the real meaning of any policy (Pressman and Wildavsky, 1973), but appears to have an even greater impact in taxation than in other policy areas. Even more than most other policy areas, citizens have an interest in finding ways to circumvent the laws, and the implementors must determine which ways out of paying more tax are legal. Further, most citizens often are afraid of the tax authorities and may not contest the tax bureaucracies' rulings, thus giving greater latitude and authority to those bureaucracies.

With both the similarities and dissimilarities of tax policy to other types of public policy in mind, a number of possible political explanations for the policy choices made by governments will now be considered. These explanations will range across the various subfields of political science and policy studies, but all must take into account the pronounced difficulties that governments encounter in formulating and implementing a set of policies that are so essential to their survival, but which are almost never popular among the public. Further, an attempt will be made to take into account the different political circumstances of the OECD countries, and the consequences those political differences have for tax policy.

Political Culture

Perhaps the most general possible explanation for the differences in tax policies found among countries is that there are national styles of taxation, or that the political culture of a country tends to drive government toward formulating one type of solution rather than another for its tax problems. For example, it is often argued that the anti-statist values of many French and Italian citizens, and the consequent high levels of evasion of direct personal taxes, produce tax systems highly dependent upon indirect taxation (Haycraft, 1985, 107–8). Similarly, the tradition of property taxes as a means of financing local government (at least until Mrs Thatcher and the community charge) in the Anglo-American democracies generated much greater dependence upon that form of taxation in those countries than in others. In the United States the social security tax, justified as an insurance "contribution" rather than a real tax, has been more acceptable than other means of funding social programs. My own earlier research (Peters, 1980; see pp. 58–64 below) found stable clusterings of taxation patterns among groups of industrialized democracies that persisted even with economic and political change. Thus, there does appear to be some justification for a cultural explanation of tax choices. These findings about tax policy are but a few manifestations of the argument King (1975) advanced that the best way to understand public policies is to understand the ideas and values which undergird them.

There may be good political reasons for a government to accept the political culture argument, in the form of the status quo, as its tax policy. This is, if a system for raising revenue exists already, and the taxes in operation are generating revenue at a reasonably acceptable rate, then that structure is probably at least minimally acceptable to the population. It therefore makes sense for the government simply to permit that system to continue to function and to generate such revenue as it will. Marginal adjustments to the tax system may be made for ideological or practical reasons, but the status quo ante may be a good guide to current policy (Rose and Karran, 1986). This argument assumes, as do other incremental arguments, that the past has been functional and has produced an array of policies which the public finds congenial and which corresponds to the basic political values of that public (March and Olsen, 1989). This is a very conservative proposition, but one which may be substantially safer politically than are adventurous forays which require altering the existing tax policies to suit a new government's ideological or economic precepts.

Further, it is important to note the extent to which tax reform has proceeded differently in different political systems. Although there has been a sense of world-wide tax reform, the major action has been in the Anglo-American democracies rather than in the continental systems – with the exception of the Federal Republic of Germany (pre-reunification) (Hagemann, Jones, and Montador, 1988) – although some important reforms have occurred in these countries. Some nations, such as France, have resisted reform even though their tax systems are extremely complex and seemingly inefficient (Graham, 1990). Further, tax reforms have had a number of similarities in both the logic behind them and the details of the policy changes. While this may have occurred because the Anglo-American systems of taxation were the most in need of change, there also appears to be a cultural element involved. If nothing else, a general cultural belief about the meaning of "fairness" appeared to have informed these tax reform packages.

On the other hand, the direct linkage between taxes and the

cultural environment of politics is difficult to make. If indeed tax policy reflects some very difficult and potentially dangerous political decisions for politicians in power, it appears more likely that they would want to make more calculated choices (Alt, 1983). Culture may exert some influence over political choices, but it appears that more proximate values may offer a superior approach. In particular, the politicians may want to implement the values that they believe won the election for them. Further, in most societies "culture" is not a unitary concept, and there may be a number of different political cultures (sometimes parading as ideologies) attempting to exert their influence over policy choices. For example, Mogens Glistrup was able to find a strong anti-government subculture within Denmark, presumably a model Scandinavian Welfare State. This subcultural route may be, in fact, the way in which the ethical values mentioned above enter into the political fray; as noted there, values must be incorporated through the political process before they can be expected to have any significant influence over policies.

Public Opinion

Somewhat related to the above idea that political culture will determine or at least influence tax policy is the argument that public opinion should have a direct and determinate impact on policy. This influence typically works, if it works at all, through the mediating role of political parties and interest groups discussed below. On the other hand, there are ways in which public opinion can have a more direct impact on tax policy. The most obvious method is through initiatives and referenda on tax issues. Some states in the United States and the cantons in Switzerland permit citizens to propose changes in the law directly, and then to vote on the issue (Rhinow, 1984; Delley, 1978). The most famous example of direct lawmaking in tax policy is Proposition 13 in California, but some states in the United States require popular votes on all changes in state or local property tax and these votes can occur frequently (Ranney, 1985; 1987). In the case of referenda, voters are given an opportunity to approve or disapprove a tax proposal put to them by elected officials, while in the case of an initiative they are given the opportunity even to frame the proposal to be considered. These opportunities exist in relatively few countries, and then primarily at the subnational level, but are important instances in which public opinion can determine tax policy directly.

At a more general level, advocates of the public choice approach to political questions have argued in favor of a "median voter model" to explain tax and expenditure policy (Romer and Rosenthal, 1979; 1982; Chicoine, Walzer, and Deller, 1989). The argument of the public choice school is that in a functioning democracy tax and expenditure levels that go above the level desired by the average (median) voter will ultimately produce political retribution against the officials responsible for adopting them. This model of political behavior makes a number of assumptions about the ability of complex political systems to transmit discontent about taxes directly into policy changes. In reality, these assumptions come close to working only when there is an option for referendum (Pommerehne, 1978; Santerre, 1986). The public choice approach also makes the assumption that voters respond only, or perhaps primarily, to aggregate levels of taxing and spending, rather than to the quality of the services being provided, the personal characteristics of political leaders, or any of a number of other possible influences on their behavior. Although some assumptions underlying the public choice approach do appear suspect, it constitutes yet another theoretical point at which to begin the exploration of the politics, especially the mass politics, of tax policy.

There may be even more direct manifestations of public opinion about tax policy. Americans still remember that public opinion (of a sort) concerning tax policy in 1775 helped to spawn the separation of the United States from Britain, and have seen the power of more recent tax revolts (Beito, 1989; Sears and Citrin, 1985). Less dramatically, the manifest public dislike of the community charge, or "poll tax" in Britain helped to produce some modifications in the government's proposals (Evans, 1990). The riots that occurred in London may have hardened Mrs Thatcher's resolve to implement the policy; there was, however, a substantial softening of the proposals, and the introduction of a much larger social "safety net" to assist the poor, after numerous large-scale and peaceful protests took place throughout the United Kingdom (including in some Tory strongholds in the suburbs). Moreover, Conservative defeats in safe by-elections in 1990 and 1991, and the resignation of Mrs Thatcher made it possible to consider a major overhaul, if not complete abolition, of this extremely unpopular tax. The public rarely speaks loudly or with one voice on tax policy, but when it does there appears to be some chance that it will be heard.

Parties and Ideologies

Culture begins to have more clearly political and policy manifestations once it is converted into party programs and their associated ideologies. Everything else being equal, we would expect parties of the political left in office to adopt more progressive (personal and corporate income with high marginal rates) taxes, and parties of the political right to adopt more regressive (sales, insurance contributions) taxes. Some quantitative analyses have demonstrated this effect for tax policy in some time periods and some countries (Castles, 1982; Peters, 1976; 1980). Other more qualitative research has demonstrated a significant influence of political parties on tax policy (Elvander, 1972a; Hadenius, 1981; Morrissey and Steinmo, 1987; Steinmo 1989) in some settings. Neither the quantitative or qualitative evidence, however, is overwhelming in its support for the point that parties have a major influence over tax policies.

Although there are some observed effects of party ideologies on tax policy, there is by no means an overwhelming tendency for differences in political parties to be manifested directly through differences in tax structures. The failure of Socialist Party in France to implement a more progressive tax structure and the increased reliance of Sweden under the Social Democrats on indirect taxes in the late 1980s are but two recent and obvious examples of the slippage between ideology and policy. There appears to be a large number of barriers standing between the promulgation of an ideology by a political party in an electoral campaign, and the implementation of that ideology through a new tax program once the party is in government.

In the first place, a party must win an election in order to implement its program. This is rather basic, but it is important to remember that in most industrialized democracies coalitions, rather than single parties, form the government of the day; of the 22 OECD countries only six had single party governments in 1990. Therefore, even if a political party is successful in getting into government, it generally will not be there alone and may have to compromise with its partners to make tax and other policies. Any one party may be able to get some of its program adopted by the coalition, but by no means all, and the resultant tax program may be a hash of many ideas rather than a clear statement of any single ideology. Even in the United States, which does not have coalition governments in the usual sense, tax reform appears more likely (at both the state and federal levels) when the legislature and executive are from the same political party (Portney, 1980).

The existence of a coalition government can be argued to influence the shape of the tax policies adopted, and it may affect the amount of revenue which a government is likely to be able to extract. Beginning with the basic assumption that taxes are not popular public policies, coalitions often attempt to minimize taxes, and especially to minimize the taxes paid by their constituent groups. That is, political parties with agrarian bases will attempt to minimize the amount of tax paid by farmers, while labor parties will attempt to minimize the amount of tax paid by the working class, and so on. Needing agreement among a number of parties will mean that it will be difficult to get agreement on enough taxation to pay for all the services the government must offer, and hence coalition governments may tend to run larger deficits than single party governments. Further, coalition governments may have to spend more, to be able to "pay off" all the members of the ruling coalition (Robertson, 1989) and that will only increase the deficit.

In the second place, once in office any government will find that any number of factors will impinge upon its ideological purity. Not the least of these factors will be the desire to be reelected. As noted above, changing the tax system is often not the best way to win the hearts and minds of the voters. Even if the changes in the tax system introduced are beneficial to most citizens, they may still create uncertainty and simply direct media attention to the amount of money which citizens are already paying in taxes and which they will continue to pay after the reform. Therefore, the best strategy (politically) is often to ignore the tax system and allow it to continue pretty much as it has been – perhaps with a few changes around the margin (Rose and Karran, 1986).

There are, of course, some good examples of political leaders who have been able to introduce large-scale tax policy measures and retain their popularity (President Reagan in 1981 and Helmut Kohl in 1986 are among the most obvious), but these successes appear to be the exceptions rather than the rule. Following from that statement, it appears that most politicians have been attempting to hide the true costs of taxes from citizens rather than to make bold ideological statements about their tax policies. Even if a public statement is more bold than ideological, any statement about more taxes is likely to be political suicide, as Walter Mondale found out in 1984. It will be pointed out in much greater detail later that there has been a tendency among the industrialized countries of the OECD world for tax systems to become increasingly similar over time. Countries such as France and Italy which have relied on indirect taxes have been increasing their direct tax burdens, while countries such as Sweden and Australia with very high direct tax burdens have shifted somewhat more toward indirect taxes. Ideology implies clear statements and placing most of a government's tax eggs in a few baskets, but tax politics appears to call for hiding the total burden in as many baskets as possible. The introduction of the "community charge" or poll tax to finance local government in Britain was a clear ideological move on the part of the Thatcher government, and one which met initially with severe political discontent (Game, 1988).

The final point which should be raised about the mass political considerations involved in tax policy arises from the literature on the "political business cycle" (Tufte, 1978; Schneider, 1984). The argument here is that the action of governments in taxing and spending will constitute a major portion of their attempts to be reelected. Further, a government's actions may not be the same throughout their term of office, but rather will be timed to coincide with the electoral cycle. If a government believes that it must increase taxes, or change the distribution of the tax burden, it will tend to do so early in its term of office so that any negative repercussion of the change (they hope) will have been forgotten by the time of the next election. Likewise, governments will attempt to increase public expenditure, especially for programs that benefit a number of individuals directly, late in their terms of office so that citizens would more likely remember the good deeds of the government and return them to office. Thus, as we examine the politics of tax policy, politicians must be cognizant of the temporal as well as the ideological dimension of political actions. Thus, Mrs Thatcher may have erred seriously in not introducing the poll tax until rather late in her third term of office, while President Reagan made a safer choice, and perhaps his only available choice, by pushing for his major tax change early in his first term. In both cases, there may have been little real choice for the leaders, but it does appear that timing does make a real difference in the political effects of a decision.

The reverse side of the above argument is that governments may be able to make any changes in the tax system early in their terms, but that opportunity will vanish later. Governments appear to enjoy "honeymoon periods" after their election in which they have greater influence with the rest of the political system (Bunce, 1981). A new government can claim a mandate from the people, and although that mandate is often very indistinct, the claim is a powerful political weapon. Unless the government acts promptly that window of opportunity will vanish, and other actors in the political system will begin to wonder by whom the next government will be composed. This closing of windows of opportunity may be especially evident for tax policies, given their general unpopularity. Again, timing counts for a great deal in politics, and making tax policy is little different from other policies in that regard.

Group Politics

Another possible explanation for the shaping of the tax system in democratic political systems is that the universe of pressure groups plays a significant role in the process. This should not be surprising, given that a general finding is that interest groups have significant political influence in all these systems – whether pluralist (Dahl, 1973) or corporatist (Schmitter and Lehmbruch, 1979). In the case of interest groups we would not, however, expect highly visible impacts on broad issues of tax policy – the amount of total taxes extracted or perhaps even the general distribution among different types of taxes. Rather, we would expect greater influence by those interest groups on the fine detail of tax policy, and in particular the pattern of deductions and exemptions – "loopholes" – made available to special interests through the tax system. Interest groups are sometimes argued to be more successful in tax policy than in other policy areas because its complex, technical character makes it easier for them to disguise their real influence in legal and economic jargon. Further, the relative secrecy in which tax policy is made in most countries provides interest groups with an arena in which their impact may not be as evident as in other policy areas (McQuaig, 1987).

The literature recounting the influence of interest groups on taxes is rather extensive, although most of it tends to be condemnations of the influence of special interests, and the consequent inequities written into the tax system. One of the most interesting of the analytical essays on the role of special interests in tax policy concerns their role in Canada. Good (1980) argues for an anticipatory model of tax policymaking in which the principal interest groups do not have to make overt representations of their positions to government. Morrissey (1990) argues much the same for Ireland, when he notes the importance of scanning alternatives, and the political coalitions around them, before making a policy choice. The positions of interest groups on tax policy changes are well known, or are readily predictable, and the decisionmakers in government will act so as to avoid conflict with any powerful groups. In this approach, if there is much overt political activity on the part of interest groups, both they and the policymakers have not done their jobs well.

If we look at the relationship of interest groups to tax policy from the perspective of James Q. Wilson's analysis of policymaking in the United States (1980; 1989), we would expect tax policymakers to have a great deal of influence over the final outcome of the process. Wilson argued that in a decisionmaking situation such as tax policy where there are a large number of interests involved with none being dominant – what he called an "interest group" situation – then the political institution involved has more opportunity for making the final policy decision based on its own values. Certainly tax policy is the target of any number of interests, and the decisionmakers therefore may have the opportunity to pick and choose among those groups. This opportunity is available especially in pluralist settings which do not require conflicting interests to work out compromise arrangements (Pen, 1987, 331–2) as might be required in corporatist interest group settings.

We should, however, expect somewhat different relationships between interest groups and government concerning tax policy, depending upon how those political relationships are structured. In pluralist systems, for example, the competitive involvement of interest groups in policymaking will tend to produce differential influence by groups over policy, and the creation of perhaps more specific deductions and exemptions, most favoring powerful producer groups (Freeman, 1965; Jordan, 1981). If policymakers have the ability to pick and choose, those are the types of interests picked most often to be rewarded. On the other hand, more corporatist systems with the legitimate involvement of a range of interest groups in policymaking should produce more balanced policy outcomes. The same total number of "loopholes" may be created, but they can be hypothesized to be more widely distributed among social groups. Likewise, corporatist structures tend to generate equal shares of many sorts of taxes, rather than greater reliance on only one or two major sources of revenue (Peters, 1981).

Given the conventional wisdom about the power of interest groups over policy, and particularly tax policy, the spate of tax reforms that occurred during the late 1980s and early 1990s is extremely surprising. A general characteristic of these reforms has been to eliminate many of the special privileges granted to special interests through the tax law. This has broadened the tax base and permitted decreased average and marginal tax rates for many taxpayers. Although many interest groups lobbied long and hard to protect their privileges, the reforms were adopted and implemented (Birnbaum and Murray, 1987; Pechman, 1988; Gretschmann and Kenis, 1990). Also, some interest groups appeared to avoid the fray, sensing perhaps the limits of their power and legitimacy in democratic political systems bent on reform (Mucciaroni, 1990).

The successes of tax reform legislation, and their implications for understand tax policymaking, will be examined in much greater detail in a later chapter (chapter 10). However, it should be pointed out in the present context that the successes of the reform efforts to some degree point to the development of a new type of interest group in tax politics, and to some degree in other types of politics as well. The conventional wisdom (Olson, 1965) has been that it is impossible to organize taxpayers qua taxpayers effectively. Their interests in any one tax are too diffuse, and their individual tax situations sufficiently different, that they will not organize in the same way as will more specific interests to gain special treatment. In contrast to this conventional wisdom, however, a number of public interest and taxpayer groups were involved in the tax reform process, generally pressing for fewer loopholes and a simpler tax system (Mucciaroni, 1990). This was especially true in the United States, but analogous groups have been seen in other countries as well. It does appear, therefore, that the policy community (Freeman and Stevens, 1987) surrounding tax policy has become much broader, and that broader citizen interests cannot now be excluded.

Policy Reasons

All tax decisions are policy decisions, but at times governments choose to make tax policies in order to produce other policy outcomes, rather than just to raise revenue. Taxes are but one among many instruments at the disposal of government (Linder and Peters, 1989). We have been discussing the preferences built into tax policy using the pejorative term "loopholes," but such preferences can produce positive benefits for the society as a whole. Not only may having the policies adopted be easier as a part of a tax bill than as an expenditure program, but they may be easier and less expensive to administer in the form of taxes as well. The subsidies given homeownership in most countries through tax benefits are widely distributed, generally beneficial, and much easier to administer than would be a direct housing subsidy to that large a segment of the population (Comeau, 1979). Thus, not all tax preferences are merely special preferences for the wealthy and powerful; some are more generally beneficial to the population. The difficulty, politically and socially, is determining which tax expenditures are which.

In addition to the above examples, earmarked (hypothecated) taxes may also be a positive means of reaching certain policy goals when other methods might generate large-scale conflict. Citizens may resist any new general taxes, but may be willing to accept a tax if its revenues go for a specified and popular purpose. For example, widespread concern about the rather poor state of the National Health Service in Britain has prompted some to suggest a new tax just for that single purpose. This proposal certainly would not fit well with the general policies of the Conservative government against taxation and public expenditure, but earmarking may make the proposal more acceptable even to that administration. Earmarking is doubly acceptable when it taxes "sin" (alcohol, tobacco, gambling) for "good" purposes (health or education).

Finally, taxes can be used as a mechanism for social control, and to produce general good, as well as a means of conferring special benefits. For example, there is concern in many countries about global warming and the "greenhouse effect" resulting in large part from emissions of carbon dioxide. A number of countries have advanced proposals for a carbon tax, on the use of carbon in the form of coal or petroleum, as a means of reducing consumption of fossil fuels (Johnson, 1990; Samuelson, 1990). Similarly, taxes on alcohol and tobacco, in addition to their revenue effects, are also intended to reduce consumption of those potentially harmful substances. There is some question about how effective any of these taxes intended to be control devices are (Cook, 1989; Baker and McKay, 1990), but they do constitute yet another policy option available to government in attempting to reach its goals.

The Institutions of Taxation

The final variable to be considered when attempting to explain the tax policy decisions taken by a government are the formal governing institutions involved in the process. We have already discussed the role played by the elected government of the day in that policymaking process, and the difficulties it may encounter in implementing its own tax policy priorities. A President or the Prime Minister and the Cabinet are not, however, the only actors involved in the tax policy process, and other institutions have a vital role to play.

First, although it is now conventional to denigrate their influence over policy, parliaments may have a great deal to say about taxes. Parliaments in some systems received their initial powers in conflicts over public money, and have sought to maintain the purse strings. Even the relatively weak parliament in the European Community has some control over the budget (Shackleton, 1990). Thus, the manner in which these legislative institutions are structured to make tax and expenditure policy may have a significant impact on the outcomes of the process. For example, to the extent that the parliament is structured with autonomous financial committees and specialized staffs to consider fiscal issues, it can play a more important role in policy. The legislature in a parliamentary system of government will tend to be at something of an informational disadvantage in comparison to the executive, but the extent of that disadvantage varies (Peters, 1990, 81–3) and some parliaments do manage to have substantial influence over fiscal policy. In the few presidential systems extant among the OECD countries the legislature may be able to play a more significant role, with a sizeable staff of its own and the expertise to counteract the executive (Schick, 1988). In whatever system, however, parliament does have the ultimate lawmaking power and cannot be discounted too readily.

Tax policy is a technical subject, and the experts in the public bureaucracy often come to dominate the process of making it. As experts, they may apply their own particular visions of the world to that policy (Wilson, 1989). So, for example, if lawyers dominate the tax agencies, then the tax legislation which emerges from the process may suit a lawyer's need for greater tidiness in the law. On the other hand, if economists dominate, then there may be greater attention to the effects of the legislation on business but less on the legal niceties. Finally, if career civil servants dominate the process, there may be greater attention to the ability of the proposed legislation actually to collect revenues for government, and in the ease of adminstration rather than in the policy's distributive effects.

It may be that different agencies charged with making parts of tax policy within a single country may employ differing types of personnel, and that this will produce even more "bureaucratic politics" than might otherwise have been expected. For example, the Tax Policy Division of the Treasury in the United States has been dominated by economists concerned that the law be written in a way to minimize negative impacts on the economy of the United States and be able to raise sufficient revenue given that economy and its performance (Campbell, 1983, 116–18). This view often has come into conflict with the Internal Revenue Service (IRS) and its career civil servants more concerned with their own ability to implement the legislation once it is passed. The IRS may make rulings as it implements policy that run counter to the intentions of the other parts of Treasury simply to ease its own administrative problems. Similar conflicts emerge in other countries where different professional training, and differences in organizational cultures, produce conflicts over tax policy within government itself.

Any differing organizational cultures which are found need not result only from the professional backgrounds of public employees, but may represent the values which an organization has built up over time. For example, Johnstone (1975) found the HM Customs and Excise in Britain had developed its own distinctive organizational perspective on how to implement indirect taxes, and carried that culture over into its implementation of the (then) new value-added tax. Likewise, many of the problems which the members of the European Community are encountering in harmonizing their tax structures are the result of differing organizational cultures and differences in operational definitions of some of the important elements of taxation, rather than the product of any overt hostility to European integration.

The above point leads to another institutional factor concerning tax policy. This is that there may not be a single tax policy in a country, but actually several different tax policies. This is obviously true when different levels of government have independent authority to raise taxes, and may use very different philosophies when they do (even when using the same type of tax). Differing organizational values also may be present within the same level of government when different organizations are involved in the process. The above example in the United States illustrates one potential type of conflict: that between the policymaking organizations and an implementing body. This potential conflict is made more intense because of the power of the IRS to issue administrative rulings defining tax policy as it is being implemented that may go against the desires of the formulators of the legislation. These differences may arise even though the IRS and the tax formulators are both employees of the Department of the Treasury.

Another potential for institutional conflict arises if there are several organizations involved in tax policy, each responsible for implementing different types of taxes and using somewhat different methods to do so. For example, in the United Kingdom, the Board of Inland Revenue is responsible for implementing the income tax, while the Customs and Excise is responsible for implementing the second large tax in that country, the Value-Added Tax (VAT). This division of responsibility was adopted when the VAT was perceived to be very much like the earlier, and very simple, purchase tax. As the VAT has become more complex and more inclusive of considerations about economic differences among individuals, there is some discussion of combining the two organizations (Ridley, 1990; Sandford, 1988). This combination might minimize the impact of two very different approaches to taxation being applied to the same population of taxpayers, but might have the negative consequence of too little differentiation of taxes actually fulfilling different purposes.

It is not, however, only these types of institutional differences among tax bureaucracies themselves which must be negotiated when making tax policy. Rather, there may be more significant differences among the political institutions making policy which will generate perhaps even greater difficulties in governance. The most important of these differences may be the degree of institutional separation of tax and expenditure policymaking. In the large majority of political systems these two categories of fiscal decisions are the responsibilities of different organizations, or at least of different components of the same larger organization. For example, in the United States the Office of Management and Budget is responsible for making expenditure policy, while the Department of the Treasury has a greater impact on tax policy. Within Congress, these two important sets of decisions are the responsibilities of different committees in the two houses, and are brought together formally only twice each year during the budget cycle (Ott and Ott, 1977). Much the same division is found for fiscal policymaking in other industrialized democracies (Peters, 1991).

The division of fiscal responsibility should make it little surprise, therefore, that there is a tendency for budget deficits to occur in these countries on a regular basis. It is always easier to spend than to tax, and there is no means of forcing joint consideration of the two sides of the budget. Further, it should not be surprising that the distributive effects of taxes and expenditures are not well-coordinated in most public sectors, and that taxes that are intended to be redistributive may end up by actually being proportional. The numerous institutional divisions make the effective management of the financial side of government that much more difficult, and tend to generate some unexpected and undesirable consequences for governments and their citizens.

International Influences

A final source of influences on tax policy is the international environment within which any individual country's tax system must operate. As the economies and societies of the industrialized democracies have become more internationalized, the actions of other countries and international organizations have an increasing influence over domestic policies. In some instances the influence of the international environment may be extremely remote, and only establish broad parameters for action by an individual government. In other cases, however, the international context of taxation is extremely important and will virtually determine domestic tax policies. It is now almost impossible to consider domestic economic policies, including tax policy, without also considering their possible international sources, and their possible international consequences.

The more remote international causes of domestic tax policy are associated with the openness of economies and the need to maintain international competitiveness. Any one country, even one with a large internal market and a large endowment of natural resources such as the United States, can no longer afford to go it alone in the world economy. Therefore, there will be some tendency to homogenize national tax policies in order to ensure that a country is not at a competitive disadvantage as a result of its tax policies. Capital is more mobile than ever in the 1990s, so it is relatively easy for a company to move its financial operations if it finds that the tax laws of one country are operating to its disadvantage. Likewise, even private citizens may organize their financial affairs to utilize the numerous international tax advantages if governments provide the taxpayers a sufficient incentive to do so.

Another somewhat indirect international influence on tax policy is mimicry, and the diffusion of policy innovations (Collier and Messick, 1975). A number of industrialized countries adopted rather similar tax reforms during the 1980s, and those that did not appeared to wonder why they had not, or why they were moving so slowly (Sodersten, 1989). One of the laggards – Sweden – did implement a staged tax reform during the early 1990s (Taylor, 1989). The countries adopting and/or implementing the reforms all reduced the top rates of income tax, reduced the number of tax brackets, and eliminated a large number of "loopholes" (see chapter 10). A portion of this reform activity appeared to be a function of the need to remain competitive, but some of it also appeared to be an international fad in tax policy. Even in an area as important and as politically sensitive as this there may still be fads, and those fashions may even be enacted into law. The extensive contacts that fiscal policymakers now have with one another, in part through international organizations such as the OECD, the European Community, and the International Monetary Fund, make it easy for new policy ideas to spread among the industrialized countries.

The more direct influence of the international environment on domestic tax policies also tends to be centered around issues of competitiveness. In particular, the European Community is attempting to harmonize the taxes (especially commercial taxes such as the VAT and excise taxes) charged by its twelve member nations (Puchala, 1984; Buchan, 1990). This harmonization is designed to ensure that no country gains an unfair economic advantage through the manipulation of its tax system. One of the principal goals of the EC is to eliminate all barriers to the free movement of goods and services, as well as the promotion of fair competition among its members, and the harmonization of taxation would be a major step toward those goals. Predictably, the full harmonization of taxes is proving very difficult both politically and economically, but the Commission of the EC appears willing to engage in this struggle (Bos and Nelson, 1988; Pearson and Smith, 1988). Even countries seeking to trade extensively with the EC must consider realigning their own tax systems to more closely conform to the Community system (Schneider, 1989). Further, although less powerful, the General Agreement on Tariffs and Trade organization (Jackson, 1990) has also sought to reduce the tariffs charged by all countries in the world – not just those in Europe – and to ensure that these taxes are applied fairly.

Summary

Any number of factors can be used to justify tax policies. Taxes certainly have pronounced effects upon the economy, and those effects must be taken into account when making choices about tax policies. Likewise, taxes come into being through legal instruments, and their correspondence to legal norms must also be considered thoroughly. Taxes also have distributional effects on the citizens of a society, and those effects must also be reviewed and understood carefully. In the end, however, political considerations will dominate in the selection of tax policies. Taxes are simply too important as political actions – in both real and symbolic terms – to permit other types of factors (important as they certainly are) to have anything other than a secondary influence over the final selection of tax instruments. Politics is itself, however, a very broad category of concerns and activity. We have already specified a number of possible political variables that may influence the policy choices made by government. We have also specified a number of avenues through which those factors may operate to influence policy choices. The exact manner in which each political factor influences policy in each country is, however, something which depends very much upon their interaction within the particular institutional and cultural setting. It further depends upon the external constraints imposed on policy choices. Specifying the influence of these factors thus requires some understanding of the political system within which the policies are being made.

Understanding tax policy choices, therefore, is inherently a comparative process, and this book will attempt to explain as much as possible about the differences (and the similarities) of tax policymaking within the industrialized countries belonging to the Organization for Economic Cooperation and Development. This explanation will not be undertaken on a country by country basis; rather, we will develop some important questions about tax policy and tax politics to organize the inquiry, and then pull together the optimum information from as many OECD countries as possible to help illuminate the dynamics and the constraints of making this important type of public policy.

2
Variations on a Theme: The Nature of Taxation

Governments are required to make a number of choices about how they will finance their many programs and services. A fundamental choice is just how much they will tax. This decision is in part driven by others about how much they want to spend, but if there is a great deal of political resistance to taxation, the possibilities to spend may be constrained. Also, governments can choose to spend more than they will collect in taxes. If they do choose to do this, they can borrow the difference, or simply print enough money to cover their debts. Governments can also raise revenues from other sources, such as charging users for particular services rather than having all citizens pay general taxes to finance those services, or selling off assets that they have acquired in the past. Deciding how much tax revenue they *want* to raise (the real amount collected will depend upon a large number of factors, many beyond the control of government) is not a simple political decision, nor is it totally dependent upon prior decisions to spend.

Once there is a decision to tax at a certain level, there must then be decisions about how to apportion the total tax bill among different types of taxes – taxes on income, expenditures, wealth, etc. Again, the process is not as linear as this implies; many of the decisions will be simply to keep the existing tax structure and let it produce the tax revenue that it can with only marginal adjustments. Large-scale overhauls of tax systems are possible, however, and are becoming a popular political exercise (Pechman, 1988; Goode, 1984). Further, in most countries, there a number of governments involved in determining the final tax bill to the society, each government with different goals and different revenue requirements. The final amount of tax revenue raised therefore depends upon a large number of decisions, often made without regard to that final bill.

Even though the choices made about raising revenues very rarely reflect a conscious and rational ordering of priorities by the political system, they do reflect a great deal about the politics of the society. Those choice processes, and the outcomes they produce, allow us to understand both the political process and the political values of a country. Hence, taxation and tax policy are very suitable subjects of a comparative political inquiry. That comparison should obviously be trans-national, but should also attempt to compare tax policy and tax politics with what occurs in other policy areas. Tax politics appears to be different from other types of policymaking in a number of countries (Elvander, 1972a; 1972b; Johnstone, 1975; Birnbaum and Murray, 1987), and we will need to determine to what extent differences among nations override the general technocratic and elite style that tends to dominate tax policymaking.

This chapter provides a great deal of basic information to begin to unravel the tightly knit cloth that is tax policy. First, the question of just how much tax goverents extract from citizens is addressed. The numerous different taxes that governments levy and the different tax rates charged in different nations are also examined. Again, a more elaborate explanation is reserved for a later chapter. Not only is what is taxed important, but so is who taxes; therefore the way in which tax revenue is distributed among levels of government and the impact of different degrees of local autonomy on revenue raising are also discussed. Third, taxes can be evaluated according to a number of dimensions, and the criteria and some discussion of how different types of taxes rank on those criteria are presented. Finally, we will examine some observed clusterings of tax policies in the OECD countries and relate those to the criteria developed in this chapter, and the ideas about tax politics developed in chapter 1.

Total Levels of Taxation

The governments of all industrialized democracies extract a great deal of tax revenue from their citizens. The amount of revenue collected efforts made by OECD countries is reported in table 2.1. The information in this table shows that although all governments are involved in their economies through taxation (an average of 37.2 percent of Gross Domestic Product was taken as tax revenue in 1986), there are substantial variations. Sweden, the country with the highest level of taxation relative to economic resources, extracts more than one kroner in every two produced in the economy for the use of the public sector. This is over three times as much tax proportionately as Turkey extracts, and 80 percent higher than the next lowest

Table 2.1 Revenue from specific taxes as percentage of total tax revenue, 1987

Country	*Personal income*	*Corporate income*	*Employees' social security*	*Employers' social security*	*Payroll*	*Property*	*General consump-tion*	*Specific commod-ities*	*Estate and gift*	*Customs*	*Wealth*	*Other*
Australia	55.6	10.2	–	–	5.4	4.4	8.2	11.5	0.0	3.9	–	0.8
Austria	22.7	3.4	13.5	15.9	5.9	0.7	20.9	10.2	0.2	0.1	0.9	5.6
Belgium	32.7	6.6	11.1	20.3	–	0.0	15.7	7.8	0.6	1.5	–	3.7
Canada	38.7	8.2	4.6	8.5	–	7.8	14.1	10.0	0.0	2.3	1.0	4.8
Denmark	49.2	4.5	1.9	1.8	0.7	2.4	18.9	12.9	0.6	0.5	0.5	6.1
Finland	45.5	3.9	–	9.0	–	0.3	24.6	11.7	0.4	0.7	0.1	3.8
France	12.7	5.2	12.3	27.2	1.9	4.7	19.5	6.4	0.8	0.4	0.4	9.5
Germany	29.0	5.0	16.1	19.1	–	1.1	15.7	6.5	0.3	0.8	1.3	5.1
Greece	12.3	4.4	14.1	14.2	1.1	0.1	26.9	16.9	1.0	1.5	–	7.5
Ireland	34.6	3.2	5.1	8.8	1.3	2.9	20.2	17.2	0.3	1.2	–	5.2
Italy	26.2	10.6	6.7	24.1	0.5	–	14.6	10.3	0.2	0.6	–	6.2
Japan	24.0	22.9	10.2	14.8	–	5.6	–	11.1	2.7	0.7	–	8.0

Luxembourg	25.3	17.1	10.9	14.1	–	0.5	13.8	9.1	0.3	0.3	3.5	5.1
Netherlands	27.4	7.7	18.8	17.0	–	1.7	16.4	5.7	0.5	1.3	0.5	3.0
New Zealand	49.8	8.9	–	–	0.9	5.7	16.7	12.5	0.2	2.3	–	3.0
Norway	26.4	6.7	6.5	16.3	–	0.6	20.8	18.0	0.1	0.5	1.3	2.8
Portugal	29.6[a]	–	6.1	17.8	–	–	21.0	17.3	0.8	4.4	–	3.0
Spain	21.3	6.7	6.1	27.6	–	3.7	16.9	12.4	0.6	3.1	0.4	1.2
Sweden	41.3	4.1	–	23.3	4.5	1.1	13.3	8.7	0.2	1.3	0.4	1.8
Switzerland	34.0	6.2	10.2	10.1	–	8.5	9.7	8.1	0.7	1.3	3.8	7.4
United Kingdom	25.8	10.6	8.3	9.4	–	11.0	16.1	13.7	0.7	1.2	–	5.2
United States	36.2	8.1	11.1	16.6	–	9.2	7.4	7.2	0.8	1.1	–	2.3

[a] Personal and corporate income tax cannot be disaggregated.
Source: OECD, annual a

country in terms of taxation (Japan). In general the Scandinavian and Benelux countries lead the taxation league, while the lesser developed European countries, Japan, and the United States trail the other industrialized democracies.

These now industrialized countries have not always been as heavily involved in revenue collection. Table 2.2 shows the development of taxation for all OECD countries since 1965, and for selected countries since 1865.[1] Since 1965, there has been a steady increase in the level of taxation, relative to economic resources, in almost every country. On an annual basis in only two years did the average level of taxation in OECD countries decrease as a proportion of Gross Domestic Product (GDP – a standard measure of economic output). Tax levels of individual countries vary relative to GDP, with fluctuations based as much on changes in economic performance as on tax policies, but the general trend is almost always upward. The trend rarely, however, reflects conscious decisions to tax more, and certainly rarely reflect decisions that more taxation is desirable; rather, it reflects decisions – frequently made in several different governments within a single country – about the needs to finance programs.

Over a longer time span the upward movement of taxation is less of a secular trend, and the increases following the Second World War are more pronounced. Taxes appear to remain about the same relative to economic resources for much of the period from 1865 to the present. In addition, there was much less variance among countries prior to the Second World War than there is in the 1980s; countries appeared to have rather similar expenditure and revenue needs. To be sure there were some significant fluctuations in tax levels, but these appeared related to wars or other significant socioeconomic and political upheavals. It is only in the period following the First World War, and especially the period following the Second World War, that taxation begins to get on the steady upward track (Webber and Wildavsky, 1986). We will return to some explanations of the development of tax policies over time in a later chapter. These will focus on changing demands for government services, and changing economic systems that make extraction easier. It is sufficient now to understand that fiscal policies have not always been as they are today, and governments have not always been engaged in a search for every shred of additional revenue they could find.

Table 2.2 Growth of total tax revenues of government, 1865–1985 (percentage of GDP)

	1865	*1900*	*1920*	*1950*	*1955*	*1965*	*1975*	*1980*	*1985*
Australia					21.6	23.2	27.7	28.6	30.2
Austria				16.6	30.0	34.7	38.6	41.2	43.1
Belgium					24.0	30.8	41.1	43.5	46.4
Canada					21.4	25.4	32.4	31.6	33.1
Denmark					23.4	29.9	41.4	43.5	46.4
Finland					26.8	29.5	38.6	33.0	37.0
France			16.7	20.6		34.5	38.7	41.7	44.5
Germany		5.3		29.3	30.8	31.6	38.6	38.0	38.0
Greece						20.6	27.3	29.4	35.1
Ireland					22.5	26.0	35.0	34.0	38.3
Italy		12.8	14.6	17.2	30.5	25.5	27.1	30.2	34.4
Japan					17.1	18.3	21.8	25.5	28.0
Luxembourg						30.4	39.2	40.1	44.0
Netherlands		7.7	11.8	21.8	26.3	33.2	43.2	45.8	45.9
New Zealand					27.0	24.7	31.0	33.1	34.0
Norway	8.5	9.0	8.8	16.6	28.3	33.3	46.2	47.1	47.6
Portugal					15.4	18.4	26.8	28.7	31.6
Spain						14.5	19.6	24.1	28.8
Sweden	8.4	8.2		22.0	25.5	35.4	48.2	49.1	50.4
Switzerland					19.2	20.7	31.3	30.8	32.0
United Kingdom	7.8	7.0	22.0	31.1	29.8	30.4	35.5	35.4	38.0
United States	6.0	3.3	7.5	12.8	23.6	25.9	28.3	29.9	29.2

Sources: Mitchell, 1980; Flora *et al*., 1983; US Bureau of the Census, 1979

Types of Taxes

In addition to knowing what the total tax bill being charged in a country is, we also need to understand the number and types of taxes that citizens pay. There is a wide variety of taxes that the average citizen pays, often without being aware that government is receiving the money, and it is difficult for most people to identify all the tax money they pay to government. This dispersion of the tax system among a number of different instruments has several effects. First, as has already been pointed out, it tends to obscure the total amount being paid to government, and it may therefore reduce the popular resistance to taxation (Winer, 1983). In addition, collecting a variety of taxes on different economic activities enables government to catch almost every citizen in the tax net. People who may not earn a sufficient income to pay income tax (or who are able to evade that tax successfully) must still pay when they purchase goods and services if there is a sales tax, or a value-added tax, or excise taxes on specific commodities. Thus, the variety of "tax handles" which governments employ enable them to catch almost all citizens and to force them to bear at least some portion of the burden of running their government.

The latter point brings us to a third reason for distributing the costs of government over a variety of different taxes; it prevents any single form of economic activity or asset from bearing too great a burden of taxation. Concentration on a small number of taxes may introduce inequities or substantial economic or social distortion. Consider, for example, financing local government through the property tax in the United States and a few other countries. For many local governments this is their only significant source of tax revenue, and therefore as the costs of local government increase so too do property taxes. In cities – which tend to have larger expenses and therefore higher taxes than do suburban and rural localities – the property tax provides an incentive for citizens to move to the suburbs, where, everything else being equal, property taxes are lower. If the total expense of running the city could be distributed across a variety of activities, for example also taxing payrolls to capture some revenue from suburban commuters, then the disincentives to live in the city might be lessened. This is one reason why the Thatcher government in the United Kingdom introduced a "poll tax" for local governments. Although not without its own problems (Midwinter and Mair, 1987), the poll tax makes all citizens over 18 share the costs of government, rather than concentrating all of those costs on property owners. This tax produced a political storm that has led to its modification to take account of the income of the taxpayer. Still, the changes introduced in 1991 require almost all households to make some contribution to the costs of government rather than having all the burden fall on property owners.

Taxes on Incomes

Probably the most familar "tax handle" is income. We usually think of this in terms of the personal income tax which is now the principal source of revenue for most national governments in the industrialized world. The personal income tax is not, however, the only tax levied on incomes. Corporations also have incomes and governments in all nations extract some revenue from that source. Also, taxes on payrolls – the most important being taxes for social insurance – are also taxes on incomes. Although using the same basic tax handle, each of these forms of revenue collection has its own characteristics which are important for understanding it specifically, and tax policy in general.

The personal income tax In most industrialized countries personal income tax is the largest single source of revenue. It ranges from 60 percent of total tax revenues in New Zealand to only 12.7 percent in France. The tax averages almost one-third of all tax revenues in all OECD countries, and is the largest single tax in all but three of the countries for which we have reliable data.[2] However, despite the personal income tax being such a dominant revenue source, it accounts for one-half or more of total taxation only in New Zealand. The principle of distributing revenue collection among a number of different sources remains a powerful one for both political and economic reasons. Further, in a number of the countries that rely heavily on the personal income tax, e.g. Sweden and the United States, it is not a single tax. Both the central government and subnational governments use the income tax as a revenue source so that again taxing is distributed. In Sweden, for example, local governments extract three times as much revenue by income taxes as does the central government.

Although the personal income tax is administered somewhat differently in different countries (and at different levels of government within a single country), there are some common features. The first is that income tends to be defined very broadly, so that it is difficult for anyone living in the country and earning substantial income to escape paying some income tax. In most countries, social benefits such as unemployment benefits or pensions for the elderly are excluded from taxation (although not necessarily if a pensioner has substantial income from other sources). In addition, to the extent that employees receive a portion of their compensation through fringe benefits (health and life insurance, retirement funds, etc.), they can escape taxation. Governments are tightening these loopholes, but many fringe benefits still qualify for exclusion as "income." There are some other possible means of escaping (legally) the income tax, but in general if the individual receives an income the government has the right to levy a tax on it.

Another common feature of the personal income tax is that it is a progressive tax. Everything else being equal, the more the individual earns, the higher the percentage of those earnings that will be paid to government as income tax. The rate of progression has been reduced in most countries during the 1980s as a wave of "tax reform" has eliminated some of the disincentives for the more affluent to earn larger incomes. In addition, the need to charge very high rates on the highest incomes has been reduced as many exclusions and deductions (which had differentially benefited the wealthy) have been eliminated to broaden the tax base. Even with these changes, however, higher income earners have a higher marginal tax rate than will lower income earners. The major exception to the generalization about progressivity is that subnational governments are more likely to charge flat-rate income taxes. So, for example, in the United States, of the 40 states that charge an income tax, six use a flat rate, as do almost all local governments with an income tax. Local income taxes in other countries tend to be less progressive than central government income taxes.

Finally, although governments do have the legal right to tax any form of income, in most tax systems all sources of income and all types of expenditure are not treated the same. We will discuss the concept of "tax expenditures" in some detail later (see pp. 193–208), but we should note here that tax systems are used for a variety of purposes in addition to just collecting revenue. By granting preferences for certain sources of income, e.g. capital gains from investments, or for certain types of expenditures, e.g. contributions to charities, the tax system can be used to subsidize any number of social or economic activities. The desirability of using the tax system for all of these policy purposes can be questioned (Surrey and McDaniel, 1985; McDaniel and Surrey, 1985; Bradley, 1984), but exemptions and deductions in the income tax remain a major source of benefits to social groups. Interestingly, these "loopholes" appear to be most prevalent where taxes are highest, and serve as a means of reducing taxation to more tolerable levels for the average citizen.

Corporate income taxes Individuals are not the only source of revenue through an income tax. Corporations, as legal persons, also pay a tax on their income or profits in all industrialized societies. This tax is generally a politically easier tax to adopt or increase since corporations do not vote and their stockholders might identify less with the plight of the corporation than with their own problems with the individual income tax. There is also a populist strain in the politics of many countries that advocates taxing corporations heavily to protect the "little man." Administratively, collecting the corporation tax is also easier than personal income taxes because corporations keep better records than do most citizens. Despite the political and administrative appeal, the corporation income tax is not used to collect as much tax revenue as might be expected. As shown in table 2.1, in only five countries does the corporation tax account for more than 10 percent of total tax revenue, and the average across all the OECD countries is only 8.2 percent. Why is this the case, when it would appear that revenue from a corporation tax should be much higher?

One reason for not taxing corporations more heavily is that, although they do not vote, they do organize rather effectively for political purposes, and tend to have among the most powerful lobbying organizations in capitalist economies. In addition, corporations have financial resources which they can direct toward one candidate or another, or toward one party or another, and can exert political influence in that way. Thus, politicians are often reluctant to place too much of the tax burden on corporations directly. Numerous electoral reforms have sought to limit the power of corporations over politics, but have been less than successful, so tax policymakers still must be aware of the political "clout" of the business community.

In addition to the political reluctance to place too much of the tax burden on corporations, there may also be economic reasons for that reticence. Placing a heavy tax burden on corporations may impede economic growth, especially through reducing the amount of corporate capital available for investment (although this does not appear to be the case in Japan, which relies heavily on corporate taxation). Therefore, it might be desirable to keep the corporate tax rate lower, with the hope of promoting economic growth. Politicians, even those on the political left, must be cognizant of the need to balance their desire to collect relatively easy revenues from corporations with the economic necessity of not killing the goose that lays the golden egg of economic growth and employment.

Social insurance taxes We are not yet through with taxes on incomes, because governments have still more means of extracting revenue from the incomes of individuals and corporations. The most important of these are taxes, or "contributions," paid for social insurance. All advanced industrial democracies, as welfare states, spend a substantial proportion of their public budgets for social purposes (see chapter 3). While some of this spending is financed out of general revenues such as the income tax, a good deal of it comes from taxes earmarked for social purposes, e.g. social security contributions in the United States or National Insurance contributions in the United Kingdom. Although these levies are as obligatory as any other tax, they are frequently referred to as "contributions" to preserve the concept that these are insurance programs and not "welfare." This concept helps to make the programs (and the taxes) more palatable to citizens who might object to receiving (or paying for) welfare. The credibility of the contribution concept is enhanced by not charging the tax, at least in some countries, on income over a certain amount. The idea is that after an individual has made his or her maximum "contribution" for the year, there should be no more tax; that individual has "bought" full insurance for that year.

In most countries, social insurance contributions are divided between the employer and the employee. In some countries the two pay equally, while in others the employer pays a higher percentage. In either case, however, social insurance contributions can be regarded as a tax on the income of the employee because: (a) the employer would not pay the tax if it were not for the existence of the employee on the payroll, and (b) the contribution by the employer is a portion of the total compensation package for the employee, and hence has the effect of reducing wages by approximately the amount of the tax (Brittain, 1972). Placing a larger share of the social insurance contribution on the employer, however, has some of the same political appeal as the corporation tax, i.e. it is perceived as less of an imposition to tax an employer than to tax an individual. Further, economically, if the net cost (total of wages and taxes) would be the same for the employer, it makes relatively little difference. Finally, administratively, employers tend to be less mobile and to keep better records than individuals and therefore it is easier to extract revenue from a company than from an individual.

The question of financing social insurance through social insurance contributions will be returned to later, in the discussion of public expenditures, but here it should be noted that the same organization which collects the income tax may not collect social insurance contributions. Often the organization responsible for distributing benefits also will be responsible for collecting contributions. In many European countries, these are quasi-governmental organizations into which employers pay the contributions (including those withdrawn from employees' paychecks). For example, there are some 1,600 *Krankenkasse* (sickness funds) in former West Germany responsible for administering health insurance programs financed by social insurance contributions; these are considered private organizations. Although these organizations are parastatal, they enjoy the same legal authority as a state organization in collecting contributions (taxes). This is but one of several instances of institutional fragmentation of the State in the collection of revenue. Fragmentation tends to produce administrative difficulties within government, but also helps perpetuate the fiscal illusion of lower taxation.

A final point should be made about this approach to taxing income. This, unlike other forms of income taxation, is relatively difficult to evade if an individual works for an organization of any consequence at all. This is one reason why some governments which historically have been plagued by tax evasion have adopted extremely high rates of social insurance contributions, as well as other forms of payroll taxation. France, for example, collects almost 48 percent of its tax revenue (1986) from social insurance and other payroll taxes. Social insurance taxes can be collected prior to the money being paid to the employee and, since the employee has a definite interest in having his or her rights to a pension and other benefits up-to-date, is likely to assist the State in policing employers. As it has become more acceptable to withdraw personal income taxes from payrolls, the special appeal of social insurance taxation is decreasing, but it remains an important means for a State to ensure that it will be receiving its desired share of taxes on income from one source or another.

Summary. There are a number of different ways to tax income, and almost all governments use all available to them. These taxes on income, taken broadly, are the major source of revenue for all OECD countries (table 2.3). Even Ireland, which uses this tax handle

Table 2.3 Taxes on income as percentage of total revenue, 1985

	Personal and corporate income taxes	*Social security contributions*	*Total*[a]
Australia	54.4	0.0	59.9
Austria	26.4	31.8	58.2
Belgium	40.6	33.2	73.8
Canada	44.3	13.3	57.6
Denmark	56.8	3.8	61.4
Finland	50.6	9.0	60.1
France	17.1	43.6	62.8
Germany	34.8	36.5	71.3
Greece	17.6	34.9	52.5
Ireland	34.6	14.8	52.0
Italy	36.8	34.7	72.1
Japan	45.8	30.2	76.0
Luxembourg	44.4	25.5	70.5
Netherlands	26.5	43.9	70.4
New Zealand	69.0	0.0	69.7
Norway	39.5	20.6	60.1
Portugal	25.9	26.0	54.4
Spain	28.0	41.5	69.5
Switzerland	40.8	32.1	72.9
United Kingdom	38.9	17.5	56.5
United States	42.8	29.4	72.2
Average	39.1	24.0	63.8

[a] Includes payroll taxes and other small taxes on income. Therefore the total may be greater than the sum of the other two columns.
Source: OECD, annual a

the least, receives over 50 percent of their government revenue from taxes on incomes. Further, when all taxes on income are added together, the variance among the countries is diminished. For example, there is a 403 percent difference between the highest and lowest levels of reliance on the personal income tax (New Zealand with 69 percent and France with 17.1 percent) but only a 42 percent difference between the highest and lowest reliance (Belgium at 73.8 and Ireland at 52 percent) on all taxes on income. Since some countries do not charge any social security taxes, calculating the differences is impossible. However, for those countries that do use this tax, the highest reliance (the Netherlands) is 1,055 percent higher than the lowest (Denmark). It thus appears that all industrialized democracies have decided to base their fiscal well-being on the success of taxes on income, finding sufficient ways to extract the revenue they need even when citizens are somewhat adverse to paying the conventional personal income tax.

Taxes on Expenditure

The second major tax handle is taxes on expenditures. These taxes also come in a variety of forms and catch money being spent in a number of different ways. If anything, they affect an even broader spectrum of the population than do income taxes, because anybody – whether a millionaire or living on a small government pension – will pay the same amount of tax on the same purchase. Because of this equal treatment of consumers, expenditure (or consumption) taxes are often considered to be regressive and unfair (but see Kaldor, 1955). On the other hand, the taxes do treat all citizens identically (Pechman, 1980), and force all or almost all citizens to make some contributions to government, thus others (Warren, 1980) regard consumption taxes as the fairest form of taxation.

Sales and value-added taxes Governments can extract income as people earn their income, and they can also collect revenues as people spend the money remaining. Almost all money in the economy passes through both of these sets of transactions (savings and investments are a major exception), and therefore government can catch most citizens in its tax system. Even though most sales and value-added taxes do not collect a tax on unprocessed food, clothing, and other necessities of life, it is collected on almost everything else. Therefore, unless a citizen is eking out an extremely modest living, and spends money only for food, clothes, and rent (even though that may be taxed), he or she will make some contributions to government through a sales or value-added tax.

We have to this point been discussing sales and value-added taxes (VAT) as if they were identical, but, although they do have some important elements in common, they do operate somewhat differently. Both are taxes on general consumption, so that most commodities are treated the same and are taxed at the same rate. Some necessities, or a few items with special political appeal, may be excluded or taxed at lower rates (table 2.4), but the sales tax and

Table 2.4 Exclusions from VAT taxation[a]

	Food	*Clothing*	*Rental housing*	*Medical services*	*News-papers*
Belgium	X		X	X	X
Denmark			X	X	X
France			X	X	
Germany			X	X	
Ireland	X	X	X	X	
Italy	X		X	X	X
Netherlands			X	X	X
New Zealand			X		
Norway			X	X	
Portugal	X		X	X	X
Spain			X	X	X
Sweden			X	X	X
United Kingdom	X	X	X	X	X

[a] Including zero rating.
Source: Tait, 1988

VAT are general taxes on expenditures. How they differ is in the way by which they are collected. The majority of countries using this form of taxation use the VAT; of the 22 countries in table 2.3, eight use a sales tax rather than VAT.

With the value-added tax, at each stage of production a tax is levied on the difference between the price of the materials that go into the product and the cost of that final product. For example, for an automobile, the value-added tax would be levied when raw materials are made into steel, glass, rubber, etc. needed for the car, and again when those materials are fashioned into the automobile, and again on the difference between the wholesale and the retail prices.[3] At each stage, the tax is included in the price of the product, so the consumer sees a single price and not a separate tax bill. For a very large item such as our automobile the VAT may be shown separately (in part so the automobile itself does not appear as expensive) but for most products purchased in a shop there is only a price. The buyer/taxpayer may know that there is 15 or 22 or whatever percent VAT included in that price, but after the initial shock of this form of taxation (seen as higher prices) has been absorbed, the prices appear more normal and consumers just pay them. Sales taxes, in contrast, are single stage taxes. They are levied once, either at the wholesale level (New Zealand) or on the price of the commodity at the retail level (state and local government in the United States). With the wholesale tax the tax is computed as a part of the price of the commodity, like VAT. With a retail sales tax, when a consumer picks an item off the shelf and takes it to the cash register, an additional percentage will be added to the price in the form of the sales tax.

The VAT (and the wholesale sales tax) has the advantage for government that it is relatively invisible; unless the consumer is thinking about the issue at the time, he or she will not be particularly aware that a tax is being paid. The retail sales tax, however, is more visible, as a few cents or dollars are added to the price of the product after the consumer sees the nominal price. The tax rates for sales taxes are generally lower than for VAT. The highest rate for the sales tax in the United State where it is commonly used in 8.25 percent (combined state and local), while the highest VAT rate is over 30 percent. Despite that, the sales tax is more visible and hence is more of a potential political liability. The VAT may be less visible to the consumer/taxpayer but its complexity may make it more so to the businessman who must keep detailed records about the value added to products, the amount of tax they are paying for semi-manufactured goods that should be credited or rebated, etc. Keeping records and filling in forms about the VAT requires even small businesses several hours a week. The sales tax is easier to administer even when merchants have to make decisions about which items (food, medicine, etc.) are not taxable. Thus, there is something of a trade-off between these two methods of taxing general consumption. What is almost certain, however, is that governments will use this tax handle; of the 22 OECD countries only Japan has not had a significant general consumption tax, but did pass a 3 percent national sales tax at the end of 1988.

Customs and excises Sales tax and the VAT are taxes on general consumption, but this does not end government's taxation of consumption by its citizens. There are also a number of taxes on specific commodities, or on some imported products. A tax on a specific commodity is called an *excise* tax while *customs duties* or *tariffs* are taxes on goods imported from abroad. Again, almost every country uses these forms of taxation as a part of their revenue-raising portfolio, although reliance on customs for revenue has been declining as economies become increasingly internationalized and countries depend upon foreign trade for their own economic prosperity. Excise taxes are sometimes called "sin taxes" because they tend to fall most heavily on commodities such as alcohol and tobacco, and on services such as gambling. There are several reasons why governments may choose to single out these goods for taxation, and to charge rather high tax rates. One is that excise taxes are a relatively sure source of revenue. In economic terms, the demand for alcohol and tobacco is relatively inelastic, and up to a very high threshold no price will deter the individuals who want to consume them. Therefore, a high tax rate simply produces greater revenue for government. On the other hand, high tax rates are also used to deter consumption. High prices certainly will not eliminate consumption, but they may reduce it from excessive and destructive levels (Lewit and Coate, 1982; Cook, 1983). The evidence about the effects of taxation on alcohol and tobacco consumption is somewhat mixed, but there appears to be some limited effect of higher prices on levels of consumption. Finally, there is a moral element to having higher prices charged through taxation for these goods; some people believe that if their fellow citizens want to "sin" they should have to pay for it very dearly (in this world if not the next).

Excise taxes are not, however, confined to alcohol, tobacco, and gambling. They are also charged on other, less "sinful" products. One common target for excise taxation is gasoline and other motor fuels, while luxuries of all types – jewelry, perfume, furs, etc. – may also attract excise taxes at very high rates. Finally, in some countries such as France and Italy the practice of levying numerous excise taxes as a means of generating revenues in societies resistant to taxation continues. So, for example, in 1985 France charged more than 30 different excise taxes and Italy had 20 (including one on bananas); the leader however is Denmark with 47. As a number of the commodities which have been burdened with excises are virtual necessities of modern life (lightbulbs in Denmark), this is again a means of ensuring that all citizens will make at least a minimal contribution to the expenses of the State, even if they are able to evade or avoid other taxes. Also, excises like the VAT are included in the selling price of the commodity so that these are invisible, and therefore less politically sensitive, forms of taxation.

Taxes on fuels for automobiles and trucks raise the point that excise taxes are frequently dedicated, or earmarked, taxes much as are social insurance contributions. That is, it is common to allocate the revenue from the tax collected on motor fuels to highway construction and maintenance. Also, in some countries, all or a portion of the revenue derived from the tax on alcoholic beverages is used for treating alcoholism and other addictive diseases. Other smaller excise taxes also may be earmarked for specific purposes, and there is a general tendency to think of excise taxes as a ready source of revenue for specific public purposes. Further, because those who pay the tax tend to benefit from earmarking, there is a tendency to think of excises as user charges as much as taxes.

Finally, customs duties are taxes on goods and services imported from another country. Historically, customs have been a major revenue source for most countries, when economies and tax administration did not generate adequate tax handles for governments to collect the income they needed. So, for example, in 1850 customs duties amounted to almost all the revenue for the federal government in the United States, over 40 percent for Sweden and the United Kingdom. Some countries, e.g. France and Italy, relied less on customs but extracted very heavy excise taxes (Flora 1986a; 1986b). Governments could afford to be financed by customs duties so long as the international economy was robust, and so long as they did not undertake a large number of expensive programs. Customs duties remained an important source of revenue for less economically developed countries in the 1980s, with approximately 25 percent of the tax revenues for Kenya coming from customs and almost 20 percent for Paraguay (International Monetary Fund, monthly).

Customs are used for a variety of purposes, as are excise taxes. The first is simply to raise revenue for government, although this function has been largely superseded in most industrialized countries because of the need to raise larger volumes of revenue. The income tax and the value-added tax are more efficient at generating large volumes of revenue. In addition, as economies become more internationalized, few countries want to restrict the flow of trade with tariffs – a sentiment reinforced by international agreements such as GATT.[4] Despite that, customs duties still account for, on average, 2 percent of all revenues of the OECD countries; not a very high pecentage but a huge amount of money. The second function of customs is to regulate the flow of goods, and to a lesser extent services, into a country. Customs are a means of protecting the industries of a country against competition from other countries, especially when it is believed that the other country may be using unfair tactics, such as selling products below the cost of production (dumping) in order to gain a larger share of the international market. In some instances customs duties may be sufficiently high to make it impossible, or at least extraordinarily expensive, to import certain products. This raising of prohibitive duties is now most commonly practiced in the less developed countries as a means of protecting their "infant industries" or to prevent scarce foreign exchange resources from being used on consumer goods. Prohibitive customs duties may still be used in more developed countries to protect industries (computers, electronics, etc.) believed to be vital either for defense or for future economic development. Some countries also use non-tariff barriers to restrict imports, e.g. quotas or regulations on types of products, but as these do not generate any revenue they will not be discussed here. Even this regulatory function of customs is now losing its importance as the internationalization of domestic economies makes prohibiting importation of most goods less desirable. To limit imports is also ultimately to limit exports, and few economies can now afford that luxury. Even with internationalization some relatively minor customs duties will remain to generate some modest revenues for government.

Taxes on Property

The final major "tax handle" for government is the property owned by its citizens and by corporations. The most commonly used tax on property is the tax on real property – land and the buildings that occupy it – but other forms of property also can be taxed. Some governments impose a tax on the wealth of citizens, so that it is not only the income that the individual earns each year which is taxed, but also the accumulation of income over time. This is true even if that wealth is held in a form other than real property. Finally, almost all governments extract some revenue when a person dies and passes along any sizeable assets to others (estate taxes), or if he or she attempts to avoid estate taxes by giving gifts while still alive (gift taxes). Government is not interested in the modest gifts that all families give at holidays, but they may be very interested in large gifts of cash or land that the wealthy may be able to make to their families.

Real estate taxes Real estate taxes, usually referred to as the property tax, are the principal form of property taxation. Although used in some form in most countries, the property tax is used most extensively in the Anglo-American democracies, where it is the traditional means of financing local government. For most local governments in the United States, for example, the property tax is the major (and often sole) source of local tax revenues. The same was true in the United Kingdom, but the Thatcher government changed the revenue source of local governments to a poll tax, or per capita tax, charged on all citizens over the age of 18. However, the political reaction to the poll tax has since prompted a reintroduction of a property tax element in local government finance in Britain. The property tax is also an important source of revenue in Canada, the Antipodes, and Ireland, and is used extensively in several Continental European countries as well, especially Switzerland. The property tax has been a declining source of revenue for local governments in Scandinavia as it replaced by the more buoyant and progressive income tax.

The logic underlying the property tax to finance local government is that property owners are the principal beneficiaries of the services provided by local governments. Their houses are protected by the fire department and the police department, and their houses receive water, sanitation, and the other services usually associated with local government. Reliance on the property tax does, however, place substantial burdens on local governments. The property tax is somewhat more difficult to administer than are many other taxes. It is charged on the value of property, and therefore if the tax is to be applied fairly, the value of property must be assessed. This requires a skilled staff to do properly. In addition, unless property is assessed annually, the stated value of property on the tax books will almost certainly lag behind its real value. This means that property taxes will also tend to lag behind the costs of providing local government services. Therefore, local governments may have difficulties in keeping their revenues equal to their expenditure needs (Meltsner, 1971; Clark and Ferguson, 1983).[5] As local governments are usually prohibited from running operating deficits in the countries where it must rely so heavily on the property tax, they may experience real budgetary difficulties.

There are also some real political difficulties with the property tax. Because it does involve assessment, and local governments frequently send out revised tax bills and new assessments for the tax, it may be more visible than other forms of taxation. Even if government does not raise the property tax rate (the amount charged per dollar or pound of assessed valuation), it still *appears* to citizens as if the tax has been increased when new assessments arrive in the mailbox. This is to some extent what happened in California to trigger Proposition 13 and the "revolt" against property taxation there, and political discontent about assessments is a common occurrence when there is a property tax of any magnitude. Most local governments would like to be able to use other forms of taxation (with or instead of property taxes), but commonly are prohibited by laws or even by constitutional provisions.

In addition to the political woes that the property tax creates for local government, it also creates some real problems for taxpayers, especially the poor and the elderly. As property has increased in value in most industrialized countries, especially rapidly in cities, many elderly people have found themselves owning relatively valuable pieces of property without an income sufficient to afford the ever-increasing property taxes. There have been numerous newspaper stories about the elderly – and even some working-age people – being driven from their homes by a heartless government and its property tax. Although some local governments have made arrangements so that people need not be forced from their homes by the property tax (homestead exemptions and so-called circuit breaker provisions) there is still a problem when the value of property, and therefore liabilities for property tax, are increasing rapidly.

Wealth, estate, and gift taxation Taxes on estates and gifts also require administrative expenses that other types of taxes may not. This is also true of general taxes on accumulated wealth. In all these cases the nature of the wealth and its market value must be ascertained, and this may be difficult to achieve. In countries with a wealth tax citizens have an incentive to disguise how much they own. This can be done in a number of ways, but often it is achieved by keeping the wealth out of the country in places such as Switzerland and Luxembourg that have strict banking laws guaranteeing secrecy. In addition to identifying any wealth, a value must be placed on that which is known. This may be difficult when the wealth is held in the form of art or similar assets. At times governments negotiate with a taxpayer for a certain piece of art to satisfy estate or wealth taxes that are due, with the belief that it would be more valuable to keep the art in the country than to receive the immediate cash flow. In addition to art and other tangible assets, trusts and other complicated financial arrangements may make it difficult for governments to identify wealth and the flow of funds in order to be able to extract what it is due, either at the time of death or as an annual wealth tax. While wealth and estate taxes may have a number of administrative difficulties, they do serve several purposes for government. First, they are a means of allowing government access to yet another source of revenue. Wealth taxes further allow government to distribute the total costs of its operations over a larger variety of sources. This helps prevent any single source of revenue from becoming so visible and onerous that it would provoke a public outcry, or from distorting economic activity. Finally, since they are intended to fall most heavily on the most affluent, these taxes are often perceived as being "fair" by citizens, and they may allow governments to address more readily any redistributive goals they may have. Unfortunately for government, however, the more affluent usually can hire the best tax advice, and are often able to avoid legally paying estate or gift taxes of any consequence (Cooper, 1979).

Non-tax Revenues

Although this is a book about taxation, we should not forget that governments derive a large proportion of their revenues from sources other than taxation (Schick, 1986; OECD, 1990c). These non-tax revenue sources have become increasingly important as citizens have become less enamoured of paying taxes and have placed an increasing number of roadblocks in the path of any government attempting to raise or even maintain taxes (Ladd and Tideman, 1981). Further, some politicians make extravagant pledges not to raise taxes in order to get elected but must confront budgetary realities once in office. Therefore, governments are looking for other sources of revenue, and have found them in a number of places. The most significant non-tax revenues are from borrowing and from fees and charges for services provided by government.

The most important non-tax revenue source, in terms of the amount of money raised, is borrowing (table 2.5). This may be borrowing by central governments simply to fund the deficits they have incurred by spending more than they have been willing to tax, or it may be borrowing by local governments for capital improvements to roads, water systems, schools, or whatever (Sbragia, 1979). In countries with large nationalized industries, there is also a great deal of borrowing to construct new plants and to purchase new equipment for the industries. While borrowing is a simple expedient for governments in need of money in the short-run, the difficulty is that those loans will have to be repaid, and repaid with interest. This commitment to repay will limit the capacity of the borrowing government to undertake new programs. For example, in the United States, debt interest alone has become (1988) over 14 percent of the total federal budget, thereby restricting the amount of money available to spend for the programs that citizens are demanding (Mills

Table 2.5 Public debt as a percentage of Gross National Product, 1950–1987

	1950	*1960*	*1970*	*1980*	*1982*	*1985*	*1987*
Australia	60.0	14.1	39.6	20.7	19.1	19.5	20.0
Austria	NA	NA	NA	26.3	30.4	38.7	47.4
Belgium	63.5	57.1	47.8	51.6	78.3	102.1	105.5
Canada	83.6	29.2	28.9	27.5	31.1	41.1	45.3
Denmark	34.3	18.8	9.1	12.4	17.7	15.8	19.2
Finland	25.6	9.0	8.7	9.4	12.4	14.7	14.9
France	33.4	28.6	13.2	14.7	17.0	22.7	18.7
Germany	9.9	7.6	6.9	15.7	19.5	20.9	22.1
Ireland	42.8	59.7	66.0	77.5	NA	NA	NA
Italy	30.1	34.9	36.8	60.7	71.1	96.3	81.0
Japan	10.5	6.0	6.8	NA	NA	NA	NA
Luxembourg	NA	NA	NA	5.1	5.3	6.3	5.9
Netherlands	92.2	43.5	28.6	29.2	39.3	54.7	58.3
New Zealand	95.6	NA	NA	51.8	61.9	74.7	74.7
Norway	24.3	28.8	24.0	38.2	27.6	27.6	28.6
Spain	40.0	38.5	NA	17.3	24.4	27.9	37.8
Sweden	42.6	34.9	21.2	30.6	44.4	57.3	53.8
Switzerland	39.0	16.0	6.0	13.8	12.2	12.1	10.4
United Kingdom	233.2	NA	NA	46.3	44.4	47.0	47.1
United States	90.0	56.9	28.2	30.3	31.1	39.9	43.5
Average[a]	48.3	29.2	23.0	27.3	32.4	40.4	40.1

[a] Average for the thirteen countries for which we have information in every year.
Source: International Monetary Fund, monthly *Washington, DC: International Monetary Fund, monthly*

and Palmer, 1983). The debt and debt interest situation of many Third World countries (as well as Ireland and Italy) is even more serious, with governments borrowing one-quarter to one-third of all government revenues. The debt burden has become so great that some Third World countries have had to make unilateral decisions about suspending or reducing interest payments if they are to be able to provide even basic public services.

In addition to borrowing, governments collect increasing revenues as fees and charges (table 2.6). With the "conservative revolution" in many countries, governments have found that many services they have always provided free could actually be marketed and charged

Table 2.6 Non-tax revenue as percentage of total revenue, 1988

	Property	*Fees, sales*	*Other*	*Total*
Australia	8.1	6.2	0.3	14.6
Austria	3.8	9.3	1.7	14.8
Belgium	NA	NA	NA	5.2
Canada	10.1	4.2	2.0	16.3
Denmark	8.8	4.0	1.2	14.0
Finland	NA	NA	NA	14.1
France	2.5	2.5	1.8	6.8
Germany	4.3	6.8	2.4	13.5
Greece	7.2	2.7	1.9	11.8
Ireland	7.2	5.7	NA	12.9
Italy	NA	NA	NA	NA
Japan	NA	NA	NA	NA
Luxembourg	8.3	2.5	1.4	12.2
Netherlands	12.4	3.2	0.5	16.1
New Zealand	8.9	4.5	0.2	13.6
Norway	13.3	4.0	0.8	18.1
Portugal	NA	NA	NA	NA
Spain	4.2	4.5	2.5	11.2
Sweden	13.0	1.5	5.6	20.1
Switzerland	4.7	12.6	NA	17.3
United Kingdom	7.9	3.8	1.5	13.2
United States	11.5	5.3	2.3	19.1
OECD average[a]	8.0	4.9	1.5	14.4

[a] This is an average of the 17 countries for which we have data.
Source: OECD, 1990b

for (Seldon, 1981). Charging fees for services helps governments in several ways. First, it enables them to keep taxes down, or in some cases actually to reduce taxes. In addition, fees and charges make the people who actually want a service pay for it, and frees those who do not want the service from having to finance it through taxation. Also, charging fees enables governments to collect some revenues from people who live outside their boundaries but who nonetheless use the services provided by the local government – frequently a major benefit for large cities. Finally, using charges is a means of rationing access to facilities that might otherwise be used excessively or unwisely. If citizens have to pay a fee for those facilities, they will perhaps make wiser decisions about their use.

Fees and charges are not, however, without their own problems. First, they may prevent the poor from using facilities. User charges may deter the very people who need a service most from receiving it and therefore turn the targeting of public programs completely on its head. Therefore, most governments do not impose charges on all facilities, e.g. libraries, public health clinics, for which they could in principle charge. Second, if the fees being charged for a service are small, collecting and administering the money could cost more than they yield. Finally, some would argue more philosophically that the institution of government should be concerned with providing services rather than marketing them, and that the nature of government is fundamentally altered by this approach to fiscal needs.

Who Collects the Taxes?

Now that we know what types of taxes governments are collecting, we need to look at which levels of government are responsible for collecting those taxes. As with taxes in general, we need to understand first the total amount of revenue being collected at each level of government and then which particular types of taxes are administered by which stratum of government. The first discussion highlights the degree of independence of subnational governments from central control; local governments with more independent revenue sources can, everything else being equal, do more of what they choose rather than what the central government wants them to do (Newton, 1980; Levine and Posner, 1981). The types of taxes that each level of government has at its disposal are also important in defining the autonomy of local governments. For example, the property tax is not a buoyant tax, and if local authorities are dependent upon that tax their autonomy is severely constrained. In addition to low buoyancy, subnational governments also frequently are given more visible taxes than those retained by the central government; retail sales taxes tend to be subnational taxes while the VAT is a national tax. This allocation of taxes makes the political task of regional and local governments more difficult because they have to overcome more overtly the natural resistance of citizens to taxation.

Countries differ in the proportion of revenues derived from their own sources, and in the manner in which they raise their revenues. The level of own-source revenues for subnational governments varies

Table 2.7 Central government grants as percentage of total revenues of subnational governments, 1985

Australia	50.7
Austria	17.6
Belgium	59.9
Canada	17.3
Denmark	43.7
Finland	32.7
France	39.0
Germany	8.5
Greece	42.5
Ireland	73.4
Italy	84.3
Japan	NA
Luxembourg	50.7
Netherlands	83.8
New Zealand	18.6
Norway	40.1
Portugal	NA
Spain	40.3
Sweden	21.9
Switzerland	12.7
United Kingdom	48.7
United States	12.6
Average	39.9

Source: International Monetary Fund, *Yearbook*, 1987, Washington DC: IMF, 1987

significantly among the OECD countries. The country permitting the greatest local autonomy in revenue-raising (Canada) has 2,000 percent more locally generated revenues than does the country with the greatest centralization of revenue collection (Greece). Federal political systems allow subnational governments substantially greater latitude in revenue collection than do unitary systems. In the six federal countries in these data, subnational governments collect an average of 31.6 percent of total revenue. The average level of local government revenue in unitary governments is 12.1 percent. The Scandinavian countries, although unitary, have a tradition of local democracy and in those four countries subnational governments raise an average of

25.6 percent of all revenues – almost as large a percentage as for the federal countries.

In addition to the total revenue that subnational governments raise, the sources of those revenues are important in determining the autonomy of subnational governments. As shown in table 2.8, subnational governments utilize a variety of revenue sources, but many have to rely on some of the least buoyant, and most politically awkward, revenue sources possible. Most countries now permit subnational governments to charge income taxes, but only in a few countries are local income taxes as significant a source of revenue for local governments as for national governments (Bogason, 1987).

Table 2.8 Sources of local government revenues (in percent), 1985

	Income	*Property*	*Goods and services*	*Other*
Australia	0.0	38.0	33.7	28.3
Austria	46.8	5.1	37.0	11.1
Belgium	78.9	0.0	15.3	5.8
Canada	35.9	21.0	40.0	3.1
Denmark	93.4	6.4	0.2	0.0
Finland	99.0	0.9	0.1	0.0
France	16.0	32.6	9.7	41.7
Germany	68.1	9.0	22.8	0.1
Greece	14.5	9.0	33.8	42.7
Ireland	0.0	100.0	0.0	0.0
Italy	66.7	0.0	10.5	22.8
Japan	58.0	23.7	17.2	1.1
Luxembourg	83.0	4.2	8.1	4.7
Netherlands	0.0	75.4	24.6	0.0
New Zealand	0.0	93.0	7.0	0.0
Norway	91.4	5.5	0.4	2.7
Portugal	64.4	1.6	32.9	1.1
Spain	40.3	10.4	39.9	9.4
Sweden	99.7	0.0	0.3	0.0
Switzerland	81.3	14.2	4.5	0.0
Turkey	NA	NA	NA	NA
United Kingdom	0.0	100.0	0.0	0.0
United States	25.5	30.7	43.8	0.0
Average	48.3	26.4	17.4	7.9

Source: OECD, annual a

In federal countries, e.g. the United States, the power of local governments to charge income taxes depends on state governments, and only eleven states allow local governments to use this revenue source. Further, as shown in table 2.8, subnational governments increasingly depend upon fees and charges for revenues. For example, in the United States in 1985, fees accounted for almost 24 percent of revenue for subnational governments, but less than 19 percent in 1975. In general, therefore, subnational governments depend upon sources that are less likely to produce additional revenue without some political action, and hence they have substantial restraints imposed on their fiscal autonomy.

The absence of autonomy of subnational governments is enhanced, or perhaps just indicated, by the flow of grant money from central governments to subnational governments. Although tracking the flow of funds among levels of government is a complex task (Anton, 1980; Hesse, 1978), the best evidence indicates that grants from central governments to regional and local governments in 1985 averaged 37.7 percent of their total expenditures. The greatest dependence on central government was in Italy, with over 84 percent of local expenditures financed by central government grants (see Table 2.7). The least dependence at that time was in West Germany, with only 8.5 percent of subnational expenditures financed centrally. As noted with their capacity to raise own-source revenues, local governments in federal countries depend less on the central government than do local governments in unitary countries. An average of less than 20 percent of total subnational revenue comes from the central government in federal countries, as compared to over 45 percent in unitary countries. Again, the Scandinavian countries, although unitary, allow greater latitude for local revenue collection, with an average of only 34.6 percent of local expenditures being financed centrally. Although not all grants are equally destructive of local autonomy (Oates, 1977), in general the more dependent local governments are financially, the less they will be able to make their own policy decisions.

Evaluating Taxes

The principal sources of revenue used by contemporary governments of industrialized countries have now been described. The following is a discussion of the logic underlying these taxes, and the criteria which can be used to evaluate both individual taxes and national systems of taxation. Some criteria are derived from economics, others are political, and some are concerned with the administration of the taxes. No tax could be judged the best by all these criteria, but it is important to understand what values are enhanced when specific tax instruments are selected. Further, these multiple criteria are yet another argument for the multifacted approach to taxation adopted by most countries. Excessive reliance on one tax instrument will promote a few values and advantage a few citizens, but a broad system of revenue collection provides some support for a range of values and a broad range of citizens.

The Basis of Taxation

There are two fundamental principles which undergird most taxes and have different economic and political ramifications. These are the "ability to pay" principle and the "benefit" principle. Both are concerned with equity and fairness in taxation, and can inform discussions about who should bear the burden of running government, and at times bear the burden of financing specific programs. As the name implies, the former principle argues that taxes should be levied in rough relationship to citizens' abilities to pay those taxes and still be able to maintain a reasonable standard of living of their own. This is the justification for the income tax and other progressive taxcs such as thc wealth tax. As well as being practical to tax where there is money available, there are several more theoretical points involved. One is the economic question of attempting to equalize the utility loss of the taxes across income classes (see Witte, 1985, 32–41). The assumption is that the marginal dollar or krona has less utility for a wealthy person than for a poor, or even middle-class, person. Therefore, more revenue can be extracted from the wealthy without a disproportionate reduction of utility. Empirical research appears to confirm this logic, as even very high levels of taxation have little impact on labor market participation by the very affluent (Hausman, 1981). Measuring utility directly may be impossible, but the inverse relationship of marginal utility to income is largely accepted. The second more theoretical point underlying the ability to pay approach is the philosophical (and political) point of equality, and the desire to make society more equal through progressive taxation.

The second principle justifying tax policy choices is the benefit principle (Musgrave, 1969). We have already mentioned that one option available to governments to finance many of their programs is to levy charges rather than to pay for them by taxation. That is an example of the benefit principle being applied in the extreme, but the basic idea of this approach is that citizens who benefit from a government program should pay for it. Property taxes, for example, are to some degree premised on the assumption that property owners benefit more from local government services than do other citizens. Similarly, all earmarked taxes (social insurance, motor fuels, etc.) tend to plow the receipts of the tax back into programs benefiting the people who paid it. Many government programs cannot be funded by benefit-based tax schemes (table 2.6); if the poor could pay for the programs that benefit them, those programs would not be necessary. However, just as some people consider ability to pay a fair way to apportion taxes, others consider the benefit principle so.

Economic Criteria

This is not a book about the economics of taxation. That subject is a study in itself, and there are a number of excellent books providing that information (Atkinson and Stiglitz, 1980; Davies, 1986). Still, we should understand something about the economic logic of choice that may undergird the selection of taxes before we can understand how political logic may conflict with it, and why the more technical criteria applied by economists do not often win in making tax policy. In fact, it appears that the economic criteria that will be discussed win very infrequently, despite the degree to which economists have dominated thinking about tax policy. It appears that politics is often the factor requiring economists to accept what is to them definitely a "second best" solution, if the solution is even that high on their list of preferences.

Fiscal neutrality One of the most important economic criteria concerning taxes is fiscal neutrality. This criterion argues that the tax system should not impose any special barriers, or provide any special advantages, to citizens or businesses choosing to use their funds or energy one way versus another or to invest in one industry versus another. Instead, the tax system should be neutral among all uses of resources, allowing the market to determine what is the most productive utilization of those available. All sources of income and all expenditures should be, according to this criterion, treated equally. A more discriminatory tax system will distort the operations of the market and, at least in theory, produce lower real economic growth and income.

While this criterion appears very good as economic theory, most politicians would regard it as a hindrance on their use of the tax system as a broad-scale policy instrument. It has already been pointed out that the tax system is used not only to collect revenue but also to achieve a variety of other social and political goals. If this criterion of fiscal neutrality were applied strictly, most or all of the special preferences that are built into tax laws would have to be abandoned. Tax reforms in a number of industrialized countries have already gone some distance in eliminating these preferences, although usually to broaden the revenue base rather than to promote fiscal neutrality. Most politicians, and perhaps most citizens, still appear to want to retain the capacity to utilize taxation for political goals other than financing government. So, for example, after governments go through the long and often painful exercise of eliminating preferences in tax reform legislation, there is often a bill in a subsequent legislative session (or even the same one) restoring old preferences, or creating new ones. For example, the Tax Reform Act of 1986 in the United States itself contained a number of one-time special preferences for organizations and individuals. Then, a year later, a "technical corrections" bill added a number of additional preferences to the legislation.

Buoyancy A second criterion derived from the economics of taxation is the buoyancy of a tax. This refers to the extent to which a tax increases in line with economic growth, inflation, or some other significant economic aggregate. Everything else being equal, a good tax will enable government to keep its revenue constant relative to its needs without continual rate adjustment. We have already pointed out, for example, that the lack of buoyancy of the property tax presents a significant problem for local governments that depend upon it heavily. Some taxes, the progressive income tax for example, actually give governments enhanced revenues relative to economic resources when there is either economic growth or inflation. This buoyancy gives the government a "fiscal dividend," which it can then spend without needing to increase taxes.

The above point demonstrates that, although I have classified buoyancy as an economic criterion for my purposes here, it also has a very important political dimension. If government is able to receive a continuing dividend from growth, or even if it is able to keep pace with growth and inflation, then politically it can appear more responsible and sensitive to the needs of its public than a government that must continually adjust tax rates (usually upward) in order to meet its expenditure requirements. If a tax is sufficiently buoyant, a government may be able actually to reduce the tax rate and still receive sufficient income to finance its operations. This is, of course, an extremely desirable political position for a government in which to find itself.

Fiscal conservatives attempt to find ways to restrain the buoyancy of taxes. They do not like governments receiving a bonus from the tax system that can be spent on new programs or used to enhance existing ones. They have sought to limit buoyancy in tax systems by two devices – in addition to their continuing pressures to lower taxes in general. The first is to index tax thresholds and brackets in progressive income taxes. If there is inflation, and brackets are not adjusted, people with the same real income will pay a larger proportion of their income as tax without government ever passing tax legislation. If the brackets are adjusted automatically, then there is no fiscal dividend and governments must act if they want more money. The second way to limit buoyancy is to reduce the progression of taxes. This has been done in the majority of countries around the world, with many now using income taxes with only three or four brackets. For example, the income tax in the United States in 1976 had 25 brackets, and as late as 1986 there were 12 brackets. In 1988 there are only two brackets, with a surtax on part of the upper bracket making in essence a third. Of the 22 OECD countries for which we have data, 16 reduced the number of tax brackets between 1975 and 1985 (New Zealand from 22 to 5), 6 increased the number, and 2 remained the same (OECD, 1987).

Distributional consequences It has already been mentioned that taxes differ in the extent to which they redistribute income, and from whom they take and to whom they give. Income tax, for example, is for the most part progressive, and takes a larger share of income the more an individual earns. The sales tax and other consumption taxes, on the other hand, are for the most part regressive (Institute for Fiscal Studies, 1988). Because the poor spend a larger proportion of their income on taxable goods and services (as opposed to saving it or paying mortgages) consumption taxes tend to be regressive. In both examples, the exact impact (incidence) of the tax can be manipulated; exemptions and deductions may make the income tax less progressive, and excluding food, clothing, and the like from consumption taxes can make them less regressive. However, taxes do have significant consequences for the distribution of income in a society.

To understand the impact of taxes on income groups in society, we must distinguish nominal taxpayers from those who actually bear the tax burden. This is the question of the *incidence* of the tax. For example, although corporations nominally pay corporation income and profit taxes, depending upon the administration of the tax and economic circumstances the real incidence of the tax may be on purchasers of the corporation's products, or shareholders, or perhaps even employees (Mieszkowski, 1969; Stiglitz, 1976). Similarly, although employers pay a share of social insurance, the incidence may be on the employees (lower wages) or consumers (higher prices). In short, we must determine who really pays the taxes, rather than simply where the check is written (Pechman, 1986; Browning and Johnson, 1979).

The distributional impact of taxation is a political as well as economic criterion, especially for politicians on the left. Distribution, however, will be discussed as an economic criterion because of its relationship with economic policymaking. If, for example, a Keynesian model is assumed with effective demand as the principal regulator of the economy, then during a recession government would want to manipulate the tax structure to put more money in the hands of the less affluent. On the other hand, if a government adopts a "supply-side" (Bartlett and Roth, 1983) notion of economic management, it would use the tax system to permit the wealthy to retain more of their earnings so that they would (presumably) invest savings in productive enterprises that would produce economic growth. Although the underlying models are very different, both approaches to economic management use the tax system as an important policy instrument.

Economic class is not the only dimension along which a population is divided politically or economically. The distributional consequences of tax policies must therefore be considered somewhat more broadly. For example, some tax policies have pronounced regional implications (Bennett, 1980; Paddison, 1983); in the United States the special depletion allowances for oil exploration and production have differentially benefited oil producing states such as Texas, Oklahoma, and Louisiana. These benefits are very important to that industry and have been a political touchstone in those states.[6] Although often less successful than energy producers, all regionally concentrated industries and interests have sought to use tax legislation to gain benefits for themselves. Given the prevalence of this type of tax politics (Good, 1980), the distributional criterion (in practice if not in theory) may run counter to the criterion of fiscal neutrality.

Political Criteria

Although it is difficult to isolate the political from the economic or even from administrative criteria, several characteristics of taxation do have a special political flavor. Economists may have dominated the academic discussion of taxation, but political criteria appear to have dominated tax policymaking in the real world. To every neatly phrased economic theorem about taxation there appears to be at least one political lemma that obviates its austere logic. The fact is that taxes are important political instruments and express important political values, and their evaluation must therefore greatly or even disproportionately reflect their political characteristics and political consequences.

Visibility When we discussed the value-added tax, we noted that one of its several virtues was relative invisibility. Although citizens may know in the back of their minds that they are paying the tax, they are not reminded of this directly. Popular resistance to the VAT may therefore be less than it would be to a tax, such as the sales tax, collected in ways that make its impact more clearly visible. Although the concept of visibility is somewhat imprecise (Wilensky, 1976), and we can debate whether one tax is more visible than another, this is an important political consideration. Governments therefore attempt to make taxes as invisible as possible. For example, using "pay as you earn" (withholding) schemes to collect income taxes does not lessen the tax rate, but because the individual does not have to make out a big check at the end of the tax year (in fact he or she may receive a refund), the tax's visibility is minimized. If they employ invisible taxes governments can impose substantial taxes on the public, and even manipulate rates, with little or no reaction. Wilensky's (1976) analysis of tax protest found that the visibility of the tax system was the principal variable explaining the development of tax protest parties and interest groups. The visibility of the property tax (as well as the availability of referenda and initiatives at the state and local level) helps to explain why it has been such a common target for attack by tax protesters in the United States. In short, if governments want to collect as much money as possible with a minimum amount of resistance and rebellion, they should attempt to make their tax structures as invisible as possible.

It may be possible to stand the visibility argument on its head if the benefits created by government are included in the analysis. Governments may want to make it clear to people just how much service they are purchasing with their tax money and that, on average, the public sector is good value. This need to emphasize the value of the goods and services produced by government is particularly pronounced for public goods – those goods and services such as defense and clean air created by government which do not specifically benefit any particular citizen. It has been argued (Downs, 1967) that citizens tend to undervalue public goods and therefore are less willing to support government with their taxes than perhaps they should be. If the volume of publicly provided goods (and especially public goods) could be made more visible then perhaps citizen resistance to taxation could be lessened.

Political acceptability Everything else being equal, less visible taxes will be more acceptable politically, but everything else is not always equal. Different forms of taxation appear to be more acceptable to citizens of some countries than to those of others. This simple fact is to some degree illustrated by the presence of some zero cells in table 2.1. Those governments have chosen not to use that particular form of taxation, even though there is also a compelling political argument to be made in favor of using every available tax instrument and distributing the costs of government as widely as possible. Either the governments not using a tax do not understand all their options (unlikely) or there are even more compelling political reasons for them not to use the taxes in question.

Political acceptability is related to a number of attributes of a tax, as well as to a number of attributes of politics in a country. For example, there may be a strong preference for redistribution through the public sector which would favor concentrating on direct, progressive taxes such as the income tax (see New Zealand). On the other hand, governments may want to make their tax system as invisible as possible, given public hostility to taxation and other impositions of government (see France and Italy). Other countries (Norway and Sweden) may consider alcohol and tobacco major social problems, and impose very high excise taxes to deter consumption – so high that they are in all probability suboptimal from the perspective of raising revenue. In short, as I will discuss in greater detail in a later chapter, there are a number of factors which affect political acceptability of taxes and which must be considered when attempting to understand tax policy decisions.

Administrative Criteria

Finally, taxes rarely collect themselves, and we must be cognizant of administrative characteristics when tax systems are designed. The best tax in the world, in terms of fairness or buoyancy, or lack of adverse economic impact, will be of little use to government if it cannot be collected. It will be of only slightly greater use if it is so expensive to administer that benefits only slightly outweight costs, or so intrusive that citizens and businesses rebel. For example, some governments still have so-called nuisance taxes on their lawbooks allowing them to collect small amounts of money on stock ownership or moveable personal property. These taxes may be so easy to evade and produce so little potential revenue that they simply are not collected. Similarly, the British income tax included for a number of years "imputed rent" from homes owned by the taxpayer as a component of taxable income.[7] This provision became so difficult to administer equitably within any reasonable cost that it was dropped. In short, an uncollectable tax is not really a tax but rather simply a piece of paper that can create public cynicism, but no revenue for government.

As well as the administrative ease of individual taxes, the administrative characteristics of whole tax systems should be examined. Countries are more or less centralized in tax collection and these administrative arrangements may influence the effectiveness and perceptions of tax systems. For example, in many countries, personal income taxes, social insurance contributions, and the value-added tax are collected by different organizations within central government. This means that corporations must submit reports to three different revenue bureaucracies (assuming personal income tax is withheld by the employer), each with its own forms and its own ways of calculating tax liabilities. To these central government organizations can be added subnational governments which collect their own income or wage taxes. This can create a confusing and inefficient picture for businesses and individual citizens alike.

There are several ways to reduce duplication in revenue collection. One method is to have a single organization collect all taxes of a certain type, e.g. HM Customs and Excise in Britain collects almost all consumption taxes. Another is to have one level of government collect all taxes of a certain sort and then apportion the proceeds among the levels, as is done in Germany (Hesse, 1978). Another means is to standardize definitions to reduce confusion; some states in the United States levy an income tax which is simply a percentage of the federal income tax. Some redundancy, however, can be beneficial in any administrative system (Landau, 1969) as it helps check on the performance of the individual organizations. For example, several different organizations taxing income may identify some potential taxpayers who have slipped through cracks in one organization's monitoring system. This is especially valuable for subnational governments with less sophisticated systems for monitoring employers and employees (Penniman, 1980).

Summary

Collecting government revenue is not a simple task, and making choices about how to do it involves weighing a number of criteria. Criteria from economics are most often cited in academic circles as means of assessing taxation, but there are numerous others which can be invoked. Political and administrative criteria may be as dominant in the real world as those from economics are in the academic world. Politics, with its imperative to make benefits visible and direct and to make costs invisible and indirect (Wilson, 1980), appears to run almost directly counter to economic criteria. While economists might want to make tax systems as neutral as possible, politicians attempt to hang as many benefits on a tax bill (the "Christmas tree" approach) as they can. We must remember, however, that tax laws are made and implemented in a real world, not the more abstract world of economic dogma.

Patterns of Taxation in the OECD World

This last portion of the chapter investigates patterns of taxation within the member countries of the OECD.[8] We will base that analysis on the patterns of taxation found in those 22 countries in 1965, and then look at the evolution of the patterns across time until 1987. This analysis will be based on the percentage of total tax revenue for all levels of government derived from each of eleven types of taxes in table 2.1. We also are using several other variables, such as the centralization of taxation at the national level and the total level of taxation, but the bulk of the analysis is based on yields from the eleven taxes. The data are taken from a common source

(OECD, annual a) and hence have as few problems of comparability as possible when dealing with such a complex subject. These data are the yields of each of these taxes and do not address issues of nominal rates or the real incidence of the taxes. They do, however, reflect categories that citizens contend with when they pay taxes, and categories among which governments choose when they adopt tax laws.

Clusters of Countries, or is Japan Really Like Canada?

This analysis concentrates on differences among the OECD countries in the way in which they raise revenue. There are also similarities, however. The eleven taxes identified (plus a residual "other" category) account for the vast majority of taxation in all countries. Further, all the countries tend to use almost all the taxes, although two countries collect no social insurance contributions, two others collect no contributions from employees, and nine collect no payroll or wealth taxes (table 2.1). Thus, all OECD countries appear broadly similar in their choices of taxes, although each employs the instruments in its own particular pattern.

To simplify the task of trying to understand tax policy choices of 22 countries with eleven possible tax categories, we use the statistical method of cluster analysis (Aldenderfer and Blashfield, 1984). Stated simply, this considers all variables (taxes in this instance) describing a series of cases (countries) and then places the cases into groups in a manner which minimizes the variance within each group and maximizes the distance from other clusters. Further, the technique can provide measures of the distances between the clusters to give an idea of the overall distribution of cases. This method permits examining the whole range of tax yields of the 22 countries and gives some idea of the similarities and differences among them. The initial clustering of the countries in 1965 serves as the basis of the discussion, with changes from that observed pattern showing the dynamics of policy adjustment over the two decades for which we have data. Several different versions of cluster analysis for the OECD countries were attempted for 1965, using from three to seven clusters as possible solutions. The most satisfy solution – theoretically as well as mathematically – was a four cluster solution. The four clusters derived in this analysis are shown in figure 2.1. They are reasonably homogeneous internally, capture a good deal of the variance within the tax data, and also make sense given what else we know about the tax policies and the politics of these countries. Ultimately, each

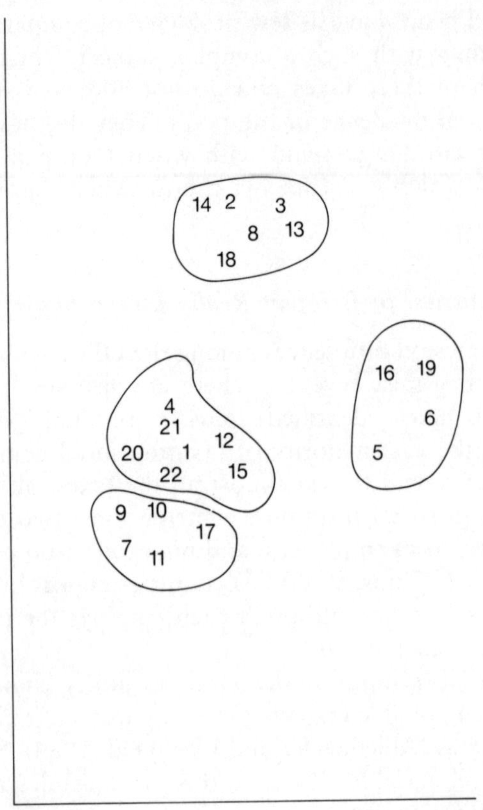

1 = Australia
2 = Austria
3 = Belgium
4 = Canada
5 = Denmark
6 = Finland
7 = France
8 = West Germany
9 = Greece
10 = Ireland
11 = Italy
12 = Japan
13 = Luxembourg
14 = Netherlands
15 = New Zealand
16 = Norway
17 = Portugal
18 = Spain
19 = Sweden
20 = Switzerland
21 = United Kingdom
22 = United States

Figure 2.1 Clusters in two-dimensional space, 1965

country's policy choices must be understood as *sui generis*, but there are also interesting similarities among the countries that can be identified through this technique.

The Anglo-American Democracies and Their Friends

The first cluster extracted by the computer program, and therefore the most distinctive grouping, is composed of the Anglo-American democracies – the United States, the United Kingdom, Canada, Australia, and New Zealand. The cluster also includes Japan and Switzerland, but excludes the Republic of Ireland, which might have been expected to be a part of this grouping given its long (if troubled) political and economic links with the United Kingdom. This cluster is characterized by much higher than average reliance on the property tax, as well as on corporation taxes, and a somewhat higher than average reliance on personal income taxes. Most countries in this cluster also have used both employers' and employees' contributions approximately equally to fund their social insurance programs,[9] and have tended to have lower than average consumption taxes, especially general consumption taxes. This is a pattern of taxation which almost any British or American citizen would find very familiar, although he or she might not recongize that it is distinctive.

Swiss and Japanese membership in this grouping appears to require some explanation. For Japan, the tax system may be to some degree an inheritance from its occupation by the United States after the Second World War (Ishi, 1989, 28ff). For both Switzerland and Japan (as well as the United States), the importance of their corporate communities might have been expected to be associated with low levels of corporate taxation. It may be, however, that because corporations have been successful in so many ways in extracting benefits from governments, those governments cannot be said to be the enemies of business and can therefore employ corporation taxes more heavily.[10] Politically, these taxes are more palatable since they appear to fall on amorphous entities rather than on citizens, although economists would point to their real incidence on consumers and/or shareholders. Finally, Switzerland becomes an even more central member of this cluster if the centralization variable is included in the analysis (centralization is the proportion of total public revenues collected by the central government). When this is done, the United Kingdom and New Zealand appear somewhat more as outliers in the cluster, although the United Kingdom at that time had a somewhat higher proportion of local revenues than most unitary regimes.

The Scandinavian Countries

The second cluster extracted was composed of the Scandinavian countries – Sweden, Norway, Denmark, and Finland. As might have been expected from their social and political similarities,[11] these countries have similar tax policies with a heavy reliance on the personal income tax but relatively low corporate income taxes. They also tended to use the employers' social insurance contribution extensively, but to extract relatively little, or nothing, as the employee's contribution to social insurance. Both citizens and their employers contribute to the tax systems, but in different ways. The manner selected may conform to social democratic ideology, but it also tends to make the tax system rather visible to citizens and may be in part to blame for "tax revolts" in Denmark and to a lesser extent in Norway (Wickman, 1977; Wilensky, 1976).

The impact of taxation in the Scandinavian countries does not end with taxes on income. The Scandinavian countries also extract high consumption taxes, both general consumption taxes and excises, in large part because these governments require a great deal of money to finance their extensive programs in social welfare and, in at least two instances, defense. Consumption taxes are generally less visible to the public than are taxes on income or property, and using these taxes tends to ensure that all citizens will pay at least something toward the cost of government. In addition, excise taxes on tobacco and alcohol are very high in the Scandinavian countries in an attempt to deter consumption of these products, although the evidence of the effectiveness of that strategy is mixed.

Broad-based Taxation

The third cluster extracted from the OECD countries includes Austria, Belgium, Luxembourg, the Netherlands, Spain, and West Germany (pre-reunification). The countries in this group tend to use all tax instruments at their disposal, but to do so in moderation. The pattern followed here is in essence to have no pattern, but rather to use all possible taxes at something around the mean level for all OECD countries. This level is not selected consciously by the governments, but appears rather to emerge from the political and economic systems within which the policy choices are being made. This pattern of taxation tends to reduce the visibility of the tax system to citizens. No one tax stands out as being particularly oppressive, and citizens may not perceive that the total tax bite is large when the individual taxes are taken as nibbles.

As well as a means of limiting visibility, using a number of taxes in limited ways fits well with the general political dynamics of these countries. All of these countries have had, or developed, corporate structures for the management of relationships between the public and private sectors (Schmitter, 1974; Bekke, 1985). That is, in each case private interests were accorded substantial rights of representation in government, and policymaking tended to require some agreement among the interests. These arrangements are particularly prominent in Austria and West Germany and less dominant in Spain but still evident there (Perez-Diaz, 1987). In a policymaking setting with corporatist structures, it is difficult for governments to make any decision which adversely affects, in a very serious way, any organized interest. Therefore, policies may tend toward accommodation and toward a rather low common denominator.

The Latin Cluster

The final cluster extracted by the analysis contains four countries in Southern Europe – France, Greece, Italy, and Portugal. It also contains the Republic of Ireland, but not Spain. These five countries rely heavily on indirect taxation, including customs duties, employers' social security contributions, and consumption taxes (general and specific excises)[12] to meet their revenue needs. To the extent that they have utilized any significant taxes on income, they have been employees' contributions for social insurance. Further, when the centralization variable is used, the countries in this cluster are even more distinct from other clusters because of their high degree of centralization and minimal local autonomy in fiscal affairs.

The pattern of taxation found in these five countries is often argued to reflect the difficulties of their governments in collecting taxes directly from citizens. Since the population generally is unwilling to pay direct taxes on their income, and the pattern of tax administration makes evasion relatively easy, governments must find other means to collect the revenues they need. It is easier for a government to supervise thousands of employers and commercial establishments than it is to scrutinize millions of individual income earners, especially when many of the latter are independent farmers and artisans. Further, consumption taxes make it difficult for any citizen to escape paying some part of the costs of government, especially when excise taxes are levied on virtual necessities of life.

This tax system tends to be regressive, but has been the only effective means of generating revenue in these societies.

Explaining the Differences

Four patterns of taxation have now been identified among the 22 countries of the OECD world. These patterns are interesting and make intuitive sense, but a better understanding is needed of why they have emerged. The explanation will not be like the several statistical explanation of taxation which have been offered; an attempt will be made, however, to explain some of the apparent relationships between tax policies and the political, social, and economic characteristics of the several countries belonging to this universe of affluent democracies.

Politics Given that stress has been laid on the importance of a political analysis of tax policy, the first factor which should be considered is the influence of politics on tax policy choices. It seems somewhat obvious to argue that politics is important for explaining tax policy, given that taxes are some of the most important political decisions which must be made by a government. In some academic circles, however, there is a tendency to forget the real political influences in favor of the search for optimal tax systems, or the true incidence of particular taxes. Still, the clusters that have been identified do show some very clear impact of politics on taxes in several of the countries.

Perhaps the most interesting influence of politics on tax policies is found in the third cluster of countries, which have "broad-base" tax policies. It was argued above that these countries adopted such strategies in part because of the impact of corporatist political structures, and the consequent need to raise revenue without offending major economic or social interests. The impact of corporatist politics may extend well beyond the "politics of anticipation," in which governments seek to anticipate and avoid negative reactions to tax proposals (Good, 1980). The impact may extend to having representatives of those interests involved directly in bargaining over policy. The outcomes of this process appear to be distributive, with all parties benefiting some, or in the case of taxation it may be better to say all parties only being hurt some. In this setting there are no big winners and no big losers.

An opposite influence of politics over tax policy can be seen in the Scandinavian countries, which have tax programs structured to be more redistributive. These programs are designed around high personal income taxes and very low contributions by employees to social insurance programs. These policies reflect the domination of politics by social democratic and labor parties; in the four Scandinavian countries, parties of the left controlled government an average of twelve out of the 20 years from 1946 to 1965. These parties were committed to redistributive policies and were successful in having those policies adopted. This is one of the relatively few instances in which a party government model clearly is related to major policy choices, although there also may be some important linkage to the egalitarian political cultures found in the Scandinavian countries.

Culture Culture is often used as a residual variable to explain social phenomena when all else fails. That casual treatment is perhaps an unfortunate use of this variable, because the values and beliefs of a society can have a profound influence on the policies which their governments select. If nothing else, taxes may be of cultural importance themselves so that indeed "an old tax is a good tax." The influence of political culture over tax policy can be seen most clearly in the Latin cluster. It has often been argued that the culture of these countries is characterized by *incivisme*, and that many members of the population are unwilling to recognize the claims of government – of perhaps even other social institutions – on the resources of individuals and families. While the claims of *incivisme* frequently are overstated, and these societies have been modernizing rapidly, there does appear to be some truth to the belief that French, Italian, and Greek citizens are less willing to participate in organizations outside the family and that they are more reluctant to pay taxes (Peters, 1989, 53–63). In such a setting the strategy of indirect taxation adopted by the governments in this cluster appear very rational.

Another way to look at the influence of culture on tax policies is to examine the use of property taxes in the Anglo-American democracies in the first cluster. At least until 1989 this form of taxation has been the pillar of local taxation in all these countries. This is to some degree a product of history and tradition, and to some extent the product of having a relatively large proportion of the population which has owned property – especially their own home. The use of the property tax also reflects in the culture something of the benefit which citizens can derive from the local public sector, and therefore is a measure of what those citizens should be willing to pay to provide services such as police and fire protection.

Economic and social structure Finally, we should recognize that the tax policy choices made by a government are constrained by the socio-economic environment within which they work. Although some apparent influence of these factors may be attributed to culture and habit, they can also be seen as the direct influence of economic conditions. For example, the use of consumption taxes within the Latin cluster was attributed to cultural variables above, but it might also be a reaction to the relatively low level of economic development in some of the countries in that cluster. As one example, Ireland does not appear to display nearly as much *incivisme* as the others in that grouping, but does have a very large agricultural sector. This structural factor makes consumption taxes an easier approach to revenue collection than more direct forms of taxation. Similarly, the relatively high level of property ownership in the Anglo-American democracies makes the property tax more viable than in countries where fewer people might be concerned about maintaining their own home. We could multiply the example of these influences, but the general point that socio-economic structures must affect policy choices appears clear.

Changing Patterns of Taxation

We have been describing the patterns of taxation that existed in the OECD countries in 1965. This may appear a very ancient time in which to start this discussion, but a great deal about the influences of various factors in policy choices can be gained by looking at policies over time. Even though the 1965 data may appear to come from antiquity, however, in reality very little has changed in the tax policies of these countries. The same clusters identified in 1965 persist, with the few changes discussed below, until 1987. The analyses undertaken in each five years from 1965 to 1985 and then again in 1987 revealed little major shifting of countries among the groups. Thus again we can point to the conservatism that appear to exist in making tax policy. Few politicians have had the ability or desire to push through major changes in tax policy. In fact, even the much vaunted tax reforms of the 1980s and 1990s have done little to alter the distribution of revenue derived from the various taxes. The reforms have had a great deal of impact on who pays the income tax but little on what proportion of total revenues come from that source.

The Move Toward Broad-Based Taxation

Having said that there is a great deal of conservatism in the tax policy choices of governments, it can also be said that there has been some movement. The general direction of that movement has been toward more broad-based taxation of the type found in Cluster 3 discussed above. The most dramatic shift of this type was that France moved from being a part of the Latin cluster in 1980 to being a part of the broad-based cluster (along with its neighbor Spain). Along with that move, the four clusters have moved closer together when various statistical measures of their proximity are used.[13] There is some sense that the countries of the OECD are becoming much more alike in tax policies than they have been. This appears to be happening for a variety of reasons.

Political change There are some good political reasons for countries to be moving toward more broad-based taxation. Perhaps the most important is that this is a means of reducing the visibility of taxation in an era of tax revolts and manifest citizen discontent with "big government." As argued above, the use of a large number of taxes, each charged at a relatively low rate, may create a "fiscal illusion" that taxes really are not so high (Pommerehne and Schneider, 1978). Likewise, the use of a broad spectrum of taxes helps to minimize the probability of mobilization around a single high tax, as occurred in relation to the property tax in California during the time of Proposition 13 (Sears and Citrin, 1985), or is now occurring around the community charge (poll tax) as virtually the sole personal tax financing local government in Britain. Moving toward a broad-based tax system may also mean that governments might actually be able to *reduce* some taxes. Any capable politician would advertise such an event widely, while trying to hide any need to raise other taxes to keep the accounts in balance.

Administration of taxation Administrative institutions also appear to have had some influence on the tendency toward broad-based taxation. Countries that have relied on indirect taxation (largely the Latin cluster) have made greater efforts to collect income taxes due to them (Stathopoulos, 1982). This effort has been aided by technological developments such as computerization of financial records. This has meant that income tax yields have increased substantially – almost doubling as a percentage of total taxation from 1975 to 1987 in Italy – during the later portion of the time period considered. For countries which have relied on direct personal taxes, there has been an increasing use of consumption taxes in part because these taxes are relatively to collect and produce a high return for the money invested in administering them. Some additional return from consumption taxes has come from new or increased tax rates, but some has come simply from more stringent enforcement of existing laws.

International pressures A third source of change in tax policy has been the increasing internationalization of business and finance. This is obvious within the European Community as a crucial part of the movement toward supranational integration has been harmonization of taxation (Puchala, 1984). The EC pressure for harmonization falls most heavily on consumption and corporation taxes (Pearson and Smith, 1988) but to some extent is felt in all areas of national tax policy. Even in countries which are not members of the EC, there are some pressures from the international economy to harmonize their tax systems. This can be seen in the move by the Swiss government to adopt a value-added tax similar to that used within the European Community as a way of making business between the EC and Switzerland easier (Schneider, 1989). The ease of movement of capital and persons in the world economy means that it is increasingly difficult for any country to maintain a very distinctive tax profile.

Economics Last but not least we should point out that there have been some economic pressures toward greater harmonization of taxes across the OECD world, and toward broad-based tax systems. One of the most important pressures has been the strong desire of many governments to reduce the impacts of direct personal and corporate income taxes on their citizens as a means of encouraging economic growth. This strategy was most clearly seen in the Reagan tax cut in the United States, but less dramatic examples have also been implemented in other countries. Even the Scandinavian countries have had some pressures for reducing income taxes and either reducing spending or shifting some of the burden of taxation (Haskel, 1987). Associated with that also have been a number of tax reforms that have sought to make the effects of taxation more neutral across a range of industries and individuals (Hagemann, Jones, and Montador, 1988).

Summary

The above catalog of changes and reasons for change points to the growth of broad-based taxation, and rather similar patterns of taxation, among the OECD countries. Although countries do retain some distinctive patterns of revenue collection, they have tended toward homogenization. There have been pressures operating in almost all of the countries that would aid this process. The countries that have relied very heavily on personal income taxes now find reasons to use more consumption taxes, and those that have used consumption taxes now find reasons to use more direct personal taxes. The basic logic which has driven these changes appears to be political, motivated by the need to minimize the visibility of taxation and its apparent impact on citizens. There are important economic and international forces at work as well, but politics appears to be trumps in this game. These changes indicate the continuing needs of governments to raise revenue while facing populations that have demonstrated that they do have limits on the amount of taxes they are willing to pay.

In considering the general pattern of change, the United Kingdom appears to be moving in a somewhat opposite direction. The UK government has, with the poll tax, adopted a visible and controversial tax, while eliminating a well-tried one. This "all or nothing" approach to tax reform is markedly different from the tendency in other countries to use any available tax instrument at least a little, and to rely on old taxes as much as possible to make taxes less visible. The logic of the United Kingdom's government's strategy is, however, also apparently political. The poll tax was designed make clear to voters the differences in local government spending and place pressure on high-spending local councils (mostly Labour dominated) to reduce spending and thereby reduce taxes. There is some evidence that this strategy worked to some extent in the local elections of 1990, but not perhaps enough to counter the adverse reaction caused by the introduction of a highly visible and unpopular tax.

Conclusion: Similarities and Differences, Persistence and Change

The lessons drawn from these data may depend upon the perspective which the reader applies. On the one hand, there are some important similarities among the OECD countries in the ways in which they choose to extract revenue. On the other hand, this analysis has emphasized the differences among the countries and the choices that each has made about tax policy. Similarly, there is a grat deal of persistence in tax policies, and very few countries change places within the clusters. There is, however, some change and almost all countries appear to be moving toward a rather similar pattern of revenue collection. Tax policy is no different from any other policy area, and the policies found at any one time are a mixture of recent choices and older inheritances.

Tax policy is also no different from other policies in that political considerations are a dominant, if not the dominant, consideration in their formulation. The complexity and technical content of tax policy should not obscure the fact that decisions about the policy must satisfy political as well as economic constraints. As the political cultures of many Western societies shifted from a period during the 1960s and 1970s in which government was seen as the solution to most social problems to an era in which government itself is seen by many as a major problem, there has been a definite political movement toward minimizing the visibility of taxes. The tendency toward tax systems using the entire spectrum of available tax instruments appears to be an outcome of pressures arising in that process. That change in taxation will almost certainly beget still other changes, as governments and citizens continue to play the game of hide-and-seek over taxation.

Summary

This chapter has provided a great deal of basic information about taxation in industrialized democracies. It has pointed to the variety of options open to governments when they must tax, and further that almost all governments exercise all the policy options available to them. When governments do exercise their options, however, they do so in different ways and to different degrees. These differences represent the effects of political culture, some cumulative effect of political and economic history, as well as more proximate political choices. Some explanations for the differences in tax policies encountered in this chapter have been offered. These notions are extremely preliminary, however, and the bulk of the book will be devoted to more extensive explanations of the observed differences. Unlike most examinations of tax policy, however, the majority of the explanations will arise from political and social processes, rather than from the machinations of the economy. In this, I am interested in processes of choice about taxation, whether those choices are rational calculations of economic costs and benefits, incremental adjustments of functioning policies, decisions attempting to maximize political gains, or simply products of the "garbage can" that determines so much of what happens in government. The persistence of clear patterns of taxation within individual countries over time indicates that there are some systematic relationships in tax policy, but the explanations offered must remain tentative and preliminary.

NOTES

1 The data prior to 1965 is from a different source than the OECD data used from 1965 onward. In years in which the two overlap, however, the figures are close, indicating that the longer time comparisons are valid.

2 Data for Portugal did not disaggregate personal and corporate income taxes prior to 1984, and hence this calculation could not be performed for that country.

3 The administration of the value-added tax is not nearly as simple as this implies. See McClure, 1987.

4 GATT = General Agreement on Tariffs and Trade.

5 This is an indication of what is sometimes called "Baumol's disease." The efficiency of services provided by government tend to be less affected by investment than does the production of private goods and services. Therefore, the costs of government relative to the private sector will rise even to provide a common volume of services (Baumol, 1967; Beck, 1980). This is also referred to as the relative price effect.

6 Texas, Oklahoma, and Louisiana have been fortunate in having chairmen of the Senate Finance Committee (especially Russell Long of Louisiana for over a decade) who came from their states.

7 Several countries in Western Europe, including Belgium, still charge a tax on the rentable value of residential property (including owner-occupied property) owned by a taxpayer.

8 Because of weaknesses in the data we have had to exclude Iceland, Turkey, and Yugoslavia from the analysis.

9 The similarity of the two appears more important than the taxes themselves, given that Australia and New Zealand have not used this form of taxation.

10 The logic here is much like that of Nixon and China. Only a

dedicated anti-Communist like Richard Nixon could have made the first gestures of openness to China. Likewise, pro-business governments may have an easier time taxing corporations than more leftist governments.

11 Although seen from afar the Scandinavian countries have many similarities, they also have substantial differences among them. See Einhorn and Logue (1989).

12 The emphasis on excise taxes would be even clearer if the number of different excises (in the dozens) was used along with the total yields of those taxes.

13 Specifically, the Mahalanobis measure of D^2 decreases across time.

3

Spending Public Money: More Variations on a Theme

Governments do not collect taxes just for the love of it. Everything else being equal, most people in government, being human and preferring not to be disliked, would just as soon not do it. They must do so, however, simply because they spend a large volume of money each year and that money must come from some place. Not only do governments already spend a great deal of money, but there are almost always pressures present to spend more. Thus, one necessary component in any examination of the politics of taxation is a discussion of the reality of public expenditure, and the political pressures that have produced that reality. Expenditure is the great engine of growth that provides the dynamism in the system of public finance. Certainly there are developments in taxation, and some might occur without the pressure from expenditures, but this will be the source of most change.

As with public revenue, it would be a mistake to consider changes in public expenditures to be driven entirely by conscious political choice. Certainly an immense number of choices are made each year as the public budget is constructed, but those are commonly decisions at the margin. The bulk of decisions made are really non-decisions, and involve merely continuing to fund a program at a level that is necessary for its survival and for it to deliver its mandated services to clients. Some choices must be made about just how generous that level of survival and service delivery will be, but in the scope of total public expenditure the possible differences will be very small amounts of money. Those amounts may be very important to the workers in the program, and to the clients receiving their services, but they will make little or no difference to aggregate levels of public expenditure. Really to influence aggregate levels of public expenditure, old programs must be terminated, or new ones initiated.

Thus, there should be a great deal of stability from year to year in the relative amounts of money spent for specific functions by a government; the public budget in the industrialized countries we are discussing can be described very readily as changing only incrementally (Wildavsky, 1986, 31ff). In addition, up to some point, the patterns of change in public expenditure may be largely beyond the control of the government of the day. A great deal of the amount of money to be spent will be determined by commitments made by previous governments. This is especially true for programs such as unemployment insurance and pensions, often referred to as "entitlement programs." These expenditures are more dependent upon the number of people eligible for benefits and changes in consumer price levels than upon marginal government decisions. Even programs which do not involve entitlements of citizens may involve contracts and long-term arrangements which any incumbent government will find difficult to terminate or change.

There may be substantial stability in public expenditure from year to year for any one government, but there is some evidence pointing to individual choices being made when the patterns of public expenditure for different governments are compared. Although governments in all industrialized countries now spend heavily for social services, health care, education, and defense, there are marked differences in the relative amounts they spend. For example, approximately 37 percent of public expenditure in France is for social welfare, but only 18 percent of the total in Australia goes for this purpose; defense spending in the United States is 18 percent of the total, but is only 2 percent in Italy, while Luxembourg spends only 1 percent of its budget on defense.

In addition to differences in spending priorities, there are marked differences in the manner in which governments spend. Some governments are very centralized, and provide most services and spend most money through the central government itself. Other governments rely heavily on subnational governments to provide programs. We have already seen that subnational governments usually do not collect nearly as much tax money as does the central government, so relying on them for service delivery will require moving a great deal of money from central government to the lower levels (see Anton, 1980). Finally, some governments spend a great deal of money through off-budget and quasi-governmental organizations rather than through line agencies in government itself (Schick, 1986). For example, in some countries the social insurance system is technically not a part of government, or may operate through a separate financial system, although large volumes of tax money are channeled through it to pay for pensions or health services. Again, in broad aggregate terms, who spends the money may not make a great deal of difference. It may, however, make a significant difference in terms of the controllability of expenditures and the manner in which citizens assess the performance of their governments.

Even more than taxation, patterns of public expenditure constitute a set of variations on a theme. A few governments have eschewed using some categories of taxes entirely, but no government has avoided spending at least something for almost every public purpose imaginable. Even the government of the United States, theoretically one of the most committed to the free market and least interested in government intervention among the OECD countries, spends substantial amounts of money for social policies and spends some money for its own versions of nationalized industries (e.g. the Tennessee Valley Authority, AMTRAK, plus many more enterprises at state and local levels). The variations in spending are important and interesting, but the similarities are equally as important. The most important similarity for our purposes is that all governments have vast (and often increasing) commitments to spend public money, and those commitments must be funded by some means. The usual means is through taxation.

Types of Expenditures

Just as we found with taxation, there are a variety of ways in which to disaggregate the total amount of public expenditure. Each of these methods of breaking down the totals is valid for its own purposes, but should not be taken as the only or even the "best" measure of what government is doing. Governments and their expenditures are multi-faceted, and unless we can gain a variety of perspectives on what is being done in the public sector, we are likely to misunderstand and misinterpret government and its economic role. For our purposes here, we will look at functional classifications of expenditure – defense, health, etc. – and at several economic categories of expenditure, e.g. transfers and consumption expenditures. First, however, we will examine the total level of public expenditures and their development since the end of the Second World War.

Total Expenditures

Government spending has increased markedly since the end of the Second World War in the industrialized democracies. This is hardly a revelation to anyone who has followed the development of government during the period. However, three things stand out for special comment. One is the extent of growth. If we were to calculate public expenditure growth from 1950 to 1986 in current monetary units the rate of growth would be immense, e.g. 2,696 percent for the United States, 4,297 percent for the United Kingdom, and 15,687 percent for Italy. A large part of these huge changes is the product of inflation, but even if we deflate the expenditure figures the growth is still substantial, with the average increase for all OECD countries being almost 800 percent. The economies in these countries are now also vastly more productive than they were in 1950, and a good deal of the growth in public expenditure is simply spending the same percentage of a larger economic base. However, if we look at public expenditure as a percentage of available resources (Gross Domestic Product), that figure has also, on average, increased. For all OECD countries the average was 115.8 percent. However their activities are counted, governments are simply spending more money now than they did (table 3.1).

These increases in expenditures may be attributed to a number of factors, to be discussed in greater detail later (see chapter 8). There did appear to be a belief during the 1950s and 1960s, however, that the economy was manageable and that future economic growth was virtually assured (Heller, 1966). Governments could afford therefore to make expenditure commitments believing that those commitments could be paid for out of future economic expansion. In addition, the destruction and deprivation of the World War produced deepened commitments to the principles of the Welfare State – at least in most West European countries – and it was seen not only as possible and desirable but essential to spend more for social and health programs. Other demands on the public sector did not vanish, however, and the Cold War produced continued expenditures for national defense, and permitted less disarmament after the end of a major conflict than had been the experience after previous wars. In short, there were a number of factors permitting and encouraging growth of public expenditure.

The second factor worthy of note in the expansion of total public expenditure is that this expansion has slowed or in some cases actually reversed (table 3.2). Governments continued to increase their spending rather rapidly during the 1950s and 1960s. Those halcyon days ended, however, in the first and then the second oil crises in the 1970s (Rose and Peters, 1978). No longer did it appear certain that economic growth in the industrialized world would, or could,

Table 3.1 Public expenditure as a percentage of Gross Domestic Product, 1950–1980

	1950	*1960*	*1970*	*1980*
Australia[a]	18.8	21.4	24.3	34.5
Austria[a]	18.0	35.7	40.6	48.9
Belgium	22.6	30.3	36.3	50.7
Canada	24.4	28.6	32.3	40.5
Denmark	19.0	24.8	36.3	56.2
Finland	28.6	26.6	32.8	36.6
France	36.0	34.6	40.3	46.4
Germany[a]	32.0	32.4	39.1	48.3
Greece	NA	17.4	23.5	30.5
Ireland	32.1	28.0	35.2	50.9
Italy	22.2	30.1	34.7	41.6
Japan	NA	NA	18.3	32.6
Luxembourg[a]	25.0	30.5	37.3	54.8
Netherlands	26.5	33.7	43.9	57.5
Norway	27.6	29.9	37.9	50.7
Portugal	NA	17.0	20.9	35.9
Spain	NA	NA	21.3	32.9
Sweden	16.2	31.0	42.8	61.6
Switzerland	19.8	17.2	20.7	29.3
United Kingdom	32.1	32.3	39.2	45.0
United States	24.4	27.0	30.7	33.7

[a] Estimated.

Source: OECD, monthly; national sources

proceed unabated. The magic of Keynesian economic management had disappeared, and real resource constraints as well as managerial restraints within government were being highlighted. From that time onward economic growth became problematic and with that loss of confidence came severe questions about the level of public expenditure. In the 1980s, four OECD (table 3.2) countries reduced their levels of public expenditure relative to Gross Domestic Product, and in most of the remainder growth slowed dramatically. Most of the countries in which public expenditures continued to expand rapidly (Greece, Spain) had relatively less developed public sectors and had to "catch up" with their peers.[1] The major exception was France, where the election of a Socialist government to power in the early 1980s after several decades of right and center-right domination

Table 3.2 Public expenditure as a percentage of Gross Domestic Product, 1970–1987[a]

	1970	*1975*	*1980*	*1985*	*1987*
Australia	26.9	33.7	34.5	38.5	34.5
Austria	39.2	46.1	48.9	51.5	50.6
Belgium	36.5	44.5	50.7	57.9	50.7
Canada	34.8	40.1	40.5	47.2	44.4
Denmark	40.2	48.2	56.2	59.5	60.2
Finland	30.5	36.1	36.6	41.4	40.2
France	38.9	43.5	46.4	52.4	50.3
Germany	38.6	48.9	48.3	47.4	46.6
Greece	22.4	26.7	30.5	43.8	45.7
Ireland	39.6	46.5	50.9	53.9	53.4
Italy	34.2	43.2	41.6	50.8	50.7
Japan	19.4	27.3	32.6	33.2	33.4
Netherlands	43.9	52.8	57.5	59.9	60.7
Norway	41.0	48.4	50.7	47.7	51.1
Spain	22.2	24.7	32.9	42.1	41.7
Sweden	43.3	48.9	61.6	64.6	59.0
Switzerland	21.3	28.7	29.3	31.0	30.1
United Kingdom	39.0	46.3	45.0	46.7	43.2
United States	31.6	34.6	33.7	36.7	36.3

[a] Total outlays; information not available for New Zealand and Portugal.
Source: OECD, monthly

produced increased public expenditures. Even that government, however, was forced to curtail expenditures after several years of rapid increases (Hall, 1987).

The questions about public expenditure were more than economic, however, and the mid- to late 1970s saw the election of a number of politicians committed to reducing public expenditure and taxation. The two dominant figures here were Ronald Reagan and Margaret Thatcher, but Malcolm Fraser, Ruud Lubbers, Helmut Kohl, and others were cut from some of the same cloth (if somewhat less dramatic parts). These leaders in the attack on the public sector appeared to reflect accurately public skepticism about the costs of government and people's desire to keep a larger portion of their earned income for personal consumption. Government leaders have attempted to implement this more privatized view of the good life, although in most cases they have succeeded in slowing the expansion of expenditures rather than actually cutting them in real terms. The pressures built into programs through indexing benefits to meet price increases, entitlements to benefits based on contributions, and increasing costs for technology (e.g. in defense and medical care) have made real "cuts" almost impossible to achieve (Rose, 1980). The rhetoric of both the proponents and detractors of the public sector, however, have made it appear that those real cuts were occurring.

The third point, worthy of a more extended discussion (see chapter 4), is that governments generally spend more than they choose to tax. It has already been pointed out that few, if any, leaders in government choose to tax because they think that it is a desirable thing to do; they do so because they have to, and they are vulnerable politically if they tax more than citizens want to pay, or think that they should pay, for the services they receive. On the other hand, government officials know that they can create political good will if they spend for programs that citizens want. Opposition parties find it easy to criticize tax levels, but then find that they too must tax and spend once in power. Because of the basic political imbalance in incentives (see Downs, 1967; Brittan, 1975; Buchanan and Wagner, 1977) governments tend to incur deficits, and run them even when resources are relatively plentiful. In the 1950s and 1960s, when there was rapid economic growth and a positive conception of government by the majority of citizens, governments still ran deficits. In the 20 years between 1950 and 1970, each government in the OECD countries for which we have full data on average ran a deficit in 15.6 years (table 3.3). Those deficits were often substantial. The largest was over 8 percent of GNP, and the average across all countries in all years was approximately 3 percent of GNP. Thus, when we discuss deficits and public sector borrowing in more detail in the next chapter, we are in fact talking about a major issue of government finance and one which is *not* just the product of the relatively poor economic conditions in which governments have found themselves since the mid-1970s.

A final point which should be raised here is that the actual definition of what a public expenditure is is not entirely clear. It is clear that money which is spent directly for old age pensions, or to pay soldiers, or to purchase paperclips is a public expenditure. It is less clear, however, whether other types of financial transactions of governments should be counted as expenditures (Peters and Heisler, 1983). For example, some systems of public accounting do not count government loans as expenditures in the year in which they are made.

Table 3.3 Number of public deficits

	1950–9	*1960–9*	*1970–9*	*1980–6*
Australia	1	8	6	7
Austria	10	9	6	7
Belgium	5	10	9	7
Canada	3	9	9	7
Denmark	5	1	5	7
Finland	4	9	3	3
France	10	9	6	6
Germany	5	8	9	7
Greece	NA	NA	4	7
Ireland	10	10	10	7
Italy	10	10	10	7
Japan	4	8	5	7
Luxembourg	NA	NA	1	5
Netherlands	3	9	8	7
New Zealand	9	8	9	7
Norway	9	8	1	0
Portugal	NA	8	6	6
Spain	8	10	6	7
Sweden	9	5	3	7
Switzerland	4	2	1	2
United Kingdom	9	8	9	7
United States	6	8	9	7
Average	6.8	7.8	6.1	6.1

Sources: International Montary Fund, monthly; OECD, annual b

The assumption is that these loans are to be repaid and, therefore, they are not money which is gone forever as an expenditure would be. If there is a default on the loan and it must be written off as a bad debt then it might be counted as an expenditure in the year in which the default occurs. Even if the loan is repaid, any interest subsidy which may have been included as part of the loan program is not counted as an expenditure (USGAO, 1989). Similarly, "tax expenditures" or revenues foregone for specific purposes (see chapter 6) are not counted as expenditures although many of their effects may be the same as direct expenditures. Even more indirectly, soldiers reporting for short-term active duty in the militia in Switzerland continue to be paid by their private employers rather than by government, significantly reducing the apparent cost of defense policy. These are more than issues of accounting. The campaign speeches of many conservative politicians about "big government," and the political support which this has engendered makes the quantity of public expenditure a real political issue. Therefore, to the extent that a government can provide services while appearing to minimize the costs of those services, they are likely to be more successful politically.

Spending for Public Purposes

With those general thoughts about public expenditure functioning as a background, we can now begin to discuss spending for specific public purposes. Although all governments spend a great deal of money for a huge variety of purposes, we will concentrate on the five categories of public expenditure which account for the large majority of total expenditures in all OECD countries. These categories are: social policy, health, education, defense, and debt interest. As shown in table 3.4, these expenditure categories account for, on average, almost two-thirds of total public expenditure for all OECD countries. Everything else, e.g. law and order, nationalized industries and other economic subsidies, agriculture, and tax collection itself, only account for an average of 35 percent of total public expenditure.

There are, of course, variations around those average figures. The United States and Canada, in part because of their large expenditures for debt interest and defense, have only 21 percent of total expenditures remaining for purposes other than the five major programs. The largest spenders for purposes other than the "big five" are Luxembourg and Switzerland, which have relatively less developed social service programs than most European countries. Also, Greece and Spain, as two of the less economically developed West European countries, spend a good deal more on economic functions than do the majority of the industrialized democracies. Likewise, although Italy has experienced substantial economic growth in the post-war period, it continues to have large public expenditures for economic functions and for regional development in the south of that country.

As we discuss patterns of expenditure for different functions, we should be aware of the difficulties in calculating these figures, and hence of their approximate nature. First, there are problems in cumulating expenditures across a number of levels of government, especially with the numbers of transfers of funds which occur across levels of government. In addition to these problems, there are a number of gray areas among the functional categories. For example,

Table 3.4 Spending by function, 1985 (percent of total public expenditure)

	Social	*Health*	*Education*	*Defense*	*Interest*	*Other*
Australia	18	14	15	8	6	39
Austria	31	10	11	3	6	39
Belgium	30	10	10	5	14	31
Canada	33	17	19	6	14	21
Denmark	34	10	11	4	13	28
Finland	31	13	13	4	4	35
France	37	13	11	8	5	26
W. Germany	31	16	9	7	6	31
Greece	32	6	4	12	4	42
Ireland	25	13	12	3	16	31
Italy	19	11	10	2	16	43
Luxembourg	28	3	14	1	2	52
Netherlands	36	11	10	5	10	28
New Zealand	32	10	9	4	10	35
Norway	32	7	8	6	9	38
Spain	26	11	6	6	5	46
Sweden	36	13	12	5	12	22
Switzerland	27	7	5	6	4	51
United Kingdom	30	6	5	11	10	38
United States	24	11	14	18	12	21
Averages	30	11	10	6	9	35

Sources: International Monetary Fund, annual; International Labour Office, 1988; UNESCO, 1988

in the United States, should the program providing medical care of dependents of servicemen be counted as a defense expenditure or as a health expenditure? Should programs providing special benefits to veterans in a number of countries be counted as military expenditures or as social and educational expenditures? The figures reported here are, in so far as possible, standardized by international organizations, but there is still room for some interpretation and error in the classification of expenditures.

Social policy Social policy, taken broadly, is the largest single item of public expenditure in most OECD countries, and accounts for an average of almost 30 percent of public expenditure in those nations.

The Welfare State is now well institutionalized in industrialized democracies and concomitant with that institutional structure is a large volume of expenditures for programs such as old age pensions, sickness and accident insurance, unemployment insurance, and public relief for those few citizens[2] whose needs are not adequately covered by social insurance programs. Of all the components of the public sector, spending for social programs increased the most rapidly during the post-war years, and these expenditures have been the most difficult for the conservative governments of the 1980s to control. The entitlement basis and insurance principles of the social programs prevent even the most committed conservative government from reducing, or perhaps even slowing, their expansion. Further, politically, these are among the most popular public programs, and proposals even to slow the rate at which benefits increase in relationship to inflation are likely to produce very large, negative political consequences (Weaver, 1988).

Social expenditures are not, however, an undifferentiated whole. The category is actually made up of a number of components which vary in their target populations, their methodology of service delivery, and their patterns of change. The largest single category of social expenditures is old age pensions (table 3.5); on average over 60 percent of total social expenditures goes to pensions. As the populations of almost all industrialized countries age day by day, so too the level of expenditure for pensions increases. Pensions are placing a double bind on the revenues of industrialized countries. Many citizens think that when they made social insurance contributions while working that money is invested and pays for their pensions after retirement. The fact is, however, that public pension programs are not actuarially based, and current tax revenues pay for current pensions. As the population ages, the number of pension recipients increases, and the number of workers paying for those pensions, on average, is declining (OECD, 1988b). This means that each worker is supporting, through his or her taxes, that many people who are no longer working.

The implications of those changing demographics are presented in table 3.6. On average, a retiree in an OECD country is now "supported" by over five workers and their contributions to the tax system. By the year 2000, the average will be just over four and one-half per retiree, and then the number drops rapidly to an average of less than three by 2040 (OECD, 1988b, 32). In a few countries (Switzerland, Germany) there will be only two active workers per retiree by 2040. Most of the revenue for public pensions is collected

Table 3.5 Pensions as a percentage of total social expenditures

	1960	*1981*
Australia	68.3	68.3
Austria	73.9	71.8
Belgium	34.8	36.0
Canada	40.8	47.3
Denmark	36.6	38.9
Finland	50.7	60.6
France	54.0	68.9
Germany	65.6	63.4
Greece	73.8	75.7
Ireland	44.3	40.2
Italy	55.1	79.2
Japan	51.0	61.4
Netherlands	50.3	58.1
New Zealand	61.9	70.7
Norway	55.7	54.3
Sweden	60.0	65.4
Switzerland	94.7	88.5
United Kingdom	59.8	58.9
United States	70.4	66.6

Source: OECD, 1985; supplemented by national sources

as social security contributions, although countries other than the United States do have subsidies from general taxation for their pension programs. This will mean that there will have to be substantial (almost doubling on average), and therefore increasingly visible, increases in social security contributions, or a change in the formula financing pensions. In any case, pensions will likely be an even more major expenditure item for governments in the future.

The costs of social policy programs other than pensions have been a stable, or even slightly declining, portion of total expenditure in most countries. Given that old age pensions have been almost untouchable politically, budget cutters have had to make attacks on other social programs, even if there was not as much money to be saved by controlling those expenditures. The non-entitlement portions of social expenditures – public assistance, counseling, child protection, and the like – have been especially vulnerable to budget cutters. Despite the seeming ascendance of conservative politicians in many industrialized countries, social programs are still popular

Table 3.6 Number of workers per retiree

	1980	*2000*	*2020*	*2040*
Austria	4.1	4.4	3.3	2.4
Australia	6.7	5.7	3.4	3.1
Belgium	4.6	4.5	3.7	2.8
Canada	7.1	5.3	3.5	2.6
Denmark	4.5	4.6	3.3	2.4
Finland	5.6	4.7	2.9	2.6
France	4.6	4.3	3.3	2.6
Germany	4.3	3.9	3.0	2.1
Greece	4.9	4.4	3.6	2.9
Ireland	5.5	5.9	5.3	3.7
Italy	4.8	4.4	3.4	2.4
Japan	7.4	4.4	3.0	2.6
Luxembourg	5.0	3.9	3.1	2.7
Netherlands	5.7	5.1	3.5	2.4
New Zealand	6.5	6.1	4.3	2.8
Norway	4.3	4.4	3.6	2.6
Portugal	6.2	4.8	4.2	3.0
Spain	5.8	4.6	3.9	2.6
Sweden	3.9	4.0	3.0	2.7
Switzerland	4.8	4.0	2.6	2.0
United Kingdom	4.3	4.5	3.9	3.0
United States	5.8	5.5	4.0	3.1
Average	5.3	4.7	3.5	2.8

Source: OECD, 1988b

among the majority of the population and may not be able to be reduced any further without possibly severe reactions.

Health Expenditures Although public expenditures for health care might be treated as but one component of social expenditures, they do have some features that make a separate discussion of them desirable. One is that, although health care is an entitlement program like pensions, it can also be rationed somewhat more effectively. Although in emergencies health care is life-saving, beneficiaries do not depend on this program for their daily existence. Many operations can be postponed, or hospital construction deferred for a year, without serious damage being done. There must be some means of rationing access to medical care, and when money is eliminated time may be used in its place (Wildavsky, 1977). Thus, if government wants to, it probably can control health expenditures more readily than many social expenditures (especially the big one – pensions). The largest component of expenditure for health care is personnel, and this is more controllable than direct transfers to pensioners, or even people on unemployment benefits. Interestingly, in fact, the countries that have had the greatest success in controlling the costs of medical care are those with a largest public sector presence. In countries such as the United States, where the public sector is weak relative to private sector providers, health care costs have soared.

On the other hand, there are a number of factors tending to drive up the cost of medical care in any country very rapidly. One is that medical care employs a large number of highly paid and professionally powerful people; the impact of their salaries is extreme in the United States but formidable in other health care systems. Also, the cost of providing medical care is impacted by increases in technology. Modern medicine can do wonders, but the machines central to those wonders – CAT scanners, NMR scanners, etc. – are expensive to purchase and maintain. The costs of processing pensions have probably been reduced by technology (computers) but the costs of providing medical care have been increased. In addition, many patients know about the technological advances and may demand high-quality (and high-cost) services for themselves. Especially where malpractice suits are common, as in the United States, doctors would be loath to refuse such demands for fear of being considered negligent.

Finally, it should be pointed out that the same demographic changes which have influenced the costs of pensions have also influenced the costs of health policy. Older citizens are the largest consumers of medical care, and the very old are extremely large consumers of these services. Therefore, the demographic trends are bringing the same bad news to this policy area as they have brought to social policy. In some ways the news for health care may be worse. Pensions pay the beneficiary a fixed sum per month, but there is no real limit to the amount which a single episode of illness may cost.

With all these factors at play in determining health expenditures, plus social and cultural norms about the use of medical care, it is not surprising that there is a good deal of variance in the range of expenditures on health, and the changes which have been occurring. In almost all countries health care is a major expenditure item, but is especially large in Canada and Germany, and rather small in Luxembourg, Greece, and the United Kingdom. Further, public health care expenditures have been increasing rapidly in Canada, Spain, and the United States while remaining relatively stable in the majority of OECD countries. Even more than for most other types of expenditures, these simple figures about health care may be insufficient to demonstrate or make intelligible the complex changes which are occurring in the delivery and financing of medical care through the public sector (De Swaan, 1988).

Education Education is another major government expenditure which might be classified as a form of social expenditure, but which has a number of important economic elements as well. As developed economies become more "knowledge-based" (Bell, 1973), and technological change plays a larger role in promoting economic growth, education should be seen as a major economic investment as well as a way to keep children off the streets until they are old enough to work. Skilled workers have always been important for economic success, but have become increasingly so with change from industrial to post-industrial economies. In addition, the rapid economic changes which appear to characterize the 1990s will require frequent retraining and reeducation of workers, so that the impact of education (as well as its costs) will be extended beyond its traditional age groups.

Spending for education varies significantly among OECD countries (from 4 to 19 percent of total expenditures), and varies as much or more in the locus of expenditure as it does in the total amount being spent. Education is more of a subnational government function than almost any other of the major expenditure categories. For a variety of reasons – parental concerns and influence, cultural and linguistic differences, and church provision of some educational services – education traditionally has been more decentralized than other services. A few countries, France for example, have chosen to make education primarily a central government function. Therefore, central government spending for education varies between 3 percent of the total to 18 percent. With these differences in expenditures go equally pronounced differences in the levels of control, and in the independent revenue needs of the local governments.

Spending for education has been increasing, but only slightly, in most OECD countries. Although the number of children being educated is, on average, lower than it has been, costs have been increasing. Teachers demand more pay and increased demands for training in computers and other technologies drive up costs. In addition, the university sector of education has been increasing in size. This is especially important in the European countries, where higher education is almost entirely public. European countries have tended to educate a much smaller proportion of their age-eligible population in universities than have their North American counterparts. With the increasing need for higher education for economic growth, and its consequent expansion to a much broader segment of the population, have come demands for enhanced public spending for education, especially higher education.

Defense Debates about where to spend public money often resolve into debates betwen "guns and butter." The first three categories we have discussed are "butter," but most governments of OECD countries continue to spend significant amounts of money on guns, although these have tended to decline as a proportion of total public expenditures and may decline even more if there is really a "peace dividend" with the winding down of the Cold War. Defense is one of the categories of public expenditure that is most readily cut in the short-run, and many governments when faced with fiscal problems have found it more convenient to reduce military expenditures than to attack social entitlement programs. There are several factors which facilitate the relative ease with which defense expenditures can be cut.

One factor is the nature of defense expenditures, a large and growing percentage of which is for equipment. Military strategists and procurement experts have tended to replace manpower with firepower, and to spend large amounts of money for increasingly sophisticated weapon systems. The purchase of these weapons can be delayed or even cancelled without the public reaction that would arise if social programs such as pensions were to be cut. Even the personnel component of military expenditures can be reduced without much reaction, except by citizens concerned with maintaining a strong national defense. Unlike pensioners, a significant portion of the personnel in the military do have other options (most more lucrative) for making a living, and many would as soon get on with their life's work as remain a soldier.

In addition, although there are advocates for national defense in every country, the effects of defense cuts are not as politically sensitive as cuts in social programs. There certainly will be lobbying on behalf of maintaining or increasing military expenditures – from veterans' organizations, from committed defense advocates, from defense contractors – but not the mass mobilization that has surrounded any attempt to tamper with pensions or health care. Survey evidence indicates that citizens in most countries at most times regard military defense as one of the few policy areas on which government spends too much money, and therefore cutting will almost certainly be easier than in other policy areas.

Finally, military expenditures have been receiving bad publicity in a number of countries. This has been most pronounced in the United States, where $700 toilet seats and $400 wrenches have become symbols of the waste associated with defense expenditures. The perception of fraud and waste is not confined to the United States, and a number of European countries have witnessed scandals about military purchases and defense management in general (Linklater and Leigh, 1986). Therefore, there is a perception that there is a great deal of "fat" in the defense budget of most countries which can be cut without harming national defense at all. Defense expenditures are still sizeable, and will remain so, but they have been decreasing and are vulnerable to even greater reductions in the future.

Debt interest The final major category of public expenditure in OECD countries is interest on public debt. We noted above that governments tend not to collect as much in taxes and other revenues as they spend, and this has a cumulative effect of increasing the public debt. For most industrialized countries the public debt was not an important issue prior to 1973, because it had not increased as rapidly as total economic productivity (GNP) during the post-war period and debt and debt interest payments were in line with increasing revenues. Since the first oil crisis and the economic uncertainties which it engendered, debt and its interest payments have been an increasing problem for many governments. The effects of economic slowdowns were exacerbated by decisions by conservative governments (especially the Reagan administration) to reduce taxes without cutting back as sharply on expenditures. Interest on the public debt now constitutes an average of 9 percent of public expenditure in the OECD world we are studying, with Ireland and Italy paying a high of 16 percent of their public expenditure as debt interest payments.

In some ways debt interest is just another type of public expenditure. It is a transfer from government to persons or organizations which have loaned it money in the past. In other ways, however, debt interest constitutes a major problem. The more government must spend for debt interest, the fewer services it can provide during the current year. Thus, large debt interest payments place a mortmain on the activities of the government of the day and restrict its flexibility. Whether by design or by accident, one legacy of the Reagan administration in the United States (Jones, 1989) will be a reduced ability of the federal government to undertake new programs; it will still be paying interest on the debts incurred between 1980 and 1988.

The remainder In addition to the big five programs discussed above, governments do spend money on a huge number of areas. There is almost no region of human activity which the governments of industrialized democracies do not presently regulate and/or subsidize. Although there is by now a bewildering array of programs in agriculture, industry, housing, justice, foreign affairs, environmental protection, etc., these do not add up to a very large percentage of total public expenditure. On average, the "big five" account for 65 percent of all public expenditure in OECD countries, leaving just over one-third of expenditures to cover everything else.

Although none of the other programs of government amounts to much in the way of public expenditure, relative to the total amount being spent, there is still a great deal of money involved. In the United States, the 21 percent in addition to the "big five" is, including all levels of government, some $500 million. There may also be a great deal of controversy about programs other than the five largest. Agricultural subsidies, for example, have excited a great deal of political interest in the United States and in the members of the European Community (Moyer and Josling, 1990). Likewise, programs in criminal justice may excite substantial controversy between advocates of human rights and advocates of strict treatment of offenders. Few programs in government, regardless of their relative size, are immune from political pressures and political controversies.

This "everything else" category of public expenditure also has been particularly subject to cuts during the 1970s and 1980s. A relatively small proportion of these programs are entitlement programs and, although some citizens may still depend upon the benefits, they can be cut without the political or even legal difficulties which cutting entitlements would produce. In addition, the more conservative politics of the 1980s has meant that the goals of regulatory and even subsidy programs are less acceptable, so that the programs may be cut for ideological as well as strictly financial considerations. Similarly, a significant portion of the expenses of many of these programs are personnel costs (in contrast to pensions and health in most countries) and given that "the bureaucracy" is another of the targets of conservative politicians, eliminating personnel is also desirable for them. Being small does not eliminate controversy for a spending program, nor does it eliminate the possibility of becoming even smaller.

Economic Classifications of Public Expenditures

As well as being classified according to the functional use to which the money will be put, public expenditures may also be categorized according to their economic characteristics. To politicians, all public expenditures may appear to be the same. All expenditures come through the budget, they add up to a percentage of total economic resources which, depending upon ideological persuasions, may be too large or too small, and the money all has to come from some place (mostly taxes). The manner in which the money is spent will have, however, rather different economic impacts. Those impacts, in turn, may also have some real political importance.

Consumption and transfers One of the standard economic differentiations is between consumption (or exhaustive) expenditure and transfer expenditures. As the name implies, consumption expenditures involve government making decisions to use some real factors of production – labor, capital, or materials – for its own purposes. Transfer expenditures, on the other hand, merely provide money to individuals or organizations in the society who are then able to make the final consumption decisions. Because they do not involve government directly utilizing resources, some scholars do not count transfer expenditures when they measure the putative size of government. From the perspective of taxation and the average taxpayer, however, transfer expenditures must be counted as a part of public expenditure. These expenditures still require the collection of revenue (or borrowing) and hence may be seen by the taxpayer as just one more government expenditure, regardless of who makes the final decisions about how to spend the money.

Consumption and transfer expenditures are usually associated with certain functional programs. Defense, for example, tends to be very heavily a consumption expenditure program. The government buys or builds airplanes, tanks, and the like, and it hires a large number of people to provide defense. Social programs, on the other hand, tend to be transfer programs; all pension programs do is to give older citizens a weekly or monthly check that they then decide how to spend. Although there are these associations, there may be alternative approaches to service delivery as well. For example, education is at present largely a consumption expenditure for government; it builds schools, hires teachers, and purchases books and supplies. Proposals to institute voucher programs for education, however, would change this into a transfer program (Seldon, 1986; Lieberman, 1989). Government would simply send a check to the parents of each child, and that could be used to purchase educational services of the parents' choosing. Unlike the pension check, however, the voucher check would only be good for education, while the elderly citizen is permitted to gamble away their pension if they so choose.

Although we have said above that to most taxpayers transfer and consumption programs are very much the same, for the recipient of the program they may be seen differently. A pension program which preserves the freedom of choice of the individual is preferred by most citizens to a program which would require the recipients to spend their money in certain ways, or which at the extreme might institutionalize the elderly for their own good. By preserving freedom of choice, transfer programs tend to maximize the human quality of independence, and to treat clients more as adults than do direct service delivery programs. Also, conservatives have argued that transfer programs such as vouchers would enable markets to operate in place of public monopolies, and that the resultant competition will improve the quality of services available to all citizens. The evidence for this contention is rather uneven, but transfer programs continue to have strong advocates on both the political right and left.

Current and capital Another classification of public expenditure is current and capital. Current expenditures are funds spent for the normal, annual expenses of running a government – salaries, supplies, etc. – as well as transfer payments to individuals and organizations in the private sector. Capital expenditures imply some sort of investment. This investment may be in public buildings, in highways and other parts of the physical infrastructure, or in equipment. Again, although these are primarily economic criteria, they may have some political importance. This will lie in how the two types of expenditures are treated in the budgetary process, as well as how they are perceived by citizens.

Capital expenditures are in some ways politically preferable to current expenditures. First, the idea of investment has a positive appeal to most citizens, even if the investment is made through the public sector. Second, capital expenditures tend to create positive physical symbols of the operations of government, and those symbols can be located in the districts of representatives, creating the image that the politician in question has been successful in "bringing home the bacon" for the folks back home. Whether it is called "pork barrel" or "saupoudrage," this is a powerful political weapon for incumbent politicians (Fiorina, 1989). Finally, capital expenditures can be reduced, or even eliminated, more readily than can current expenditures. Government has to pay the salaries of its employees every month, and must send out pensions checks every month, but it can postpone or even cancel many capital projects with relatively little furor. Thus, a budget with a larger capital component provides a good deal more flexibility to decisionmakers.

Capital expenditures are not, however, without their problems. First, if the symbol being created with capital expenditures is to be a school or a hospital or some similar facility, the operating costs will soon surpass the capital costs and will have to be met annually. If a politician seeks to build a monument, it is cheaper to build a statue than a hospital. Also, although capital projects can be slowed or stopped, few things are more offensive to taxpayers than a half-finished project. Such a "white elephant" rapidly becomes a symbol of ineptitude and failure in the public sector. Finally, citizens are beginning to resist new capital facilities – the NIMBY phenomenon of "Not in My Backyard" – that may affect their lives directly. This has been true for some time for facilities such as prisons and nuclear power stations, but is now becoming increasingly true for highways, and even schools and hospitals. What were once symbols of the benefits produced by government may become symbols of its intrusiveness into the social environment if the values of the population change.

Who Spends the Money?

Taxation is a game in which any number of players have been able to participate, and this characterization is even more true of expenditure. Some governments, e.g. special districts, which have no taxing power of their own, do spend tax money that has been transferred to them by other governments. If we look only at broad aggregates of public expenditure for all governments within a country, we would ignore a good deal of the politics of that country. Important decisions must be made about how the responsibilities of government are to be divided, how the total sum of expenditure is to be allocated, and how the money that is raised at one level of government is to be moved to other levels. On one hand, this division of responsibility may not matter to many citizens so long as the services they want are provided, and the tax costs of providing them are not exorbitant. One the other hand, a number of questions about intergovernmental relations, financial accountability, and democratic responsibility can be raised by looking at the movement of public money within a country.

Spending Agents

Countries vary significantly in the expenditure powers granted to local governments. Even countries which are nominally unitary and centralized allow (or require) local governments to spend a great deal of money, and in federal countries the central government may exercise little real control over how much those subnational governments spend. In general, local governments spend much more money that they raise in taxes, even in federal governments where state and local authorities presumably have a great deal of autonomy. The revenue instruments available to central governments are, on average, more flexible and buoyant than those available to subnational governments, and it is therefore somewhat more convenient to allow central government to raise revenue and then allocate a portion of that revenue to local authorities. Of course, even in federal countries, the strings attached to this money and other central government grants are a major instrument of policy as well as financial control (Levine and Posner, 1981).

In addition to subnational governments, other organizations spend tax money on behalf of government. The most significant of these are the social insurance funds. In a number of industrialized democracies, the social insurance system is not (technically) a part of government, and its funds do not appear as public sector expenditures or revenues. This is true despite the fact that social insurance "contributions" are as obligatory as any other tax and that the organizations and their spending programs exist largely because of public laws. The social insurance funds, and a variety of "off-budget" organizations (especially in the area of economic development activities), do spend money and must be counted as a part of government, but they are also the subject of a great deal of financial movement.

Some idea of the patterns of public expenditure according to the spending agents is provided in table 3.7. In this table total expenditures are divided among central government, subnational governments, and other organizations. In a few countries social insurance is just another spending program in central government (with some components perhaps in subnational governments as well) so that this off-budget component is relatively small. This table demonstrates the

Table 3.7 Public expenditure by types of government

	Central	*Subnational*	*Other*
Australia	53.3	46.7	–
Austria	38.0	37.0	25.0
Belgium	51.6	12.0	36.4
Canada	21.6	74.1	4.3
Denmark	41.3	54.5	4.2
Finland	39.4	47.4	13.2
France	38.1	17.7	44.2
W.Germany	20.5	44.9	34.6
Ireland	70.0	30.0	–
Italy	53.4	29.4	17.2
Japan	38.2	61.8	–
Luxembourg	42.4	16.4	41.2
Netherlands	34.1	33.1	32.8
New Zealand	90.4	9.6	–
Norway	34.6	35.3	30.1
Spain	35.5	24.6	39.9
Sweden	45.6	44.1	10.3
Switzerland	16.5	53.6	29.9
United Kingdom	70.9	29.1	–
United States	60.0	40.0	–

Source: International Monetary Fund, annual

degree of variance in patterns of expenditure among these countries, all of which are highly developed economically and have democratic forms of government. At one extreme almost all public expenditure in New Zealand is made by central government; at the other in four countries over one-half of all expenditures are made by subnational governments, and in five over one-third of all expenditures are made by through "other" organizations or accounts.

Perhaps the best way to compare these countries is through the spending powers of subnational governments. First, there is a marked contrast between federal and non-federal systems. On average subnational governments in federal systems spend 49.4 percent of total public expenditure, while subnational governments in unitary systems spend on average 31.5 percent of the total. Second, there is a lingering legacy of Napoleonic centralization, with France, Italy, Belgium, and Spain having among the lowest levels of subnational expenditures. Finally, the Scandinavian countries, despite being nominally unitary, behave to some extent like federal systems in financial terms. A number of important functions, e.g. health care, are left largely to the subnational governments there, and this is demonstrated in relatively high levels of subnational public expenditure.

Where Will the Money Go?

Although decisionmakers in government make the nominal decisions about levels of public expenditure for the numerous functions of government, they must respond to a variety of pressures. The most obvious of these are political. During the 1960s and 1970s, when there was a sense that government was able to accomplish great things, almost all the political pressures were in the direction of new programs and increased spending. When economic scarcity was reinstated in the 1970s and when many conservative politicians were elected in the 1980s, the pressures shifted toward reducing expenditures and eliminating programs. Political pressures for specific programs may wax and wane as well, as the emergence of the environmental movement in the 1960s and then its reemergence in the late 1980s indicates (Peters and Hogwood, 1985). Not all pressures for and against public expenditure are so overt and political. In many cases government decisionmakers must respond to pressures coming from the social and economic environment of programs. In some cases, the effects of environmental change may be virtually automatic, as when pension expenditures must rise to meet a growing number of elderly citizens, but in others the reaction will be mediated through the political process. This section will discuss several important pressures on public expenditure and the ways in which the political process may be able to cope with them. Most of these factors will be discussed in a somewhat different context later as explanations for changes in total taxation by government are developed.

Demography

The impact of demography on social and health expenditures has already been mentioned. The number (and proportion) of elderly in Western industrialized countries has been increasing and this is projected to continue. The largest increases are projected for the "old old", those over 80 years of age, who tend to be the very largest consumers of medical care. Although the age profiles of these countries do differ (see table 3.6), the general pattern is one of an increasingly elderly population requiring larger public expenditures for pensions and for medical care. At the other end of the age spectrum, there is a declining population of children of normal school age in most industrialized democracies, although there is some evidence that the birth rate may increase again slightly at least in some countries. On average, however, it appears that there will be less demand for elementary and secondary education in the next several decades.

There have been several attempts to estimate the impact of these demographic changes on public expenditures. The OECD estimated that for a sample of its seven largest member nations, changes in demography accounted for almost one-third of increased pension expenditures from 1960 through 1981. Those changes also accounted for approximately 12 percent of increases in health expenditures over the same time period. The projections made in the mid-1980s (OECD, 1985) were that demography would account for two-thirds of the anticipated real increases in pension expenditures through 1990 and almost one-third of increases in health expenditures. The accelerating demographic effects are a result of both the rapid increasing of the populations and the declining political willingness to spend more *real* money per recipient; pensions will keep pace with inflation but are unlikely to become more generous in real terms. Education expenditures, on the other hand, are expected to decrease for demographic reasons, although there will be a net increase because of other factors.

Politics

As implied above, the political climate within which expenditure decisions are made has changed dramaticaly in most industrialized democracies. The climate for public expenditure is now much less supportive than it had been in the 1960s and early 1970s. Although there is a general skepticism about public programs and public expenditures, the greatest doubts are saved for social programs, so that the political pressures to reduce (or at least restrain the growth of) social programs is very strong. This climate can be contrasted to the experiences from 1960 to 1981 in which the OECD (1985) calculated that approximately three-quarters of the growth in health expenditures and one-half of the growth in pension expenditures came from increases in the real benefits being delivered.

Another way to look at the question of the potential political pressures for increases (or decreases) in public expenditure is to examine survey data reporting what programs citizens want increased and what they want decreased. This question will be examined in greater detail in the following chapter, but it is important to note here that citizens in most countries do not appear to be as negative about public expenditure as many of their political leaders appear to be. The majority of citizens are not strongly in favor of cutting existing programs, and there is often a majority in favor of *increasing* expenditures for programs. Thus, although political elites may want to reduce expenditures, they will tend to meet opposition from the beneficiaries of those programs, and even from ordinary citizens who believe that the programs are beneficial.

Not all of the politics of public expenditure is determined by either mass political pressures or the actions of partisan political leaders. The permanent bureaucracy of government plays a major role as defenders of existing programs being threatened with cuts, and as advocates of new programs to serve their clients. The success of these bureaucratic "entrepreneurs" may depend upon the availability of resources, and upon the favor or disfavor in which their programs stand at any one moment. However, these program advocates have the advantage of permanency (unless their organization is terminated entirely) and thus may have the ability to outlast their partisan opponents. A number of ideas, e.g. Medicare in the United States, remain in the bureaucracy for years before the right combination of political circumstances permit their adoption (Kingdon, 1984).

The Economy

The money which governments raise through taxes and then spend comes from the economy. Thus, when the economy is robust there is more money to spend as citizens and businesses pay increased amounts of taxes on their increased earnings. In addition, a robust economy will mean that there are fewer demands for social programs such as unemployment insurance and public welfare. Government will have to meet fewer commitments of this sort and therefore may have greater latitude to make discretionary expenditures and to initiate new programs. The problem is that since the mid-1970s the economy in most industrialized democracies has not been particularly robust. More specifically, the economies have not been *predictably* robust, and as a consequence decisionmakers in government have had a more difficult time in making a realistic annual budget (see Wildavsky, 1987).

In addition to these general effects, movements in the economy will have some more specific effects on public expenditures. One such effect is through changes in price levels and wage rates. Many public programs (including taxes) are now directly linked to changes in prices, with a few also being linked to changes in wage rates. Pensions are the major example. All industrialized countries have now indexed pensions to one or both of these variables so that pensioners' real income at least stays approximately in step with changes in the economy. When the pension is linked to wage rates, the concept is that pensioners' standards of living should remain roughly comparable to that of their income group during their working life. In either case, indexing benefits is costly for governments and contributes substantially to increasing levels of expenditures.

Another factor worthy of note is that governments are labor intensive organizations, and have relatively limited returns on capital investment. Although some government services have been improved and made less expensive by technological change, e.g. check writing by computer for pensions, most still require relatively large numbers of people. As wage rates rise (and they have tended to increase more rapidly than general prices), therefore, the costs of doing government business increase more rapidly than the cost of other "industries" (Baumol, 1967; Beck, 1976). This Relative Price Effect means that just to continue to provide the same volume of services government must absorb an increasing share of Gross Domestic Product. The impact of this characteristic of government services will vary depending upon just how labor intensive they are, and upon the nature of the economy in the private sector. All governments, however, face some expenditure growth relative to the private sector if they are to continue to provide the quantity and quality of services they are already providing.

Summary

A number of forces come to bear when decisions about public expenditures are being made. Some of these pressures are general; the total increase in revenues in the fiscal year may be better or worse than average and therefore requests will be scrutinized more or less carefully. Other pressures will be more specific, as when increases in the elderly population require additional money for pensions, or when escalating international tensions produce demands for increased defense expenditures. One of the more important pressures for change in the 1980s and into the 1990s is the power of the political right, and its agenda of reduction in public expenditures. This has been general, directed at reducing the overall size of government. The pressure has also been more specific, directed at certain expenditure programs, particularly those which the dominant political persuasion have considered particularly wasteful or frivolous. A dominant question about public expenditure, therefore, has become: What can be cut?

What Can be Cut?

In principle, everything that government does could be cut almost immediately. Governments created programs and governments could abolish those programs. Even the defining programs of government (Rose, 1976), such as defense or criminal justice, could be largely eliminated, possibly through privatization, as has already been done with some police services. That extreme point having been made, however, elimination of many programs is not likely to happen. Given political realities, few programs in government are targets for total elimination. Even the popular and largely successful Reagan administration in the United States in fact found it impossible to terminate all the programs it had targeted. Once created, organizations and programs tend to persist in the face of attacks on their existence. They may not be immortal (Peters and Hogwood, 1988), and they may be trimmed at the edges, but they will usually survive.

Although most are likely to persist, some types of programs are more vulnerable to cutbacks or terminations than are others. The Office of Management and Budget in the United States, for example, classifies expenditures as "controllable" and "uncontrollable" depending upon the ease with which Congress and the President can eliminate the expenditure within a single budget year. Uncontrollable expenditures are primarily entitlement programs, especially social insurance programs. Citizens have made contributions to these programs while they were working and when they are not working (through unemployment, disability, or retirement) they belive they have the right (and they probably do legally) to receive the benefits for which they have "paid" in the past. Other types of uncontrollable expenditures include long-term contracts and debt interest payments. The government could renege on all these commitments, but to do so would be to indicate that it was financially (and perhaps morally) bankrupt.

Although the United States is thought by many critics to have a small public sector, and very small social service sector, the large majority of the federal budget is considered uncontrollable. In 1989 the estimate is that over 75 percent of the federal budget is not controllable in that year. The percentage of uncontrollable expenditures has been increasing, as the Reagan government cut the more vulnerable programs and social insurance payments continued to increase. Although as exacting a calculation cannot be made for other countries, lacking detailed information on long-term contracts, some estimates of the controllability of the budget in different OECD countries are available. For example, in the United Kingdom, the proportion of the budget which is subject to cash limits can be used as a measure of controllability. As shown in table 3.8, more than half of the budget for the United Kingdom is uncontrollable, but the figure is not so high as in the United States. As in the United States,

Table 3.8 Cash limits on expenditure in the United Kingdom, 1982 (as percentage of total budget)

Northern Ireland	100.0[a]
Education	95.5
Defense	94.8
Other services	91.2
Law and order	81.1
Health	79.5
Other environmental services	73.0
Wales	70.9
Scotland	69.4
Transportation	50.6
Industry	43.3
Common services	32.3
Agriculture	30.9
Overseas aid	30.1
Social Security	1.9
Housing	1.3
Average	59.1

[a] Northern Ireland Office also administers programs analogous to those in Great Britain. Those programs are cash limited to approximately the same degree as expenditures in Great Britain.

Source: HMSO, 1981

defense is the most controllable category of expenditure, while social services tend to be the least controllable.

For most governments in industrialized democracies, only a very small percentage of the budget can be touched in any budget year. Governments have sought to increase their control and, for example, those of the Netherlands and Sweden have greatly expanded their command over the budget (Tarschys, 1985); over half the Dutch budget is now considered controllable. In most countries, of the portion that is apparently eligible for elimination, a large portion is defense expenditure which, at least in the United States and the United Kingdom, incumbent political leaders have been reluctant to decrease. This then places a great deal of pressure toward cutting domestic discretionary programs such as subsidies for agriculture and industry, transportation, the environment, and the like.

Although it does reflect some political reality, the use of the word "uncontrollable" to describe types of public expenditures to some extent creates a new reality of its own. If an expenditure is labeled "uncontrollable" or if a decisionmaker is told that only a small fraction of the budget is controllable in that year, then that decisionmaker will have to have extraordinary fortitude to persist with any plans that he or she may have to reduce some programs and increase others, or perhaps reduce expenditures in total. Thus, the ready use of this classificatory scheme, although it does say something about differences in expenditure, also may place a mortmain on the ideas of politicians coming into office, and institutionalize the priorities and decisions of the past.

Summary

Although we are primarily concerned about how governments raise their revenues, we must remember that they are raising that revenue in order to finance public expenditures. Therefore, to understand the dynamics of revenue, we need also to understand expenditures. This is especially true because the expenditures – and the programs that they pay for – are what most citizens want from government, and therefore there are almost always pressures to spend more. Those pressures to spend more may be especially manifest in the presence of a revenue surplus, as Peacock and Wiseman (1961) argued, and even when there is a surplus there will be more bids to spend than there is money. Thus, although revenues may respond to economic fluctuations (Rose and Karran, 1976), the real dynamic moving public financial systems along tends to come from the expenditure side of the equation.

The public economy, just like the economy of a household or a business, is very much an equation. Governments have much more latitude to incur debts than do private organizations; national governments can print money and subnational governments can increase taxes to pay off debts. In the end, however, governments cannot accumulate debts with total impunity. This is especially true as national economies are becoming increasingly internationalized and the holders of debt are as likely to be foreign investors as the country's own citizens. The International Monetary Fund and other international organizations also monitor the financial soundness of governments and can impose stringent policies on the less circumspect. Governments have to present the appearance, if not always the reality, of fiscal responsibility to the international financial community. They must do that while attempting to satisfy the wishes of their own citizens, and sustain their own possibilities of reelection. Therefore, public debt and the management of that debt is an important political issue.

NOTES

1 Even in these countries, however, the rate of increase in public spending has tended to decline in the late 1980s and early 1990s.
2 Social assistance ("welfare" in the United States) accounts for only 1 or 2 percent of public social spending in most OECD countries.

4
Putting the Two Sides Together: The Budget Deficit and Income Redistribution

Patterns of tax collection in the industrialized countries that comprise the OECD universe have now been described in broad brushstrokes. The patterns of public expenditure in those same countries have also been outlined. The two sides of the equation will now be put together in an examination of the macro- and micro-level impacts of taxing and spending. At the macro-level, these two activities of government combine to produce a budget deficit or, at times, a budget surplus, and this fiscal balance in the public household may have important political and economic consequences for the entire country. At the micro-level, the fiscal activities of the public sector combine to alter the distribution of income and wealth among citizens, generally taking from the more affluent and giving to the less affluent. This redistribution is a very important outcome for individuals and households, and it will influence their well-being and their evaluations of their government. Despite the importance of these combined impacts, governments have not developed very effective institutions for considering and implementing policy options which involve both taxing and spending. Taxation and expenditure decisions are generally made separately, and are combined only at a later date, sometimes with surprising results. These two outcomes of public sector fiscal activity will now be looked at in turn.

Deficits and Debt

Governments must balance their desires to spend and their needs to tax. It should surprise few people to be told that the balance has been in favor of spending. A handful of governments for a few years have been able to run budget surpluses or balance their budgets, but the greater number have run budget deficits in most years since the Second World War. A few countries – Italy and Ireland – have managed to run budget deficits in every year since 1948, despite rapid economic growth (especially in Italy). Several others are very close behind those two in their *apparent* fiscal irresponsibility, managing to run a surplus in only one or two years in the presence of sustained economic growth for most of the period. Clearly balancing the public budget is not something which political leaders in the post-war years have considered a very high priority, or if those leaders have considered it important, they have been noticeably ineffective in achieving their goal.

An unbalanced budget has been blamed for almost all the ills of humankind except fallen arches. At a personal level, Charles Dickens's Mr Micawber provided a simple test for personal happiness based on the balance budget. At the national level, the decline of nations and the fall of empires has been attributed to financial profligacy (Eisenstadt, 1963). A few sovereign nations actually have had to declare bankruptcy, and for other countries fiscal problems have produced at least metaphorical bankruptcy (Rose and Peters, 1978). At less extreme levels the public deficit, and the debt service payments which inevitably result from it, places a number of economic and political restraints on a country's public finances. Government debt and large interest payments also may place a substantial burden on the finances of individual citizens and private corporations, because of higher taxes and higher interest rates. Despite all those real and potential problems, most industrialized democracies continue to run substantial deficits, and to run them very frequently.

This section will be an analysis of budget deficits and public debt in the population of the industrialized democracies that have been discussed. The debt problem in these wealthy countries is not so pressing as that in many Third World countries, but for some it is nonetheless a major economic and political question. This discussion of deficits will seek to answer the following four questions. Firstly, what are the dimensions of the problem, across countries and across time? Secondly, why do countries – even very wealthy countries – continue to run significant public deficits? There appear to be some economic and political patterns associated with running deficits, and an attempt will be made to document those correlates of deficit spending. Thirdly, what are the presumed impacts of public deficits and debt on the political economy of a country, especially in the modern world of global economic interdependence? The public debt of industrialized countries is now more likely than ever to be held by foreigners and the fiscal balances of a country are a matter of international, not just national, concern. Finally, the policy options available to a country faced with large-scale public debt, or one faced with large recurring budgetary deficits, will be of interest. Is there any way out, short of repudiating the debt, or radically reducing public expenditures, or passing massive tax increases? These are not simple questions, and attempting to discuss them within a single chapter is ambitious. It is, however, necessary to understand the fiscal options facing industrialized democracies, and the types of tax policies they may have to adopt to meet their continuing financial obligations.

What are Deficits and Debt?

In the preceding chapter something of the patterns of deficit financing and debt creation in industrialized democracies was documented. It was pointed out that most countries had run deficits on the public budget in most years since the Second World War. This reliance on borrowing was present even though these were, for the most part, years of rapid and sustained economic growth with few active military conflicts. If ever there was a time period in which governments should have been able to balance their budgets, this was it. Still, however, there was a significant accumulation of debt. In the period since the mid-1970s, when the economic fortunes of Western countries have been less certain, the number and size of public deficits have been increasing. Just how big a problem have their deficits and accumulated debt become for the governments involved? As with most issues in government finances, the answer depends upon how the issue is addressed, and how debt is counted.

A prior question is what do we count as debt in the public sector. In any accumulation of financial statistics for any country there will be a figure given for public debt. This is very important, and provides a measure of the amount of formal instruments of indebtedness which the country has actually issued and which it is servicing with interest payments. Some have argued, however, that this conventional figure is too high, as domestically held debt is not a particularly difficult problem for governments (Cebula, 1987). The principal problem created by domestic debt is having to extract revenue in order to pay the debt interest. Even these interest payments, however, are internal transfers with the tax money being paid to citizens who have purchased the debt (often the same people who pay the most taxes). If the debt is broadly held by people throughout the society, as it might be with instruments like savings bonds, then debt service need not even affect economic inequalities very adversely. It might be argued, therefore, that the important debt figure is the amount of public debt held by foreigners. This is the debt that is potentially the most disruptive to the domestic economy and to the government's economic plans.

It may also be that the focus on debt and deficits is too much on the central government. Especially in federal systems, subnational governments may make their own decisions about issuing indebtedness, and make their own decisions about taxing and spending. So, for example, even though almost all state and local governments in the United States are forbidden from running a deficit on the current budget, they are permitted to issue bonds for capital projects, and each year borrow billions of dollars – 75 billion in new borrowing, and 33 billion "rolled over" in 1988. On their current accounts, however, most state governments have been running significant surpluses rather than deficits and the fiscal balance across the public sector may not be as negative as would appear from looking only at federal figures.[1] Other federal countries also permit some of the same fiscal autonomy for subnational governments. For example, in 1988 the *Länder* and local governments in West Germany were servicing substantially more public debt than was the federal government. Even in unitary countries complex financial relationships for capital projects among levels of government require careful scrutiny (Sbragia, 1986; 1979) in order to understand the scale of a debt and where it actually resides. In short, great care must be taken when attempting to calculate which countries are really spending more in the public sector than they take in as revenue.

On the other hand, the published figures for public debt may underestimate the true liabilities of many modern governments. In addition to the amount of debt already issues, most governments have used loan guarantees as an inexpensive (at least in the short-run) manner of intervening in the economy (Lund, 1989). Among other measures, governments now guarantee credit for exporters in order to encourage foreign trade, they guarantee home loans to encourage housing construction and home ownership, and to farmers to promote agriculture, and they guarantee a variety of industrial borrowing in order to promote economic growth (Towe, 1991). Governments therefore have a great deal of contingent liability. The British government in 1987 had contingent liabilities equal to 19 percent of the issued public debt (Central Statistical Office, annual). The contingent liability figure for the federal government of the

United States in 1987 was over 22 percent of the federal debt, and that was more than double the amount of direct federal loans in that year (Office of Management and Budget, annual). It is unlikely that all these guaranteed loans would be forfeited at once, but there is a danger that some could, and that the real obligations of governments to pay for debts in any year may be even higher than they initially appear.

Other types of public debt may be even less tangible than guaranteed loans. One type which many countries will have to face is unfunded pension liabilities (Boskin, 1984; Hills, 1984). We have noted that no industrialized country fully funds its social security system with the "contributions" made by individuals. Rather, these pension programs depend upon future contributions from people still of working age in order to be able to meet the obligation to pay pensions to people who worked in the past. With declining working age populations, and declining economic growth, the optimistic assumptions upon which earlier obligations were made will be potentially very burdensome in the near future. The burden is even more pronounced for subnational governments (especially in the United States) which have huge unfunded pension obligations for their employees. During the fiscal crises of the 1970s and 1980s these governments often purchased labor peace with promises of future pension benefits rather than increasing current wages. This approach appeared very cheap at the time, but it soon will place substantial burdens on the governments which adopted that strategy.

Measurement

One approach to the measurement of public debt is simply to enumerate the gross amount of identifiable public debt which has been accumulated by a country across time. This exercise produces very different pictures, depending upon how that accumulation of debt is portrayed. First, if we just present the gross amount of public debt in current monetary units, the rates of increase in public indebtedness have been immense (see table 4.1). For example, debt in the United States has increased by 852 percent since 1950 and that in France has increased by over 2,200 percent, when measured in current monetary units.[2] If those gross figures are adjusted for inflation, the resulting figures make it appear as though governments have not been quite so profligate (US debt increased by "only" 189 percent in real terms), although the amount of public debt has still increased substantially in almost all countries. Finally, if we examine public

Table 4.1 Public debt in current monetary units

	France	West Germany	Italy	Sweden	United Kingdom	United States
1950	41.2	1.08	5,000	12.4	25,802	219.6
1960	71.7	2.55	6,329	20.8	27,733	231.2
1970	89.2	47.32	23,189	36.2	33,079	291.2
1980	404.4	232.32	205,313	159.6	95,314	737.7
1982	751.0	314.44	332,161	272.8	147,640	987.7
1985	1,027.0	399.15	654,261	480.5	189,460	1,598.5
1988	955.4	446.57	850,000[a]	510.3	205,050	2,091.2
Change (in %)	2,219	41,249	16,900	4,015	695	852

[a] Estimated.
Source: International Monetary Fund, monthly; Mitchell, 1980

debt as a percentage of Gross National Product, governments appear to have been very responsible fiscally (table 4.2). At least until the 1980s, the public debt of most industrialized countries had been a *declining* proportion of Gross National Product. In other words, governments gradually were reducing their debt (often incurred during the Second World War) relative to the total resources available in the economy, and public debt was becoming less of a real or even potential problem. If we look only at the figures of debt as a

Table 4.2 Public debt as percentage of Gross National Product

Year	France	Germany	Italy	Sweden	United Kingdom	United States
1950	40.9	1.1	51.5	41.4	227.5	96.3
1960	23.8	8.4	32.8	55.0	122.9	57.4
1970	11.4	7.0	36.9	50.6	64.8	38.6
1980	14.4	15.6	53.0	49.8	42.3	34.2
1982	20.7	19.7	60.9	34.1	52.8	36.5
1985	21.9	21.6	80.5	55.5	53.2	46.4
1988	16.8	20.9	78.5	54.7	43.7	54.6

Source: See table 4.1.

percentage of GNP it appears that although Keynesian economics released some of the inhibitions of government financial managers, those managers still behaved very responsibly – at least until the economic problems of the last 1970s and the 1980s began to exert their influence.

There are several exceptions to the generalizations in the above paragraph. The most obvious ones are Italy and Ireland and – for exactly opposite reasons – Switzerland. The first two countries were not able to reduce their debt relative to Gross National Product during the prosperous years of the 1950s and 1960s, but rather continued to accumulate additional debt. This deficit spending did not appear to be a function of economic performance because Italy had one of the most rapid rates of economic growth among industrialized democracies during the period and Ireland had one of the lowest. Italy, however, was able to reduce its debt ratio slightly toward the end of the 1980s. Switzerland, in contrast to Italy and Ireland, continued to reduce its level of debt relative to GNP throughout the entire period. It accomplished this feat despite a lower rate of economic growth – albeit a very stable and predictable one – than Italy and most other industrialized countries. Rather than reflecting economic differences, these varied patterns of fiscal policy appear to reflect divergencies in political performance, and perhaps even in the "fiscal culture" (Beichelt *et al.*, 1969) of the three countries.

Again, we can see that the volume and importance of public debt and deficits are often a matter of definition and measurement (Catsambas, 1988; Buiter, 1983). A number of government contingent promises and guarantees can be included in a definition of debt, and if included they increase the apparent obligations of government dramatically. On the other hand, if only foreign debt is counted as important, the obligations of most industrialized democracies appear less significant, albeit of increasing significance in some countries such as the United States. Likewise, if we look at the amount of debt of any industrialized country in current monetary figures, it appears to have been escalating rapidly. If, on the other hand, debt is examined relative to economic resources, it has tended to decline since the Second World War. Issues of public debt are political issues, and there is no shortage of figures to "prove" the validity of positions; the difficulty is in understanding the basis of the arguments and just what the figures mean in a less emotional context.

The Politics of Deficits

We have already pointed out that the governments of most industrialized democracies have tended to run budget deficits in the post-war period; they have found it easy to spend and difficult to tax. That tendency has been exacerbated by the economic problems of the 1970s and by the ideological changes of the 1980s (Tarschys, 1983), but deficit financing has been a staple of the post-war political world. There are, of course, very good political reasons for this persistent behavior. There are also a variety of other reasons why governments tend to produce budget deficits and, in fact, why they tend to produce budgetary outcomes which are very different from the ones intended when they construct their budgets. There are biases in the political and economic systems which tend to drive the budgetary outcomes toward deficits. If the budget is to be a tool of economic management, however, the overall level of error introduced may be as important as the general tendency to produce public deficits.

On the expenditure side of the budget, governments find it difficult to reduce spending as the means of producing a more balanced budget. Almost all citizens receive some direct benefits from government – pensions, farm subsidies, research grants, etc. – and all receive numerous indirect benefits – police protection, national defense, highways, environmental protection (Rose *et al.*, 1985). Almost no citizen would want to have his or her own benefits reduced, and survey evidence tends to indicate that there are majorities in favor of spending the same amount, or more, for most public programs (Sears and Citrin, 1985; Taylor-Gooby, 1985; Hadenius, 1986). This may be because citizens do not understand the true "tax price" of public services, but it is a real problem for governors nonetheless (Kristensen, 1986; 1984). It is very easy and politically desirable for governments to spend money, and to continue to spend even when faced with the prospect of a large deficit. This tendency may be exacerbated in parliamentary regimes where it is rarely certain when the next election will occur, and incumbents therefore are to some degree always preparing for that next election. Governments may be unwilling to impose even short-term austerity for fear of provoking a new election and losing office. Furthermore, even if governments were willing to make difficult financial decisions, a good deal of public expenditure is difficult for government to control without direct repudiation of its existing spending commitments (see pp. 100–102).

On the other side of the ledger, it is relatively difficult for governments to tax. Governments, of course, have the legal power to tax and can extract money effectively whenever they have the will. It is summoning the will to tax that more often is the stumbling block to more closely balanced budgets. Although governments historically have encountered difficulty in mustering the will to levy new or increased taxes, that tendency appears to have been exacerbated in the 1970s and 1980s. Both public opinion and a number of elected politicians came out very strongly against taxes. Unlike previous periods in political history, many of the politicians elected during the 1980s were able to keep their electoral promises about cutting taxes, or at least not increasing the existing levels of taxation; George Bush's need to go back on his pledge of "No new taxes" was the exception rather than the rule. Perhaps more than ever in peacetime, governments are having genuine political problems in making their income equal to their outflow. The few politicians who have said in campaigns that they would raise taxes if elected have had to find other types of employment, and candidates and parties have been contending with one another to see who can be the strongest opponent of taxes.

In addition to the political problems encountered in producing a balanced budget, there may be economic questions about whether this is actually a desirable goal for fiscal policy. Any number of economists have pronounced Keynesian economics dead, but it still appears to hold sway over a number of policymakers in government.[3] At times, old Keynesian ideas may be repackaged as something new, e.g. "supply-side" economics (Bartlett and Roth, 1983). Whatever label may be applied, the basic ideas are often the same: government can stimulate the economy and minimize unemployment by putting more money in circulation by spending than they remove from the economy by taxing. Many public officials (and a few economists) may have read Keynes with only one eye open and have seen the justification for deficits, but not the arguments for budget surpluses (Rose and Peters, 1978, 135–41). That selective perception does not, however, negate the potential importance of the budget balance as an instrument of economic policy.

In addition to the economic and the partisan political reasons for deficits, there may be factors within the institutions of government which make balancing budgets more difficult than it really needs to be. For example, legislatures tend to consider taxes and expenditures at different times and in different bills (see Coombes *et al.*, 1976). The committees which consider these pieces of legislation are usually also different and, as a consequence, there is rarely any procedure in the legislative process which forces parliament to consider the two sides of the budget together. The executive may be somewhat more unified, but even for it the legislative timetable and differentiated structures below the cabinet level may not facilitate simultaneous consideration of the two components of the budget. A number of governments have separate organizations responsible for taxation and tax policy and their administrative decisions often have a substantial impact on the revenue yield for government. The Inland Revenue and the Customs and Excise in Britain, the Internal Revenue Service in the United States, and Direction Générale des Impôts in France are all relatively independent actors in making and implementing tax policy. Spending decisions will be made in some other institution. In short, governments are often not very well organized to make the decisions that would produce a balanced budget – even if that were a high priority for them. Some of the same problems of divided decisionmaking also occur when there are transfers among levels of government and multiple governments provide services to the same geographical areas (Winer, 1983).

Even if the underlying structure of government were well-designed to produce effective fiscal policy decisions, the politics within government itself might make producing such decisions difficult. We have already pointed out some of the problems which electoral politics produce for fiscal policymaking, but the internal management of governments themselves may produce yet another impediment toward effective fiscal management. The governments of most industrialized democracies are coalitions. In some instances these coalitions are fragile unions among a number of parties – the government of Italy in the late 1980s had five parties and that for Belgium for part of the 1980s had six. The members of these multi-party coalition governments represent their own particular policy priorities and interests, and the bargaining for forming and perpetuating the coalitions often is concerned with making the "side-payments" to satisfy the policy preferences, and the constituents, of the parties involved (Franklin and Mackie, 1984). In short, coalition governments will tend to spend more (everything else being equal) than would a single party government. Further, the fragility of a governing coalition may make accepting difficult decisions about tax policies especially unlikely. Therefore, we would expect coalition governments, especially ones involving more than two or three parties, to find producing balanced budgets and effective fiscal policies extremely difficult. Some have been able to do this successfully, but they were overcoming very long odds when they did.

Finally, producing a balanced budget, or an imbalance of a certain level desired for fiscal policy reasons, requires accurate forecasting of revenues and expenditures (Behn, 1981). Those forecasts, in turn, depend upon accurate forecasts of economic conditions; the difficulty is that these are not often available (Penner, 1982; Plesko, 1988). A government may be behaving in the most fiscally conservative manner possible and still have its policies upset by using inaccurate forecasts in making its policies. It should not be surprising that economic forecasts, as well as spending and revenue forecasts, are often quite inaccurate. A huge number of factors are involved in making an economic forecast, any one of which – including uncontrollable events like the weather and natural disasters – may influence the final results. Further, as economies become more internationalized, the economic fortunes for any one country are increasingly beyond its own control, and projections can be made virtually meaningless by external forces. These factors are compounded by the fact that budgets must be based on forecast economic outcomes that are as much as eighteen months or two years in the future. Again, even the best intentioned and most circumspect member of a government would find it difficult to come up with the right answers for a budget laboring under these restraints.

Finally, it should be noted that governments, or at least some of the people within them, are not always well-intentioned (in fiscal policymaking) and they may manipulate the economic forecasts to suit themselves. Thus, official economic forecasts tend to be optimistic about economic growth, unemployment, and revenues, thus allowing governments to budget greater discretionary spending. For example, in the United States, official forecasts from 1970 to 1988 underestimated expenditures and the deficit in 13 of 19 years, often by a wide margin; during the same time period, official projections in the United Kingdom were optimistic in 14 years. Even countries with reputations for fiscal responsibility, e.g. West Germany, tended to overestimate economic growth (in 10 of 19 years). Japan appeared to have erred systematically in its estimates, but in the opposite direction, in order to allow greater spending discretion during the budget year (Ishi, 1990).

Explaining Deficits

A number of factors which may influence the size of the final fiscal balance which a government achieves have now been enumerated. Some of these have already been employed to attempt to explain the fiscal policy decisions of nations, most often the United States. In particular, there is a growing literature attempting to explain the decision to run a deficit as a function of either electoral pressures or fiscal policy reasons (Lowery, 1985; Beck, 1982; Laney and Willett, 1983). The argument is that as election time nears the incumbent party (meaning largely the President) has an incentive either to increase the benefits offered to citizens, or to lower the apparent tax "price" of public services, or to do both. Any of those electoral strategies will tend to produce, or increase the size of, the public deficit. Therefore, everything else being equal, the years closest to elections should have higher deficits than other years. This analysis appears to be confirmed in analyses across time in the United States, and to some degree in time-series analyses in other countries (Cowart, 1978; Tufte, 1978).

The other major set of reasons for running deficits have been argued to be due to fiscal policy. Again, although Keynes has been pronounced dead many times, his ideas appear to live on, and there is still a pronounced tendency of governments to utilize the public budget as an instrument for economic management. Therefore, again with everything else being equal, deficits should be higher when there have been high rates of unemployment or when economic growth has been lower. Likewise, higher rates of inflation should require a dampening of the economy through running smaller deficits or (*mirable dictu*) perhaps even a budget surplus. Governments may now employ a variety of other instruments (such as monetary policy) to influence economic conditions, but the budget deficit generally remains a significant component of their armory. As noted above, however, politicians and other budget makers in government have tended to read Keynes's policy prescriptions very selectively and economic management may be the *justification*, rather than the real reason, for incurring deficits. As Buchanan and Wagner (1977) argued, Keynes's theories made some deficits legitimate, but this came to be interpreted as all deficits are legitimate.

The above discussion of deficits assumes, of course, that governments have a great deal of control over the final balance of their budget, and that the only political reasons for budgetary manipulation are electoral. It has, however, already been pointed out that any number of factors can upset governments' calculations. A projected balanced budget or surplus can be upset by inaccurate forecasts of revenues and expenditures. The internal dynamics of coalition governments – or even one party governments with factions – may mean that side-payments are necessary to keep the government together. More institutionally divided governments may find making any decisions which confront expenditures with revenues unlikely if not impossible. In short, when looking across a range of democratic countries we should not expect a very high degree of predictability by simple economic or electoral factors operating alone; the final outcomes may be determined by a process that is too complex for such simple explanations.

The dependent variable In examining the causes of deficit financing among the OECD member countries which constitute the "sample" for our analysis of tax policy, the deficits in every country will not be analyzed separately with a time-series analysis. This would produce a huge amount of data, much of it perhaps contradictory, that might confuse rather than illuminate the causes of public deficits. Therefore, I have decided to examine deficits cross-sectionally, and to consider the average level of the deficit, measured as a percentage of GDP during the period from 1980 to 1986, as the dependent variable. By selecting deficits in a segment of time rather than a single year, it is possible to eliminate some of the potential random error which the selection of any one year could produce – through poor planning, poor weather, or whatever. The use of the seven-year period does, however, make isolating the effects of anticipated elections or the effects of cabinet crises somewhat more difficult.

The independent variables A variety of independent variables will be used to attempt to explain the differential performance of governments in balancing their budgets – again if a balanced budget is indeed a central goal of a government. Some of these variables are economic, and are indicators of the degree to which the economy in question may objectively be said to require stimulation. In addition, the structure of contemporary public policies creates automatic fiscal effects of changes in the economy. As unemployment increases, fewer people pay income and social insurance taxes, and more people receive social benefits. This creates pressures toward a deficit even if the budget were projected to be in balance. Thus, some observed effects of the economy on deficits may be a result of conscious policy choices, but some others may be automatic effects.

In particular, the average annual growth rate of Gross Domestic Product and the average rate of unemployment will be used as the measures of legitimate fiscal policy reasons for running a deficit. These two economic measures tend to vary inversely ($r = -0.59$), but not as strongly as might have been anticipated. There are still pronounced differences in the abilities of national economies to translate economic growth into jobs, to some degree a function of differences in labor productivity, and to some extent a function of government policies encouraging or discouraging changes in the labor force when economic conditions change.

A variety of political variables will also be used to attempt to explain the occurrence of public deficits. One of these variables will be concerned specifically with the pressures which elections create for greater spending and/or lower taxes. The others will be more indicative of the difficulties which governments may encounter in maintaining their unity without being able to spend money as their members wish, or conversely the difficulty a government, especially a coalition government, might encounter in making the politically dangerous decision to increase taxes. Specifically, the number of elections occurring within the seven-year period will be used as a measure of electoral pressures for deficit spending. Several countries had one or three elections during this period, while most had only two. It would be expected that political leaders under greater electoral pressure would perceive a need to use the budget for electoral purposes much more than would those with more stable political arrangements.

Although elections are the most obvious indications of potential external political influences on government fiscal policy decisions, this may be inadequate to capture the real political dynamics of many countries. Statistically, the election variable has too little variance to generate acceptable explanations. More substantively, there are differences in the timing and meaning of elections which are related to the operative political stability of a country. For example, it is the tradition in several parliamentary regimes, and the law in at least one case, not to have elections other than at the previously determined three- or four-year intervals. The parliament which is elected at the time may create and dissolve several governments without holding an election. The most obvious example would be Italy, which had only the two scheduled elections between 1980 to 1987, but which had at least ten changes of government during the period, with some government changes occurring over fiscal matters. The Norwegian parliament elected in 1989 has no politically compatible majority coalition and may also have unstable governments during its three-year life. The sense that governments could be changed may not be as potent a motivator as the threat of a new election, but it could still motivate governments to attempt to use fiscal policies for political purposes.

The literature on coalition formation in parliamentary democracies indicates substantial difficulty in developing good measures of coalitions and the conditions for their formation (Franklin and Mackie, 1984; Robertson, 1989). In this analysis two relatively simple measures of the possible influence of coalitions on deficits will be utilized. The first will be simply whether the current government is single party or a coalition. This variable becomes almost a surrogate measure for Anglo-American democracies, with only a few other countries able to form a government from a single party; most single party governments in non-Anglo Saxon countries were minority governments. The two presidentialist or quasi-presidentialist systems (the United States and France) will, of course, be counted as having a one party government, although they will have institutional weaknesses of their own which are discussed in a subsequent part of the analysis. A second measure, which will capture something of the potential effects of extreme multi-party membership in a coalition, will be a simple count of the number of parties included in a coalition, ranging from one (a single party government) to six, every year. These will be averaged over the time period used in the analysis.

As well as knowing the number of parties involved in a government, we will want to know the persuasion of those parties. Cowart's work (1978) on the fiscal policy of European governments for an earlier time period found that governments of the political left (Labor, Socialist, Social Democratic, etc.) tended to be more likely to run deficits, or to incur larger deficits, than were parties of the right. Such a finding would be consistent with the fiscal policies traditionally associated with those ideological persuasions. In the 1970s and 1980s, however, the association of partisanship to deficits may be less clear. The supply-side economic policies of some governments on the right have produced very large deficits, while Socialist and Social Democratic governments increasingly have adopted rather conservative fiscal policies (Olsen, 1983; Hall, 1987) in order to meet the economic demands of the world market. However, I would still expect that governments of the left would have larger deficits than other governments.

The institutional weaknesses alluded to above for France and the United States comprise part of a broader institutional variable attempting to measure the internal division of governments, and hence of their potential difficulty in reaching decisions. A division between two branches of governments, or the presence of alternative executives, is an extreme version of such institutional cleavage, but more moderate versions may also influence fiscal policy formation. Therefore, building on the information contained in table 4.3, a variable has been constructed that should indicate the capacity of a government to gain control over the budgetary process and implement policies which would reduce, or even eliminate, the public deficit. This measurement assumes, of course, that the government

Table 4.3 Strength of parliaments in the budgetary process

	Right to amend	*Separate budget committee*	*Referral to functional comm.*	*Staffing*	*Summary*
Austria	yes	yes	no	low	medium
Belgium	yes	yes	yes	medium	high
Denmark	yes	yes	no	medium	medium
Finland	yes	yes	yes	medium	high
France	no	yes	no	low	low
W. Germany	yes	yes	yes	high	high
Greece	no	yes	yes	low	low
Ireland	no	yes (several)	no	medium	medium
Italy	no	yes	yes	medium	medium
Luxembourg	yes	yes	no	medium	medium
Netherlands	limited	no	yes	low	low
Norway	yes	yes	yes	medium	high
Portugal	yes	yes	yes	low	medium
Spain	yes	yes	no	high	high
Sweden	yes	yes	yes	high	high
Switzerland	no	yes	no	high	medium
United Kingdom	no	no[a]	no[a]	low	low

[a] Referred to various select committees rather than to standing committees.
Source: Inter-Parliamentary Union, 1986

in question desires to impose this degree of fiscal control. This variable is a simple ordinal measure ranging from 0 to 5, depending upon the presence or absence of the factors outlined in table 4.3.

Finally, the structure of demands being placed upon government, and their incorporation into the political process should be of concern. Mancur Olson (1982) has argued that the presence of a number of interest groups competing for, and receiving, benefits from government may have a deleterious effect upon economic growth in a country. The same may be said for the balance of its public budget; the more multiple interest groups are able to make legitimate claims on government the more difficult it is for government to balance its budget. To some extent the argument about the influence of coalition governments makes the same type of point, but in this instance the direct access of groups is of interest rather than parties. Furthermore, Wilensky (1976) argued that the presence of corporatist-technocratic linkages were important in explaining the tax backlash in industrialized countries, and the same may be true by inference in explaining the degree of deficit financing in those countries.[4]

All democratic governments face pressure groups; the important question is how the demands of those groups are processed and aggregated. Although far from a perfect representation of the complexities involved in Olson's theories, a measure of corporatism (Schmitter, 1981; Beyme, 1981) will be used as an indicator of the nature of the pressure group structure of a country. This indicator might be thought to be related to public deficits in one of two alternative ways. On the one hand, corporatism would be an indication of legitimate involvement of interest groups in policymaking, of their capacity to press demands on government, and of consequent difficulties in balancing the budget. On the other hand, corporatism would indicate the aggregation of demands from multiple groups into "singular, hierarchical and non-competitive" organizations (Schmitter, 1974), which would eliminate the scramble of multiple, competing interests which Olson associates with problems in economic management; therefore corporatism may actually minimize the budget deficit.

Finally, the tendency to run deficits may be explained by the fiscal system itself. In particular, deficits may occur because governments have to continue to fund programs regardless of the volume of revenues, so that when revenues diminish a deficit occurs. In a more extreme version, governments may have to continue planned increases in expenditures regardless of their revenues so that the size of the deficit may even tend to escalate. Kristensen (1986) makes this argument very strongly for the OECD countries after 1979. He argues that citizens had become accustomed to government benefits coming to them on a regular basis, and that to keep delivering those benefits during a period of financial problems, the easiest course of action was to finance the services through a deficit. Some empirical work (Shibata and Kimura, 1986) has contested this interpretation, but it is sufficiently important in the literature to merit some examination.

The tendency of governments to continue to provide and pay for programs, even when there is not sufficient revenue to finance them, may itself be explained by the political variables discussed above. For example, having relatively weak coalition governments may make it desirable to keep spending for all services rather than risk offending the constituents of one or another of the member parties. Likewise, the direct connections of interest groups to government through corporatism may make it difficult to reduce or eliminate benefits going to those groups. In the first instance, we can test whether there is a strong independent relationship between increases in spending and deficits. This need not be a tautology, as increases in spending could be financed through increased taxation. If there is a significant relationship, this variable can potentially be included in a multivariate model with the political and economic variables.

Results of the analysis Given the limited number of cases available for the analysis, a series of bivariate correlations have been used to test the relationship between the various independent variables and the dependent variable of average deficit during the seven-year period. Of the normal complement of twenty-two OECD countries, three – Portugal, Luxembourg, and New Zealand – are missing because of inadequate data reported in the OECD publications used as sources; this reduction of the size of the sample makes the use of bivariate analysis even more of a necessity.[5] The results of this analysis are presented in table 4.4.

Economic explanations The strongest single correlation with the average level of deficits for these seven years was the unemployment rate. That level of correlation (r = 0.51) was statistically significant, and could be taken as indicating one of at least two relationships between the labor market and fiscal balances. One would be that governments did respond in good Keynesian fashion to poor labor market conditions in their countries by attempting to reflate the economies using budget deficits. The other interpretation would be

Table 4.4 Correlations of level of deficit with economic and political variables (including Norway)

Unemploy-ment	*Economic growth*	*Number of elections*	*Changes of government*	*Party control*	*Institu-tions*	*Corpor-atism*
0.51	−0.44	0.18	0.33	0.19	−0.31	0.36

that these deficits were the result of automatic fiscal stabilization. With high unemployment less money was flowing into the Treasury, and more was flowing out to make social payments, and hence the deficit increased almost on its own. Of course, government policy was responsible for establishing the programs producing this result, but government did not have to make fiscal policy decisions to incur deficits. This point will be returned to somewhat later in the analysis.

The level of economic growth was not related to the deficit as strongly as was unemployment ($r = -0.44$), although the relationship was statistically significant. The period of the 1980s did not have the stable and assured economic growth of the 1950s and 1960s for most of these countries. Economic growth was occurring, and the national leaders did not appear to be reacting strongly to their economic fortunes relative to history when making fiscal policy decisions. They did, however, appear to react more strongly to levels of unemployment which might mobilize citizens much more readily than would comparative rates of economic growth. This is especially true since some growth was occurring (an average across all the countries of 2.3 percent real growth annually during the period). Again, however, we cannot be sure whether the deficits were a political response to pressures, or merely the consequences of the automatic fiscal stabilizers inherent in modern welfare state programs. Unemployment increases social expenditures and reduces revenues more directly than does less-than-hoped-for economic growth, so that these findings may not reveal conscious policy choices by governments.

Political explanations The relationships of most of the political variables to deficits were rather weak. As noted, the number of elections did not have sufficient variance to predict deficits well, and the more elaborate surrogate of number of cabinet changes did show some relationship but does not appear to be as strong a predictor as unemployment. The political persuasion of the government also appears to have little relationship to deficits, with several conservative governments (Netherlands and Canada) producing large deficits and several social democratic (Finland and Sweden) governments producing relatively small deficits. Also, if we look at countries where the political composition of the government changed during the course of the seven years, there were few appreciable impacts on the level of deficits; deficits in Ireland and Australia were not significantly different before and after changes in the partisan composition of government. The presence or absence of a coalition government had a somewhat stronger relationship to deficits, but several important outliers lessen that variable's explanatory capacity. For example, Ireland had one-party or limited coalition governments throughout but has incurred among the largest deficits, while Switzerland with a permanent coalition government has had one of the smallest average deficits.

The two political variables which do appear to have substantial explanatory power for deficits are the institutional variable and corporatism. As noted above, with the first of these variables we are attempting to measure the degree of fragmentation within the institutions responsible for making expenditures about revenue and expenditure. This combines factors such as separation of powers in the United States, the special position given to the finance ministers in countries such as West Germany, and requirements for parliaments to consider revenue and expenditure levels simultaneously in several countries. There are still some outliers in this analysis. The most important would appear to be the United Kingdom which, with a strong Treasury in a unitary regime, might have been thought to be able to control the deficit, has not been very effective. The corporatism variable, on the other hand, may address the extent to which non-governmental interests are incorporated directly into government and therefore may make it difficult for the very institutions mentioned directly above to make the types of difficult decisions required to minimize a deficit.

Fiscal explanation The simple test of the fiscal explanation – increased public spending produces increased deficits which in turn create more spending – generated very little support for this hypothesis. The correlation between the rate of increase in public expenditures in earlier years and the average size of the public deficit were quite low in these data. It appears that governments are perhaps not so driven by expenditure decisions, and the need to finance those expenditures through deficits, as some analysts (especially conservative analysts) have argued. Rather, it appears that deficits are generated more from the need to meet changing economic circumstances, especially unemployment, with appropriate policy responses (automatic or not), and the need to manage the political process, especialy to create or preserve government coalitions.

Combining the two sides While unemployment rates are rather strongly related to deficits, the explanation is far from perfect. It is interesting to note that the cases which the level of unemployment is not very successful in explaining do appear to have ready political explanations. For example, the deficits in Italy and Switzerland are both higher than might have been expected from their relatively low levels of unemployment. The presence of this higher deficit may be explained by the coalition governments, and the relatively rapid changes in government, in both countries.[6] On the other hand, the public deficit in France is somewhat smaller than would have been expected by its level of unemployment, and this may be explained by the powerful set of political institutions at the center of French government, including restrictions on the ability of the National Assembly to interfere with the budgets of the executive (Lord, 1973). Even with a Socialist government, this level of institutional control appears to generate greater budgetary restraint. Table 4.5 demonstrates that when political and economic explanations for deficits are

Table 4.5 Multiple correlations of deficits with economic and political variables (including Norway)

Unemployment with:				
Number of elections	*Changes in government*	*Party control*	*Institutions*	*Corporatism*
0.53	0.34	0.64	0.55	0.56
Economic growth with:				
Number of elections	*Changes in government*	*Party control*	*Institutions*	*Corporatism*
0.46	0.29	0.44	0.52	0.51

combined in multiple regressions, some very high levels of explanation are achieved. These data cover only a limited number of cases for a relatively short time period, but the results are suggestive of an important interaction between economics and the political system in generating the balances between the taxing and spending components of the public budget. As in so much other comparative policy research (Peters, 1972; Cameron, 1978; Castles, 1982) selecting political *or* economic explanations does not produce as satisfying results as selecting economic *and* political explanations.

The case of Norway In the data on public deficits, Norway stands out because of its very high budget surplus – an average of almost 6 petrcent over the seven years. This may have been in part a function of successful economic management, but was to a large extent due to the windfall of North Sea oil impacting on a very small domesic economy (see Laegreid, 1988). The high economic growth and low unemployment generated at least partially from this windfall combined with the budget surplus to skew the statistical findings somewhat in the direction of economic effects on deficits.[7] Therefore, it appears justified to remove the case of Norway from the data and run the analysis again to determine just what impact that single exceptional case did have on the findings. The results of that analysis are presented in tables 4.6 and 4.7.

As expected, these data do not demonstrate as stong an effect of economic variables on deficits as did the data including Norway. Economic explanations are still statistically significant and stronger than political variables, but not to nearly the same extent as they were previously. Also, the explanatory capacities of the political variables were increased, albeit slightly, especially for the institutions and corporatism variables. Again, the fiscal explanation was very poorly correlated with deficits. Even more clearly than in the data with Norway included, neither economic nor

Table 4.6 Correlations of level of deficit with economic and political variables (excluding Norway)

Unemployment	*Economic growth*	*Number of elections*	*Changes of government*	*Party control*	*Institutions*	*Corporatism*
0.44	−0.31	0.15	0.39	0.21	−0.33	0.36

Table 4.7 Multiple correlations of deficits with economic and political variables (excluding Norway)

Unemployment with:				
Number of elections	*Changes in government*	*Party control*	*Institutions*	*Corporatism*
0.42	0.51	0.53	0.45	0.52

Economic growth with:				
Number of elections	*Changes in government*	*Party control*	*Institutions*	*Corporatism*
0.31	0.49	0.36	0.35	0.41

political variables were sufficient by themselves to explain deficits, but combinations of the two did provide substantially improved and acceptable explanations. This is especially true when unemployment is used as the economic indicator. Therefore, I would accept a combination of economic prosperity (and particularly the strength of the labor market) and political demands as the most reasonable way of explaining the extent to which countries rely upon deficit financing.

Summary The final balance of the public budget does not occur because of any one simple factor or any single decision. The whole public budget – the spending and taxing sides alike – is the product of a bewildering number and variety of decisions, many of which are private and taken in the marketplace rather than by governments. Both the performance of the economy and of the political system appear to be contributory factors in producing a deficit. As a consequence, those who seek to rid their countries of continuing budget deficits will also have to address both the economic and political dimensions of the problem. It will be pointed out below that any number of proposals for quick and easy solutions are around, but these appear likely only to generate cynicism on the part of the public, and perhaps more red ink on the pages of the budget document.

Do Deficits and Debt Matter?

Much of the discussion in this chapter has been premised on an implicit assumption that the level of public deficit, as well as the accumulated public debt, are important considerations for a government. This may be based on a very American, or at least Anglo-American, notion of the importance of a balanced budget (Savage, 1988) and fiscal propriety. All manner of ills are supposed to befall countries which go into debt, just as they would individuals who regularly spend more than they earn. These conservative values have persisted in the United States long after the initial victory of the Keynesian revolution, and dominate much of American discussion about public finance. The deficit crisis of 1990 is but the latest of many manifestations of the concern about deficits and debt in American politics. These values, however, have little apparent effect on political behavior. The question, therefore, is how important are the deficit and public debt as indicators of the fiscal well-being of a country? Should this obsession with a balanced budget be a real concern, or is it only so much political rhetoric? Further, does the ability to produce a balanced budget say more about the strength of the political system than it does about the future strength of the economic system?

Economic Effects

The major effects which are alleged to derive from an unbalanced budget are economic. These presumed negative effects include rising interest rates, lowered savings rates, and slower economic growth (Congressional Budget Office, 1990). This is not a book about the economics of public finance, but these potential effects must be discussed in order to understand some of the potential political effects of deficits. The conventional discussion of these economic effects of borrowing is based upon the analogy to the private household, and the bankruptcy which almost inevitably comes to individuals who spend more than they earn. The governments of almost all countries in the industrialized world have spent more money in almost every year in the post-war period than they have taken in as taxes (see table 3.3 in the previous chapter). All these governments have, however, been able to remain in business, and indeed most have enjoyed flourishing economies. There does appear to be some relationship between unemployment rates and the size of a deficit (although not between economic growth rates and the deficit) but this is usually taken to indicate government's reaction to poor economic performance, rather than the deficits being the cause of poor economic performance. Further, there appears to be virtually no empirical relationship between accumulated public debt and economic performance, as measured by either unemployment or economic growth. Some high deficit countries (Italy) have experienced strong economic growth, while other high deficit and debt countries (Ireland) have had poor growth. Some low deficit countries (United Kingdom) have had high unemployment while others (Sweden) have not. Why have some of the apparently more profligate countries – one would probably choose Italy, Belgium, and Ireland as the prime examples, but there are other candidates such as the United States – not actually gone bankrupt with so much continued deficit financing?

The most obvious answer to that question is that public finance and private finance are different. In the first place, most of the money spent by the public sector goes right back into the economy of the country. This is true whether the money is spent for pensions for the elderly or tanks for the army. Some money may flow overseas but most stays at home to circulate in the domestic economy. This may mean that there is simply more economic activity for government to tax in subsequent years. These positive (or perhaps only neutral) effects of government expenditure may be even greater if the money is spent on economic development activities, or long-term investments such as education. Although some economists would argue that the economy would be better off it private individuals could make the final decisions about how to spend all that money, it is still important to remember that money spent by government (whether it comes from taxes or is borrowed) is not lost forever but goes back into the economy.

Although deficits and debt may not have produced cataclysmic problems for national economies, they may have other, more subtle effects on them. One of the most important would be on levels of investment in the economy. If government must borrow a great deal of money to pay for its expenditures, then it must compete with private borrowers for the same stock of funds. Government may "crowd out" the private investors – in part because government securities are usually considered very safe investments – or force interest rates up to a point where it is difficult for a private investor to earn a reasonable profit on an investment (Evans, 1985; Niskanen, 1978). If these types of effects should occur within an economy, the long-term consequences would obviously be extremely bad; the economy would, over the long-term, stagnate without new investments. This negative effect of crowding-out is likely to be especially pronounced in contemporary economies requiring large-scale investments in research and development to keep pace with an accelerating product cycle (Krasner, 1978).

Although the logic of "crowding-out" appears superficially to be very strong, the empirical relationship between deficits or debt and investment is not especially great. Many economists have detected only a minimal effect of crowding-out, and argue that the impact of deficits in stimulating the economy is substantially more important (Friedman, 1978; Roley, 1981). Some analysts have argued that there may be a "crowding-in" effect, in which the increased economic activity generated by deficits makes private investment more attractive to businessmen (Tobin, 1984). There may be longer-term relationships between deficits, debt, and investment which do not appear in these data, but most available data suggests little negative impact on savings or investments from government deficits.

The other possible consequence of continuing deficit financing is inflation. If the deficit of a country is financed not by borrowing from the domestic or international financial markets but is covered simply by printing more money, there is a greater likelihood of inflation. There simply will be more money in circulation relative to the amount of goods being produced in the economy and that will produce, or is almost a definition of, inflation. Even very prosperous and well-managed political economies experience some inflation; the question becomes how much inflation, and the tolerance of the particular country of inflation. Even within OECD countries, there is substantial variance in the willingness of populations to tolerate inflation, or to tolerate the unemployment which might result if government did not run a deficit (Schmolders, 1969).

The problem for the critics of deficits is that the empirical relationship between deficits and inflation is not particularly compelling. There does appear to be some moderate inflationary impact of deficits in the contemporary economy, but much less than is often assumed (Brooks, 1981; Guess and Koford, 1984). These major empirical studies concluded that the inflationary impact of the deficit was not nearly as significant as its stimulative impact on the economy. In other words, inflation coming from deficit may be a problem, but it does not appear to be a problem of the magnitude (unemployment, possible recession) that might have resulted from not running the deficit.

Foreign debt The potential economic effects of public debt may become greater if a large percentage of the debt is held by other countries, or by the citizens of other countries. In the short-term the effects may be positive, given that money from elsewhere can be used to fund the debtor country's internal public expenditures. The large deficits of the 1990s in the United States, for example, were funded largely by overseas borrowing. If that money is being well-spent and is promoting economic growth, then the long-term consequences of borrowing may be positive. If, on the other hand, the borrowed money is not being spent wisely and is not producing substantial economic growth, then the long-term consequences will be less positive. Obviously, the debtor nation becomes dependent upon its creditors and to some degree must tailor its policies to ensure a stable environment for borrowing.[8] Further, the economy becomes vulnerable to rapid movements of capital out of the country. Even without the threat of large-scale disruption, borrowing from abroad will mean that debt interest must be paid abroad and, rather than being just an internal transfer of funds, it becomes a net loss to the economy.

Political effects Not all the effects of deficits and borrowing are economic. The public budget is a political statement as much as it is an economic one, and hence some of the impact it makes will also be on politics. That impact may differ, however, according to the particular political context within which the deficit is occurring. For example, given the rhetoric surrounding the balanced budget in American politics, we might expect politicians who produced large deficits to be punished severely, but that does not appear to have been the case. Ronald Reagan produced larger deficits by far than any peacetime President (and larger ones in current dollars than any President including Franklin Roosevelt during the Second World War) but departed the office with very high approval ratings. Over 95 percent of the Congressmen who cooperated with President Reagan in producing these deficits were reelected during the period between 1982 and 1988. The American voting public certainly did not retaliate through the ballot box against their leaders who had produced deficits. Surveys following the deficit crisis in October 1990 indicated very strong disaffection with the politicians responsible, but most still won reelection in the November elections. In other cultures with less manifest concern about the existence or size of a budget deficit, it appears even less clear that voters have thrown out, or would throw out, a government just because it spent more than it collected in taxes.

As with so many other policies, the real effects of running deficits consistently may not be felt until any one President or any one party has left government. President Bush in 1990 began, in the words of one analyst, to pay for President Reagan's party. One effect of the deficits that one government incurs is higher levels of debt interest payments for subsequent governments. The deficit producing government can reap the political benefits of spending more and/or taxing less, and this will have to be paid for by governments which come after. This will mean that the fiscal and policy options of those subsequent governments will be constrained by having to make interest payments. If a subsequent government decides it wants to retire some of the debt, it will have to face very severe restrictions on its other options unles there is very large-scale economic growth or equally considerable inflation. In short, the political costs of deficit financing tend to be borne at a later date, and hence most politicians are willing to borrow during their time in office and let the next person worry about paying the costs.

Finally, it has been argued (Rizzo and Peacock, 1987) that one significant impact of deficit financing is more deficit financing. In the first place, once governments lost the constraint of a balanced budget through the Keynsian revolution in public finance (Buchanan and Wagner, 1977; Brittan, 1975), they found it easy initially to finance their spending programs through deficits. After deficit financing became more routine, the amount of money borrowed began to fund a "normal" level of public expenditure which was higher than the tax price being paid by citizens. Therefore, any politician seeking to balance the books with more taxing or less spending will be acting against the established expectations of citizens about what they will receive and at what cost. Further, borrowing money in one time period means that interest will have to be paid in subsequent time periods, and therefore that the costs of government will continue to increase. If political leaders are expected to continue providing a constant volume of services, make increased interest payments, and keep taxes down, they will have to respond with even greater deficits. Brittan describes this downward fiscal spiral as the "debt trap."

It may also be that the political effects of running deficits are more systemic. They may go to the heart of public confidence and support, rather than being specific political targets remediable by defeating an incumbent. Consistently producing deficits may indicate to citizens, if they really care about the matter, that government is out of control and is incapable of managing effectively the affairs of State. This may be true for any particular government of the day, but if deficits occur over a long period of time, and with different types of governments, citizens may come to assume that the system as a whole is incapable of doing the job for which it is designed. Later (chapter 6) it will be shown rather conclusively that tax evasion has been on the increase in most OECD countries, and that this increased evasion is as much or more a political as an economic act. Also, "tax revolts" in the American states and in some European countries appear as much related to disaffection from the political system as levels of taxation. The popular cynicism about the use of public money and the qualities of public management engendered by governments consistently running deficits may be related to this decline in the willingness of citizens to "contribute" their money to the public sector. Even if it is not related directly to evasion or voting against taxes, it may be related to some popular and pervasive ideas that contemporary government is not very effective at governing.

What to do About Deficits?

One of the most pervasive questions in American politics in the late 1980s and early 1990s has been what to do with the public deficit. The same question is being asked in other countries, but not with the air of apparent urgency which has surrounded the American debate. As mentioned above, the concept of a balanced budget holds a particular attraction for Americans and the large-scale and persistent deviations from that ideal have provoked an intense political discussion. All this discussion has not yet, however, gone very far toward remedying the deficit problem. This inaction is especially evident because the most obvious solution – increasing taxes – has been kept off the political agenda by the past two Presidents. Just what options – other than the unpalatable step of increasing taxes – are available to governments who want to deal with their deficits? This discussion will focus on the problems of the United States federal government, but many of the same options and much of the logic would be applicable to a number of other countries. Other countries may be able to avoid taking harsh measures because their political economies are not so central to the world economy, but the United States has been forced by its own ideology and by circumstances to confront the issue.

A Balanced Budget Amendment

Beginning at one end of an implicit continuum of control of fiscal decisionmaking, one option available to government would be to ban running deficits. This has been discussed in the United States in terms of an amendment to the Constitution which would make deficits illegal except in time of declared national emergency (Moore and Penner, 1980; Wildavsky, 1980). This amendment would be analogous to amendments in most of the American states which forbid running deficits on the current budget. To fiscal conservatives, this amendment is a simple, if somewhat extreme, means of eliminating the problem of the deficit forever. The size of the deficit and its persistence enabled conservatives to get almost enough state legislatures to endorse a convention for discussing this amendment during the 1980s. The critics of the amendment argue that it would create more problems than it could ever solve, and would produce even greater citizen cynicism about government than persistent budget deficits have. The clamor for the balanced budget amendment has subsided somewhat in the early 1990s, but this change to the Constitution remains a real possibility to some critics of current fiscal practices in Washington.

The major problems in the balanced budget amendment arise from the possibilities of its requirements being met at the planning stage but not being reached in reality. Planning for the public budget must begin well over a year in advance of its first implementation, and therefore must be based upon projections of economic conditions. Even if calculated with great care and integrity, these predictions can err significantly (see above), and a budget which was in balance when planned may go into deficit once it is implemented. The possibility of error leaves the leaders of government with the options of making adjustments in programs throughout the budget year, with the attendant uncertainties for managers or clients, or running a deficit which is considered to be not only illegal but actually unconstitutional. Neither of these outcomes is very palatable, and may be substantially worse outcomes than a planned budget deficit.

We noted above that American state and local governments have been working within the restraints of constitutional requirements of a balanced budget for some years. They have adjusted to these strictures with "revenue budgeting" (Wildavsky, 1986, 18–9; Meltsner, 1971). In this form of budgeting, the probable revenues of government dominate budgetary decisions, rather than expenditure priorities having at least an equal role in determining the outcomes. The dominant position of revenue is made even more important in some states where a quasi-autonomous tax commission determines what government income and therefore what expenditures will be. Revenue budgeting has worked reasonably effectively in these subnational governments, although the results are often very conservative. For example Rudy Perpich, the Governor of Minnesota, was unable to fund a favorite economic development project in 1988 because of a revenue forecast that turned out to be $206 million lower than real revenues (Fessler, 1988). Similarly, state governments which have enacted tax and/or expenditure limitations have also found ways of avoiding the caps imposed by those measures (Howard, 1989), so that simply mandating lower expenditures, lower revenues, or a balanced budget often appears to produce greater creativity concerning accounting and forecasting strategies rather than genuine fiscal responsibility.

Although requirements for a balanced budget have worked reasonably well at the state and local level, it is not clear that this approach would work as well for a national government. One reason is that neither the revenues nor the expenditures of the federal government in the United States are as predictable or controllable as the activities of subnational governments. There are too many entitlement programs, and taxes fluctuate somewhat more with economic conditions at the federal level than at the state and local level. The same would be true of the revenues and expenditures of other national governments. Further, subnational governments do not have the responsibilities for managing an economy that a central government does. Even if there were not the financial emergency required under the proposed amendment, most leaders at the federal level would like to attempt to manage the economy. Even if such an amendment (or other legal constraint) were desirable, it is not at all clear that it could work as intended.

The Wizard of OB

Another “solution” to the problem of the public deficit is to define it away, and to create accounting systems which move expensive public functions “off-budget” (OB). Again, this option has arisen most commonly in the United States as the President and Congress have struggled to find ways to meet the Gramm–Rudman–Hollings targets (see below). The idea is a simple one: find an excuse to move a spending item off the budget and then simply not count it as public expenditure for purposes of determining the deficit. Money is being spent, but simply is not counted. The largest spending program proposed for this category has been the Savings and Loan bailout bill, estimated at around $5 billion. The justification is that this is a one-time expense associated with one of the contingent liabilities of government mentioned above. Why this justification makes the money being spent less important than money being spent for defense or education is not clear to critics of the move, but it removes that necessary expenditure from competition with other necessary public programs.

Although this blatant use of off-budget expenditures to mask, or minimize, a real deficit is peculiarly American, the use of off-budget expenditure programs is more universal. As noted above, the social insurance programs of most countries are managed off-budget and appear in national accounts to be private or quasi-private (Lepelmeier, 1979). Thus, when national accounts are presented for the budget appears smaller and perhaps somewhat more in balance.[9] Furthermore, public enterprises are also often managed off-budget because monitoring their economic activities may be substantially different from the type of accounting and control needed for other public sector activities (Anastassopoulous, 1985). Especially when there is a great deal of capital subsidy and the writing off of loans to public enterprises, their treatment as off-budget entities can mask substantial flows of funds within the public sector. A variety of other government activities may be administered off-budget or in special budgets in all the OECD countries; in short, almost everyone tries to use the Wizard of OB to help make the budget picture look brighter to citizens and to the financial community. Even if the budget is in balance, OB can make government appear smaller to citizens and therefore perhaps appear to be less of an intrusion into their lives and pocketbooks.

As with so many of the budgetary tricks which can be employed to mask the true state of public finance, the acceptance of off-budget spending may produce as many problems as it is able to solve for government. Some of these problems will be economic, if indeed deficits and debt do have deleterious economic consequences. Simply glossing over the true state of fiscal affairs will not force decisionmakers to confront the difficult choices which perhaps should be made about taxing and spending. Further, the same public cynicism that can arise from other tricks and "quick-fixes" can arise here. A significant portion of the public may never understand the nature of the maneuvers being undertaken when spending is moved on or off budget but the announcement of a "solution," followed by actual negative consequences, risks producing public disillusionment and alienation.

Load-Shedding

To some extent privatization and other programs to reduce the burdens of government represent the extreme version of the Wizard of OB. To many people, if a program is given to the private sector the function almost disappears. In reality, however, most services of government which are privatized will continue to be provided, albeit by someone else. This is true whether a program such as a nationalized industry is sold to the private sector, or if the service is merely contracted out to private suppliers. The private sector may be able to provide the service less expensively and perhaps more efficiently, but some or all of the cost will still exist, and will be paid by someone. The only thing which really will have changed through privatization is whether the cost of the function will appear in the public or the private side of the ledger.

It cannot be denied that privatization (especially getting rid of expensive continuing programs) could reduce costs for the public sector, and thereby may reduce the deficit. But, like so many other of the relatively quick and "easy" remedies to real problems, it could not be done without real costs. Some of the costs might be imposed on services, especially in terms of their quality and equality. Government services may be expensive in part because their program structure is designed to serve all legally qualified clients, not just the ones it is easy or profitable to serve. Ironically, privatization may increase rather than decrease alienation from the public sector because the public programs which are the easiest to privatize may also be the public services which are most visible to citizens – health care, water, telecommunications, etc. Taxes may go down a little, but the perception of service delivery may go down a great deal. The programs least likely to be privatized – public goods – are also the ones which most citizens do not think about when calculating the benefits they buy with their taxes (Downs, 1967). Finally, some governments (notably the United Kingdom) have managed to balance their budgets in the short-run by selling off assets. For a while their budget figures look very good, but the long-term consequences of selling such assets are less clear to many observers (Veljanovski, 1987).

Tax More, Spend Less

Finally, the simplest solution to the deficit problem is to tax more or spend less. This is a much easier propostion to write than it is to implement. A number of conservative governments in the 1980s in a variety of countries have attempted to implement just that simple formula (or at least the expenditure side of it), but few have produced anything like the results that they promised or desired. Most governments have been content with reducing projected levels of increases in expenditures, or with "revenue enhancements" rather than significant boosts in revenue. Also, some of the political leaders – most notably Ronald Reagan – were so keen to reduce taxes that they ignored the deficits produced by their actions. The political problems on each side of the taxing/spending equation have already been mentioned at some length, but it is worthwhile to remember them briefly in this context.

It is also important to note here that despite the rhetoric of balanced budgets, taxpayers – even those in the United States with its particular fetish about a balanced budget – are not anxious to have taxes raised to pay for deficit reduction. Almost 70 percent of respondents in an October 1989 poll disapproved of raising income taxes to reduce the deficit (Gallup, October 5–8); a Yankelovich survey (January, 1989) found 72 percent opposing any type of tax increase for that purpose. Even the budget crisis of October 1990 found two-thirds of respondents to surveys saying that they did not believe that increases in taxes were needed to balance the budget (*USA Today*, October 2, 1990). Voters prefer to hold down expenditures as a means of reducing the deficit, at least until specific expenditure programs that might have to be cut are mentioned.

When unable to implement this simple solution easily, governments have had to resort to playing tricks on themselves (and perhaps on citizens). The most common have been to remove any volition from making budget cuts and to attempt to make them automatic. Perhaps the most famous incarnation of this strategy is the Gramm–Rudman–Hollings program in the United States, which has mandated reducing the federal deficit to zero within five years. While we do not need to engage in a detailed description of this "solution" to the problem (Collender, 1988), the basic idea is that Congress and the President are first offered an opportunity to reduce the budget deficit to meet the targets of the Act through the normal budgeting process. If that is not successful, then automatic cuts ("sequestrations") are implemented, with the total coming half from domestic spending (other than entitlement programs) and half from defense spending.[10] Portions of this legislation have been declared unconstitutional by the Supreme Court (Bowsher v. Synar), but the bulk of the program has been put into effect, or at least been used as a sufficient threat to generate a political compromise on the budget.[11]

Althoug it is perhaps the most visible of automatic budget cutting devices, Gramm–Rudman–Hollings is by no means the only program of its type. The government of the Netherlands experimented rather early on with a program to relate increases in total public spending to economic growth, allowing government to spend the "structural budget margin" in addition to expenditures in the previous year (Diamond, 1977). This program would have kept government at approximately the same size relative to GNP, with some adjustments to take into account the needs for countercyclical fiscal policy. The consensus surrounding this approach broke down during the fiscal crises that swept the industrialized democracies during the 1970s and 1980s, and it has been replaced by a less ambitious, and less automatic, program for reconsidering spending programs on a systematic basis (Heroverwegingen, 1980–1; Schick, 1988). The Swedish government has used a device called the "main alternative" as a way of attempting to reduce spending (Erickson, 1983). This is a very simple idea – budgets are automatically cut by 2 percent and agencies must bargain to have any cuts restored. The British government has used "cash limits" as a means of controlling public expenditure during an inflationary period (Pliatzky, 1989). The volume budgeting system used in the United Kingdom would permit expenditures to increase with inflation, but cash limits place a ceiling of total possible expenditures. The envelope budgeting system in Canada (McCaffrey, 1984) has required ministers who want to spend more to find commensurate spending reductions in other programs within the same broad policy area (envelope). A similar "scrap and build" budgeting system has been introduced into New Zealand and Japan (Tarschys, 1985, 40–1).

There are a number of other innovations to control spending which could be mentioned, with most systems attempting to remove discretion from political leaders (Schick, 1988; Tarschys, 1985). As pointed out above, the politics of the public purse are such that it is easy to spend but difficult to tax. Thus, one way to attempt to impose control on the public sector is to remove the discretion of politicians, whose incentives all tend to point in the one direction.

No program or gimmick, however, can eliminate that discretion entirely. Congress in the United States has voted to exempt certain spending from the limits imposed by Gramm–Rudman–Hollings, and to delay implementing the process. The reconsideration process in the Netherlands often has focussed on entitlement programs that would be almost impossible to reduce. Politics and governing are about exercising discretion, and attempts to limit discretion will meet with attempts to circumvent them. As with so many other gimmicks in the public sector, they therefore run the risk of creating cynicism and decreased respect for government.

The Micro-Level – Redistribution

Public deficits (and the occasional surpluses) appear to have some real importance for government and for the performance of whole economies. That importance may not be so great as has often been assumed, and may only be symbolic, but yet it is something to which political leaders must attend. In addition to those societal effects, the budget also plays a very important role in balancing the books for a large number of ordinary citizens in all industrialized societies. It has already been pointed out that, on average, governments in OECD countries receive approximately 39 percent of the total production in society as taxes. This tax money is not buried in boxes in the ground but is transferred through a variety of spending programs (chapter 3) back into the economy. How government taxes, and how it spends, will determine to a great extent how well-off specific individuals in the society will be. The OECD world remains capitalist and the distributions of income generated by the market tend to dominate the final distributions; these in turn remain unequal even after the operations of government. The question we will be asking, and partially answering, here is what does the public sector in these countries do to help make the final distribution of income more egalitarian.

Given the rhetoric about the "Welfare State" in most of the countries in the OECD world, we might expect government to do a great deal to make income more equal. In almost all of these countries, social spending (broadly conceived to include health and housing) accounts for at least one-third of all public expenditure – the average level of social spending is over 41 percent of total public expenditure. Likewise, we showed in chapter 2 that on average almost 40 percent of all government revenues are derived from personal and corporate incomes taxes, which should be the most progressive form of taxation; another 6 percent of total tax revenue, on average, comes from property and wealth taxes, which also should have a pronounced redistributive effect. These patterns of taxation and expenditure should combine to make the distribution of income more equal after government operates than was the distribution created in the market.

The operations of government certainly do create greater equality, but the effects of government are not as pronounced as they may be thought to be a priori. First, although a significant share of revenue is derived from the income tax, that tax is not as progressive as it appears on the law books, because of the ability of taxpayers to avoid payments legally through a series of "loopholes" (chapter 6). The presence of loopholes has made the income tax less progressive; in the 1980s the numerous tax reforms undertaken by governments have had the same effect on the nominal tax structures.[12] The affluent do pay more income tax, but not as much more as is usually assumed. Further, if government is to be successful in raising the volume of money it needs to provide all its services, it must tax the middle classes rather heavily – that is where the most money is. In almost all industrialized societies the bulk of the money in the economy is earned by people in the middle ranges of the income distribution, and therefore that is also from where the bulk of tax revenue must come. For example, in the United States, even confiscatory taxes on incomes over $1 million per year would increase tax revenues by only about 8 percent; the same process applied to incomes over £500, 000 in Britain would yield only approximately 6 percent additional income. Finally, property ownership – at least in the form of a first home – is now also widely distributed in OECD countries, so that the property tax is often as much a middle-class and even working-class tax as it is an upper-income one.

On the expenditure side of the equation, although there is a very large element of social expenditure in all of the OECD countries, this is not as redistributive as might be assumed. The bulk of social expenditure derives from social insurance programs, and that spending is funded heavily from insurance contributions paid by all wage earners and their employers, but *not* generally paid on income earned from investments. Further, in some countries social security contributions are not paid on wages above a certain total amount each year, a decision taken in order to preserve their appearance as insurance premiums rather than as tax. This limitation is understandable politically, but does limit the redistributive effects of social programs.

A very large share of social expenditure goes to the elderly as pensions, in rough proportion to the amount of income they earned during their working lives. Since many of the elderly may have little or no market income during their retirement this appears to be redistribution across classes, but when we can ascertain the incomes of pensioners while working, the apparent redistributive effect of social expenditure is actually much less. Thus, this component of public spending tends to be more redistributive across time than it is across income classes. People pay these taxes while they are working and then receive benefits when they retire, or are disabled, or are unemployed. Other social programs, e.g. means-tested benefits, are more directly redistributive across income classes but these are relatively small component of social expenditure (see chapter 3). In addition, some expenditures, including social expenditures broadly conceived, such as education and even health, tend to be consumed more by the middle and upper classes than by the working class (Deleeck, 1978; Deleeck, Huybrechs, and Cantillon, 1983) and hence tend to redistribute real income away from the poorest people in society and toward the more affluent.

Perhaps one reason why governments do not do a better job of redistributing income (assuming that this is indeed a goal for welfare states) is that the data on the two sides of the public sector are rarely considered together. In most countries, tax decisions and expenditure decisions are the responsibilities of two separate organizations in the executive branch, and the choices are generally made according to the criteria and values of those organizations, rather than a criterion of redistribution. Taxing organizations, for example, tend to be more concerned about their ability to collect revenue (see below, pp. 250–255) than they are about the redistributive effects of the taxes. Spending organizations – whether central organizations (Campbell and Szablowski, 1979) monitoring all expenditure, or the specific spending agencies – are more concerned with managing and defending their programs than with the net redistributive effects of those programs. Likewise, taxing and spending decisions tend to be taken at different times, and by different committees, in legislative bodies, and those bodies do not have to consider the joint effects. Further, the legislative committees concerned with fiscal decisions tend to be different from the committees most concerned with redistribution, e.g. social policy committees. In short, if income redistribution does occur as a result of the public budget, it is usually as a subsidiary effect of all the other activity.

The failure to consider the joint effects of taxing and spending on individuals is very visible in the "poverty trap" which exists in a number of industrialized countries (Piachaud, 1980; Dilnot and Stark, 1989). This "trap" results from a failure to synchronize tax and expenditure policies affecting the poorest members of society, especially those who do earn some income in the economy. In the poverty trap, as earned income increases, benefits are decreased and taxes are imposed. This often occurs in a way that the individual can have a net reduction in disposable income if he or she earns the extra dollar or pound through work. The existence of this anomaly is widely known to policy analysts,[13] but governments have managed to avoid doing anything about it, largely because the taxing and spending organizations are not forced to coordinate their activities, and the policies concerning taxing and spending make good sense when considered in isolation.

Not only do different organizations within central government often make independent decisions about taxing and spending, but often different governments also can make their own, autonomous decisions. We pointed out in chapters 2 and 3 that subnational governments in some countries have a great deal of autonomy in making taxing and spending decisions. This level of government spends an increasing amount of money, and their activities can have almost as much effect on income distribution as does the central government. Rose (1985, 296) has estimated that the average citizen in OECD countries is subject to 20 taxes, each of which will have its own distributive effects. That same citizen will be the beneficiary of at least that many expenditure programs, each one also having a number of complex distributive effects. The only people who really are forced to put all these distributive effects together in a budget are the citizens who pay the taxes and receive the benefits, and that can usually be done very subjectively.

Some idea of the effects of government taxing and spending in several countries can be gained by examining the data provided in tables 4.8 and 4.9. The first table shows the distribution of income prior to government action, and then the effects of government taxes and transfers. In some cases, e.g. the United Kingdom, Ireland, and Finland, the effects of government are disaggregated substantially, and we can see just what effects different components of public sector activity (direct versus indirect taxes, transfer vs. in-kind benefits) have on citizens' incomes. In most cases, however, we have only figures

Table 4.8 Redistribution through the public sector

Finland (1976) Quintiles	I	II	III	IV	V
Factor income	545	4,538	7,751	11,229	18,017
Direct taxes	309	1,097	2,103	3,225	6,166
After-tax income	236	3,261	5,648	8,004	11,851
Transfers	3,140	1,726	1,174	820	742
Disposable income	3,376	4,987	6,822	8,824	12,593
Indirect taxes	562	1,037	1,404	1,865	2,318
Final income	2,814	3,950	5,418	6,959	10,725

United Kingdom (1987) Quintiles	I	II	III	IV	V
Factor income	130	2,800	8,030	13,180	24,790
+Cash benefits	3,370	2,730	1,250	870	680
Gross income	3,500	5,530	9,280	14,060	25,470
−Direct taxes	−10	330	1,490	2,710	5,650
Disposable income	3,510	5,200	7,790	11,350	19,820
−Indirect taxes	880	1,540	2,280	2,900	4,250
Cash income	2,620	3,650	5,520	8,450	15,560
+Benefits in kind	1,510	1,500	1,500	1,670	1,700
Final income	4,130	5,150	7,020	10,120	17,260

Ireland (1970–3) Quintiles	I	III	V
Factor income	3.79	95.05	322.58
Direct taxes	0.32	12.68	66.71
After-tax income	3.57	82.37	255.87
Transfers	31.66	8.44	6.90
Disposable income	35.23	90.81	262.77
Indirect taxes	7.32	16.82	36.04
Cash income	27.91	73.99	226.73
Non-cash benefits	18.46	18.18	27.74
Final income	46.37	92.17	254.47

Sources: Alestalo and Uusitalo, 1986 (Finland); Central Statistical Office, 1988 (United Kingdom); Maguire, 1986 (Ireland)

Table 4.9 Inequality before and after government operations (Gini coefficients)

Gini coefficients	*Canada*	*Germany*	*Norway*	*Sweden*	*United Kingdom*	*United States*
Gross income	0.374	0.429	0.356	0.329	0.365	0.395
Net income	0.348	0.389	0.311	0.292	0.343	0.370
Equivalent net income[a]	0.299	0.340	0.243	0.205	0.273	0.326

[a] Adjusted for family size.
Source: O'Higgins, Schmaus, and Stephenson, 1989

for income distribution before and after the operations of the public sector, or the summary impact of taxes and expenditures. The measure reported in some parts of table 4.9 – the Gini coefficient – quantifies deviations from pure proportionality in the distribution of income, with higher values of the coefficient indicating greater inequality.[14]

The income distribution generated by the market in almost all industrialized democracies is quite unequal. The lowest quintiles of income earners averaged receving 2.6 percent of the income, while the upper quintiles averaged 45.5 percent. For those countries where there is income information available by deciles, the level of maldistribution is even more apparent; the lowest deciles averaged only 1.6 percent of total income while the upper deciles averaged almost 25 percent of total income. These figures are to some extent a function of the number of retired people whose principal source of income is a public sector pension, but even when pensioners can be excluded the bottom echelons of the economy receive only a very small share of total income. The public sector does help to improve these maldistributions – the lowest quintiles averaged almost 8 percent of total income after government operates, but income remains skewed.

Likewise, the Gini coefficients demonstrate very skewed distributions of factor income, even in countries (Sweden, West Germany) which in addition to having well-developed welfare states are also noted as having wage policies pushing market incomes toward greater equality (Scharpf, 1987; Gourevitch *et al.*, 1984). Those wage policies cannot, however, counteract the skewed distribution of incomes received from sources, e.g. dividends and corporate ownerships, other than wages and salaries. Further, the loss of a number of high-paying manufacturing jobs in many economies (Kosters and Ross, 1988) has tended to increase the unequal distribution of income, leaving more for government to do after the market operates. Industrial workers often could make a middle-class income, but unskilled or semi-skilled employees in service industries have little opportunity to earn incomes at that level. In short, even with an active government we should not expect any great reductions in inequality in contemporary democracies.

Although most countries in the OECD world are considered "welfare states," there is still substantial income inequality, and substantial variations in that inequality. There is not, however, as much difference in levels of inequality as might be expected from discussions of the low level of development of some social welfare systems (the United States) and the wide-ranging benefits in the Scandinavian countries. In the data available for most countries in the 1970s, the Scandinavian nations do have less inequality, but not substantially less than some other European countries. In addition, the US income distribution is rather unequal, but not much more than some European countries such as France, Italy, or even West Germany. Levels of socio-economic development appear to have some relationship to levels of inequality, although that relationship is far from perfect (see, for example, Switzerland). Likewise, the political complexion of a country's government appears to have relatively little relationship to inequality, although longer-term political changes, e.g. democratization, do appear to bear some relationship (see Flora, 1986a; 1986b). Income inequality results from a complex interaction between the market and government that may defy simple explanation.

Redistribution Across Time

For a limited number of countries, we have some evidence about the redistributive effect of government taxation and expenditure across time that may help unlock some of the puzzle about inequality. This is an especially interesting question as government in industrialized democracies have had to respond to a variety of changes in their economies, and in public receptivity to "big government." Everything else being equal, we might expect governments to be less capable of redistributing income in the late 1980s than they were in the 1960s and 1970s. Governments now have fewer uncommitted resources than they had, and there are more political parties, groups, and individuals prepared to challenge public expenditure decisions. This restraint, however, is being imposed at the same time that changes in national economies, such as the declining number of manufacturing jobs, may make redistribution even more important for many citizens.

The impact of these economic changes on government, and the changing political complexions of governments, are seen in the changes in inequality (tables 4.10). For example, in the earlier data the United Kingdom in table 4.10 shows that income distribution after the public sector operated was almost as equal as Sweden, the most egalitarian country, and more egalitarian than Norway. By the late 1970s and early 1980s the United Kingdom had become less egalitarian in its income distribution and Norway had remained egalitarian (O'Higgins, Schmaus, and Stephenson, 1989). The United Kingdom had undergone a number of economic shocks in the 1970s and the public sector was operating under substantial restraint even before the Conservatives came to power in 1979 (O'Higgins, 1985). Norway, on the other hand, had discovered oil and was able to spread that windfall income over a much smaller population (4.2 million in 1987) than could the United Kingdom (population 56.9 million), which also had discovered oil. Later data, though less complete, indicate that the Conservative government has continued the trend toward greater inequality in the United Kingdom, while the Norwegian government has continued to share mineral income rather broadly. The basic finding is that if a government wants to

Table 4.10 Changes in inequality

	Pre-tax		*Post-tax*	
	Early 1970s	*Early 1980s*	*Early 1970s*	*Early 1980s*
Canada	0.382	0.374	0.354	0.348
Germany	0.396	0.429	0.383	0.389
Norway	0.354	0.356	0.307	0.311
Sweden	0.346	0.329	0.302	0.292
United Kingdom	0.344	0.365	0.318	0.343
United States	0.404	0.395	0.381	0.370

redistribute income, it is extremely advantageous to have a great deal of income to share.

Other countries have persisted along their consistent national paths. Sweden still had the most equal distribution of income, even after a period of rule from the political right and some economic difficulties, and government was considerably responsible for generating that equality. The United States and West Germany continued to have the least egalitarian income distributions, despite a well-developed social insurance system in West Germany and increasing commitments to its own version of the "Welfare State" in the United States – at least until 1980 (Phillips, 1990). In both countries the income received from market activities dominates the impacts of government policy in the final distribution of incomes. Both of these countries have a more capitalist ideology concerning the economy and the importance of economic growth than do most other industrialized democracies, and the impact of this market ideology continues to affect their policy profiles, as well as the economic conditions of their citizens.

Other Forms of Income Redistribution

As well as vertical income redistribution, there is also a great deal of horizontal income redistribution occurring through government programs. The "iron law" (Cuzan, 1981; Wilson, 1980) operating here is that income is redistributed to the well-organized from the poorly-organized. Thus, economic and social groups which have been able to organize to press their demands upon government – farmers, industries, the professions – have been able to extract benefits from it. Those groups which are less well-organized – consumers, the poor – have been able to extract fewer benefits and may actually be paying for special benefits created for other interests. For politicians, taxation may be an efficient activity as long as the benefits obtained by spending to benefit organized groups outweigh the more general tax resistance that this activity may generate.

Although usually discussed in terms of socio-economic groups, the organized groups at work in distributional politics may be regional and ethnic as well as socio-economic in origin (Bennett, 1980). Potentially rebellious or fractious regions of countries have been able to extract substantial expenditure concessions from national treasuries in Britain, Canada, and Spain. Even when rebellion is not the threat, most politicians represent a geographical area and may find it advantageous politically to capture as many benefits for that region as possible. The characterizations of "pork-barrel" and "saupoudrage" reflect a fundamental political phenomenon, namely that, to be reelected, politicians must be seen as being capable of generating benefits for their constituency (Fiorina, 1989; Arnold, 1979; Roig, 1964; Gremion, 1976). Hence, some redistribution occurs in favour of areas represented by powerful politicians with great longevity.

The benefits created for special socio-economic or geographic groups tend to come at the expense of greater income redistribution among income classes. In general, lower income groups tend to have fewer organizational skills and resources than do more affluent groups, and thus they find political organization more difficult. This may be especially the case since labor unions – the logical groups to represent some of these lower-income concerns – themselves have become rather bourgeois in their orientation in many industrialized countries. Further, many consumer and middle-class interests are diffuse and difficult to mobilize, while specific producer interests have found such mobilization rather easy – this is the familiar politics of concentrated benefits and diffused costs (Wilson, 1980). While consumers, taxpayers, and other diffuse interests showed much greater organizational capacity during the 1970s and 1980s, their political successes then remain the exception rather than the rule.

It is also important to remember in this context that the success of socio-economic interests does not necessarily manifest itself in the expenditure budgets of public organizations. Rather, many of the successes are to be found in the tax expenditure budget, which is more difficult to identify and quantify. Some important successes certainly do appear as expenditures – farm subsidies, research and development grants, etc. – but most are more carefully hidden. The tax expenditures may, however, confer just as large benefits on groups as do direct subsidies, and further may have the same effect of limiting the redistributive impact of public sector activity on income classes. If some groups do not pay, other groups will have to pay more to fund government programs. Tax expenditures are more difficult to target geographically than are direct subsidies, but even those (special provisions for cattle ranching, for example) may have decided regional effects. The principal difference between tax benefits and expenditure benefits will be that the politics of tax expenditures are generally less overt and visible than are decisions about spending programs.

Conclusion

This chapter has pointed to the importance of considering public revenues and public expenditures together. This is nominally a book about tax policy, but attempting to understand those policies in isolation from the expenditure purposes to which the money will be put would be only half the story. This is true both for government as a whole and for individual citizens who pay taxes and receive the benefits created by those taxes. The problem is that it may be easier to look at both sides of the public household together in an academic text than it is in the real world of policymaking. Any number of institutional and political barriers make looking at revenues and expenditures together difficult in government, often with disappointing results for politicians and citizens alike.

Whether a result of institutional weaknesses or economic weaknesses, deficits appear to be a stable component of the political economy of mosts industrialized democracies. In the late 1980s and early 1990 deficit spending appears to have reached some sort of equilibrium point in most countries. Deficit spending is present and citizens do not have to pay the full tax price of the goods and services they receive from government. This keeps governments stable and citizens reasonably happy. On the other hand, governments are able to extract sufficient revenue to keep the public debt from increasing as a proportion of Gross National Product so that the public debt is not an increasing real burden on the society – especially future generations. This equilibrium has not been reached in all countries, and indeed may be a short-lived phenomenon in most, but for the time being it represents some stability in the macro-level balance between taxing and spending.

At the micro-level, there is less of a stable equilibrium. The distribution of income in a country, even a welfare state, is more of an outcome of multiple decisions and events than is even the public deficit. At least the public deficit is reported rather frequently in the media as an indicator of the strength or weakness of the political economy. The distribution of income is almost never reported unless indirectly, by reporting on poverty, or greath wealth. Further, unlike the balanced budget, there is no absolute criterion against which to judge a distribution of income; very few voters on the political left in Western countries would advocate absolute equality of income. Therefore, income distribution becomes something which may be judged mostly by citizens, and mostly in terms of whether they have enough rather in terms of comprehensive assessments of the operation of the economy and the system of taxing and spending.

NOTES

1 The recession in the early 1990s has forced a number of states into real deficits, although they could not have a planned budgetary deficit. After the deficits in 1991, the states will have to develop means of balancing their budgets for fiscal 1992.
2 Some of the apparent differences among countries are a function of differing rates of inflation, as well as real differences in their fiscal policies.
3 The name of Keynes is rarely invoked to justify policy decisions but the logic of manipulating effective demand through taxes and spending is still employed.
4 Corporatist linkages may be especially important in that they provide the interest group(s) with direct access to decisionmaking, and make refusal of a demand that much more difficult politically.
5 Any attempt to use more independent variables would produce very high, but possibly largely meaningless, correlations because of the few degrees of freedom in thc data.
6 This may be true even though the changes in Swiss government are predictable and not a function of political instability in any meaningful sense of the term. Swiss governments are, however, broad coalitions that may require at least some side-payments to form and maintain.
7 One outlying case such as this will tend to skew the entire statistical relationship, and mask an underlying relationship among the other cases.
8 This logic is usually applied to Third World countries, but is to some degree also becoming characteristic of economic and industrial policy in the United States.
9 In the United States the social security system has been included in the on-line budget in part to balance that budget. In most other countries the social insurance system tends to run a substantial deficit.
10 In the domestic side of the sequestration, entitlement programs would be almost entirely protected against cuts.
11 The budget compromise surrounding the Fiscal Year 1991 budget was made in the Fall of 1990, under the threat of

the imposition of Gramm–Rudman–Hollings and the adverse impact that would have on Congressional prestige as well as public programs.

12 This is especially true of President Reagan's Economic Recovery Act of 1981 in the United States described below.

13 The British government has been publishing charts and tables on the "poverty trap" for several decades now, but some of the anomalies continue to exist.

14 This curve is based on the assumption that if there were a perfectly equal distribution of income the first 1 percent of income earners would earn 1 percent of total income, the first 2 percent would earn 2 percent, and so on. The Gini index measures the extent to which there is a skewing of income distribution away from that ideal. A value of 0.0 for the index would indicate perfect equality, while a value of 1.0 (one person earning all the income) is theoretically if not practically possible.

5
Voice: What Do Citizens Say About Taxes?

This chapter is concerned with what citizens say they think about taxes, and what they do when they have a chance to make political decisions about them. Citizens' perceptions of taxes are of interest here, as is their exercise of the "voice" option when they have an opportunity to do something themselves about taxes and spending. In one way, this could be a very short chapter. All that really needs to be said is that citizens do not like taxes. The reality is, however, somewhat more complex than that and we can discuss differences in citizens' assessment of total levels of taxation across countries as well as across time, in addition to their evaluations of different types of taxes. Furthermore, as has been pointed out above, taxation is really only one part of the picture and we need also to discuss citizens' assessments of public expenditures and what they believe they are "buying" with their taxes. Predictably, the two sides of the equation balance no better for citizens than they do when governments attempt to balance their own budgets. Citizens like the benefits they receive through the public sector, but do not like to pay the price for those services, which are their taxes.

While it is easy to denigrate the average citizen for his or her unreasonable desire to have public services without paying for them, this is a real political problem for the political elites who must manage the public sector. Many of those elites find it convenient to promise no new taxes, as well as enhanced services, when running for office; George Bush promised to be the "education President" and the "environmental President," but asked voters "to read my lips – No New Taxes." Once in office, elites face the virtual impossibility of delivering on all their promises; President Bush had to ask citizens to read his lips again and that time they talked about several new taxes. Political leaders must attempt to find ways to raise revenues sufficient to fund services without also provoking the voters.

As one commentator put it, they have to get the most down from the goose with the least amount of hissing.

Policymakers have responded to their seemingly conflicting mandates from the public in a number of ways. One response has been to create a "fiscal illusion" (Pommerehne and Schneider, 1978; Wagner, 1976) by using a number of different taxes, all at relatively low levels of extraction (see chapter 2). More recently government leaders have imposed charges for government services rather than increase taxes. Another response by governments has been high levels of public borrowing, as well as the use of innovative methods of funding public programs. That innovation has in general produced positive results, but it has also created an extremely complex system of revenue extraction, and with that perhaps greater public cynicism about government finances. Further, as V.O. Key (1966) said, the average voter is no fool; he or she generally understands what is being done with taxes and services. Politicians often have promised that they could produce services and reduce taxes at the same time, and a citizen would be justified in attempting to have the best of both worlds if publicly promised that was possible. Public finance, however, is much more complex than campaign speeches, and citizens and politicians in the late twentieth century are being forced to confront a number of harsh realities about it. The positive evidence is that although citizens would like both low taxes and good services, most are sufficiently realistic to understand that it probably is impossible to produce that outcome. Therefore, citizens will be forced to choose between higher taxes and reduced services, and attempt to find some desirable balance between the two.

This chapter looks at evidence on four aspects of public opinion about public finance. First citizens' opinions on the overall levels of taxation and expenditure will be examined: are they too high, too low, or just right? Then their evaluations of specific taxation and expenditure programs will be considered. Which taxes do citizens prefer (assuming they have to pay taxes)? Which expenditures do they think should be increased and which decreased? The third issue is citizens' evaluations of the existing system of public finance: is the system fair? Whom do they believe is advantaged by the existing system? Further, what could be done to make the taxation system more fair? Finally, the behavior of citizens when they have the opportunity to vote on taxes and expenditures directly will be looked at. Do they walk the way they talk? Does voting for "anti-tax" parties, or for anti-tax referendum issues, reflect specific rejections of taxes alone, or does it imply a more complete repudiation of the existing system of government?

The evidence to be used in this chapter will come from a variety of countries and a variety of time periods. It has not been possible for me to conduct my own comprehensive survey of tax attitudes in all the OECD countries, and hence information will be assembled from a number of disparate sources. The survey questions reported will be different and differences in languages, even for ostensibly identical questions, may produce slightly different interpretations by respondents. In addition, citizens in most countries do not have the opportunity to vote directly on tax changes, and the evidence therefore must be limited largely to state and local government in the United States, Switzerland, and a few scattered fiscal referenda in other countries. This data can be supplemented with information on voting for anti-tax parties such as the Progress Party in Denmark and Norway, and for more general anti-government political parties in other countries. In addition, all elections are to some extent referenda on the taxes and benefits created by government, and some idea about the reactions of voters to taxes can be obtained from general election results. Despite those important limitations in the data, it will be possible to assemble a reasonably thorough picture of what citizens say and do about taxes in the OECD countries.

In interpreting this evidence, we also must be cognizant that citizens often function with imperfect information about public finance. They certainly recognize that government needs revenues if it is to provide services; the analogy to the private household is very clear. On the other hand, citizens may not have a very good idea of what the total amount of taxation is, what the distribution of revenues among different taxes is within their own country, or how much government spends for different programs (Lewis, 1983; 1980). Given the complexity of taxation in most countries, and the number of different taxes the average citizen pays – Britain levies 40 different taxes while France has 137 (Rose, 1989, 94), and Denmark has 41 different excise taxes alone – it is difficult for him or her to know what is being paid personally, much less keep track of national totals.[1] This basic ignorance of the facts may produce distorted perceptions of the impact of government on daily lives, and therefore different policy prescriptions than might be made if individual citizens had more information when they responded to surveys about taxes and expenditures. What is clear, however, is that – informed or not – citizens do have opinions.

The Goldilocks Question: How Much is Just Right?

The most commonly asked questions about taxing and spending in social surveys is whether government is spending too much, and whether it is taxing too much. These questions are often asked in reference to total taxing and spending, and then asked again in reference to specific spending programs, and sometimes in reference to particular taxes. In more sophisticated versions of these questions respondents are asked to accept more taxes if they also want more spending, which produces a predictable reduction in respondents favoring greater spending. Broad survey questions of this type are subject to some skepticism on a number of grounds, but they do provide some general idea of what citizens think about their government, and what they may be willing to pay for with their tax money.

Also predictably, these data tend to demonstrate several forms of a fundamental "schizophrenia" about the public sector held by many citizens. In the first place, the respondents often report that government is spending too much in general; they see "big government" and large government expenditures as a danger to themselves, and even to the national economy.[2] On the other hand, respondents commonly favor more spending, or at least the same level of spending, for most public programs. This is often true even for spending programs that do not benefit the respondents personally. Government as a whole may constitute a danger, but each individual program is beneficial. Similarly, while citizens are very desirous of more expenditures for the specific programs they favor, and often think that government is not spending enough, they may also believe that taxes are too high. When confronted with the option of paying more to spend more for a program, they are not always willing to do so, even though they might say more money is needed for that program. Free and Cantril (1968) argued that Americans were "ideological conservatives but operational liberals," and this characterization appears to apply well beyond the borders of the United States.

There are, of course, several ways in which these contradictions in tax and expenditure attitudes are apparent rather than necessarily real. Citizens may think that the budget is too large because of a few wasteful programs and poor management, and that a smaller budget would necessitate greater efficiency. In the United States, for example, conservatives tend to believe that the federal budget is too large because of a few wasteful welfare programs, while liberals tend to think the total budget is too large because of wasteful defense spending. Defense spending, however, is rather widely believed to be wasteful; almost twice as many respondents believe that defense programs are more wasteful than private industry (Opinion Roundup, March/April, 1988). Respondents may believe that greater fiscal restraint would force managers in the public sector to become more concerned with efficiency – this is the first stage of "cutback management" (Levine, 1978). Some sophisticated citizens may not be willing to pay increased taxes claimed to be linked to specific services because they know it is difficult to target tax money for specific expenditures. They would think that their tax money would likely just go into one big "pot" to be spent on the whole range of public programs. Even with these attempts to make the average citizen appear sophisticated about taxation, a great deal of their thinking about public finance does appear on the face of it to be unrealistic.

The Evidence: Total Taxing and Spending

As noted above, we have assembled a good deal of evidence about attitudes toward taxing and spending from a variety of sources. Some of these data come from time-series covering several decades in a single country, but most come from discrete surveys in one country at one time. In several instances the same survey questions were used in several countries simultaneously. The differences in time-frames, combined with all the differences in wording and interpretation, make genuine comparisons across countries difficult. In spite of those problems, the data presented in tables 5.1 to 5.3 reveal some interesting aspects of citizens' general assessments of government and the financial operations of the public sector.

Table 5.1 shows changes in attitudes toward government taxing and spending in the United Kingdom and the United States from the late 1950s to the present. These are two of the longest runs of comparable data available for questions of this type. What these data show is substantial change across time in citizens' attitudes toward government. Public spending is always more popular than taxes, but both vary with changes in political fashion and economic circumstances. Especially for the United Kingdom, during the 1950s and 1960s there appears to have been a widespread belief that government was a positive force and that more government expenditure could create a better society. This feeling was also apparent in the United States, although less strongly. The belief in the beneficial nature of government waned during the late 1970s and 1980s and government became, if not a negative symbol, certainly a question-

Table 5.1 Attitudes toward taxing and spending in the United States and the United Kingdom

	United States		*United Kingdom*	
	Percent agree, "Government wastes a lot of tax money"	*Percent agree, "Income tax too high"*	*Percent confidence in leaders of executive branch*	*Percent prefer current level rather than more spending*
1966	61	52	41	
1967	58			
1968	61			
1969	66			
1970	70		51	
1971			23	
1972	67			
1973		64	19	47
1974	76	69	28	
1975		72	13	
1976	76	73	11	
1977		69	23	
1978	80	70	14	48
1979	80	74	22	
1980		72	26	
1981	68		35	26
1985	76	75		24

Source: Peters, 1989; *Public Opinion*, 1987

able way for citizens to spend their money. Interestingly, after over a decade of rule by the Conservatives in the United Kingdom and almosts a decade by Republicans in the United States, there is some apparent resurgence of the belief that more public spending, and perhaps even more taxes, might benefit the two countries. Some recent surveys (Opinion Roundup, May/June, 1989; Gallup, September, 1989) indicate a willingness to spend more money for almost all programs (one major exception is defense), often even if this spending produces increased taxes.

Table 5.2 contains some more scattered data from a number of other OECD countries, all addressing the question of desirable levels of government taxation and expenditure. In the first instance, these data demonstrate substantial differences among the member of countries of the OECD. Citizens in some countries, particularly the

Table 5.2 Evaluations of taxing and spending

Sweden

Social reforms have gone so far that spending should be reduced rather than increased: (%) agreeing

1967	41
1968	52
1973	60
1976	60
1980	62
1984	65

Japan

Do you feel that your taxes are too high, about right or not very high (%)?

	1978	*1982*	*1986*
Heavy	50	59	70
Tolerable	40	35	24
Not heavy	3	1	1
No answer	7	5	5

Sources: Peters, 1989; Hastings and Hastings, 1984, 1987

Scandinavian countries and the Netherlands, demonstrate very strong support for the public sector as a whole, and generally are willing to accept large levels of public taxation and expenditure. Citizens in other nations, especially the Mediterranean countries, are much less willing to accept a large public sector and are certainly much less willing to accept high levels of taxation. The evidence for changes in attitudes across time is sporadic, but the findings from the United States and the United Kingdom are largely substantiated. There did appear to be a decline in levels of support for the public sector in the late 1970s and into the 1980s, with some greater acceptance of "big government" returning in the late 1980s. For some of the countries undergoing rapid economic and political modernization during this period – Portugal and Greece in particular – there was some general increase in levels of support for government taxing and spending across the time period.

Table 5.3 Opinions about the tax system, 1987 (in percent)

	Taxation is much too high/too high for those . . .		
	a	*b*	*c*
	. . . with high incomes	*. . . with middle incomes*	*. . . with low incomes*
West Germany	12	49	80
USA	17	68	67
Italy	18	61	84
Britain	24	40	85
Netherlands	25	57	76
Australia	34	59	69
	Supports progressive taxation		
Italy	77		
Britain	75		
West Germany	73		
Netherlands	70		
USA	64		
Australia	63		

Source: Smith, 1989

These data raise an interesting point about the relationship between public opinion, politics, and tax policy. From the cross-sectional data, it appears that public opinion does influence the tax policy choices made by governments. For example, the public in Scandinavia has been supportive of government and hence government can tax rather freely and use relatively visible means such as the income tax to collect its money (but see pp. 210–222 below). In the Mediterranean countries, on the other hand, popular resistance to taxation makes collecting revenues more difficult, and governments have had to rely on more indirect taxes, such as the value-added tax and employers' social security contributions. Across time, it is not so clear to what extent popular attitudes toward government paved the way for politicians like Ronald Reagan and Margaret Thatcher, and to what extent those politicians shaped the popular view of government taxing and spending. There is no simple one-to-one correspondence between public opinion and policy choices (Kristensen, 1982), but it does appear that politicians and tax administrators do not stray too far from the values of their citizens when they make their decisions.

Value for Money

Another way to approach the question of the trade-off between taxes and spending is to ask citizens if they receive value for money from the public sector. In other words, is the value of the benefits produced equal to the costs imposed by taxation, and if this were a market transaction would they be willing to pay the price being asked (Braak, 1983). The responses to questions of this sort vary a good deal across countries. For example, in Sweden, over 60 percent of the respondents asked (Hadenius, 1986) believed that they did receive a fair return in services for their taxes. This is not an overwhelming endorsement of government, but it is an endorsement. That support can be contrasted to respondents from the United States and the United Kingdom who, by a very small margin, did not think they got back what they paid for from government. At even more of an extreme, almost 60 percent of a Spanish sample did not believe that they received back from government service commensurate with the amount of taxes they paid (Centro de Investigaciones Sociologicas, 1988).

Most questions about trade-offs between taxing and spending are asked about specific spending programs, but in some instances a general trade-off possibility has been presented to citizens. In those instances, citizens have demonstrated that they are not really as naive about public finance as is sometimes assumed. Most citizens appear to recognize that if they want more services they will have to pay for them through taxes. They have been perfectly honest in answering more general questions: they would like lower taxes and they would like more spending for their pet programs. Citizens do appear to understand, however, that those two views may be incompatible and they will have to make difficult choices about whether to accept more taxes, or accept the same or reduced level of benefits. Although some would like more spending in general, it appears that most citizens would like to keep things about where they are, whether from satisfaction with the status quo or simple fear of the unknown.

When citizens say that they do or do not receive benefits back from government commensurate with their taxes, most are actually looking at a variety of governments. In the United States, for example, the Advisory Commission on Intergovernmental Relations asked citizens what level of government they believe gave them the most for their tax money over the last decade and a half (ACIR, annual). The responses over that time have been relatively consistent. Approximately one-third of the population asked has said that the federal government provides the most for the money, while another quarter to one-third of the respondents say local governments provide the most services for the money. State government usually come in third with around 20 percent of the respondents saying that it provides the most for their tax money. These variations among levels of government are not dramatic, and demonstrate that individual citizens may value alternative types of services very differently. Further, citizens may pay different levels of state and local taxes (although there are not marked divergencies in evaluation of state and local governments by regions), and therefore perceive the impact of state and local taxes very differently.

The Evidence: Specific Programs

We are again presented with a variety of evidence to address the question of whether citizens believe government should spend more or less money for certain specific programs. Again it is possible to analyze reactions to this question in two stages. In the first place, citizens can be asked which programs they want more money spent on, without reference to the tax prices involved in greater spending. This is an easy choice for citizens, and if they like the program in question they can say more should be spent, without having to think about where the extra money will come from. It appears, however, that many citizens have in the backs of their minds the obvious fact that more spending for a program implies the money will have to come from somewhere – either more taxes or reduced spending in other policy areas. The second level of analysis requires citizens to say whether or not they would be willing to spend more money on a program even if it cost them more in taxes personally. This is a more difficult choice since it forces the respondent to make a choice between a public program and private consumption.

A few public programs appear very popular in almost all countries (table 5.4), and that government would have a clear mandate to spend more for them (at least until the tax price is mentioned). Health, old age pensions, and, to some extent, education are generally supported by citizens and very few voters would find more spending for those programs objectionable. A few programs tend to have only a handful of supporters in any country; for the most part these are "public goods" with few direct constituents, or subsidy programs (e.g. agriculture) with relatively small clientele groups perceived as profiting at the expense of average taxpayers (Wilson, 1980). Finally,

Table 5.4 Preferences for public expenditure

Wanting much more/more state spending on	*Britain*	*USA*	*Australia*	*West Germany*	*Austria*	*Italy*
Health	88	60	62	52	61	81
Old age pensions	75	44	55	46	50	76
Education	75	66	64	40	38	63
Unemployment benefits	41	25	13	35	16	57
Police and law enforcement	40	51	67	30	23	48
The environment	37	43	32	83	74	61
The military and defense	17	20	46	6	13	12
Culture and the arts	10	16	10	14	12	33

% feeling budget priority should be given to:	*France (1982)*
Public Health	26
Professional Training	20
Education	16
Science	14
Housing	5
Defense	4
Agriculture	4
Public Works	4
Environment	3
Youth, Leisure	3
Culture	1

Table 5.4 Continued

Sweden (1982)
Should the amount of money spent for these purposes increase, remain unaltered or decrease (%)?

	Increase	*Remain unaltered*	*Decrease*	*Don't know*
Employment policies	69	21	6	4
Environment	50	40	5	4
Health care	45	50	3	2
Higher education	39	49	6	6
Police	39	54	5	2
Housing construction	36	43	14	7
Child care	31	55	12	2
Pensions	30	67	1	2
Education	26	64	6	4
Defense	19	44	33	4
Culture	18	57	20	5
Social assistance	16	58	21	5
Housing subsidies	13	46	36	5
Aid to developing countries	11	52	32	3
State and local administration	2	34	56	8

Sources: Taylor-Gooby, 1989; Hastings and Hastings, 1984; Hadenius, 1986

some public programs appear to polarize citizens. Defense and social welfare other than pensions, for example, are often mentioned by a large number of people who want to spend more for them, and also by large numbers of people who want to spend less. Defense programs in particular are facing an increasingly difficult time generating support as tensions between East and West lessen the apparent need for large defense budgets. This appears to be true even after the good publicity which defense establishments in several countries received during the Gulf War. These polarizing programs constitute the partisan and ideological battlegrounds of contemporary democracies, and tend to experience more significant shifts in emphasis depending upon which type of political party or coalition controls the government (Keman, 1982).

As expected, support for additional spending drops for all

programs when the tax price is mentioned (table 5.5). However, the reduction in support is not as great as might have been expected, given the common characterization of the unreasonable citizen demanding more benefits but no tax increases. This appears to indicate again that the average citizen is no fool, and that he or she understands that there are no free programs. The same pattern of support or opposition for specific programs arises when the tax price of the program is mentioned as does when it is not. The same programs are popular, the same ones are unpopular, and there are the same divergent views about a few important programs. Citizens in several countries, e.g. the United States, are more sensitive to the introduction of "tax prices" than are respondents in others, and support for a few policy areas, e.g. housing and the environment, is somewhat "softer" than it is for other programs, e.g. pensions, but the general findings about popular support for programs stand up even after tax prices are introduced.

It is especially interesting that support drops more when specific amounts of taxes are mentioned than when the general topic of taxes to pay for services is introduced. For example, in the United States,

Table 5.5 Public spending and willingness to pay more taxes in the United States (in percent)

Favor increased spending on	*In general*	*Willing to pay more taxes (general)*	*Willing to pay $100 more*	*Willing to pay $200 more*
Education	76	63	59	54
Drugs	75	57	56	52
Homeless	71	58	59	46
Health care	67	57	52	48
Pollution	59	36	34	29
AIDS	59	45	42	38
Job-training	56	40	30	29
Low-income families	56	43	38	35
Farmers	48	38	35	29
Child care	41	29	28	23
Space	21	13	13	14
Defense	14	10	11	11

Source: Kohut and Hugick, 1989

the average drop-off in support for greater spending for 15 programs when inspecific amounts of taxes are mentioned is 12 percent from the levels of support when taxes are not mentioned (Kohut and Hugick, 1989, p. 6). If the tax price for the increase in services is made $100, the level of support drops by an average of almost 16 percent. Support drops off by an average of 19 percent when a tax price of $200 is introduced. To put it another way, when there is no tax price there are majorities in favor of increased spending for eight of the 15 programs. That drops to four programs for the vague tax price, and to only two for a tax price of $200. Support for increased public spending is broad, but it does not appear to be deep.

Another way to understand public support for specific programs is to look at the trade-offs citizens may be willing to make among them, rather than trading-off spending for taxes. In other words is a citizen willing to accept a cut in defense spending, for example, in order to have more spending for pensions or health. Most of the research that has been done using this approach has, in fact, taken the guns versus butter trade-off as the central element of the question. Most citizens do, in fact, appear willing to trade a few guns for more butter, and in these comparisons defense fares rather poorly among the public. We may speculate as to the reasons about this public willingness; it may be an image of waste in the military (especially in the United States but also true elsewhere), or it may be a desire for enhanced domestic programs without paying more taxes. For whatever reasons, it appears that if the public were in charge directly they would spend less for defense and more for social programs. This is true even in countries which already have large and expensive welfare state programs. The willingness to trade defense spending for other programs is also likely to increase as the tensions of the Cold War abate.

Finally, just as people can be asked to provide an overall assessment of the "value for money" of public programs, they can be asked to assess the rate of return of specific programs. The answers to this type of question vary markedly in the individual countries where it is asked, depending upon the characteristics of the specific national programs. In the United Kingdom, for example, the National Health Service has been rated very highly as have protective services such as police and fire (Taylor-Gooby, 1982). On the other hand, despite the general support for more spending for this purpose, public pensions are rated as providing rather little value for money, perhaps because they have been flat-rate and on the whole provide rather little cash. In the United States, social security tends to be rated as "good value for money," as do law-and-order expenditures, but social welfare and defense rate poorly. In Sweden, most public services tended to be rated highly, but even in that welfare state there is some skepticism about social welfare expenditures (Hadenius, 1986).

Summary

Citizens do have apparently contradictory opinions concerning public finance. They tend to deplore government spending in the abstract, but to welcome it for the specific programs that benefit them (and for some that do not benefit them so directly). Citizens also would like something (more benefits) for nothing (the same or lower taxes). On the other hand, they also appear to understand that they are not likely to get this, and that expenditures involve taxes, or lower taxes involve reduced benefits. The rather small drop in support for spending for specific programs when taxes are introduced as the price implies that most citizens do understand the connection between spending and taxing. Further, citizens are able to make rather sophisticated choices about what they want government to do. They know which services they want to have government spend more for, and which they are willing to accept cuts in. They also know tht the big trade-off in most countries is between guns and butter, and they appear increasingly willing to accept fewer guns for greater social and education spending.

Types of Taxes

It has now been established that, everything else being equal, citizens would as soon not pay more taxes. It has also been established that citizens are not as naive as they are sometimes portrayed, and that they appear to understand that more spending really does involve some costs. Those costs may be more taxes, or they may be reductions in some other program(s). We will now move on to investigate how citizens would like to pay for programs. In other words, if citizens can "name their poison," what potion would they name? Analysts and politicians often operate from preconceived ideas about how people evaluate the taxes they must pay, but those notions are often incorrect. In fact, citizens often appear to prefer taxes which analysts would argue are poor choices – regressive, difficult to administer, non-bouyant taxes. It appears that the criteria that the "experts" apply and those that citizens use are often very different.

This variance between expert opinion and popular evaluations is demonstrated in table 5.6, drawn from the series of surveys on taxes and spending performed by the Advisory Commission on Intergovernmental Relations in the United States (annual). These data show that citizens have shifted their assessments concerning unfairness of particular taxes away from the local property tax and toward the federal income tax. The property tax remains unpopular, but not to the same extent as the federal income tax. This is true despite the several efforts to reform the income tax and to make it fairer by removing the numerous "loopholes" in the tax law (Verdier, 1988).[3] Despite its regressivity and other problems, the state sales tax remains, relatively speaking, a popular tax, with only one respondent in six thinking that it was the least desirable tax. State income taxes, which are lower than the federal tax but often flat-rate with few deductions and exemptions, remain the most popular of the taxes asked about in these surveys. Again this is true despite the fact that these taxes are often proportional or regressive rather than progressive in their impact on citizens (AFSCME, 1988).

The preference of Americans for the sales tax manifests itself in other ways as well. For example, when respondents are asked (1983) how they would want to raise the money if their state or local government were forced to increase taxes, the sales tax was the most preferred form. Likewise, when asked what taxes the federal government should increase if it needed more revenue, the respondents chose a national sales tax over the income tax or other taxes. This was chosen even though it would be a new tax. The popular preference for the sales tax may arise from several sources. One is that citizens believe consumption taxes are fairer because almost everyone will have to pay them, while there are numerous ways for a careful citizen or corporation to avoid paying the full income tax rate on all income. Further, because many states exclude food (28 of the 45 with sales tax), prescription drugs (43 of 45), and perhaps other necessities of life from sales taxation, it appears that with the sales tax the average citizen does not have to pay for the necessities, while the income tax hits before he or she begins to purchase whatever is needed. This fairness is, however, largely illusory and sales taxes are for the most part regressive.[4] Finally, because the sales tax is collected in small amounts, many citizens may not ever realize just how much of their income actually goes to the sales tax.[5]

The popular dislike of the income tax in the United States is

Table 5.6 Support for different taxes by income (in percent)

United Kingdom (1982)

Income	*Income tax*	*VAT*	*National insurance*	*Rates*	*Charges*
High	49	29	14	18	5
Medium	43	28	22	3	4
Low	46	14	27	10	3

United States (1987) (a) If the federal government had to raise taxes substantially, which would be the better way to do it (%)?

Annual income	*Individual income tax*	*New national sales tax*	*Don't know*
Under $15,000	22	47	32
15,000–24,900	23	54	23
25,000+	28	59	13

(b) If your state government had to increase revenues substantially, which would be the better way to do it (%)?

Annual income	*Individual income tax*	*Sales tax*	*Don't know*
Under $15,000	23	50	28
15,000–24,900	23	61	16
25,000–29,900	23	65	10
30,000–39,900	22	67	11
40,000+	23	69	8

(c) If your local government had to raise more revenue, what would be the best way to do this?

Annual income	*Local income tax*	*Local sales tax*	*Local property tax*	*Charges for services*	*Don't know*
Under $15,000	11	20	9	43	17
15,000–24,900	8	30	5	52	5
25,000–29,900	5	32	9	45	9
30,000–39,900	10	23	8	55	4
40,000+	10	30	6	52	2

Sources: Beedle and Taylor-Gooby, 1983; ACIR, annual

mirrored in a number of other countries. For example, in Australia, when citizens were asked (1984) what tax they would prefer if government had to raise more revenue, they chose the sales tax three to one over the federal income tax. Respondents in Spain, when presented with the hypothetical need to increase taxes, found the income tax objectionable at least twice as often as any other tax (Centro de Investigaciones Sociologicas, 1988). The Spanish respondents preferred to pay more excise taxes on alcohol and tobacco than to pay more personal income tax, or even corporate income tax (over 50 percent). In a sample of Japanese taxpayers (1987), only 2 percent would prefer to raise the income tax if more revenue was needed; most would prefer increasing the corporation tax or alcohol taxes. Although the income tax should be the fairest tax, with its ability to extract income with declining marginal utility through progressive rates (see Witte, 1985, chapter 2), it remains a very unpopular tax with most citizens in most countries.

The Spanish and Japanese preference for excise taxes raises another interesting point about citizens' assessments of different taxes. Citizens often express a preference for specific taxes on alcohol, tobacco, gambling, etc. – the so-called sin taxes – over more general levies, including even general consumption taxes like the sales tax or VAT. The same set of Spanish respondents that said that they would prefer raising money through increased excise taxes (57 percent) had only 19 percent who preferred increasing the VAT. This tendency to favor specialized taxes is enhanced when taxes are earmarked and their proceeds are dedicated for a specific program. These findings appear to point to several factors in citizens' perceptions of government and taxation. First, they may think that people who want to use certain products should have to pay for the pleasure, and increasingly citizens want the users of potentially harmful substances to compensate society for the external effects of their consumption. Further, citizens may think that if demand for those products is relatively inelastic (Cook, 1983), then a great deal of revenue can be collected from that source rather than resorting to general taxation. Finally, citizens may want to prevent government from using their tax money for purposes that they do not approve of, and with earmarking taxes the money can be used for specified purposes only. In short, citizens are again trying to displace the burden of taxation onto someone else, and to make sure that government does not have too much latitude in how it spends tax money.

One criterion which citizens appear to apply to their preferences for taxes is familiarity – the more they are familiar with a tax the less they appear to favor it. More specifically, the more remote the possibility of a tax being introduced, the more citizens appear to beleive it would be a good way to raise money. The general proposition about familiarity is illustrated in the changing attitudes of British citizens to the community charge or poll tax. When that tax was in the discussion stage, it appeared to a majority of voters questioned that it would be a positive change in local government finance. As it came closer to implementation, and was implemented in Scotland, the appeal waned dramatically (Game, 1988). The more specific proposition about the attractiveness of improbable taxes can be demonstrated in several instances. When British voters were asked what tax would be most desirable as a replacement for local property taxes, the improbable option of a local income tax was mentioned most frequently (*Daily Telegraph*, April 21, 1988). In the United States, when new sources of revenue are discussed, the improbable value-added tax receives high marks from respondents to surveys. Whether this is a polite way of saying that no new tax would really be a good idea, or it is the appeal of *terra incognita* in public finance, is not clear, but it does appear that citizens would often prefer something other than what they have, or what they are likely to get.

We have to this point been discussing citizens' preferences in the aggregate, but not all citizens think alike about taxes. These differences are often based on the citizens' own self-interest; he or she thinks taxes which other people pay are fair and the ones they have to pay are unfair. Income and socio-economic class play an important role in explaining the differential responses of citizens to taxes. Table 5.6 shows survey results from the United States and the United Kingdom illustrating who favors which taxes, with citizens broken down by socio-economic variables. The results reported there are largely predictable. Respondents with higher income or with better jobs tend to favor consumption taxes, while those with lower incomes and less rewarding occupations tend to favor income and corporation taxes. This finding should not be surprising, given that most people evaluate public policies in terms of their own benefits and costs. What is more interesting is the extent to which issues about fairness and justice do enter the debate over tax policy at the popular level, given the human tendency to think about the impact of a tax on oneself.

Non-Tax Revenues

So far the only options for raising revenue that have been discussed are the variety of taxes available to governments. This is a rather wide range of alternatives, but does not exhaust all the options. In particular, governments have increasingly turned to fees and charges to raise revenues. Many government activities are potentially marketable (Rose, 1976). Some goods and servies – nationalized industries, use of public lands for economic purposes, issuing licenses – have always been made available for a fee. More recently, even protective services such as fire and police have been marketed either by government or by private contractors, and a number of other public services have the potential for being priced and sold. Thus, governments have begun to consider a much wider utilization of fees and charges as a means of raising more revenue, and of rationing consumption of public programs. This has been in part a response to increasing citizen resistance to taxation, and in part a response to ideological pressures from the political right for greater efficiency and self-financing in government (Seldon, 1981).

The good news for government is that citizens appear to prefer fees and charges to taxes. For example, in the comprehensive surveys about taxes conducted by the Advisory Commission on Intergovernmental Relations (annual), when citizens were asked how they wanted to increase revenues for local governments, 49 percent preferred using fees to any form of taxation. Likewise, surveys of citizens in Canada and Japan demonstrated strong support for charging for government services. Interestingly, the public support for fees as a means of financing programs has increased as citizens have become more aware of the options of generating revenues in this manner. The apparent popular preference for fees does, however, depend upon the service upon which it is being implemented. In Britain, for example, the National Health Service has become sufficiently institutionalized and that many citizens would oppose imposing a charge for medical care. Indeed, the recent imposition of a nominal charge for routine sight and dental examinations on the NHS met with considerable resistance. This is true even though there are long waiting lists for some services and a widespread sense that services have deteriorated.[6]

Citizens appear to prefer fees and charges to other forms of revenue collection by government for several reasons. First, they have some control personally over how much they will contribute to government

(Beedle and Taylor-Gooby, 1983) and can relate receiving a particular benefit to paying a particular amount of money. We noted above that citizens find some public services to be better "value for money" than others, and using fees allows them to make those decisions just as they might if they were buying services in the private market. Likewise, unlike general taxation, which puts all the money collected into one fund and then reallocates that money through a separate decisionmaking process, the money collected from charges generally goes to the program levying that charge, and citizens can choose to support the program or not. In addition, fees and charges prevent "free riders" who do not contribute to the programs. Everyone who want to enjoy the benefit created through the public sector will have to make the same contribution. Unike the income tax, which can be avoided by the very wealthy and is not charged on the very poor, everyone has to pay a charge. The fact that all users are charged the same amount makes fees potentially regressive, but citizens (including many who might be harmed by it) do not appear to mind that possibility nearly as much as academic analysts appear to.[7]

One major exception to the popularity of charges as a form of raising revenue has been the "community charge" introduced in the United Kingdom as a way of financing local government (Game, 1988). This plan of the Thatcher government replaced personal rates (property taxes) as a means of supporting local governments with a flat-rate charge paid by all citizens over the age of eighteen. This charge was to be determined by the local council to cover the costs of local services not covered by grants from the central government. This was perceived as a means of making beneficiaries of services pay equally,[8] but has not been well-received. In the first place, unlike other types of charges this lumps together all local government services and citizens have little or no control over their payments through their own consumption of services. The community charge is in essence a tax rather than a charge, and is commonly called the "poll tax." Further, although the central government later made money available as a safety net to assist the less affluent (Cassell, 1989), the regressive impact of the community charge is very clear to most citizens. Finally, the methods of enforcing the tax, and finding all those liable to pay, have appeared to some critics to very draconian and invasive. For example, the Scottish National Party and sections of the Labour Party in Scotland have advocated boycotting the poll tax and civil liberties advocates have protested the intrusiveness of the means used to identify potential taxpayers. Thus, a charge may have to be a real charge, with the freedom of choice implied by that term, to be popular; just calling a tax a charge is not sufficient.

The Fairness of Taxes

Citizens may not like to pay taxes, but they may still think that the system is fair and thereby be more willing to pay. As will be pointed out in a subsequent chapter (chapter 6), a good deal of tax evasion appears related more to perceived inequities in the tax system than to the simple desire to retain more money from a paycheck. Citizens perceive that other people are legally avoiding paying what could be considered their fair share, and then decide they are justified in taking the law into their own hands and not paying taxes. Therefore, a tax system that appears equitable to citizens is desirable not only for reasons of social justice, but also for more instrumental reasons of improving tax collection. How do we know, however, if a tax system is fair?

One way is simply to ask citizens if they think the system is fair. The answers to that simple question vary across countries, and vary within countries across time (tables 5.7 and 5.8). That variance is not necessarily related to any objective characteristics of the tax system; systems that are based on the income tax (Australia) and those based on more regressive taxes (Spain) may both be considered fair or unfair by citizens. Some of the perception of unfairness may be a function of media and political attention to taxation. The agitation surrounding Proposition 13 and later tax reform in the United States heightened this perceived unfairness of taxes. As noted above, however, not all the variance is due to nation, and differences in an individual's location in the economic and fiscal universe may influence his or her assessment of the tax system.

Who Pays

Another means of assessing whether citizens perceive the tax system as fair or not is to determine whom they think pays the biggest share of taxation, or perhaps which groups pay the most proportionate to income. The facts are that, despite the numerous loopholes and special provisions in tax laws, the wealthy continue to pay a higher proportion of their income in tax than do middle-class and most working-class people (see Pechman, 1988; Cnossen and Bird, 1990). The major exception to this generalization is the very poor, who also

Table 5.7 Perceived fairness of taxes

Spain

In general, do you that taxes in Spain are just (%)?

	Yes	*No*	*Don't know*
1988	22	64	14
1987	16	69	15
1985	15	71	14

Australia (1982)

Do you feel the present tax system is fair or unfair for people like yourself (%)?

Very unfair	*Somewhat unfair*	*Somewhat fair*	*Very fair*	*No answer*
28	33	22	6	11

Japan

Do you think the current tax system is fair or unfair (%)?

	Fair	*Rather fair*	*Rather unfair*	*Unfair*	*No answer*
1985	6	14	33	41	7
1987	10	–	–	77	13

Switzerland (1985)

Are taxes much too high, somewhat too high, or just about right (%)?

Income	*Much too high*	*Somewhat too high*	*About right*	*No answer*
Well-off	49	17	12	22
Upper middle	32	29	17	22
Lower middle	32	28	21	19
Less well-off	34	20	18	28

Sources: CIS, 1988; Hastings and Hastings, 1984; 1987; 1988

Table 5.8 Perceptions of the least fair tax in the United States, 1973–1988 (in percent)

	1973	*1975*	*1977*	*1980*	*1982*	*1984*	*1986*	*1988*
Federal income tax	30	28	28	36	36	36	37	33
State income tax	10	11	11	10	11	10	8	10
State sales tax	20	23	17	19	14	15	17	18
Local property tax	31	29	33	25	30	29	28	28
Don't know	11	10	11	10	9	10	10	11

Source: ACIR, annual

may have to pay a very high proportion of their income in taxes – primarily through consumption taxes, the impact of indirect taxes such as corporation taxes, and social insurance contributions if they are working.

Citizens do not always perceive this progressivity in the tax bite to be the case. A popular complaint about taxes, and sometimes a justification for tax evasion, is that wealthy individuals (and corporations) are not paying enough tax relative to their income. A number of widely publicized cases – the 48 of the 250 largest corporations in the United States which paid no taxes from 1981 to 1985 for example – have made citizens very aware of apparent inequities. Citizens, especially middle-class citizens, also have a tendency to believe that people like themselves bear a disproportionate share of the tax burden. The complaint about the unfairness of the tax system is sometimes extended to the poor, and the preference for consumption taxes is sometimes justified as a means of making the "freeloaders" on government pay for a part of its costs.

Loopholes

Related to the question of the fairness of taxes and who really pays them is the questions of loopholes in the tax system. Again, citizens appear to experience a certain amount of schizophrenia in their reaction to taxes and tax laws. On the one hand, one of the most commonly expressed complaints about tax laws is the existence of so many loopholes that permit taxpayers (other than the respondent, of course) to wiggle out of paying taxes. These loopholes are often cited as being unfair and undermining any possible justice in taxation.

On the other hand, when citizens are asked about specific loopholes, there are often majorities in favor of their being retained. This is true even for respondents who do not themselves benefit from the particular loophole. Like public expenditures, loopholes are collectively evil but individually beneficial and acceptable.

Some of the evidence available about citizens' evaluations of loopholes is contained in table 5.9. Again, this evidence is far from directly comparable, given that the tax preference available in the OECD countries are very different. However, these data do provide some idea of the general assessments that citizens make about tax loopholes. As might be expected, the tax preferences which broadly benefit the population tend to be widely supported. For example, in a British survey 75 percent of the total sample supported tax relief on mortgage interest for homes; even two-thirds of renters supported that "loophole" (Beedle and Taylor-Gooby, 1983, 34). Support for preferences for homeownership are equally widely supported in other countries, although that support drops when the mortgage relief is

Table 5.9 Fairness of tax "loopholes" (in percent)

United States (1985)

	Deduction is:		*Percent who used the deduction*
	Fair	*Unfair*	
Charitable contributions	84	16	51
State and local taxes	76	24	32
Interest on loans	75	25	34
Capital gains on investments of 6 months or less	51	49	12
Mortgage interest on second house	50	50	7
Fringe benefits at work	28	72	30
Business entertainment	21	79	7

United Kingdom (1982)
Support deduction for:

Mortgage Relief	75	(Mortgagees = 100%)
Private Pensions	57	(over 51 years = 75%)

Sources: Kohut and Hugick, 1989; Beedle and Taylor-Gooby, 1983

extended to second homes. For example, in the United States, although over 85 percent of respondents have supported relief on mortgage interest for first homes, over half in some surveys favor elimination or limitation of deductions on a second home (*Public Opinion*, March, 1985 and September, 1985). Support for other common benefits, such as relief on life insurance profits, is also widely shared.

Tax preferences which advantage smaller segments of the population tend to receive less support. These loopholes which are perceived as favoring only the very wealthy, and especially those favoring businesses, are supported by a very small percentage of the population. For example, a majority of the population in a Swedish sample thought that tax preferences for company cars and other perquisites of executive employment should be eliminated (Taylor, 1989). During the tax reform drive in the United States a number of surveys demonstrated that the average American did not like many of the tax preferences in the law at that time, although these "loopholes" were often only vaguely understood. Deductions favoring business (such as business entertaining of clients) and the very wealthy (exclusion of state and local bond interest) were special targets of discontent, while the non-taxable status of fringe benefits and the deductability of charitable contributions were widely supported. As during the tax reform process itself, public support for tax preferences can be reduced when their elimination is linked to the reduction of levels of taxation for the public as a whole. It appears that tax preferences which the average citizen can enjoy, or can aspire to enjoy, are perceived as fair but more narrowly defined preferences are not considered so.

Voting: Tax Protests

What citizens say in public opinion polls is important to politicians who follow those polls. What citizens do in elections, however, is almost certain to catch the attention of political elites. Voting on taxation issues is a more active voice for citizens in coping with their governments, and one which became increasingly important during the 1970s and 1980s. In some instances the voting took place in rather traditional venues, through electing candidates and political parties dedicated to reducing taxation. At least in the United States, voting in referenda on taxation became an important indicator of citizen support for government in general, and for public spending in particular (Sears and Citrin, 1985; Jeffe and Jeffe, 1988). Referenda have been a common feature of state and local government for a number of years, especially in the Midwest and West, but gained special importance after citizens in California voted to reduce taxation through the now famous Proposition 13. Referenda also are an integral part of Swiss democracy and have restrained the growth of public revenue and expenditure there.

Protest Parties

In Western Europe, the principal manifestation of citizen protest against taxation has been voting for tax protest parties. The most famous of these have been in Scandinavia, but some less visible examples have appeared in other countries. Tax protest politics in contemporary Western Europe is usually traced to Mogens Glistrup and the Progress Party (Fremdskrittspartei) in Denmark, although the Small Farmers' Party in Finland had an anti-state program somewhat earlier. The Progress Party is a radical anti-tax party, seeking to virtually eliminate taxation in Denmark and privatize almost all activities of government. As one extreme example, the party (or at least the flamboyant Glistrup as its leader) advocated reducing the Danish defense budget to only enough money to pay for an answering machine that would tell any caller "We capitulate." A similar Progress Party, with a leader (Carl I. Hagen) almost as flamboyant as Glistrup, has been organized and met with growing success in Norway.

The Progress Party first ran in elections for the Folketing (Danish Parliament) in 1973, and received 15.9 percent of the vote, which made them the second largest party. When it ran again in 1975 and 1977, the party received over 13 percent of the vote each time, and was again the second largest party in the Folketing in 1977 (Wickman, 1977). This level of support for a party with such a radical program, and with such an unusual leader, demonstrated vividly the discontent of many Danish voters with taxation and "big government." Support for the Progress Party had diminished after the 1977, in part because taxes have been reduced somewhat and in part because Glistrup has gone to jail for overt tax evasion. Despite the decline in votes, the Progress Party has remained in parliament and continues to be something of an *eminence grise* preventing government from taxing and spending too much.

The Progress Party in Norway began at about the same time as the party in Denmark, but did not have any great success until the

1980s. First at the local level (especially in cities such as Oslo) and then at the national level in the election of 1989 the party began to attract support for its anti-tax, anti-government, anti-immigrant[10] program. Although somewhat less flamboyant and apparently more law-abiding than Glistrup, Carl I. Hagen, the leader, is very photogenic and persuasive and has been able to attract considerable media attention for the party. The Norwegian Progress Party joined in a somewhat uneasy coalition government of the right after the 1989 elections briefly deposed the Norwegian Labor Party. As noted, the Progress Party in Norway has used concerns over increasing immigration (and the costs that more immigrants would impose of taxpayers) as a part of its appeal, but the basic message remains anti-tax and anti-expenditure.

The Small Farmers' Party in Finland has not met with the same success as the two Progress Parties, but has received around 10 percent of the total vote in several elections since 1970. In Finland, the presence of several alternative versions of communism may, oddly enough, reduce the potential for a radical anti-tax party to flourish. This is true if we consider (see below) that anti-tax parties represent as much a general reaction to government and the status quo as they represent a specific right-wing reaction to big government. Voters may simply want something else and a way to express their discontent.

What explains the success of these protest parties in Denmark, Norway, and Finland, among the wealthiest countries in the world and countries which apparently have had very positive attitudes toward government and the Welfare State? Further, what explains the success of these parties and the absence of a similar party in neighboring Sweden with its even higher levels of taxation? Wilensky (1976) has argued that the visibility of the tax structure is the most important explanatory factor. Denmark (50 percent) and Finland (47 percent) had tax systems which relied very heavily on the personal income tax while Sweden (and Norway!) have a more widely dispersed tax burden. Wilensky further argues that the institutionalization of party systems and the presence of strong technocratic-corporatist linkages have a decided influence on the success of protest parties.

Wilensky's explanation for the emergence of tax protest parties is somewhat unsatisfying on several counts. First, his conceptualization and operationalization of tax visibility appears rather questionable, especially given that most taxpayers pay their personal income taxes through monthly withholding payments, and social security contributions may therefore be as visible as income taxes (see also Hanneman, 1982).[11] Second, if we accept Wilensky's definition of visible taxes, there are a number of anomalies in the data. Why the emergence of a tax protest party in Norway but not in Sweden when their tax structures are very similar? Why no significant protest movements in New Zealand and Australia with tax structures that are even more visible than that of Denmark? Why the tendency toward tax protest, or protest against government more generally, in France and Italy with their relatively "invisible" tax structures? It appears that a great deal of theoretical interpretation has been built on a rather shaky empirical foundation, with rather small differences among the relatively small sample being used to support a large argument.

If the answer cannot be gained from macro-level analyses of countries, we may be able to learn something by seeing who votes for protest parties in Denmark, Norway, and Finland. These findings indicate that a certain amount of self-interest is involved in the voting – public employees very rarely vote for the tax protest parties and tend to favor high-spending parties of the left (Blais and Dion, 1987; Lafferty and Knutsen, 1984; Andersen, 1984; Jaffre, 1986, 214). In some instances, however, the voting appears less related to employment and more related to beliefs that government has become too costly and too distant from the concerns of the average citizen. Some of the voting for tax protest parties appears to be expressing strictly populist ideals – a revolt of the "little man" against big government and perhaps other large social institutions. This populist interpretation is bolstered by the significant proportion of the industrial working class in Finland that vote for the Small Farmers' Party, a party which would hardly appear to represent their economic interests but which does have a very populist platform opposed to large-scale institutions. If this interpretation is correct, the visibility of the tax structure may not be such a crucial variable in explaining the willingness of citizens to protest.

The self-interest interpretation of voting for tax protest parties is further undermined by the finding that a significant share of voters for the Progress Party in Denmark in the 1973 (63 percent) and 1975 (40 percent) elections favored *higher* taxes on large incomes (Nielsen, 1976, 149). Thus, as much as an economic act expressing concern about the bite which taxation takes from a paycheck, voting for these parties appears to be a reflection of general protest against the modern Welfare State. Taxes became a symbol of that protest in Denmark, perhaps because of the concerns of Glistrup as a tax lawyer, but the protest has much wider targets as well. With this interpretation other protest movements, such as those of shopkeepers and artisans in France,[12] appear less distinctive; taxes are a component, but only one, of the mobilization of discontent. Further, as will be demonstrated below, tax evasion stems from some of the same roots. It too may represent a personal protest against the entire system, and decisions to exercise "voice" and decisions to exercise the "exit" option may stem from the same concerns.

Wickman (1977) discusses four possible explanations for the success of the Progress Party in Denmark. The first explanation is that the Progress Party appeals not to affluent urbanites who might have a great deal to gain economically through a reduction in taxation; rather, it appeals more to small farmers, shopkeepers, artisans, and others who may feel excluded from modern capitalist society. This interpretation would make the anti-tax movement in Denmark very similar to the Poujadist movement in France (Hoffmann, 1956). A portion of the justification for this argument comes from the differences in the distribution sides of the Danish and Swedish economies. The Danish economy (as well as the Norwegian economy) has retained more small shops and small agricultural holdings than has the more "modernized" Swedish economy, and therefore there are more people who are likely to feel alienated from economic, social, and political life. A corrollary to this explanation is that the processes of industrialization and socio-economic change have proceeded at differential rates in the Scandinavian countries (Peters and Klingman, 1980) and this has created different responses to taxation and the public sector more generally.

A second, more psychological, explanation for the success of the Progress Party in Denmark is based upon changes in the attachment of citizens to the political system and their beliefs about the appropriateness of this system. Although the danger of any significant rejection of the existing system was minimal, the 1970s witnessed substantial disaffection among the population. This was reflected in increased cynicism about politics. In addition a number of political issues, such as Danish entry into the European Community, produced questions about the nature of the existing political arrangements. This period of relative turmoil was then ripe for a group such as the Progress Party to capture the concerns and alienation of the public and express it politically. Norway faced many of the same issues (Orvik, 1975) but Sweden did not.

A third explanation for the rise of the Progress Party is based upon the general pattern of partisan realignment in almost all industrialized democracies (Dalton, Flanagan, and Beck, 1984). As political issues have shifted and allegiances to older political parties have diminished, there are niches for new political parties. In the case of Denmark, this realignment coincided with the failure of a center-right government to keep down taxes and spending, and hence some feeling that the old political parties were failing (Andersen, 1984). In contrast, in Sweden, the five major political parties have continued to attract almost all the voters (with the exception of a growing ecological party) and their institutionalization in the political process appears to have helped prevent any serious attempt at an anti-state party. Taxing and spending issues certainly helped create the niche for the Progress Party, but they alone are insufficient to explain why it enjoyed as much success as it did.

The final explanation is an entrepreneurial one. The Progress Party was developed, it is argued, because of the leadership and entrepreneurial skill of Glistrup and a few other committed individuals, just as Proposition 13 was successful in California in part through the entrepreneurship of Jarvis and Gans. This explanation is to some degree an extension of the previous one; realignment or dealignment from older political formations produced the opportunity for a political entrepreneur such as Glistrup to develop a party and a political following of the magnitude that he enjoyed during the early 1970s. It may be, of course, that such a following could have been developed simply through the leadership and appeal of Glistrup, but it appears that realignment was extremely conducive to these changes.

Tax Referenda

In the United States, citizens often have an opportunity to vote directly on whether they want to have their own taxes increased. This does not occur at the federal level, but does at the state and local level. Proposition 13 (California) and then Proposition $2\frac{1}{2}$ (Massachusetts) were dramatic instances of citizens voting to reduce their own taxes, but at this level of government voting on taxes is a common occurrence. Many state constitutions require voters to approve increases in local property tax rates (the millage), and often issuing new bonded indebtedness by a state or local government also requires a popular vote. In addition, voters in many states (Cronin, 1989) have the opportunity (called the initiative) to put issues on the ballot themselves, and have used those opportunities to put tax cutting issues to a popular vote (as in Proposition 13). Votes of this sort can serve as a valuable barometer of popular sentiment about government and the management of public money. Also, as fiscal issues have become hotly contested, initiatives and referenda have enabled incumbent politicians to avoid the onus of making difficult decisions.

The success of tax reduction initiatives, or the failure of referenda on tax increases proposed by governments, has varied substantially over time. At about the time of Proposition 13, perhaps fueled by the success and publicity of that initiative, there were numerous instances of governments having their tax incomes reduced, or not being able to increase their taxes when those in office believed they needed more money. Immediately after the success of Proposition 13, tax reduction/expenditure limitation referenda succeeded in twelve other states – including large industrial states such as Illinois, Massachusetts, and Michigan. This tendency persisted for some time: for example, in 1980, 13 of the 20 issues on state ballots concerning tax and expenditure limitations were resolved in ways providing the public sector with less money (Ranney, 1981). By the late 1980s, however, state and local governments began to have greater success in making their cases to the voters. For example, in 1984, none of the five tax limitation items on ballots were accepted by voters, and in 1988, eight of ten propositions on ballots were resolved in favor of governments being able to increase their revenues or expenditures (Ranney, 1985; 1989).

It is not at all clear why some tax limitation efforts succeed and others fail.[13] In some instances, the level of taxation or at least the level of increased taxation appears to have been the cause. For example, in California, there were dramatic increases in the property tax (the target of Proposition 13) just prior to that issue coming onto the ballot. Government had not increased tax rates, but the huge increases in property values in California had suddenly pushed property assessments of tax purposes extremely high (Jeffe and Jeffe, 1988). Many ordinary homeowners in the state were facing huge property tax bills and reacted rather predictably when they were given an opportunity to reduce them. The evidence is that property tax increases in some other states (especially Massachusetts) also helped to fuel movements to reduce or stabilize state and local taxation.

There is not, however, any clear correlation between tax rates or even increases in taxation and voting for tax-limiting propositions. Taxes were very high in California and Massachusetts, but were not particularly high in a number of other states which voted to reduce taxation. Also, although taxes increased in California just prior to the success of Proposition 13, and had been increasingly steadily in Massachusetts prior to Proposition 2½, tax reduction measures also were successful in states which had had stable tax rates. Making an analogy with Wilensky's work (1976) concerning the tax revolt in Western Europe does not appear particularly helpful either. State tax systems which are more visible (rely more heavily on the income tax) did not produce significantly greater tax revolts than did states with less visible tax structures. Further, if we argue that the property tax is the most visible tax to many voters,[14] using that as the independent variable produces no stronger explanations of tax revolts than does the income tax. Hansen (1983) examined a number of possible explanations for the "taxpayer's revolt" in the late 1970s and found only one significant relationship: states that permitted initiatives for bringing issues to a popular vote were more likely to experience the revolt.

Analyzing the individual responses of citizens does not appear any more helpful than the ecological analysis using state-level data in understanding voting for tax and expenditure limitations. Lowery and Sigelman (1981) attempted to find correlates of willingness to vote for tax reduction measures in a large national sample. They examined eight possible, and plausible, explanations for willingness to vote for such measures but found little evidence to support any of them. Although they were not statistically significant, the strongest correlates of individual attitudes toward tax protests were more general political variables such as efficacy and trust (Lowery and Sigelman, 1981, 970), while variables related to the direct impact of taxes or the economy on the individual had somewhat smaller relationships. These questions were concerned with the *willingness* of respondents to a survey to vote for tax limitation, but some survey evidence from voting for Proposition 13 had similar findings.

Thus, it appears that voting for tax limitation measures in the American states, like voting for tax protest parties in Western Europe, is motivated by reasons which go beyond simple self-interest to express some fundamental disaffection from the political system. This may not be discontent with democratic institutions or the constitutional order, but rather the way in which those institutions and that order have come to be practiced. Tax revolt may be a "style" issue (see Lowery and Sigelman, 1981, 972) reflecting more complex reactions to the political environment than would a "position" issue based on the evaluation of correct or incorrect policy responses to a problem. This also means that tax revolt is unlikely to vanish if taxes are reduced, or expenditures are constrained (DeCanio, 1979), but may represent a more fundamental realignment of political forces. That realignment may be expressed in the success of Ronald Reagan and the continuing occupation of the White House by the Republican Party.

Although they are used frequently as a means of making public policy in Switzerland, relatively few national initiatives and referenda have been concerned with tax policy. Those that have been about taxes have been more concerned with the use of specific taxes to finance specific programs, and the use of taxes to achieve other policy purposes, such as control of pollution, rather than with limiting total taxing and spending (Delley, 1978; Rhinow, 1984). This lack of an emphasis on general taxation may be because taxes in Switzerland are already low in comparison to other industrialized democracies, and the government has been generally efficient and effective. In addition, the confederal structure of the country provides citizens with substantial influence over local government, and with corresponding control over taxing and spending. Referenda have been used much more commonly at the cantonal and communal level, and governments have had a number of disappointments over their proposals for tax changes.

There is some evidence that local referenda do function as an effective brake on increases in taxes and expenditures. For example, Pommerehne (1978) found that local governments (communes) in Switzerland with direct democracy and those representative governments with referenda had substantially lower spending for public goods programs than did representative governments without the requirement of a referendum. The same finding has been confirmed for local governments in the United States, even before the taxpayer revolt. It may be, however, that the levels of expenditure found do not adequately reflect the demands of citizens, given that the options given them in referenda are usually simple yes or no choices on a package presented by the local government officials. Those votes again may conflate symbolic and real political issues over public expenditure. In short, referendum voting requires substantially greater investigation as a means of producing optimal outcomes of taxation and expenditures for governments.

General Elections as Referenda?

Although some elections on specific taxing and spending issues are clearly referenda on fiscal policy, in a certain sense all general elections are also votes about fiscal policy. Of course, those fiscal policy issues will be mixed together with a wide variety of other political questions, but they often play a significant role in helping the voter determine for whom to vote. This impact is especially evident if voting is considered to be "approval voting," or "retrospective voting" (Fiorina, 1981) with the voters deciding whether or not they approve of the actions of the incumbent political leaders, and then deciding whether or not is worthwhile to try to vote those incumbents out of office. In cases or retrospective voting, the decisions made by a government to raise taxes or cut programs may have a substantial impact on the outcomes of elections, and voters may exact "retribution" on their leaders (Eismer, 1979; Kinder and Kiewit, 1979).

Evidence from voting studies in a variety of countries indicates that taxation issues are among the most salient political issues. They often rank at the top, or near the top, of issues that voters consider important. The salience of taxation increased during the 1970s and 1980s as voters became increasingly disenchanted with "big government" and learned of the apparent successes of other countries or other local governments in cutting taxes. The salience of taxation as an election issue is, of course, accentuated when there has been a recent increase in taxes, or a new tax has been introduced. For example, the introduction of a modest sales tax in Japan in 1989 was generally considered to be a major reason for the poor showing of the ruling Liberal Democratic Party in elections that summer.[15] Also, the *Land* elections in Germany in April, 1991 became in many ways a referendum on the tax increases required to pay for reunification. In these elections Chancellor Kohl's party lost in his home state and became a minority party in the upper house of the legislature for the first time.

Some very detailed research has been undertaken on the effect of tax increases on voting behavior in the American states, particularly for governors. The states constitute a very good test for the retribution hypothesis because the political agenda at that level is less cluttered than for a national government, and taxes are often a central political issue (Hansen, 1983; Kone and Winters, 1989). The research that has been done indicates a significant retribution effect, but that this effect is not uniform across all types of tax policy changes. First, and surprisingly, increases in old taxes tended to produce greater retribution than adding new taxes. This appears to be the case because new taxes were adopted only when there was sufficient need, and sufficient political mobilization in advance, to minimize any negative impact (Kone and Winters, 1989, 16). Also, the negative impact of sales tax changes was greater than the impact of changes in state income taxes (Hansen, 1983; Kone and Winters, 1989, 17). This appears to be a populist reaction to increases in a tax that affects all voters, whereas the income tax is perceived to affect primarily the more affluent. Whatever the details of the reactions, however, an election after a tax increase appears to become something approaching a referendum on the tax, and voters will exact a political price for it.

The local elections in Britain in May of 1990 offer additional evidence on the impact of tax policy decisions on electoral outcomes. These elections occurred shortly after the initial introduction of the community charge in England and Wales – it had been introduced in Scotland the previous year (John, 1989). The electoral results were mixed and their interpretation depends in part upon party allegiance. It does appear, however, that while the Conservatives were punished somewhat by the introduction of the community charge, the Labour Party did not escape retribution (A. Smith, 1990). In particular, high-spending and therefore high-tax Labour local governments were punished severely, and several Labour councils in Greater London were thrown out of office (Rogaly, 1990).

There is not, however, much evidence to indicate that voters reward tax cutters to the extent that they punish tax increasers. This asymmetry may arise from several factors. First, voters may take a tax cut as evidence that government has been wasteful all along, and that their taxes should have been lowered much sooner. In addition, in most instances tax cuts also involve some reductions in government services, and voters may punish service reducers as much as they punish tax increasers. Finally, there is the symbolic element, with tax increases capturing public interest and public outrage while tax decreases are treated more cynically and almost indifferently by many voters. This analysis, if correct, indicates that a politican who wants to remain in office may do well to "tax by inertia" (Rose and Karran, 1986), and avoid changing the tax system except when absolutely necessary. Tax increases are almost always very costly politically, and any political benefits from decreasing taxes probably do not equal the costs of assembling coalitions to do so.

Conclusion

What do citizens think about taxes? Again, they generally do not like them, but most citizens appear to have come to the realistic acceptance that taxes are both necessary and inevitable. Citizens do, on the whole, like the benefits they receive from government, and tend to be much more willing to pay taxes when reminded of the benefits received as a consequence of doing so. Citizens like government spending programs in principle better than they like paying for them, and support for expenditures drops when the tax price is introduced. There are still, however, majorities in favour of the same or greater expenditures for most programs once the "tax price" is introduced. On balance, most respondents to survey questions appear to believe that they receive reasonably good value for money from the public sector, although certainly cases of fraud and waste anger the average taxpayer. Not all programs, or levels of government, are perceived to be equally beneficial, and citizens appear very capable of distinguishing among the programs they like and the ones they do not.

In fact, it appears that the cries of "taxpayer rebellions" have less to do with taxes per se than with many other factors. The revolt against taxes is at times a specific response to an increase in taxes, as it appears to have been in California and Massachusetts. More often, however, the disaffection of citizens from government goes deeper. Taxes and public expenditures then become a symbol of rejection of those other aspects of government, or perhaps a rejection of some values of modern urban, industrial society more broadly conceived. Even social changes such as the growth of immigrant populations may become associated with political parties and issues that nominally are oriented toward issues of public finance. Of course, many voters and party adherents are very serious about their dislike for taxes and expenditures and their desire for a smaller public sector. For many others, however, their participation in the "anti-tax movement" is an indication that there is a great deal wrong with modern societies and the taxes levied by government are a convenient target for their disaffection. The success of the taxpayer rebellion may be more a triumph of symbolic politics than it is any specific rejection of government taxing and spending.

NOTES

1 The author, for example, pays at least eight taxes to five political units (federal government, state government, county, city, and school district), plus a sizeable fee to an independent sanitary district. Any excise taxes on gasoline, alcohol, etc. would be

added to those taxes, as would taxes such as corporate income taxes paid by consumers through the final price of the product. In addition to the usual excise taxes on alcohol, tobacco, and gasoline, Denmark charges excise taxes on ice cream, electric light bulbs, and disposable tableware.

2 Over half of a Swedish sample, for example, thought that tax reductions would improve the Swedish economy (Hadenius, 1986, p. 141). President Reagan also promoted his tax reductions as the "Economic Recovery" tax act. In one survey of Japanese taxpayers, almost two-thirds thought that reduction (even when taxes are so low in comparison to other industrialized countries) had to brought down to promote greater economic growth.

3 It may be that all the discussion about tax reform in the United States during the 1980s merely raised the awareness of citizens of the apparent unfairness of the income tax as it was administered prior to reform. Further, more attentive citizens came to understand the impact of the numerous special preferences that were written back into the tax system during and after passage of the tax reform legislation.

4 This is true for several reasons. One is that lower-income people spend a larger proportion of their income on items which are taxed, even if necessities are not taxed. Rent, for example, may be taxed while payments on home mortgages are not.

5 Some citizens may have noticed, prior to 1986, when they used the table provided in the federal income tax returns to find out how much they could deduct for state sales tax. When that deduction was eliminated by tax reform, citizens lost even that indirect reminder about how much they paid.

6 The regressivity would be increased, of course, to the extent that the public services that are charged for are virtual necessities for citizens. Some charges have been used, e.g. prescription charges in the National Health Service in Britain, to pay for a part of the real costs of the service and to ration consumption. Charges, however, have rarely been imposed for necessary public services other than those which might normally be marketed, e.g. gas and electricity.

7 This may result from a confusion between total taxes and tax rates. The middle classes do contribute more total tax revenues than the upper socio-economic classes, primarily because there are so many more people earning middle-class incomes. The upper classes do pay a higher proportion of their income in tax.

8 Another purpose of this change in local government finance was to prevent local governments (often Labour dominated) from charging very high property taxes on the more affluent, i.e. on Conservative Party supporters, to pay for programs of which the central government did not approve. The earlier "rate-capping" scheme had gone some distance toward imposing central control over local government finance by limiting the amount of domestic rates which a local government could impose; the community charge has completed the move toward greater central government control.

9 This party followed closely in time the less successful Anders Lange party which also had a radical anti-tax platform. The Anders Lange party actually began operation a few months prior to the Progress Party in Denmark, but did not gain anything close to the publicity achieved by the Danish party.

10 Some of the anti-immigrant stance may be pure ethnocentrism – the threat of a "Muslim Norway" was raised in one campaign speech – but this may also be playing on the common perception that immigrants are a burden on the already costly social welfare system. See "Antipathy Rules" in *The Economist*, July 29, 1989.

11 The manner of assessment of taxes may make a difference here. Citizens who must self-assess the personal income tax will be more conscious of the total amount paid than would citizens in systems where assessments are done by the tax bureaucracy.

12 The French reaction and protest against "bigness" in the economy was typified by the Poujadist movement in the 1950s, and more recently has been taken up by the UCDA (Union for the Defense of Shopkeepers and Artisans).

13 It should be noted that on average tax limitation referenda fare better with voters than do expenditure limitation propositions. Citizens when voting appear to have the same schizophrenia about the public sector which they display when answering questions on surveys.

14 The visibility of property taxes may depend a great deal upon how they are paid. People who pay them directly to state and local governments may find them very visible and very onerous, while citizens who pay them monthly as a part of their monthly mortgage payment may not notice these taxes nearly as much.

15 This reaction to the tax was experienced even though the impact of the sales tax on domestic prices was not nearly as great as that of trade restrictions. This was especially true for food, but

much of the reaction to the tax appeared to come from housewives who saw their grocery bills increase.

The problems of the Liberal Democratic Party extended beyond the sales tax, and several financial and sex scandals also reduced their electoral support.

6
Exit: Tax Evasion and Tax Avoidance

We have already seen that citizens do not like to pay taxes. Most of them recognize this as a civic duty and a legal obligation but, to paraphrase Abraham Lincoln's comment about being ridden out of town on a rail, "If it weren't for the honor, they would decline." Many citizens do seek to find ways of declining the honor of paying for government, and they find that they have two options: to exit from the tax system legally or illegally. In most industrialized countries a *partial* legal exit from the tax system is relatively easy, and often involves doing those things that the citizens would have done anyway. Governments and their tax laws simply make it easier and more profitable to do so. Most citizens would like to own their own home, and most have an inclination to donate money to charities, and government gives them a bonus, through the tax system, for these purposes. Illegal means to escape the tax system are also readily available, although the occupation of the individual citizen and his or her other socio-economic endowments (e.g. self-employed workers and professionals appear to have the greatest opportunities) make that option more or less difficult to exercise. In any case, the citizen who has really decided that he or she has had enough of the tax system will encounter little difficulty in finding a way to exit.

The usual term applied to legal exit from the tax system is "tax avoidance," while "tax evasion" usually is used to describe illegal exit from the system. These two terms are sometimes combined into the phrase "tax avoision" (Seldon *et al.*, 1979), but this notion appears to confuse the very fundamental differences between the two strategies available to a citizen. In choosing tax avoidance the individual is only accepting the incentives offered by government through the tax laws; to some degree an individual would be a fool if he or she did not take full advantage of opportunities that are made so readily available. At the extreme, it could be argued that the legal utilization of tax avoidance allows the individual to fulfill some other public policy purposes that would not be met with a more zealous commitment to paying taxes. This may be simply building a house or supporting a university, or it may be larger public policy purposes such as managing the economy through consumer credit or bolstering the retirement income of the less affluent by making their pensions non-taxable. For whatever reasons, government has decided that it is advantageous to the society for citizens to engage in certain designated activities. Therefore, government is willing to allow citizens who do so not to pay some tax for which they would otherwise be obligated.

Tax evasion is quite a different matter, however, and in this case the citizen takes the law into his or her own hands to decide how much tax is just, and therefore how much he or she will pay. There is no public policy purpose in evasion, but only the private purpose of the individual to have more disposable income by not paying what the law states is a fair share of taxes. Unlike tax avoidance, which is perfectly legal (even if some people do regard it unjust), tax evasion is illegal and the individual may be fined or imprisoned if their actions are detected. While the threat of detection and punishment appears to be a major deterrent to an individual engaging in tax evasion (Spicer and Lundstet, 1976; Allingham and Sandmo, 1972), this has not prevented a significant portion of the population in industrialized societies from trying their luck at it. While the evidence is limited, and subject to substantial errors because of the illegality of the activity, it does appear that tax evasion is a major growth industry in almost all industrialized societies. It also appears clear that governments are not capable of adequately monitoring and punishing all the evasion that does occur. The (justifiable) belief that other citizens are getting away without paying their share in turn creates a sense of unfairness in the tax system among an even greater number of citizens.

Tax Avoidance

It has already been said that tax avoidance is, by definition, a legal means to escape taxation. This formal legality does not, however, make it any more respectable to citizens who cannot avail themselves of the benefits of tax avoidance. Any number of phrases have been applied to the provisions in the tax law that allow individuals to escape paying taxes on a portion of his or her income, with the most common being "loopholes." As with so many aspects of social life, it appears that if I can avail myself of the benefits of the tax law I perceive that it is only just, but if the provision benefits only you it is a "loophole" and unjust. This is especially true of provisions in the tax law that benefit larger corporations so that many with large earnings and even some with large profits can legally avoid paying any taxes at all (Citizens for Tax Justice, 1988). As corporations are legal persons, but only indirectly are they really individuals, many people feel personally disadvantaged by the favorable treatment given to corporate profits.

Another term frequently applied to tax avoidance is "tax expenditures" (Surrey, 1973; Surrey and McDaniel, 1985; OECD, 1984). This term implies that the decision made by government to forego taxation, when an individual spends money for a particular purpose or earns money in a particular way, is identical to making a direct public expenditure for the same purpose. In other words, if government decides to subsidize homeownership through providing tax relief on mortgage payments, the net effect is the same as if government had handed each homeowner a check for the same amount of money. Further, if we want to determine just how much money government is spending in a particular policy area, we need to sum all the money it spends directly as well as all the money which is returned to the private sector through not taxing money earned or spent in certain ways. Thus, in the United States and in many other industrialized countries, the government housing program managed through the tax system is many times larger than the housing program provided directly through housing subsidies and construction of low-income housing projects. In the United States in fiscal 1988, direct housing expenditures were $8 billion, while tax expenditures for housing were $147 billion (US Budget, 1988); a ratio of eighteen dollars in tax expenditures for every one dollar in direct housing expenditures. In the United Kingdom, which has had a substantial direct public involvement in housing, the ratio between direct expenditures and tax expenditures has still been in the order of one to one. Housing is the most extreme example, but other policy areas have tax expenditures that rival direct expenditures in magnitude.

Some experts have, however, objected to the totalling of expenditures made directly through the budget with expenditures made through the tax system to find "exactly" how much money government is spending for a certain purpose. These objections are raised for at least two reasons. The first is technical. Often, the impact of tax expenditure decisions are estimated by a variety of means, and adding those estimates to "real" figures as calculated for the budget may in effect be adding apples and oranges. The published reports on tax expenditures, in fact, warn against adding together figures derived from different portions of the reports because of the different types of estimates used to calculate the figures (Office of Management and Budget, annual; Willis and Hardwick, 1978; Comeau, 1979). Thus, although the figures would probably not be terribly different, it is stilly risky to attempt to cumulate different forms of expenditure figures into one grand total.

The conceptual reasons for not attempting to cumulate expenditure and tax expenditure figures are perhaps even more compelling. Wildavsky (1985) has argued that it is important to keep "kosher" and to keep the two types of expenditures, and the two types of government activity (revenue and expenditure), distinct. He argues that the use of the term "expenditure" with reference to tax expenditures is a misnomer for something that is indeed a benefit but not an expenditure. To Wildavsky, this term is in effect a political one, used to increase scrutiny of the tax law, rather than a meaningful description of a government expenditure. Further, with most expenditure programs there is some accountability so that the money does go for the purpose intended. Tax expenditures are, in effect, an all purpose, fungible grant to the individual taxpayer. Although the individual may receive the benefits in respect of having made a decision to buy a house, once the individual receives the money it is fully fungible and may be spent on a trip to the Bahamas rather than directly on housing. In other words, the individual may well have bought their house anyway, and giving the tax money back is simply a bonus.

Following from the above, there is the additional budgetary problem that tax expenditures are largely uncontrollable by government. In other words, when governments make decisions about making a tax "loophole" available to individual or corporate taxpayers, they have little or no control over how much revenue they will actually be surrendering. That amount will depend upon the individual decisions of taxpayers (personal and corporate). In some cases the acceptance of the benefit may be much greater than expected, while in others it may be lower. In addition, the value of the benefits will depend upon the tax status of the taxpayers using them (see below). The various governments around the world have developed their own means for estimating the take-up of benefits and the revenue losses (OECD, 1984), but they can never be sure of the real outcomes until the final returns are filed. This uncertainty makes the world of the tax officials and revenue ministries very difficult. It is not a desperate problem where, in national governments, running a deficit is not a major disaster and is, in fact, now commonly accepted fiscal policy, but it does matter a great deal in subnational governments, which may not be allowed constitutionally or legally to incur operating deficits. In those cases, either fewer tax preferences will be made available or the methods used to estimate revenue losses for the expenditure budget will be extremely conservative (Meltsner, 1971).

In addition to the difficulties in controlling aggregate amounts of tax expenditures, there may be difficulties in targeting who actually receives the benefits. This was brought to light on a large scale at the end of 1988 as tax preferences for buying thrift institutions in the United States ("savings and loans") were found to be going to a number of overseas investors. Even for the everyday tax expenditures, however, there are significant targeting problems. In particular, Surrey (1973) argued that tax expenditures constitute an "upside-down subsidy" to the more affluent. That is, the higher the marginal rate of tax for which a taxpayer is liable, the greater the value of the tax expenditure. Even though any taxpayer is eligible for the benefits, and many do avail themselves of benefits such as mortgage interest relief, the greatest value is for the high income earner (Wilkinson, 1986). For example, a mortgage interest deduction of $10,000 is worth $2,000 for someone in a 20 percent tax bracket, but is worth $5,000 if he or she must pay in the 50 percent bracket. Therefore, if tax expenditures are to benefit the less affluent homebuyer, they benefit the more affluent to an even greater extent.

A final difficulty with tax expenditures is that they create "*fiscal stickiness*," that is, tax expenditures do allow substantial tax savings, and those savings are proportional to the marginal tax rates. Therefore, to raise sufficient income governments may have to set nominal tax rates very high if tax expenditures are large. Even though more sophisticated citizens will know that the tax rates are in effect much lower because of the available loopholes, the image of the extremely high tax rates is a definite political disadvantage for an incumbent political party. The political operation of this problem can be seen in the numerous tax reforms in the 1980s. Their general pattern was to reduce tax rates while at the same time eliminating tax expenditures. While these reforms were largely revenue neutral, although different people may have paid different amounts, the lowering of tax rates was seen as an important political act for those in government. Further, this may allow subsequent governments to raise more (or even less) revenue with very slight changes in tax rates.

All that having been said, tax expenditures are still a very popular instrument of government policy. This is true primarily because of their invisibility (Hogwood, 1987). That is, by choosing not to tax rather than choosing to spend directly for the same purpose, governments may be able to provide the same benefits to citizens with much less political fuss. Not only will using tax expenditures make the public budget appear smaller than it would otherwise, but the politics of making tax policy has been somewhat less visible than the politics of making budgets and expenditure decisions (Reese, 1980; Doern, Maslove, and Prince, 1988). Tax laws tend to be quite complex and many legislators voting on them do not fully understand all their intricacies and implications. The general public, in turn, is much less likely to understand the fine points than are the legislators. Therefore, it is easier to hide benefits for individuals, and especially for corporations, in a tax bill than it is in an expenditure bill. Although the tendency to use tax laws as a means of disguising benefits is especially pronounced in the American congress, with its "Christmas tree" tax bills (Birnbaum and Murray, 1987; Reese, 1980), it is apparent too in other countries (Rose and Karran, 1986; Elvander, 1972a) which also have extremely complex tax codes conferring special benefits on groups in the society through tax "loopholes."

In addition to their relative invisibility, the very features that make tax expenditures less desirable for government administrators concerned with balancing the budget make them desirable for taxpayers. The amount that an individual or corporatioin can benefit from a tax expenditure is usually unlimited. For example, if an individual chooses to buy a more expensive house, he or she can receive proportionately larger benefits than from a less expensive home. Some governments have at times sought to limit the amount of benefit provided through tax expenditures, e.g. the limitation of £25,000 on mortgages eligible for tax relief imposed by the British government prior to 1986. A component of tax reform in the United States has been to limit mortgage interest deductibility, albeit to the generous figure of $1 million. In general, however, the availability of tax relief is open-ended and dependent only upon the capacity of the individual to arrange the other portions of the required financial deal, e.g. the capacity to pay a larger mortgage even with tax relief.

The use of tax expenditures as a policy instrument is not, however, without its benefits for government. In addition to their invisibility, mentioned above, tax expenditures are also less expensive programs to administer than direct expenditure programs. In essence, a tax expenditure program depends upon the taxpayer, whether individual or corporate, to do most of the work required to receive the benefit. This work will have to be monitored and checked by the tax authorities, but if most taxpayers are honest (see below), then this need not be an especially extensive monitoring process, and may involve checking mathematics as much as detailed examinations of taxpayers' income or expenditure records. Likewise, a large proportion of the cost of administering tax expenditures can be imposed on private sector organizations, knowing that taxpayers will be sure that those organizations report to the tax authorities. So, for example, banks and other organizations providing mortgages may be required to submit reports of the amount of mortgage interest paid by individuals. All government must do then is to cross-check those reports against the self-reporting of individuals to determine if indeed the claims for tax relief are correct.

Finally, with the relatively lower administrative costs of tax expenditures goes the ability of government organizations to avoid blame for almost anything that happens in the program. As tax expenditures are a policy instrument implemented almost entirely through the private sector, the public sector can be held accountable only for whether the individual received the right tax relief – what they did to get the relief and what they do after receiving it are out of the hands of the government. Even if a tax expenditure program is not successful in reaching the intended population (targeting of tax benefits is virtually impossible) or in reaching goals for housing, economic development or whatever, that may be seen as the fault of the designers of the legislation rather than the fault of the bureaucrats who implemented it.

The Volume and Types of Tax Expenditures

To this point we have been discussing tax expenditures, or tax avoidance, as if we had a clear idea of just what it was and what types of programs were available to the taxpayer. The operational definition of a tax expenditure is, in fact, less than crystal clear. The distinction must be made between those aspects of the tax system which are structural, and those which are "special" and intended to create special benefits for some portion of the public (Surrey and McDaniel, 1985, 184–239); the latter provisions would be considered tax expenditures. This distinction often is very unclear in practice.

One way to look at the issue of tax avoidance globally, however, is to determine the degree of erosion of the tax base (Tanzi, 1969).

If we begin with the assumption that government could, in principle, tax all income earned in the society, then choosing not to do so indicates some preference being granted for some reason. The level of erosion of the tax base varies across countries and across time (tables 6.1, 6.2, and 6.3), although the figure for France in table 6.1 probably indicates as much evasion as legal erosion of the tax base. In few of the countries for which we have data does taxable income constitute even half of Gross National Product. The tax preferences being used here may all be for good public purposes, but these figures indicate beyond much doubt that tax preferences do constitute a major aspect of tax policy, and do determine to a great extent who pays how much tax.

While we have some idea of the magnitude of tax expenditure, it also will be worthwhile to detail the types of activities which receive special treatment under tax codes in different countries, as well as some idea of the magnitude of benefits made available (see table 6.4). This might have been extremely difficult even a few years ago, but as the entire question of taxation and public finance has become more central politically, there has been a perceived need to document and scrutinize the facts of tax systems in each country more carefully. Hence, in the following section we will be able to note whether many countries use a particular tax expenditure, and perhaps something about the magnitude of the benefits produced for taxpayers.

We can begin by noting that tax expenditures, like taxes, apply roughly to the major types of economic decisions made by individuals and corporations: decisions to earn money in a certain way as well as decisions whether or not to spend money in certain ways. Therefore, in most tax systems, certain types of income are treated as if they did not exist, or are treated differently from other types of

Table 6.1 Erosion of the income tax base

	Reported income as percentage of total personal income	*Taxable income as percentage of total personal income*
Britain	75.1	43.2
France	23.8	23.8
United States	79.3	45.0
West Germany	92.3	79.0

Source: Tanzi, 1969

Table 6.2 Taxable income as percentage of personal income

Australia	(1987/1988)	89.8
Austria	(1982)	78.0
Belgium	(1987)	72.1
Canada	(1986)	61.2
Denmark	(1987)	76.6
Finland	(1985)	70.4
France	(1987)	70.5
Germany	(1987)	78.3
Greece	(1987)	69.0
Ireland	(1985/86)	57.7
Italy	(1985)	95.0
Netherlands	(1988)	50.0
Norway	(1987)	75.1
Spain	(1987)	92.8
Sweden	(1987)	74.4
United Kingdom	(1986/87)	56.5
United States	(1988)	65.9

Source: OECD, 1990a

income. Likewise, the tax system may treat expenditures for certain purposes as especially virtuous and enable the individual to reduce his or her earned income by the amount of that expenditure, or in a few cases actually to count the expenditure as if the money had been paid to government as a tax.

As well as being two principal types of tax expenditures, there are also two major categories of recipients of benefits through the tax system: individuals and corporations. It is usually assumed that corporations are the major beneficiaries from tax reliefs, but that is rarely if ever the case. So, for example, in the United States in fiscal 1988 approximately 78 percent of the tax benefits went to individual taxpayers, while only 22 percent went to corporations (*Budget of the United States Government*, 1988, Special Analyses, Section G). A similar type of analysis in the United Kingdom reveals that approximately 72 percent of all benefits went to individuals while 18 percent went to corporations (*Public Expenditure White Paper, 1987–88*), and in Sweden the percentages are approximately 75 percent for individuals and 25 percent for corporations. In short, although the tax breaks directed at corporations receive most of the publicity, it is individuals who benefit most from preferences in the tax laws.

Table 6.3 Erosion of the tax base

United States

	GNP	*Taxable income*	*Taxable income as percent of GNP*
		(billion $)	
1960	515.3	171.6	33.3
1965	705.1	255.1	36.2
1970	1,015.5	401.2	39.5
1975	1,598.4	595.5	37.3
1980	2,732.0	1,280.0	46.9
1983	3,401.6	1,544.9	45.4
1984	3,774.7	1,701.4	45.1
1985	3,988.5	1,820.7	45.6
1986	4,231.6	1,947.0	46.0

Norway

	Personal income	*Taxable income*	*Taxable income as percentage of personal income*
		(million NKR)	
1970	44,401	35,109	79.1
1975	83,438	67,977	81.5
1980	133,762	109,284	81.7
1985	205,416	164,538	80.1
1987	298,626	233,888	78.3

United Kingdom

	Personal income	*Taxable income*	*Taxable income as percentage of personal income*
		(million pounds)	
1970	47,095	29,300	62.2
1975	94,447	57,300	60.6
1980	202,290	123,000	60.8
1982	242,228	152,000	62.8
1985	329,820	191,000	57.9

Sources: Norway, annual; CSO, annual

Table 6.4 Major tax expenditures

	Age	Interest Mortgage	Interest Other	Pensions	Medical expenses	Charity	Union dues
Australia	−	+	−	+	+	+	+
Austria	−	+	−	−	−	−	−
Belgium	−	++	−	+	−	+	−
Canada	+	−	−	+	−	+	−
Denmark	+	++	+	+	−	+	+
Finland	−	++	+	+	+	−	+
France	+	+	−	−	−	+	−
Germany	+	+	−	+	+	+	+
Greece	−	+	−	−	+	+	−
Ireland	+	++	+	+	+	−	−
Italy	−	++	−	+	+	−	+
Japan	+	+	−	+	+	+	−
Luxembourg	−	++	+	?	?	?	?
Netherlands	−	++	+	+	+	+	+
New Zealand	−	+	−	+	−	+	+
Norway	+	++	+	+	+	+	+
Portugal	−	+	−	+	+	+	+
Spain	+	++	−	+	+	+	+
Sweden	+	++	+	+	−	−	+
Switzerland	−	++	+	+	−	−	−
United Kingdom	+	+	−	+	−	+	−
United States	+	++	−[a]	+	+	+	+

+ = Available; ++ = Mortgage relief for second homes; − = Not available.
[a] Being reduced by stages to zero after 1986 tax reform.
Sources: OECD, 1984; McDaniel and Surrey, 1985

Further, these benefits appear reasonably well distributed throughout the taxpaying population, rather than concentrated among the very wealthy (Pechman, 1987b, 78–133). The tax system may be riddled with loopholes in most industrialized societies, but the loopholes are often large enough for the average taxpayer to wiggle through.

Treatment of income When income from certain sources is not taxed, the benefit is usually called an *exemption*. Two major categories of income receive special treatment under tax laws in almost all countries. The first of these, and the largest in volume, is income received from income maintenance programs, whether received from government in the form of social insurance payments (pensions, unemployment, etc.) or from the private sector in the form of life insurance benefits, sickness insurance, or the like. The tax exemption for most fringe benefits provided by employers is a special case of this type of tax treatment of social payments (OECD, 1988a), although more luxurious fringe benefits are now taxed in many countries. In other words, governments have made conscious policy choices to exclude social payments to individuals from the tax base. In many cases this is the only meagre source of income for the individual but in other cases, e.g. fringe benefits for highly paid employees, the individual taxpayer may be affluent. This exclusion of social income is especially sensible when the payments are from the public secor and taxation would simply be "clawing back" income that government has just paid out. However, given that not all people receiving social insurance payments are poor, some governments when faced with financial problems have begun to tax social insurance payments to the more affluent. For example, in 1986 the United States federal government began to tax social security payments to individuals who had total incomes in excess of $25,000. This measure has produced relatively little income for the public sector, but has helped alleviate a perception that social security was being used by some of the wealthy as a tax-free supplement to what was already a very handsome income.

To specific income sources which can be classified as "social incomes" can be added some general relief from taxation supplied to members of the population for family and social purposes. In most tax systems there is a concept that a minimum income by the individual should not be taxed; while this would rarely be sufficient to live on, it does provide an income base. Further, this amount is increased in proportion to the size of the family of the income earner, again so that there is some basic level of income for anyone in work. This is generally the largest single tax benefit provided by government, and in the 1970s and 1980s has increasingly been adjusted to be more redistributive. For example, the Earned Income Credit in the United States is a supplement for the working poor through the tax system, and special deductions in Sweden, for example, redistribute money to the poorly paid (Swedish Institute, 1986).

The other category of income that is often treated specially in the tax system is capital gains income. That is, money which individuals realize from an investment when that investment increases in value and is sold is treated differently from ordinary income. In some instances, the difference between the buying and selling price of an asset may not be taxed at all, while in others it may be taxed at a reduced rate. There may be some constraints on the use of this particular tax preference, e.g. the asset in question may have to be held for a period of six months or a year in order not to reward speculation, but outside those restraints investors can expect very favorable treatment from the tax system. The concept behind capital gains exclusions is an obvious one – to encourage people to invest their money in profitable enterprises, therefore stimulating economic growth. Further, it should be noted that not all of the benefits of capital gains exclusions go to wealthy investors – the largest single category of capital gains benefits in many countries is exclusion of taxation on gains received from selling owner-occupied housing.

We should point out here, however, that not all tax systems are so generous with investors. At times, so-called "unearned income" from investments (both current returns such as dividends and interest as well as profits at the final sale of the investment) have been taxed at a higher than average rate. In the mid-1970s, during a Labour government in the United Kingdom, "unearned income" was taxed at 98 percent, providing individuals with resources with little incentive to invest, except abroad. In addition, we have already noted that one tax handle government has at its disposal is wealth, so that governments may want to levy a wealth tax annually on the value of investments. If this wealth tax is itself very high, it will discourage the potential investor from putting money into any visible form of wealth, and therefore may simply encourage capital flight, or the "underground economy," which will be discussed in reference to tax evasion. Also, several Scandinavian countries imposed (the then repealed) transfer taxes on sales of stocks and bonds which also have been seen as a major impediment to investment (*Financial Times*, December 20, 1988). Thus, capital gains exclusions, while appearing to advantage the wealthy excessively, may be justified as a means of getting more money to work in the visible economy and of promoting economic development within the country. Gripping the wealth tax handle too tightly may only strangle economic growth rather than redistribute income.

Treatment of expenditures Governments have provided favorable tax treatment to any number of uses of money by individuals and corporations. These are usually referred to as deductions. Almost any type of interest in society has been able at one time or another to hang its special ornaments on the Christmas tree and receive some tax relief. Again, it is assumed that there should be some public policy purpose for the "loopholes," but at times it is difficult to discern what they might be. For example, in the United States, the purchasers of race horses have been accorded tax relief, and gamblers in several countries can offset their gambling losses against any winnings. In the end, all that is required is a sufficiently strong political voice to have the desired loophole written into law. If there is a good purpose for the provision, so much the better, but it does not really appear to be crucial to the success of the proposal.

Of all the real public purposes which are affected by tax concessions, housing appears to be the most common and the most important in terms of the amount of money involved. In almost all industrialized democracies an individual receives some tax relief for mortgage interest for purchasing a house. This may be only a percentage of the interest paid, but there is still a tax subsidy. Likewise, in many countries, even if capital gains is treated as regular income, the individual will not have to declare profits made on selling a house as part of his or her income. Finally, at least in the United States, local property taxes on houses are deductible from income, giving an even greater subsidy to homeowners. In short, the tax system has made homeowning a very favored way for an individual to spend his or her income. This is, of course, not only good for the prospective homeowner but it is also beneficial to the construction industry that builds the houses, and the lending institutions which finance them. In addition to the benefits given to individual homeowners, governments may also provide special treatments for cooperative organizations and other housing suppliers (Headey, 1978) in societies that depend more on multi-family dwellings to house their populations.

A second major source of tax benefits for expenditures by individuals are contributions to charities or other non-profit organizations. In many societies individuals who make contributions to organizations ranging from their local church to educational organizations to animal welfare organizations to heaven knows what can deduct those contributions from their income. Again, many people would make these contributions with or without the tax relief that is provided, but the tax system certainly makes it easier. Further, this tax benefit may actually save government money by leveraging private money to provide services that government might otherwise have to pay for itself. This can be seen in part by a comparison of higher education in the United States and the United Kingdom. In the United States contributions to universities have long enjoyed tax relief, and universities have been able to build large endowments to finance their current operations; the book value of endowments of colleges and universities in the United States now totals more than $30 billion, developed largely through private, tax-deductible giving. Contributions to universities have not enjoyed this tax status in the United Kingdom, and dependence on government has produced very difficult times for higher education in the 1980s and 1990s.

Tax laws also confer substantial benefits for spending for personal pensions, health care, and other personal social protections. Even with the welfare state programs available in most industrialized countries, there is still often a need (or at least a desire) to supplement public programs with private programs (Rein and Rainwater, 1986). Governments often subsidize the fulfillment of this perceived need through the tax system. As might be expected, these tax benefits appear most generous in the United States, which has among the least developed social service programs, but they are also in existence in most industrialized countries. Examples of benefits would be deductions for life insurance premiums (and exemptions for the proceeds), tax subsidies for health expenditures, and special tax treatment of private pension investments and income. In short, the Welfare State has not created a public monopoly over social services, but rather has been subsidizing some redundancy through the tax system.

A final point to be made about expenditure-oriented tax benefits for individuals is that not all of them are delivered through the income tax. Consumption taxes also contain a number of benefits for consumers, especially benefits for goods and services considered to be necessities. For example, in the United States, 33 states do not tax food and 48 do not tax prescription medications through their sales taxes. Similarly, the value-added tax in most European countries excludes food, clothing, and a variety of other commodities. This form of "tax expenditure" is available to all citizens but does not have the pronounced "upside-down" characteristic of those coming through the income tax system, because all citizens pay sales tax at the same rate, and the less affluent spend a larger proportion of their income on food and other necessities. Some consumption tax benefits are also made available for goods that are clearly not necessities but which are deemed particularly meritorious, e.g. art and antiques, and these do tend to benefit differentially the more affluent.

For the corporate sector, the major source of benefits from the tax system is through subsidies to investment. If government wants to stimulate economic growth, which it usually does, one means is to stimulate business investment in productive equipment and plants. There may be general tax credits for investment, and at times governments will adopt selective credits for only certain categories of investments. One type of credit that has been of particular importance for industry is accelerated depreciation of equipment (Hulten, 1981; Alworth, 1987). Businesses have been able in most tax systems to deduct depreciation of their equipment as if it were a real, annual cost of doing business, with equipment assumed to have productive lifespans of twenty, thirty, or even fifty years. If, however, a business is allowed to depreciate its equipment more rapidly, it can have a major reduction in profits and hence a major reduction in taxes. By manipulating the rules for calculating depreciation (Gravelle, 1981), which are much more complex than presented in this paragraph, taxing authorities can play a major role in determining the profitability of industries, as well as the government's tax revenues.

Some industries receive special tax treaztment because of the type of products they produce. This is especially true of extractive industries such as mining and oil production. It is argued, by people in those industries, that the speculative nature of mineral exploration and the rapid depletion of the resources once discovered should allow them special treatment under the tax laws. In several countries, most notably the United States with its "depletion allowances," extractive industries are given preferred treatment and can deduct a portion of all their profits simply because those profits were received from a mineral resource rather than another source. Attempts by other industries arguing that their resources are also depletable, e.g. publishers, and that they therefore should have similar favorable treatments extended to them in the tax laws, have not been successful.

In summary, a number of tax loopholes exist in almost every tax system. Despite some rhetoric there is nothing inherently evil about tax expenditures, and some actually benefit the society as well as the individual taxpayer. Everything else being equal, it appears that the higher the nominal tax rates, the greater the number and value of the tax loopholes available to individual and corporate taxpayers. There may be some real threshold value beyond which taxes beome unbearable and evasion becomes a more acceptable option (see below). The major exception to the generalization of high rates and high tax expenditures would appear to be the United States, which has a rather low nominal tax rate over a long period of time, but has also developed perhaps the biggest "Christmas tree" of tax benefits of any country in the world. Even after the "tax reform" of 1986, that tree is still laden with numerous goodies for taxpayer who have the skill and financial resources to make use of them.

Tax Evasion

The other opportunity for citizens to exit from the tax system is tax evasion. This is, as noted previously, the illegal means of escape. Tax evasion results either through the failure to report all sources of income (if indeed any income is reported) or through the reporting of excess deductions and exclusions. In either case, the individual will report a lower taxable income than he or she actually has, and as a consequence will pay less tax. Citizens may go to great lengths to avoid paying taxes, and some in the United Kingdom have become non-persons to evade paying the community charge. They have removed themselves from the electoral register and other public records in order to escape the tax. It is virtually impossible for individuals to evade consumption taxes such as the value-added tax or excise taxes,[1] but for income-based taxes it might be possible. The individual would have to work alone or for a very small organization, and would have to be paid in cash, but it is possible to slip through thc tax net. The individual who evades would have to be willing, however, also to forego the possibility of some benefits based on social insurance, e.g. unemployment or retirement pension.

As might be imagined, it is difficult to undertake empirical research on tax evasion. Since it is an illegal activity, few citizens will report it openly; perhaps the only ones who do so willingly are politicians who want to make a point. One such politician is Mogens Glistrup, the leader of the Progress (anti-tax) Party in Denmark, who spent several years in jail for tax evasion. For people who do not have such a political point to make, and who do not want to go to jail, tax evasion is not discussed so openly. Indirect methods, therefore, must be adopted to estimate just how much tax evasion is actually occurring in a society. This estimation can be done in several ways. One approach is just to ask people. Again, few people will report openly that *they* are engaging in an illegal practice, but many would be willing to say if they thought their friends and neighbors were. It appears that those who believe their associates are evaders are themselves likely to be tax evaders (Laurin, 1986; Internal Revenue Service, 1984). Similarly, respondents can be asked about their perception of the illegality of evasion, and the perceived severity of the crime (Song and Yarborough, 1978; Listhaug and Miller, 1985). Those who either think that it is not a crime or it is a very trivial offense are themselves more likely to be evaders. These are imperfect means of estimating evasion, but it does provide some estimate of how people are behaving. In particular, it provides an estimate of *how many citizens* are evading taxes.

Another means of estimating the extent of tax evasion is more useful for estimating the *amount of tax revenue* which might be lost through evasion. This method is based on the assumption that a principal reason for using cash in business transactions in modern societies is to evade taxation. If transactions are in cash, there is no "paper trail" that revenue collectors can follow to determine just how much money an individual or corporation has earned. Evading taxes in this manner is difficult for large firms, which are required to keep detailed records (although they have been known to keep different records for different purposes), but it is rather easy for the small businessman or craftsman who does not have such stringent requirements. There are numerous stories about plumbers, electricians, and other craftsmen who have two prices for a job: one if paid in cash and one if paid by check. In the estimation technique for tax evasion, the proportion of cash in some monetary aggregate like M_1 is used as a surrogate measure of evasion (Cagan, 1958; Gutman, 1977). Of course, there are good reasons why people use cash, and countries differ in the extent to which checks and credit cards are used for transactions. However, within some degree of error, this statistic does provide a good estimate of the degree of evasion (but see Garcia, 1978). A somewhat similar set of assumptions is used by Feige (1979) to develop an alternative monetary measure of evasion based on the relative velocities of cash and demand deposits.

A third form of evidence, also concerning the *volume of tax evasion*, comes from national accounts statistics. In most countries, national income aggregates such as the Gross National Product and Gross Domestic Product are measured through both income and expenditure figures (Beckerman, 1968). Both how much income corporations and individuals report and how much expenditure is made are recorded and the total volume of economic activity in the country is calculated. These two means of estimating national income rarely if ever agree: one major source of the error may be the underground economy which is being hidden from tax officials (Macafee, 1980; Matthews, 1984; Blades, 1982). In particular, taxpayers will attempt to hide income, while expenditures are more difficult to hide, and there is little incentive to do so. Therefore, the difference between these two forms of measurement is one measure of the degree of evasion. If we assume for the population of industrialized countries that we are working with in this book that the reporting errors would be about equal, then differences between calculations of national income among the countries could be taken as a measure of relative levels of evasion.

The Evidence

The survey evidence about tax evasion is quite disparate and from scattered research projects done at different times for somewhat different purposes and using different questions in different languages. Therefore, assembling the data for comparative purposes creates the usual problem of mixing apples and oranges. With all those caveats in mind, however, we can still gain some sense of the willingness of citizens in several industrialized countries to engage in tax evasion. Some evidence complied from a number of sources is presented in tables 6.5 and 6.6. The first of these tables gives information about self-reported tax evasion or the "reported" evasion of others. The second table contains some evidence on the tax ethics of respondents, measuring the extent to which they considered tax evasion a really serious crime. In neither case can we be sure that an individual who says that he or she thinks that everyone else evades, or thinks that evasion is no more serious than jaywalking, is really evading taxes, but it does certainly appear to increase the likelihood.

Survey evidence Table 6.5 presents evidence on reported tax evasion in surveys. Some of this is self-reporting, but most concerns the respondents' perceptions of the activities of others. Although the reports are much higher than tax authorities in any country would desire, there are still marked differences among countries. Laurin's (1986) analysis of tax evasion in Sweden, building on Vogel (1974), is one of the most complete studies of this activity. Laurin found that over 30 percent of his sample were willing to say that they have not reported all their income to the tax authorities, and that others disclose having overreported the deductions to which they are entitled. Thus, approximately one-third of the Swedish population is willing to say that they engage in some form of tax evasion. In another thorough analysis, conducted by the Internal Revenue Service (1984) in the United States, approximately 20 percent of all

Table 6.5 Reported levels of tax evasion and tax morality

	United States				
	Percent of respondents who indicated various levels of tax evasion activity				
Activity	*Never*	*Rarely*	*Occasionally*	*Fairly often*	*Frequently*
Failing to report some income	73.0	14.7	7.4	2.5	1.5
Exaggerating medical expenses	82.4	7.9	5.4	2.3	1.1
Exaggerating charitable donations	75.7	11.1	7.2	3.1	1.4

	Acceptance of tax cheating			
	Very low	*Low/Medium*	*High*	*Very high*
	34	32	22	11

Sweden (percentages)	*1968*	*1981*
Tax evasion is inconsiderate of one's fellow citizens		
Agree strongly	62.5	51.0
Agree somewhat	25.8	30.2
Disagree somewhat	8.0	13.3
Strongly disagree	1.7	3.1
Don't know/No answer	2.0	2.4
One can scarcely complain if people use all available opportunities for tax evasion		
Agree strongly	7.6	15.4
Agree somewhat	13.1	25.5
Disagree somewhat	28.5	22.8
Strongly disagree	46.7	33.2
Don't know/No answer	4.1	3.0

Table 6.5 Continued

	1968	*1981*
Penalties for tax evasion are not severe enough		
Agree strongly	9.8	3.0
Agree somewhat	14.7	6.6
Disagree somewhat	37.6	30.4
Strongly disagree	30.3	54.3
Don't know/No answer	7.7	5.8

Sources: CSR, Inc., 1980; Hochstein, 1985; Laurin, 1986

Table 6.6 Measures of tax morality

	International Values Study		*Trettner*
Austria	–		9
Belgium	3.30	(10)	12
Canada	–		6
Denmark	2.39	(4)	4
Finland	–		4
France	3.22	(9)	14
Germany	2.51	(5)	9
Ireland	3.35	(12)	6
Italy	1.85	(2)	17
Japan	–		6
Netherlands	3.14	(8)	9
Norway	3.34	(11)	4
Spain	2.80	(7)	12
Sweden	1.79	(1)	4
Switzerland	–		1
United Kingdom	2.69	(6)	4
United States	2.04	(3)	6

Sources: Listhaug and Miller, 1985; Trettner, 1974; Frey and Weck, 1983

respondents reported cheating on their federal taxes, although most did so in a small way – usually around $100. Most cheated by not reporting all sources of income. If citizens are willing to report this much evasion in a study funded by the IRS, one can only wonder how much evasion is really taking place. Surveys in Italy and France, concentrating on "black work" as a source of tax evasion, also found that large proportions of the population were engaged in underreporting income (Pettenati, 1979; Contini, 1979; Gaudian and Schiray, 1984).

If we move from actual reported evasion to the study of tax ethics, we find a major international study of tax ethics came as a component of the International Value Systems Study (Listhaug and Miller, 1985). Respondents in this survey were asked to say whether certain types of activities were ever justified, with an answer of "Never" being assigned a value of 1, and an answer of "Always" being assigned 10. Hence, higher average scores in a nation would indicate greater acceptance of the activity. The survey data in table 6.6 given in parentheses show substantial variation among twelve industrialized countries in the acceptability of tax cheating.[2] The most "moral" countries concerning taxation were Sweden and Italy, while the most willing to accept cheating were Norway, Ireland, and Belgium.

These data are intriguing for several reasons. First, it has already been seen that one-third of the Swedish population are willing to evade, but this is the most moral country as regards taxation in the study; what must the others be doing? Likewise, Italy is often cited as a stronghold of tax evasion but yet appears to have extremely moral attitudes about obligations to the State, much more so than France, also frequently used as an example of evasion. At the other ends of the spectrum, Norwegians might have been expected to have the same respect for the law found among Swedes, but instead appear relatively very willing to cheat on taxes. These findings indicate that tax evasion is not a simple behavior and apparently evokes very complex responses from citizens. These reactions and behaviors will require additional explanation.

Although not providing the interval level measurement of the International Values Study (IVS), an earlier assessment (Trettner, 1974) of tax morality rated seventeen industrialized countries on their apparent willingness to tolerate tax evasion. These data are also shown in table 6.6. There is a good deal of agreement among the two evaluations of tax morality. The major source of disagreement is over the placement of Italy. The Italian respondents in the IVS themselves displayed a very high level of tax morality, but the

Trettner study based on a compilation of evidence ranked Italians as very low on tax morality. It may be in this case that observed behavior does not agree well with attitudes, or that respondents thought they were supposed to respond to the questions in certain ways, because there is very strong evidence of widespread evasion in Italy.

There are also some studies of tax ethics concentrating on a single country. For example, in the United States, Song and Yarborough (1978) found that although their respondents did accept that tax evasion was a crime, they did not regard it as a serious one. The large-scale study of taxpayer compliance conducted in part by the Internal Revenue Service (1984) in the United States found that one-third of all respondents did not see anything morally wrong with cheating on taxes, and another third were somewhat ambiguous about the morality of tax evasion. That figure "supporting" evasion was up substantially over earlier research on evasion (CSR, Inc., 1980). On the other hand, the success of amnesty programs in several states (Leonard and Zeckhauser, 1987; Jackson, 1986) indicates that taxpayers must feel somewhat bad when they do evade. Similar findings have come from several studies of evasion and general acceptance of corruption in the United Kingdom (Dean, Keenan, and Kenney, 1980; Johnston and Wood, 1985; Lewis, 1979), and few citizens are willing to acccpt that tax evasion is a serious crime, if it is a crime at all. The prevailing attitude about tax evasion in industrialized countries appears to be "catch me if you can," rather than any general acceptance of the obligation of citizenship to pay for government.

Macro-economic indicators The evidence gained from the analysis of cash relative to a monetary aggregate (M_1) reveals an even greater variation among nations than does the evidence retrieved from surveys. Some of the evidence here is somewhat unexpected, however, in that two countries very commonly discussed as having high levels of tax evasion – France and Italy – have substantially lower percentages of cash in M_1 than do other countries usually thought to be more law-abiding (at least with respect to taxation), such as Austria, Sweden, and Germany. The most logical explanation for this finding is that both countries have relatively low income tax rates (in part because government would not be able to collect higher taxes anyway), and tax evasion is such a part of social and economic life. Therefore, there is little incentive for citizens to attempt to avoid detection by using cash. The method of income tax collection in

France – the *forfait* or "agreed income" – allows individual taxpayers to negotiate their taxable income rather than depend upon "real" figures reported by employers, and hence there is also a reduced need to hide income.

Both the Italian and French governments have attempted, however, to crack down on evasion and to enforce their tax laws more vigorously. For example, despite the somewhat cavalier attitude toward the determination of income for tax purposes, there is a decentralized and extensive system of tax inspection in France which allows the inspectors to have a very good picture of the consumption patterns, if not the actual incomes, of citizens. The dependence of both the French and Italian governments on the income tax also has increased: in Italy from almost 11 percent to 27 percent between 1965 and 1985 although increasing only 3 percent in France. With this growing concern with the income tax, the rate of decrease in cash in M_1 has been somewhat lower than in many other OECD countries (see table 6.7). This finding in itself appears to offer some support for the utility of the cash ratio measurement of tax evasion, despite the skepticism of some about its utility as an indicator.

It is extremely interesting to note in table 6.7 that France and Italy have been decreasing the cash component of their money supply in contrast to most industrialized countries. The overall variation in those ratios among the OECD countries is even more remarkable. Most countries increased the cash component of M_1 between 1975 and 1980, but then many have had substantial decreases in the 1980s. Some countries, – Australia, Switzerland, and Ireland – have shown continually increasing levels of cash in circulation. For almost two-thirds of the countries, however, the ratio of cash to M_1 was higher in 1985 than in 1975. This movement is found despite the apparently widespread use of credit cards and electronic transfers of money. While it was once thought that cash might become obsolete with credit cards and direct debit cards, it now appears that it will continue to be a component of economic life. It does appear that one major reason for this is that government will continue to collect taxes.

All in all, the above discussion adds up to a body of evidence pointing to a rather significant amount of tax evasion in almost all industrialized countries, whether measured by the reported evasion of citizens (by themselves or by their neighbors), or by aggregate data on the amount of cash circulating in the economy, or by errors in national accounts statistics. As one respondent to a Swedish survey on the subject offered, tax evasion "is not a crime, it is merely a

Table 6.7 Ratio of cash in circulation to M_1

	1975	*1980*	*1985*
Australia	0.278	0.281	0.368
Austria	0.412	0.493	0.454
Belgium	0.440	0.451	0.386
Canada	0.275	0.299	0.200
Denmark	0.150	0.149	0.088
Finland	0.257	0.287	0.228
France	0.251	0.215	0.202
Germany	0.332	0.345	0.330
Ireland	0.390	0.393	0.429
Italy	0.187	0.146	0.146
Japan	0.232	0.251	0.267
Netherlands	0.307	0.335	0.306
New Zealand	0.199	0.228	0.216
Norway	0.368	0.413	0.261
Portugal	0.178	0.327	0.334
Spain	0.267	0.515	0.489
Sweden	0.654	0.423	0.487
Switzerland	0.347	0.370	0.376
Turkey	0.276	0.302	0.278
United Kingdom	0.338	0.330	0.177
United States	0.246	0.280	0.256

Source: International Monetary Fund, monthly

necessity" (Vogel, 1974). This cavalier attitude to the tax laws appears very widespread among the populations of most Western democracies. While it is widely shared, it is not universal and does vary markedly across countries. We therefore need to understand what factors can explain the levels of evasion that exist, and the choices of individuals to evade or not.

Explaining Tax Evasion

A limited explanation of levels of tax evasion among individual countries will be undertaken here. In so doing, two versions of the dependent variable of evasion will be used. One is the measure developed above relating cash in circulation to money supply. Despite the difficulties which have been pointed out for this measure (Barthelemy, 1988; Garcia, 1978) it does have some face validity, and further it does provide an interval level measure of tax evasion activity which does bear some relationship to the underlying (unmeasured and probably unmeasurable) "real" quantity. The second version of the dependent variable is a composite of measures developed by Frey and Weck (1983). This latter measure has the advantage of "triangulating" the concept of tax evasion (Webb, Campbell, Schwartz, and Sechrest, 1966), but has the disadvantage of being only ordinal – a rank-ordering of the major industrialized countries. A comparison of the rank-orderings of countries on the two different measurements of evasion is presented in table 6.8. These data indicate some agreement between the two measures, although that is far from strong.

The rank-order correlation (0.06) is by no means sufficiently strong to allow using one measure in place of the other. Despite some general agreement, two countries – Spain and Denmark – produced

Table 6.8 Comparison of measures of tax evasion (rank orders)

	Cash	*Composite*
Austria	3	6
Belgium	5	5
Canada	14	12
Denmark	17	4
Finland	12	8
France	13	9
Germany	7	7
Ireland	4	11
Italy	16	13
Japan	9	16
Netherlands	8	3
Norway	10	2
Spain	1	17
Sweden	2	1
Switzerland	6	14
United Kingdom	15	10
United States	11	15
	p = 0.06	

Sources: International Monetary Fund, annual; Frey and Weck, 1983

substantial apparent disagreement between the two rankings. The Frey and Weck measure, based on the probable size of the shadow economy, ranks Spain very low, but the cash portion of the monetary supply was the largest of any of the countries. On the other hand, Denmark was ranked as having a very large shadow economy by Frey and Weck, but had a very small (and declining) cash component of money. These discrepancies could be accounted for by several outside factors. For example, the relatively lower level of development of banking in Spain might encourage residents to keep more cash available, and Denmark is cited as having a high level of tax morality (Trettner, 1974; see also table 6.6). Still, in subsequent analysis both measures of tax evasion will be used, and the results compared. This will provide a more complete assessment of what is actually happening as regards tax evasion in these countries. In addition, the cash over M_1 measure can be used for four countries (Australia, New Zealand, Portugal, and Turkey) not included in the Frey and Weck data.

Independent variables A number of factors have been associated with tax evasion in the literature. Some of these concern the tax system itself, others the nature of politics, others the state of the economy, and others tax administration. If we begin with the tax system, one of the most obvious variables is the level and the progressivity of taxation itself. Everything else being equal, we would expect citizens to be more willing to attempt to evade taxes when it pays more to do so; if the marginal tax rate is 75 percent, then one hundred dollars (or kroner or whatever) not reported is a savings of 75 dollars. At lower rates of tax, the appeal may diminish. For example, one of the major justifications for tax evasion given in the surveys on the subject is that taxes are too high and ordinary people have to cheat to survive. Despite that, however, the findings of differential levels of apparent tax evasion and tax morality in Sweden and Denmark, with roughly comparable levels of taxation, and much lower apparent rates of evasion in Denmark than in lower tax Mediterranean countries, lend support to Frey and Pommerehne's (1982) comment that high tax rates were "implausible" as the sole determinant of tax evasion. Something else appears to be happening to produce higher levels of tax evasion in some countries than in others.

A second factor concerning the tax structure which could be associated with the willingness to evade is its visibility. Wilensky (1976) argued that this was a major factor explaining tax protests in industrialized countries. While visibility is a somewhat amorphous concept, the basic idea is that the more the citizen sees how much tax he or she is paying, the more willing they will become to attempt to evade taxes. Thus, indirect taxes such as the corporation tax or employers' social security contributions – even if the real economic incidence is on consumers or employees – are less likely to generate resistance and evasion than are more visible taxes such as the personal income tax. Likewise, dividing up the total tax burden among a number of different taxes and a number of different levels of government is likely to reduce the visibility of taxes and make their collection somewhat easier (see chapter 1). Finally, the visibility of taxation may be not so much a function of its structure but of increases in taxation, no matter of what type. The "revolt" against taxation in California (Proposition 13), for example, arose shortly after an increase in the property tax.

It has already been pointed out that the major purpose for taxation is to pay for services. It could therefore be hypothesized that the more citizens believe they are getting a good deal for the money they pay, the more willing they will be to pay for government. Again, it has been pointed out that some types of public expenditures are more visible to citizens than are others. Governments that have a large proportion of total expenditures as government consumption expenditures – salaries for workers, capital improvements, etc. – may produce less visible benefits for citizens than do governments which spend more for transfers and actually return a larger proportion of the taxes collected to citizens for their consumption decisions. This is especially true if government is producing more public goods (defense) than private goods (education) with its consumption expenditures (Downs, 1967). This statement contains some caveats, as the general hostility toward welfare payments in the United States brings to mind, but in general it can be hypothesized that a larger transfer component of public expenditure would make taxation more palatable, and should be associated with lower rates of tax evasion.

Politically, the availability of alternatives to the status quo may be an important predictor of levels of evasion (see Wilensky, 1976). Everything else being equal, we would expect countries which have a political movement opposed to taxation to be less concerned with evasion than countries without such a movement. If we return to Hirschman's (1970) logic, where there is the option of exercising voice there might be less concern with exercising the option to exit. This may be seen, possibly, in the case of Denmark mentioned above. Although Denmark has high and progressive taxes, it has a very low ratio of cash to total currency. One explanation offered for this is a high level of tax morality, but another could be the presence of the Progress Party, which serves as an acceptable organization through which to channel resistance to high taxation.

Finally, economic well-being can be hypothesized to be related to levels of tax evasion. If citizens are doing well economically – specifically if their real take-home pay is stable or increasing (Rose and Peters, 1978) – they will be less likely to accept the risks involved with tax evasion. This factor has been associated with the development of anti-tax parties in Scandinavia and elsewhere, as well as with the difficulties encountered by some ruling political parties and coalitions (Hibbs and Madsen, 1981). In addition to these manifestations of "voice," declining real economic fortunes may also be associated with manifestations of exit through evasion. Exit may be, in fact, a much quicker and surer means of increasing one's personal income than is political activity.

The only problem with using the exit option is the final possible explanatory factor – the chances of being caught. The probability of detection has been shown to be important in explaining ideas about evasion in surveys (Internal Revenue Service, 1984; Allingham and Sandmo, 1972), and should also be related to the actual behavior of putative taxpayers. In general, taxpayers think that the probability of their being caught, and the probability of severe sanctions, is low and are willing to take their chances. Although the probability of detection is a perceptual, psychological measure, it can also be a more objective one. This would include some assessment of the relative size of the tax administration, as well as potentially the record of enforcement for a country across time.

Analysis As noted above, two separate analyses of tax evasion using the two measures of evasion will be used (see pp. 216–17 above). In both analyses measures of the six independent variables described above (see table 6.9 for operational definitions) will be related to the dependent variable(s) of tax evasion. These will be simple cross-sectional analyses (for 1985) with 17 and 21 cases. The limited number of cases will restrict the possible number of statistical manipulations of the data, but we still should be able to obtain a good impression of the correlates of tax evasion. However, to enhance the ability to carry out some of the tricks, it will be assumed that the ordinal level measure of evasion supplied by Frey and Weck is interval; an assumption often made in social research with relatively little damage done to the canons of statistics. Even then with few

Table 6.9 Variables used in tax evasion research

Dependent Variables	
Cash/money supply	– The ratio of cash to the money supply (M_1).
Composite	– Frey-Weck (1983) measure of evasion.
Independent Variables	
Total tax	– Tax revenues as a percentage of Gross Domestic Product.
Tax visibility	– Wilensky's (1976) measure of visibility.
Take-home pay	– Per capita income after taxes.
Tax enforcement	– Tax officials per capita.
Tax protests	– Vote for tax protest parties in last election.
Social expenditures	– Social expenditures (health, welfare, housing, education) as percentage of total expenditure.

cases and many variables the repertoire of appropriate methods is very limited.

The most readily noticeable finding from the bivariate correlations of all the independent variables with the dependent variables (table 6.10) is that the two tax system variables do not appear strongly related to the level of evasion. This is especially true of the cash over total money supply dependent variable, but there is no significant

Table 6.10 Correlations of economic and political variables with measures of tax evasion

	Total tax level	*Tax visibility*	*Take-home pay*	*Tax officials*	*Tax protests*	*Social expenditures*
Cash/money supply	0.12	0.17	0.21	0.20	0.36	0.39
Composite	0.18	0.20	0.19	0.16	0.34	0.41

relationship for the composite Frey and Weck measure of evasion either. The level of visibility of taxes (as measured by the percentage of income tax in total taxation) is somewhat more positively associated with evasion than the absolute level of taxation, but only slightly so. Thus, Frey and Pommerehne's 1982 comment about the implausibility of the tax rate explaining all the variance in tax evasion appears well-justified; the simple need to keep more money does not appear to be a sufficient reason to evade taxes in these data. The measure of the visibility of the tax system also shows rather little relationship to levels of evasion (by either measure of the dependent variable). In short, the tax system itself does not appear to be strongly related to the willingness of citizens to attempt to escape it.

Much the same could be said of the relationship of economic and administrative factors to evasion. First, simply being (on average) more affluent does not appear to make citizens more willing to pay their taxes. One finds relatively poor industrialized countries (e.g. Ireland) with high rates of apparent evasion, as well as very affluent nations (Sweden). Likewise, one finds relatively poor countries (Italy) that have apparently low rates of evasion as well as rich countries (Denmark) with low rates of evasion (at least according to the cash measure). In work on individuals who say they evade or that they support tax evasion, there also appears to be rather little correlation between wealth and behavior. Similarly, the degree of enforcement effort by government does not appear strongly related to evasion, despite numerous claims that a policy of employing more tax officials will pay for itself with increased revenues (Steurle, 1986).

What does appear related to tax evasion are the two political variables, the prevalence of tax protest politics in the country, and the apparent cost/benefit ratio of government fiscal operations. The strongest relationships found were between the measures of tax protest activity (inversely to the cash measure) and the cost/benefit ratio (positively for the composite measure). Both of these findings appear to argue, despite the conventional rationalization that people must evade to survive, that tax evasion is as much a *political* act as it is an economic act. This finding meshes with the argument of Listhaug and Miller (1985) that taxation is an act of symbolic politics (see also Rose and Peters, 1978; Lowery and Sigelman, 1981). It appears that people become more willing to consider tax evasion if they believe that they are not getting from government what it should be providing. The cost/benefit ratio (albeit measured roughly) is an indication of the direct benefits that government is supplying citizens, and the less favorable that ratio is, the more likely citizens are to seek some means to reduce their obligations to support government.

The finding for the tax protest movements returns us to the logic of Hirschman (1970) and "Exit, Voice and Loyalty." It appears here that in many societies the first two options are substitutes for each other. If tax protest movements are successful in organizing, and if they are successful in reducing taxes, then it seems likely that tax evasion is unnecessary (although direct evidence is lacking for this). Given that evasion is illegal and somewhat difficult and may involve loss of some benefits (e.g. social insurance) that political protest might be a first option. That option may, however, be blocked because of weaknesses in the organizational capacity of a country, or cultural antipathy to visible anti-state political activity, or whatever. In such a case, tax evasion becomes a more viable option as a means of expressing personal discontent without the need to organize others. The meaning may still be the same one of protesting the perceived unfairness of the tax system and of government in general.

There are several other possible explanations for tax evasion that it has not been possible to explore. It may be the result of cultural factors, e.g. the legendary French *incivisme* or the American anti-state mentality. It could, as some have argued, be simply a function of the ease with which it can be done under different tax and accounting systems. What is perhaps the most important finding in this analysis is the strong rejection of a notion that high taxes per se produce tax evasion, or that relative poverty is a major cause. It appears that explanations for tax evasion are to be found in the nature of government rather than the tax or economic systems. Paying taxes is, as much as an economic activity, a political activity that defines a part of the relationship between the citizen and the State. If the citizen does not like the relationship in which he or she exists in relation to the State, then there is a readily available means of expressing that discontent – exit.

Summary

This chapter has explored means through which citizens may remove themselves and their money from the tax system. This can be done legally, through tax avoidance, or it can be done illegally, through tax evasion. Although some commentators see no moral difference between the two, governments do and have chosen to make tax evasion illegal. That illegality has not stopped all citizens from attempting to evade their taxes. Indeed, the available evidence indicates that tax evasion is almost as widespread a crime as speeding on the highways. By most accounts, the public does not regard tax evasion as any more serious a crime than speeding, and has much of the same "catch me if you can" attitude about it as well.

Despite the cavalier attitude of citizens, both tax avoidance and tax evasion are important for governments. One offers an opportunity to accomplish its policy goals while appearing to provide citizens with a real benefit. Tax avoidance for the citizen is a "tax expenditure" for government and a painless, if inefficient, means of taking actions in the economy and society. Here government offers the citizen a benefit, if he or she will only comply with the law. On the other hand, citizens may choose to reject the State and to make their own decisions about receiving benefits. They may choose the highly private benefits derived from evasion to the more public benefits which could be gained through tax avoidance. This is a financial act but, even more fundamentally, it is a political act of rejection and ultimate indifference to the authority of government.

NOTES

1 Businesses do evade the VAT and sales taxes. This is difficult for large enterprises, but reasonably common for small firms.

2 Specifically, respondents were asked about the acceptability of "Cheating on taxes if you have the chance."

7
The Development of Tax Systems

The existing tax systems of the OECD countries did not come into being over night but rather represent a long pattern of development. This policy development has a number of similar characteristics throughout the OECD countries, but there are also several important differences among those countries. It is not possible to do full justice to this complex and important history in this one chapter (see Webber and Wildavsky, 1986; Ardant, 1971; Braun, 1975), but it is crucial to provide some background for understanding developments in tax policy, and what effects earlier tax policy decisions may have had on contemporary tax policies. As was noted above, an existing tax structure may represent a workable mechanism for a government to generate necessary revenue that has arisen over a long period of time. If there is to be any major change from the existing structure, given the political hostility and skepticism that tax changes very frequently generate, then the leaders of government will require a good justification. Thus taxation represents an historical legacy, as well as a set of contemporary decisions, about what constitutes good public policy (Rose and Karran, 1986).

Some of the changes in revenues which will be documented may not, however, be a function of any real changes in policy, but rather a function of changes in the economy that, in turn, generate differential tax yields. If international economic activity increases, and there are even very small levels of tariffs (customs, or import taxes) imposed, then there should be an increase in the yield of those taxes. Likewise, if there is a high excise tax on cigarettes and all citizens suddenly begin to heed the government's warning labels about the dangers of smoking, then the excise tax yield will go down rapidly. Thus, care must be taken to separate out the effects of planned policy change from changes in the yields of existing taxes when the evolution of tax structures are examined over time.

Governments consciously utilize the underlying economic changes for their own purposes, with the most common policy choice of this type having been to allow yields from progressive income taxes to increase with inflation, even though the real income of citizens does not increase as rapidly. Inflation would move citizens into higher marginal tax brackets, even if their real income remained constant. Most governments are not constrained from using this strategy by requirements to index the thresholds of tax brackets and the values of tax allowances, but they implement that indexing as slowly as they can. Economic growth can supply the same tax benefits to governments as does inflation but in that case the real income of workers will increase along with tax revenues.

As we begin to document the evolution of tax structures in the industrialized democracies, it is also important to remember that the possibility of innovation in taxation also may be a function of economic change, and the ability of governments to extract certain types of revenue. Governments tend to want to extract their incomes in cash, although historically governments have accepted tax revenue in grain or other commodities, or even in labor on public projects (Webber and Wildavsky, 1986, 80ff). However, if an economy is not conducted heavily in monetized terms, it is difficult for government to extract cash income. Further, in economies at relatively low levels of development, it may be difficult to identify incomes and expenditures with the ease possible in more developed economies, especially those with well-developed systems of accounting (Radian, 1980). In short, governments can only tax when they can find a "tax handle" that they can pull. Until large-scale personal incomes in cash existed, and monitorable cash transactions were prevalent in the economy, the types of taxes now common in the industrialized world were difficult or impossible to implement.

The Minimalist State and Indirect Taxation

The above discussion leads quickly to an examination of the "traditional" tax structure of the countries of Western Europe and North America. By traditional, I am referring to the tax systems existing at around 1815. By this time the major nation states of Western Europe and North America had already been established (with the exception of Italy, Germany, and Canada) in something like their current forms. The Napoleonic wars had ended, and Europe was beginning to encounter the economic and social changes resulting from the continuation and culmination of the industrial revolution. Also occurring during the next century (up through the First World War and its immediate aftermath) was the gradual democratization of many of these countries, although almost all remained monarchies. These political changes, along with the rapid economic change occurring, were to place substantial pressures on governments to change their financial systems.

Indirect taxes constituted the principal revenue sources at this time for all the countries for which we have information. These sources for central governments during the early nineteenth century were taxes on trade (customs duties or export taxes) and excise taxes. One economic activity which governments had a better chance than most of monitoring was international trade. In addition, this component of the economy was almost certainly conducted in money terms, in contrast to a proportion of the agricultural sector, which was still conducted in kind. Customs duties, therefore, constituted a useful source of income for the governments of the day, and constituted (1815) approximately 15 percent of the revenue for the United Kingdom, 60 percent for the United States, and 20 percent for France. Governments also controlled directly, or taxed, the sale of a number of commodities, and these taxes totaled another 40 percent of revenues to government. Some of these excises have continued until today – especially on alcohol and tobacco – but in most countries any significant taxes on commodities such as salt and matches are things of the past (but see pp. 37–40). For many of the same reasons as today – relatively inelastic demand and relative ease in identifying the transactions – governments chose to rely on taxing the particular goods that they did. Smugglers and "bootleggers" sought to evade the impositions of government, but in most instances governments were able to extract sufficient revenue from international trade and the commodities on which they levied excises.

Governments in the early nineteenth century did extract from their citizens some revenue with direct taxes, mostly on land and other real property. Unlike income, it is virtually impossible to hide land and houses from the tax collector. These assets therefore constituted very valuable tax handles for government even at early stages of economic development. There were, however, at least two difficulties in using property taxes more extensively at this time. The first was economic. Although an individual may own or farm land, or own a house, he or she may have very little cash income. Farming at this time for many of its practitioners was little more than a subsistence activity, so that coming up with cash to pay property taxes might be difficult, with a risk of losing the farm to the sheriff. For this reason, in some instances the (then) more luxurious accoutrements of houses, e.g. windows or chimneys, may have been taxed rather than the house and land itself. The same problem of maintaining homeownership for less affluent citizens exists today – especially for the elderly – with so-called "circuit breakers" and property tax limitations being the solution rather than window taxes.

The second problem was political. Although democracy was beginning to spread its wings at this time, it was initially a property-holding democracy. In almost all countries ownership of some land, or the payment of a substantial rent, was a qualification for voting and holding public office. Therefore, the property owners making the laws were rarely willing to levy taxes on themselves when there were other options such as the indirect taxes mentioned above, or perhaps even a poll tax levied on each adult individual. The typical property tax of the period called for a small rate on property valued at over a certain (usually very large) amount. The property tax was available to government, but was not likely to constitute a major source of income so long as property owners dominated government. Much the same political problem prevented inheritance taxes, the other significant direct tax used at the time, from becoming a more appreciable part of government revenue. The only people likely to receive an inheritance of any consequence were those making the tax laws.

Governments were also beginning to experiment with other sources of revenue. In particular, the British government had used an income tax as a means of financing the Napoleonic wars. The income tax then (beginning in 1799) was very modest (ranging from 0.1 percent to 10 percent of incomes over £60), but was extremely unpopular. It was repealed at the end of the war (1817) and not revived for thirty years. The tax did, however, bring in over 15 percent of the revenue of the British government from 1805 to 1817. Further, this was the beginning of what has become the principal source of revenue for all industrialized democracies. The United States also introduced an income tax to help finance its civil war (on both the Northern and Southern sides); by 1866 it produced almost one-quarter of all Union revenues. That income tax was repealed (1871) and the new income tax passed in 1893 was declared unconstitutional (Pollock v. Farmers' Loan and Trust Co.) and could not be reintroduced until after the passage of the 16th Amendment to the Constitution (1913).[1]

In addition to the central government taxes discussed above, subnational governments also had to find sufficient revenue to operate their own services. These governments generally were a more significant part of the public sector in the early nineteenth century than they are in the late twentieth. This importance was, in part, because government as a whole simply did less and the services usually provided by local government – police and fire protection, street lighting, education, etc. – were fundamental and had to be performed, while the programs commonly associated with national governments – especially social services – were not yet developed (Rose, 1976). Therefore, local government services constituted a larger share of the total activity of the public sector during the era of "Nightwatchman" government. In addition, transportation and communications were not so well developed then as now, so managing a government from the center was somewhat less feasible – although some countries such as France certainly tried (Chapman, 1955). Subnational governments at this time financed their activities through a variety of small taxes, and often relied on a head tax (poll tax) on all adults for a significant portion of their revenue.

In addition to the continuation of old tax instruments, and limited experimentation with new ones, it should also be noted that the nineteenth century was the high-water mark of fiscal orthodoxy for most countries. A balanced budget was generally accepted as the only reasonable way of managing the fiscal household (Savage, 1988; Roseveare, 1969). This orthodoxy was especially evident for the United States and the United Kingdom, with the dominance of the Republicans in the former, and Gladstone and his followers saving candle ends in the latter. These views about taxing and spending were to continue to dominate discussion of fiscal policy for decades, even though the Keynesian "revolution" made the practice of public finance much less conservative.

War, Depression, and the Income Tax

The distribution of taxes among the various categories then available to government did not change dramatically during the nineteenth century. In 1900, the distribution of revenue sources was not significantly different from that observed in 1815, although the amount of customs revenue tended to have increased somewhat relative to other revenue sources. This increase was in large part a function of the rapid expansion of international commerce during this period, as well as of conscious choices by contemporary conservative governments to rely heavily on indirect taxes. These indirect sources remained the foundation for public finance in the countries of Europe and North

America, and were also the principal revenue sources for the (then) new countries of the Antipodes.

Some important policy innovations were, however, being introduced during this time to produce greater direct tax revenues of governments. Although a few countries (France and Belgium in particular) continued to utilize primarily land and inheritance taxes, the other nations in Europe were beginning to use a personal income tax. The date of introduction of the income tax in our "sample" of nations is given in table 7.1. These taxes generally were small, but by 1900 the yield from personal income taxes nearly equalled the yield from inheritance and land taxes in Germany, the Netherlands, and Norway (Alt, 1983). In addition, the Austrian empire introduced a tax on company profits in the 1880s, thus opening up a whole new field for taxation.

Several interesting points concerning the history of taxation in these countries arise from the above discussion. The first is that, early in the development of their fiscal states, it became clear that

Table 7.1 First introduction of the income tax

Country	*Year*
Britain	1799
Switzerland[a]	1840
Austria	1849
United States	1862
Italy	1864
Japan	1887
Germany	1891
New Zealand	1891
Canada[a]	1892
Netherlands	1892
Australia	1895
Sweden	1897
Denmark	1903
Norway	1905
France	1909
Finland	1917
Belgium	1922
Ireland	1922

[a] Initiated at subnational level

France and Italy would find it difficult to implement the income tax successfully. This difficulty has persisted until the present, although in the 1980s the yield from this source has increased substantially in both countries (OECD, annual a). In addition, it is important to note the innovative role of Germany and Austria in tax policy. It may be surprising that these two rather conservative, imperial governments were innovators with the income and corporation taxes. It was, however, because they were not dominated by the commercial classes to the extent that British or American governments were that they were able to impose these direct taxes. Economic development in Austria and Germany was more dependent upon the State than upon individual entrepreneurship, and the commercial interests looked to the State for guidance and for capital (Hall, 1986; Reich, 1990). Those economic interests therefore could not object as effectively to the new taxes on their activities. These innovations in tax policy should not be interpreted as any great desire on the part of the imperial governments of Germany and Austria to redistribute income, just as German innovations in social insurance policy (see below) were by no means a function of a conscious social policy of redistribution. The governments simply needed revenue and these were important new ways to raise it.

If the majority of the nineteenth century was relatively stable in fiscal policy terms, the first three decades of the twentieth constituted a period of great change. At least three factors influenced these rapid and momentous developments in taxation. The first was the spread of political democracy, and the extension of the franchise to larger segments of the population (Maier, 1975). This extension occurred at different rates in European and North American countries, but had profound impacts on politics in all. One of the most important such impacts was the development of socialist and labor parties. Although the existing regimes used a variety of means to attempt to stave off those organizational developments – including the initiation of Welfare State programs in Germany, followed by other European countries (see below) – in most countries there was an active socialist movement of some sort by 1910.

With the extension of the franchise and the birth of labor movements and socialist parties came demands for greater redistribution through the tax system, and particularly for greater use of income and profits taxation to raise the needed revenues for increasingly active governments. So, for example, in the United Kingdom, the Liberal Party introduced a progressive income tax with rates up to 14 percent to finance social programs in their budget of 1909, and provoked a constitutional crisis (Jenkins, 1968). In the United States a progressive coalition was able to pass the 16th amendment to the Constitution permitting a federal income tax (Ratner, 1942; Blakey and Blakey, 1940). Some of the Scandinavian countries had limited income taxes in place from the 1870s but increased their importance and progressivity from 1909 (Verney, 1957). In short, the gradual opening up of the political system to more popular pressures produced the almost inevitable beginnings of a shift in their revenue policies.

This shift was further accelerated by the First World War. In both the number of countries and the expense involved this was by far the largest conflict the world had seen until that time. Governments had to raise massive amounts of money, relative to what they had been used to taxing and spending. For example, the budget of the United Kingdom increased by over 800 percent from 1914 to 1916, and that of Germany increased by over 290 percent during the same period. Even countries not directly involved in the war increased their spending because of the tensions produced by it; Sweden's budget increased by almost 160 percent during the above two-year period, and the Swiss central government increased its spending by almost the same percentage as Sweden. Some of these changes were the product of inflation brought about by the war, but most reflected real increases in expenditures.

The need to raise massive additional revenues for the war effort shifted the burden of taxation onto the income tax. This was a more elastic form of revenue collection than the taxes then in common use, and was capable of extracting much more money than were indirect taxes or land taxes. This more progressive form of taxation may not have been as acceptable to many governments during normal periods, but these were times of national crisis and hence new and expanded revenue sources became perfectly acceptable (Peacock and Wiseman, 1961). In addition, the economies of the European and North American countries were now increasingly organized by large firms paying wages to large numbers of workers, and capable of keeping records of the amounts paid to each. Likewise, they kept their own accounts of profit and loss. The new "tax handle" therefore was available, and it was now perfectly feasible to implement the income tax and catch most workers in its net.

At the end of the First World War the participants, whether winners or losers, reduced their income tax rates; despite this, these taxes were by no means eliminated, and remained the principal sources of revenue for many countries. Other nations, such as Italy and France, however, continued their dependence upon indirect taxes, lacking the ability to collect an income tax of any significance (Tanzi, 1969). Governments also returned their spending almost to their pre-war levels, so that there was not a great deal of demand for new or increased revenue sources. To the extent that there was a need for additional revenue, the economic expansion during the 1920s was able to generate sufficient revenue with constant, or even decreasing, tax rates. The world could not quite return to the *status quo ante bellum*, but in taxing and spending terms it came very close.

This comfortable manner of economic life – personal and governmental – came to an end with the beginning of the Great Depression in the late 1920s. Some warnings of these troubles came in the hyperinflation in Weimar Germany and then in Austria, but by 1929 the economic difficulties had become general. The initial reaction of most governments to the downturn in their economies was to reduce their expenditures and taxes in order to try to return economic activity to its previous level (Stewart, 1971). That traditional remedy for depressions soon proved faulty, and there was a need for an entirely new approach to the role of government in the economy. This new approach was quickly supplied by Keynes in his *General Theory* (Keynes, 1936). As already discussed (see pp. 111–15), the Keynesian approach to economic management was premised upon maintaining effective demand through public expenditure. It countenanced large public sector deficits in times of economic crisis such as the Depression, but also argued for placing more money in the hands of those most likely to spend it – the less affluent members of the society. As a consequence, progressive income taxes were the preferred means of financing governments, even during times of normal economic progress. As well as the practical justification of that being the most likely source of the large amounts of money, heavy reliance on the progressive income tax now also had a theoretical justification.

The final event that pushed governments toward much heavier reliance on the income tax was the Second World War. This conflict surpassed even the First World War in its intensity and its costs. Again, the logical source of financing for it was progressive income tax on individuals and corporations. During the war governments extracted huge volumes of money through the income tax; in 1944 45 percent of total revenues in the United States, 55 percent in Canada, and 43 percent of revenues in the United Kingdom were extracted through this means. In addition, rates of taxation on both individual income and profits increased rapidly to become almost confiscatory. At the highest level of rates, the income tax in the United States took 94 percent of income from individuals, and 40 percent of profits from corporations. Special tax provisions were also introduced to ensure that corporations did not make excessive windfall profits from military contracts. Again, the nationalistic imperatives of a world war broke down any popular resistance there may have been to a large, and highly progressive, income tax.

Subnational governments were also busy developing their own tax structures during the first half of the twentieth century. In federal systems, or unitary systems of government permitting subnational governments some fiscal flexibility, these governments were innovating and increasing their reliance on the income tax, as were national governments. State governments in the United States were adopting income taxes at about the same time, or earlier, as did the federal government (the first was in Wisconsin in 1911). Local governments in Scandinavia were also adopting this form of taxation, and were able to obtain substantial financial independence from central governments. Subnational governments in a number of countries were also experimenting with various forms of general sales and use taxes; this system of taxation grew into the value-added taxes used in almost all industrialized countries in the 1990s. Subnational governments, therefore, have been some of the major innovators in tax policy, although they are nominally constrained by central government in most countries.

In several other countries, however, the central government maintained a strong hold over fiscal matters and confined local government revenues to more traditional sources, such as the property tax or fees for service. Further, some countries such as France and Italy kept local governments dependent upon the central government for almost all revenues so that there was no possibility or need for subnational innovation in revenue collection. The fiscal control eased financial management, as well as ensuring policy uniformity throughout the countries. This period to some degree saw the development of the fiscal constitution which was to prevail in those countries until the decentralization initiatives of the 1980s and 1990s (Keating, 1988).

The revenue system which then emerged in most countries from the crises of two world wars and a major depression was one with a heavy reliance on the personal income tax. Even after the return to "normalcy" after the Korean conflict, most countries continued to depend heavily on the income tax for revenue. As shown in table 7.2, except for some of the Southern European countries already discussed, the personal income tax remains a large, if not the largest, source of revenue for many central governments in 1955. We must remember, however, that in almost all these countries the income tax in practice was not the fully progressive revenue instrument it may have been thought to be. Although the nominal rates proclaimed in the tax laws were generally quite progressive, the presence of numerous "loopholes" and exemptions made the impact of income taxes more proportional across income classes. This greater proportionality may have blunted their social policy impact, but it did make these taxes more widely acceptable politically.

Table 7.2 Income tax as a percentage of total tax, 1955

Country	*Year*
Australia	33
Austria	17
Belgium	20
Canada	18
Denmark	42
Finland	32
France	NA
Germany	19
Greece	NA
Ireland	17
Italy	8
Japan	24
Luxembourg	NA
Netherlands	27
New Zealand	20
Norway	33
Portugal	4
Spain	NA
Sweden	56
Switzerland	28
United Kingdom	23
United States	33

Source: OECD, 1989, table 112

The Social Security System and the Welfare State

The story of the income tax above is important but by no means the only narrative in the development of contemporary tax systems. A second pattern of revenue enhancement occurring during much of the same time period was the development of social insurance programs financed by "contributions" extracted from employees and employers. The concept of social insurance was initiated in Imperial Germany by Bismarck (Köhler, Zacher, and Partington, 1982). As with the income tax, this hardly seems a likely place for a major experiment in social policy, and the motive for the initial programs had little to do with improving the living conditions of the working man and his family. Instead, it was largely to steal the thunder of the nascent socialist and labor movements in Germany. By providing first industrial accidents and sickness insurance, and then a range of other forms of social insurance – pensions, health, and unemployment – these programs provided by a conservative government provided the benefits which a more left-wing political party might use to mobilize workers.

Regardless of the motives for their initiation, social insurance programs began to spread rapidly outside Germany (see table 7.3). Although the program of benefits offered by social insurance in each of these schemes differed, they were almost all financed through social insurance contributions. These were, in effect, taxes paid by the employee and the employer based on the wages of the employee; they were in effect another form of income tax, albeit paid in part by the employer. Further, although these programs and benefits were initially available only to industrial workers and their families, they have gradually been extended to include almost all the working population. Social insurance programs became yet another component of the Keynesian approach to economic management. Their virtue was, in part, their automatic counterbalance to business cycles. If the economy slowed down and workers were laid off, then their contributions to social insurance would also cease, and unemployment insurance payments would begin. Thus, social insurance constituted a self-regulating feature built into the government finance system that tended to produce Keynesian-style economic management automatically. Social insurance would constitute a crucial, and frequently increasing, component of financing for the mixed-economy welfare state that was being developed during the early twentieth century.

Table 7.3 Introduction of social insurance taxation

Country	*Year*
Austria	1887
Belgium	1924
Canada	1927
Denmark	1916
Finland	1895
France	1910
Germany	1883
Ireland	1911
Italy	1898
Netherlands	1901
Norway	1894
Sweden	1916
Switzerland	1911
United Kingdom	1911
United States	1935

A corollary of increased program benefits has been increased costs. The social insurance share of total government revenue has increased significantly since these programs were first introduced. At the turn of the twentieth century, social insurance accounted for an average of only 4 percent of total government revenues in the 11 countries for which we have reliable data. By 1929, this form of taxation (contribution is a polite term for what is in reality a tax) amounted to almost 6 percent of total central government revenue for those countries. By 1952 this figure had increased to almost 14 percent of total revenues, and has continued to increase. These rather significant increases in tax takes indicate the extension of the programs to more and more workers, an increased range of programs (mostly adding unemployment insurance), and increasing benefits from the programs themselves.

As noted, social insurance contributions are in essence just another form of income taxation. They are, however, a form of income tax that is easier for many countries to collect than are the usual form of such taxes. They can be collected through a relatively small number of firms rather than directly from individuals. As a consequence, France, Italy, and Spain have relied on social insurance taxes much more heavily than have the other industrialized countries.

Even for countries such as the United States and Switzerland, with substantial cultural skepticism about the role of government, social insurance contributions are a more acceptable form of government finance than other types of taxes would have been. Social insurance can be presented to the population as "buying" an insurance policy, rather than paying just another tax to government. Most citizens have become sufficiently sophisticated about government to understand that social insurance contributions are really a tax, but its flat-rate and limited amount each year (in many countries) make it more palatable than a higher rate of direct income taxes. Social insurance has the additional virtue (politically if not in terms of social policy) that virtually everyone who is working contributes to the system.

As they have continued to develop, social insurance schemes have begun to move toward the limits of their utility. In the first place, these schemes have begun to reach limits on their ability to be financed through the conventional contribution mechanism. Social insurance contributions have begun to reach very high levels in almost all industrialized countries, and have begun to have effects on employment; if social insurance contributions are sufficiently high it may not be profitable for an employer to hire additional workers, but rather he or she may work the existing employees longer hours (if possible). Almost all countries finance some part of their social insurance program through general taxation, but that source of funds too is coming under substantial pressure (see below) so there appears to be some need to consider options for these programs. In addition, the aging of the populations of all industrialized countries are placing great strains on pension and health programs, again possibly requiring some rethinking of the future directions of the Welfare State.

The income tax and social security taxes developed somewhat in tandem as the two financial pillars of the contemporary mixed-economy Welfare State (Rose and Peters, 1978). Together they have produced massive amounts of revenue for government. They have the political disadvantage, however, of being direct and visible to the taxpayer. This visibility is very obvious for income taxes, but is also true for social insurance contributions. Even if the social insurance contributions are taken out of the paycheck automatically, the worker can see what he or she is contributing. What the employer is contributing to the system may be less visible, but most employees are aware that it is something. Therefore, if government is to be able to maintain its social service levels, it may have to find other means of raising additional revenues, probably through more indirect mechanisms.

Value-Added Taxes and The Return to Indirect Taxation

Governments began their modern existence with a substantial reliance on indirect taxation of goods and services. Taxes were levied mostly on certain commodities (excises) and on goods imported into the country from abroad (customs duties). These forms of revenue collection continue to be used, although they (especially customs) have become a much less significant component of total revenue collection. To those indirect taxes, have been added general taxes on goods and services. These taxes have been in some instances (the American states) a retail sales tax, added as a percentage to the final price of a product, or in others (Canada) a turnover tax on the total volume of business conducted by a firm. The more general form of general consumption tax has become the value-added tax, levied on the difference in market value between inputs and outputs at each stage of production, including the retail stage. The sum of the taxes added at each stage of production is included in the final retail price of the good, although usually not presented as a separate item.

The value-added tax (VAT) was first implemented at the national level in France and Italy, as a revenue source to compensate for the difficulty these countries had in collecting personal and even corporate income taxes. As with social insurance contributions, the VAT depends more on record-keeping by firms than on the compliance of individual taxpayers and, although there are certainly ways to evade it, is more collectable than are individual income taxes. As all European states have required additional revenues, they have begun to use the value-added tax more heavily. This is true even of countries such as Sweden that have usually sought to advance redistributive goals through their tax system. General consumption taxes of this sort accounted for only about 10 percent of total government revenues in Western Europe countries in 1952, but had increased to over 13 percent by 1970, and were almost 14 percent of revenues by 1980. For some countries, general consumption taxes will be almost one-quarter of all revenues. The differing dependence on indirect taxation constitutes a problem for the European Community and the use of similar value-added tax rates is a major component of the EC's tax harmonization schemes (Sandford and Robinson, 1988). Such harmonization is being undertaken because a reasonably common approach to indirect taxation on goods and services is considered essential to fair competition among the member countries.

Reliance on the value-added tax also fits well with the political ideas and programs of the neoconservative governments that came into office in many European and North American countries in the late 1970s and 1980s. Even if the VAT per se is not to be utilized, other forms of indirect taxation of goods and services have been introduced, e.g., the new and controversial Goods and Services Tax in Canada (Canada, 1987a; Cnossen, 1987b). The increased use of general consumption taxes has allowed governments to reduce the income tax, or at least to reduce the progressivity of that tax. Reduced progressivity corresponded with their economic views on the need to stimulate investment as the best means of stimulating the economy. Their "supply-side" approach to economic management was in contrast to the demand-side approach of Keynesianism (Roberts, 1984). In addition to fulfilling the ideological demands of neoconservative governments, this approach to taxation also served a definite political need. Consumption taxation has been a way of reducing the direct tax burden on the more affluent members of society, including members of the upper working class, who had been instrumental in putting those neoconservative governments into office.

In addition to the introduction and growth of VAT, the 1970s and especially the 1980s saw increased use of excise taxes. Taxes on alcohol, tobacco, gasoline, and the like were increased in preference to increasing or maintaining levels of income taxation. In addition to taxing specific products in the economy, governments also began to levy charges for specific services they offered to citizens. This is at once a very direct levy on the individual citizen, and a somewhat indirect means of financing government. Charges in essence allow citizens to make some choices about how much they will contribute to government. This is not the case when the services being charged for are virtual necessities of modern life (garbage collection or water), but is the case when they represent more discretionary goods or services. The greater use of fees and charges, as well as greater use of indirect taxation, has resulted in a somewhat more regressive tax structure in most industrialized countries. This was a reversal of the trends of almost a century documented above, but this shift in revenue policies may represent the limits of progressivity within contemporary political economies. The contemporary concerns about economic growth and creating (or restoring) "enterprise cultures" (especially under the Conservatives in the United Kingdom) make progressive taxation a more difficult policy to advocate successfully (but see Cnossen and Bird, 1990; Musgrave, 1989).

The development of subnational taxation is not a great deal different than that of central government. First, however, it should be said that in many countries during the 1970s and 1980s there was some decentralization of taxation, especially in France, Italy, and Spain, which had been highly centralized for most of their histories. This decentralization came in part through the creation of new regional governments (Keating, 1988), and in part through granting greater financial powers to the existing levels of subnational government. Even in countries that already were substantially decentralized, however, more financial (and policy) powers were granted to subnational governments. This was, in part, a way to make national governments appear smaller to citizens, while continuing to provide the same services that government always had provided. The decentralization was also justified as a means of strengthening local democracy and giving the public more direct control over government. Surprisingly, for all the rhetoric emanating from Whitehall about reducing the role of central government, the Thatcher Government in the United Kingdom was a major exception to this tendency, and decisionmaking about public finance – and public policy more generally – became more centralized during her time in office. The central government mandated a new and controversial tax for local authorities, and then established its own limits ("poll tax capping")on how much those local governments could actually tax their citizens.

Although they may have been greated greater financial responsibility, there was much of the same shift toward indirect taxation among the subnational governments that was found for central governments. During the 1970s subnational governments generally increased their reliance on general and specific (excises) taxes on goods and services, and to a great extent avoided using such direct taxes (often property) as local governments could employ. This tendency toward indirect taxation was perhaps especially noticeable in the United States. The adoption of Proposition 13 and other similar mechanisms of reducing state and local property taxes meant that these governments had to find new and less visible sources of revenue. In addition to indirect taxation, subnational governments in the United States and elsewhere have introduced a number of charges and fees for their services. These levels of government often were in a better position to utilize this revenue source than were central governments, given that many local government programs were services which could be marketed readily; refuse collection, recreation, and even fire protection (Savas, 1987; Ahlbrandt, 1973). In some instances these public services were, in fact, fully privatized and subsequently have been marketed to citizens through the private sector. Subnational governments also had traditionally marketed more services than had central governments, so the changes in service provision were not as noticeable to citizens, and in general provoked few serious political reactions.

The 1970s and 1980s did not represent a complete swing away from principles of progressivity and equity in taxation. The most important events attempting to maintain some sense of equity were the numerous reforms of the income tax systems of the OECD world (Cnossen and Bird, 1990). On the one hand, these reforms almost always involved a reduction of at least the highest marginal rates of taxation, a reduction of the number of tax brackets, and making the income tax function more like a flat-rate, proportional tax. On the other hand, the reforms almost all involved closing a number of the "loopholes" in the existing tax system, so that there were not as many special preferences through which the more affluent often were able to reduce their actual tax obligations. The tax reforms of the 1980s also tended to retain the tax preferences that benefited the broad segments of the population, e.g. mortgage interest deductibility for first homes. The general effect, therefore, was to make the tax system more transparent, to broaden the base on which taxes were charged, and to make the effective tax rates correspond more closely to the apparent rates. Contemporary tax reform, is, however, a sufficiently important political story, and a sufficient shift away from tax politics as usually practiced, to warrant its own chapter, which follows.

When is a Tax Not a Tax?

So far we have been discussing taxes in their primary role, as the principal means of financing the public sector. Taxes have many other uses as well. We have discussed these to some extent in chapter 6, but should talk about the non-revenue uses of taxation from a more historical perspective here. Almost from the beginning of government, by choosing not to tax certain things, governments have been providing support for certain activities through the tax system. Likewise, very early on governments found that they had the option of taxing some things out of existence. In general, however, the extensive use of taxes for non-revenue purposes is more a feature of the twentieth century. During this century, however, the use of taxes for other purposes has undergone several shifts of fashion. Even in the 1990s there are two seemingly contradictory trends in the use of taxes for non-revenue purposes.

The period following the Second World War was in many ways the heyday of the non-revenue uses of tax policy. The very high income tax rates imposed during the war were being reduced, but it was found that their real impact could be lessened, and political support from powerful interests gained, by doing so selectively as well as across the board. There was sufficient revenue being raised, especially with the rapid economic growth during that time combined with the reduction of military spending obligations, to permit governments to grant numerous tax concessions without harming themselves financially. Indeed, politically governments were able to help themselves substantially by supporting important personal (mortgage interest relief) as well as business interests (Research & Development allowances) through the tax system. Relatively soon after their adoption critics of these preferences began to question their desirability (Surrey, 1957), but these critics were swept away by the general stampede of interests to secure special tax treatment for their own favorite projects.

The period of the 1980s produced two countervailing trends in the use of taxes for non-revenue purposes. On the one hand, the movement toward tax reform has involved the termination of a number of benefits that previously had been granted through the tax codes, and the implementation of something approaching clear, concise, and fair income tax laws. Certainly some tax concessions were retained, and even a few new ones added in the course of writing the reform legislation, but the general effect of reform has been to reduce the loss of revenue from special privileges. On the other hand, the desire of many conservative governments to implement public policies without the use of direct public expenditure has meant that a number of proposals were advanced for using tax benefits, or tax punishments, as incentives for individuals and firms to do certain things. Further, because these tax provisions were labeled "incentives" they did not have the negative ring to conservative ears that regulations would have had. Non-conservatives have also joined this bandwagon, proposing things such as a "carbon tax" to promote more efficient energy use and less pollution. These two seemingly contradictory trends have been somewhat compatible because the new tax incentives have often been conceptualized as stand-alone programs, rather than as components of the personal or corporate income tax laws.

The Development of Tax Policy

This chapter has demonstrated, very briefly, some of the development of tax policy in industrialized democracies from the early nineteenth century onward. Although each country could, and should, have separate discussions of its own developments, the general patterns outlined here hold true for most (Webber and Wildavsky, 1986). In general, there had been a movement toward direct taxes on income and profits and away from taxation on goods and services during most of the twentieth century. Of course, the policy changes adopted during the 1980s run counter to this general pattern, but do appear to represent only a correction in that general trend rather than a fundamental shift in governmental priorities. Direct taxes continue to account for, by far, the greatest amount of tax revenue, and appear likely to continue to do so. The mixture of direct taxes varies among countries, with some placing greater emphasis on income taxes and others placing more reliance on social insurance contributions, but these two sources together do provide the bulk of government revenues.

Associated with the continuing reliance of OECD governments on direct taxation is the fact that all these governments remain "big governments." This means that they will have a continuing need for very large sums of income to finance the programs which citizens have come to expect. Thus, these governments will have a continuing need to search for new and better revenue sources. Fees and charges have been one popular and expanding source over the past decade; governments have always charged for some things, but the extent of possible charges has now become more evident. (Tarschys, 1988) In addition, pressure from fiscal conservatives to make governments more businesslike has led to their charging the true cost of producing the goods and services provided to citizens rather than nominal fees to deter excessive consumption. Likewise, the reforms of income and corporate taxation to be discussed in greater detail below represent an approach to making an old tax more palatable to the public, and perhaps in the long-run being able to generate additional revenue with it. What is certain about all these changes is that governments will continue to need revenues, and will, as they always will, attempt to get them any way that is economically feasible and politically acceptable.

NOTES

1 The Constitution required that direct taxes be apportioned among the states according to population. During the Civil War the Supreme Court upheld the income tax as not being a direct tax, but the Court during the conservative Republic era decided that it was a direct tax and therefore could be legal only if it were divided among states by population, not income.

8
Implementing Tax Policy

After tax policies have been made by legislatures and political executives, they must be implemented. Unless there is some mechanism for forcing action, there is a chance that nothing would happen with the laws, as indeed some small "nuisance" taxes are never enforced. Organizations within the public bureaucracy are given the primary responsibility for the task of implementing laws. These are often the same organizations who have been instrumental in providing policy advice for government during the tax legislative process. The implementation of tax law is not performed by these official organizations alone, however, and depends upon the cooperation of individuals and organizations in the private sector. Without private cooperation – mandated by law though it may be – the implementation of tax laws would be impossible, or extremely expensive.

The implementation process really has two distinct, albeit closely linked, elements. One element is deciding what the tax laws passed by the legislature are really to mean in practice; those laws are rarely sufficiently comprehensive to cover all eventualities and require substantial interpretation to match cases. The second aspect of implementation is enforcing the tax decisions reached by government in the individual cases, and identifying and collecting as much of the revenue owed to government as possible. Although components of the same implementation process, these two elements require the civil servants involved to exercise somewhat different skills. On the one hand, the civil servant must operate in almost a judicial manner deciding what the laws really mean, while on the other hand he or she must be a bloodhound, tracking the errant citizen to earth and extracting the money rightfully owed to government.

Policy Through Implementation

The process of implementing tax law, or any other type of public policy, is very difficult. Often the policy outcomes actually produced are very different from those intended by the politicans and administrators who conceived the legislation, and at other times nothing at all happens (Pressman and Wildavsky, 1973). In implementing tax policy it is rare that nothing happens, because governments do have the legal right to extract money and can enforce compliance. Revenue agencies have few qualms about seizing property, or seizing paychecks in order to obtain their legal due. Further, governments have a pressing need for the tax money to be collected and place substantial, and increasing, emphasis on prompt implementation of tax laws. Likewise, most citizens are not anxious to have difficulties with tax officials, and are willing to comply. The question is, however, comply with what?

A good deal of the meaning of tax legislation is determined as it is being implemented. The economic circumstances in which individuals and firms in modern societies may find themselves, or more often put themselves, are extremely varied. There are so many possible cases and exceptions to any general principles that it would be foolish for lawmakers to attempt to cover all the possible eventualities in a tax law. As it stands now, tax legislation, even that designed to simplify the system, is among the bulkiest legislation enacted by government. As one tax practitioner in the United Kingdom put it:

> United Kingdom tax law is Byzantine in its complexity: the basic legislation now comprises more than one million words, and reports of the relevant court judgments fill more than 50 volumes. Yet it still does not cater for every situation which may arise, and the authorities have long been conscious that a strict application of the law may sometimes cause unreasonable hardship and unfairness. (Owen, 1985, 247)

Instead of ramifying the formal legislation in an attempt to anticipate all possible cases, tax law tends to leave a great deal of latitude for interpretation by the bureaucracies charged with implementing the law. These bureaucracies confront the varied individual cases, and attempt to apply the law to those cases in ways not incompatible with the intentions of the writers of the laws. Some have argued that in so doing they may even overturn the intentions of those who framed the legislation (Owen, 1985).

As they implement the tax law, tax administrators are ramifying the law in at least two ways. First, they may issue regulations (secondary legislation) stating what they believe the law should be in particular types of cases (Levi, 1988; Bergwik, 1985). Citizens, and their tax advisors, can then use these statements as guides for determining their own tax liabilities. This is a major activity of most tax agencies and hundreds or even thousands of such statements, which have the force of law unless and until challenged, are promulgated every year by every tax agency. These decisions often must be specific for the situation of an individual taxpayer: in Canada there were separate rulings for 22,000 of the 60,000 companies paying manufacturers sales tax (Kay and King, 1986). The revenue collection agencies must be especially active in making rulings when, as during the 1980s in many OECD countries, there are comprehensive changes in the tax law. These changes require that a new body of interpretations be generated. Some of the old interpretations may still be valid, e.g. on matters such as what constitutes income (but see chapter 9), but other interpretations will have to be considered anew and perhaps revised totally in light of the new law.

The second way in which the tax administrations are involved in the creation of a body of legal rulings usable for enforcing tax legislation is by taking to court citizens whom they believe are operating outside the intentions of the tax laws, but whose real liabilities require a legal interpretation. Most tax agencies, and most citizens, will attempt to resolve their disagreements without taking such a drastic step, but sometimes there is no other recourse. In addition, a court case can establish a legal principle beyond any subsequent doubt, so that the tax agency may welcome such a determination (especially if they win their case). Finally, the revenue agencies may want to initiate a few court cases just to remind citizens that this extreme option does exist. Almost all countries have specialized courts for deciding tax issues, although many permit appeal into the regular (civil or administrative) courts. Even in law countries using a codified legal framework (such as France and Italy), judicial rulings on tax controversies amount to an important corpus of case (judge-made) law that defines the operational meanings of the tax statutes. Citizens too may appeal against rulings from the tax officials of their country, and sometimes win. The interaction of the two logics – that of the public and that of government – will define what the tax law actually means.

Even beyond the development of the formal rulings and case law about taxation, the actual meeting of taxpayer and tax official will determine what the law, in practice, is for that individual. HM Inspectors of Tax, or IRS agents, or officers from the Tax Board in Sweden are in many ways "street level bureaucrats" (Lipsky, 1980). They meet face to face with their clients to determine the individual details of a case; some commentators have noted the importance of the style of those interactions in determining outcomes (Grunow, Hagner, and Kaufmann, 1978). They then make a finding about the obligations of the citizen, just as they might determine the obligations of government to the citizen if they were civil servants working in a social service agency. In making these determinations of liabilities, the tax official has substantial latitude to enforce the law with the degree of stringency that he or she deems appropriate for the case. The same amount of unpaid tax might produce a gentle reprimand for a well-intentioned elderly person, or a stiff fine for a confrontational and ostentatiously attired younger person. The tax official has the ability to make, or at least recommend, such differences in treatment even if the law relevant to the two cases may be exactly the same. In general, however, tax officials tend to be rather strict in almost all cases, *pour encourager les autres*.

Countries do vary, however, in the extent to which they are willing and able to use the courts to promote compliance with tax laws. German tax authorities, for example, convict approximately 6,000 people a year for tax evasion, while Britain only convicts a few hundred (Grunow, Hagner, and Kaufmann, 1978; Board of Inland Revnue, annual). With a much larger population of taxpayers, the United States pursues about 40,000 thousand tax evaders each year (Internal Revenue Service, annual). The French system of negotiated taxes can eliminate most evasion cases, although even then some do arise. There is some evidence that British tax officials tend to give taxpayers the benefit of the doubt to an extent not likely to encourage strict legal compliance (Cook, 1989). In Switzerland, however, tax evasion is not strictly a crime, so that only civil penalties (interest and penalty payments) can be applied.

The above has been written from the perspective of an organization and its officials responsible for enforcing the income tax and similar types of tax laws affecting individual citizens, but much the same latitude might be available to officials enforcing customs, the value-added tax, or other types of tax laws. Customs agents would almost certainly show little mercy for a drug smuggler, but might for a tourist bringing an extra bottle of something or the other back from a Caribbean vacation. VAT officials would be more lenient on record-keeping requirements for a small family-run grocery store than they would be for a large chain store, and may even assist that small firm to meet its obligations under the law. Administration and implementation almost inevitably involve exercising discretion and the implementation of tax law is not that different from the implementation of other laws.

A final point which should be made concerning secondary legislation about tax policy and the making of tax laws through administration is that an increasing amount of tax law is being made through international agreements. These agreements may be negotiated by the diplomatic services of the countries involved, or by the tax officials themselves. As has been discussed above, international agreements mandating withholding tax on interest from bank accounts, and reporting this type of income, as well as reporting other earnings of overseas nationals to their home governments, is an increasingly important component of the fight against tax evasion for many countries (*European Taxation*, 1988). As economies have become increasingly internationalized, there is a greater need for these types of trans-national administrative arrangements, and a reading of a publication such as *European Taxation* will demonstrate that it is a flourishing source of new national tax regulations. The most extreme example, of course, is that tax policy is now being made in Brussels for the twelve members of the European Community (Pearson and Smith, 1988; Cnossen, 1987a).

Making Decisions Stick

The second part of the implementation process is ensuring that the policy decisions reached within the legislature and the bureaucracy are actually obeyed by the public. Although in principle law-abiding, citizens have every incentive to minimize their tax obligations, and have a number of ways of achieving that goal legally (see chapter 6). The job of the tax administrators, therefore, is to determine just what the citizens' legal obligations are, and to ensure that they (whether as individuals or representatives of organizations) meet those obligations. This is a difficult task, especially given the complexity of contemporary financial arrangements, and involves a variety of different administrative activities if implementation is to be successful.

To meet the need for advice and implementation, the tax collecting organizations of government have grown substantially. Table 8.1 shows the number of people employed by government to perform this function in 1960 and in the late 1980s. In almost all cases there has been a substantial increase in the number of employees, and even in the number of employees relative to the number of taxpayers. This has been true even though automation and computerization may have been thought to make the work of tax collection less labor intensive. It appears that instead of being an easier task, the pressures on government arising from fiscal stresses of various sorts have led them to employ more staff to collect as much additional revenue as possible. For example, each additional IRS auditor is estimated to bring in an additional $800,000 in tax revenue a year (Internal Revenue Service, annual; Steurle, 1986), and a German tax inspector can be expected to produce about 1 million marks (*European Taxation*, 1988). Phrased another way, a tax examination in the US on average yields 450 percent of its cost for individuals taxpayers and almost 400 percent of its costs for business taxpayers. In addition, the increasing complexity of modern financial arrangements, the globalization of economies, and the creativity of taxpayers and their accountants makes the work of the tax inspector that much more difficult, and more inspectors are needed to maintain the impression that the dishonest taxpayer will be caught.

Table 8.1 also shows that the number of employees per capita varies a great deal among the countries for which we have data. The United Kingdom, for example, employs over three times as many tax agents per capita as does the United States, and almost twice as many as Sweden or Canada (Kay and King, 1986, 54). France and Germany employ several times as many tax collectors per capita as

Table 8.1 Employees of tax collecting agencies per 1,000 population[a]

	Early 1960s	*1987*
Canada	5.5	6.7
France	2.8	2.5
Germany	2.1	2.6
Italy	1.2	1.4
Norway	1.9	2.1
Sweden	0.5	0.8
United Kingdom	1.1	1.3
United States	0.3	0.4

Sources: Rose *et al.*, 1985; national data sources

does the United Kingdom. This variation appears to be in part a function of the complexity of the tax systems in question, as well as of the degree of self-assessment permitted. Some countries have retained very complex income tax systems, such as the somewhat antiquated schedular system still used in part in Portugal (Caballero, 1986). This system charges a different tax rate on different types of income (wages, agricultural income, etc.), and requires much more administrative work than would a more unified conception of income. Tax reform has tended to make tax systems in most countries simpler, but some countries continue to use their old "bewildering" systems (Graham, 1990).

We should also note that the data in table 8.1 refer primarily to national level tax collection agencies. These countries differ in the extent to which they permit autonomous subnational taxation. That is to some extent a measure of complexity, and it would affect the apparent size of the tax administrations. For example, in Switzerland, the cantonal and local governments are as significant if not more significant than the federal government in tax collection, so that using national figures only to some extent would distort the findings. Also, in the United States, subnational governments have several times as many people employed in tax administration as does the federal government.

In addition to different levels of complexity, some countries, such as the United States, Canada, and Japan, require many of their citizens to assess their own taxes (table 8.2). The citizen reports his or her own income, exemptions, and deductions, and then tells government how much tax should be paid. Self-assessment saves government a great deal of manpower and record-keeping expense. In the majority of cases the amount of tax the citizen believes he or she owes is correct, or sufficiently correct, and that is the end of the matter. Of course, in some cases (through error or intention) the citizen arrives at an incorrect tax liability. If the error is simple mathematics, the computer check run on each return will catch that, and the Internal Revenue Service (if it is the United States) will either demand more money, or perhaps send the citizen a refund.

If the error appears to be more than just mathematics, the citizen will be asked to explain how he or she came up with the figures they did. This may be done through written correspondence or, if the case is more serious or the written communication did not clarify it, the taxpayer may be asked to come to the IRS office, and bring all the relevant records. In addition, each year the Internal Revenue Service audits approximately 3 percent of all tax returns. Some are

Table 8.2 Administrative aspects of the tax system

	Annual returns	*Self-assessment*	*Salaries*	*Withholding of interest*	*Tax Dividends*
Australia	yes	no	yes	no	no
Austria	no	no	yes	no	yes
Belgium	yes	no	yes	yes	yes
Canada	yes	yes	yes	no	no
Denmark	yes	no	yes	no	yes
Finland	yes	no	yes	yes	yes
France	yes	no	no	no	no
Germany	yes	no	yes	no	yes
Greece	yes	no	yes	yes	yes
Ireland	no	no	yes	yes	no
Italy	yes	yes	yes	yes	yes
Japan	yes	yes	yes	yes	yes
Luxembourg	yes	no	NA	NA	NA
Netherlands	yes	no	yes	no	yes
New Zealand	yes	no	yes	no	no
Norway	yes	no	yes	yes	no
Portugal	yes	no	yes	yes	yes
Spain	yes	yes	yes	yes	yes
Sweden	yes	no	yes	no	no
Switzerland	yes	no	no	yes	yes
United Kingdom	no	no	yes	yes	no
United States	yes	yes	yes	no	no

Source: OECD, 1990

picked purely at random, but most are selected because they fall outside a computer profile of "normal" returns (Internal Revenue Service, 1986). A surgeon who reports only $30,000 income may be asked to visit the local IRS office, just as might the college professor who claims $25,000 in charitable deductions. In the audit the taxpayer will be asked to present evidence of deductions claimed, and might be questioned about other sources of income.

Self-assessment removes some of the costs of administering taxes from government. Tax administration costs over three times as much in the United Kingdom as in the United States relative to revenue yield, and over 50 percent more in the United Kingdom than in Canada or Japan (National Tax Administration (Japan), 1988). Self-assessment, however, imposes those burdens on the individual citizens. For example, in the instructions for Form 1040 (the basic income tax form for individuals in the United States) the Internal Revenue Service was required to inform all American taxpayers that on average, self-assessment should require them to spend the following amount of time for the 1990 tax year:

Activities	Hours
Record-keeping	3.1
Learning about the form	2.5
Completing the forms	3.2
Copying, mailing, etc.	0.6
Total	9.4

This amount of time is required for completing the forms after the 1986 tax reform, which was supposed to simplify the tax system. An earlier estimate was that the average taxpayer spent 21.7 hours on the federal income tax (Slemrod and Sorum, 1984). Citizens with less complicated tax returns, and who can use the "short forms" (either Form 1040A or 1040EZ), would spend substantially less time complying with federal tax laws. After finishing the federal forms, most taxpayers would still have to fill out their state income tax forms, and some a local income tax form as well.

Although the amount of time required for each individual to complete the income tax form does not appear to be so great, it is substantial when it is added up over the 109 million individual tax returns filed in the United States each year. This is then some 1.02 billion hours of work Americans are doing just to be able to pay their taxes; even at the current minimum wage of $4.35 per hour, this is some $4.4 billion worth of labor carried out on behalf of the government. Of course, this labor undertaken by individuals should have the advantage of accuracy; who should know better than the individual how much money he or she earned during the year, and in particular how many deductions and exemptions are owed to him or her. This approach to tax collection then places the principal burden on the individual, who should have a personal interest in getting the answers correct, and who knows all the details of his or her particular claims. Self-assessment for taxes also fits well into American political culture, which stresses the role of the individual as to some degree the adversary of the State, especially to the State when it is operating as tax collector.

Interestingly, however, the tendency is now for governments to move away from self-assessment and individual tax filings. Sweden has instituted a system whereby people with lower incomes do not have to fill out a return. The Netherlands is in the process of combining income and social insurance contributions (levied progressively in that country) and eliminating the need for most citizens to fill out any tax forms. Even the United States is considering determining the income tax of many lower-income people by the IRS in conjunction with the employer. The move away from self-assessment is to some degree a function of tax reform (see chapter 9) and the elimination of many special treatments of income and expenditure. In addition, computers and electronic data banks have made it easier for governments to keep track of all sources of income for most citizens. There are simply now fewer details that an individual is able to include on the return that the tax agencies would not know already.

The ability of governments to uncover information about the economic affairs of taxpayers is substantial and growing. A number of governments permit their tax inspectors to use information such as the nature of the house lived in by the taxpayer, or his or her automobile, to make estimates of the real income of the individual. This information can be acted on regardless of the declared income of the citizen. Because of the tradition of income tax evasion in France, tax officials have long used the *forfait* system, with the level of tax negotiated between the tax office and the citizen (Heidenheimer, Heclo, and Adams, 1989, 187). Greece, also beset with high and increasing rates of evasion, has given its tax inspectors the right to utilize external evidence to determine real incomes (Stathopoulos, 1982). As evasion becomes more accepted and possibly easier (see chapter 6), governments may have to rely increasingly on external evidence to determine the true incomes of their citizens. This is the case, even with all the requirements for businesses, banks, and other financial operators to report income and withhold taxes (table 8.2).

Tax Advice

Of course, not all individuals fill out their own forms, and a large and thriving business of tax advice exists in the United States, Canada, and even in countries which do not employ self-assessment. The sources of advice available to citizens range from very expensive tax lawyers and accountants to simple store-front offices offering advice, or filling out the forms, for anyone who walks in off the street. The fee for the latter may be as little as $25, but for an individual who does not understand the forms required this down-market service is crucial. Also, these tax advice firms advertise – often correctly – that they are able to save the individual taxpayer money through advising them how to claim all legal deductions. In addition to professionals, a number of voluntary organizations have begun to offer tax advice to citizens – especially the elderly and the poor – who do not have the money to employ advisors, but who still confront the forms required to pay income taxes.

Table 8.3 provides some estimates on the magnitude of the tax advice business in the United States. These figures do not include the voluntary services offered to the less affluent, but only the commercial services. The figures in this table are enumerations of the number of people offering tax advice, and probably slightly overstate the actual amount of personnel time spent in the tax advice business. Many of the lawyers and accountants enumerated in the table are full-time tax advisors, but only spend a part of their professional time doing that type of work. They were sufficiently involved in tax work, however, to join one of the several national associations of professional tax advisors. Likewise, the employees of the store-front advisory firms in the US and Canada, the most widely known of which is H&R Block, are usually seasonal employees, working from late December, when the tax forms are mailed out to the public, until April 15, when they are due. Even if somewhat overstated in this table, the amount of time and money being spent on tax advice is substantial, and represents a cost of compliance imposed on taxpayers by government. One estimate is that 40 percent of American and Canadian taxpayers find it necessary, or profitable, to have someone else prepare their taxes.

Table 8.3 Estimates of tax advisors in the United States

1970	120,000
1980	280,000
1990	325,000

Sources: Gale Research Co., annual; personal communications to author

The use of tax advisors has an important impact on the compliance of taxpayers (Long and Caudill, 1987). One study (Klepper and Nagin, 1989) in the United States demonstrates that using professional preparers tends to ensure compliance with clear provisions of the tax law. The preparers, however, know which sections of the tax law are ambiguous and attempt to use those provisions aggressively to benefit their clients. Thus, there is much less error or cheating on the simple and clear portions of the tax law, but government may lose revenue through the more controversial portions of the tax code. Even when they do enforce the tax code with their clients, the professional preparers also advise their clients on enforcement priorities of government so that clients may minimize their risks of confrontation with the Internal Revenue Service.

In the United States, the Internal Revenue Service has been indirectly promoting the tax advice business. Beginning with the 1989 tax year, citizens could submit their tax forms electronically if they were due a refund; those owing money still had to file the paper work (and send the check). This electronic filing could only be done, however, through an approved tax advice service such as H&R Block. For a $25 or $35 fee, the citizen could have the form completed (if it were simple), and have it whisked away electronically for immediate action at the IRS. This service ensured that taxpayers received their refund checks at least several weeks earlier than if they had filed the paper forms themselves. The widespread availability of personal computers with links to data networks may make electronic filing available for all citizens before very long.

Taxpayers need not, however, go to the private sector for their tax advice. At least in the United States, they can go directly to the Internal Revenue Service itself. The IRS operates a free service, by telephone or in person, offering advice and assistance to the public; if the taxpayer brings in the information the IRS will even fill out the forms directly. Most taxpayers do not, however, choose to request their tax assistance from the IRS, and certainly not to the extent of having them fill out the forms. They appear to believe that the IRS will look out for the government first and for the individual taxpayer second. This perception may be correct to the extent that IRS employees may tend to be less adventurous in the types of deductions they are willing to include on the forms than would professional preparers or even citizens themselves who understand something of the tax code.

In addition to being assumed to be on the government's side, the IRS tax advisors received a great deal of bad publicity during the spring of 1989. Random telephone calls by staff of the General Accounting Office to the IRS service produced a wide variety of responses to the same tax questions, more than half of the answers being incorrect (USGAO, 1989). A repeat of this experiment in the spring of 1990 showed a significant improvement in the advice offered, but there was still a significant amount of incorrect advice offered by IRS employees (USGAO, 1990). It is not clear, however, whether private tax advisors are any more accurate, although many do guarantee their work and promise to pay any penalty and interest resulting from incorrect work on their part. The IRS itself does not make any such guarantees about its accuracy.

Business Compliance

It is not just individual taxpayers, however, who must comply with tax laws. Businesses have even greater concerns about compliance, given that they have to pay taxes on their profits, their payrolls (social insurance), their property, and on the value added by their manufacturing activities or their retail sales. Each of these objects of revenue collection involves different tax laws, and perhaps even different collecting agencies from several different levels of government. Each tax will require its own separate form(s), and have its own definitions of terms, so that the typical business firm is faced with a substantial degree of record-keeping and other paperwork just to keep itself on the right side of tax law. Larger firms can afford to have tax advisors on their staffs, but smaller businesses confront many of the same compliance problems faced by individuals in obtaining accurate and timely tax advice.

As if that were not enough, in addition to being responsible for their own taxes, businesses are responsible for collecting certain taxes owed by their employees. Governments long ago dropped the practice of "tax farming," or giving the right to collect taxes to an individual contractor in exchange for a percentage of the receipts, but they do still depend upon other people and organizations to collect taxes for them. Most OECD countries now require business firms to retain the estimated income taxes owed by employees, and to turn that money over to government directly (table 8.2). These requirements, referred to as "tax withholding" or "Pay As You Earn" (PAYE), have been a major help to government in collecting the income tax; an informal Japanese estimate is that 90 percent of income of those with taxes withheld is caught in the tax net, but only 60 percent for the self-employed and 40 percent for farmers (Ishi, 1989, 80).

Withholding taxes does, however, impose costs on businesses. The businesses must find out what exemptions and deductions are claimed by each employee, compute the tax owed, and then pay it to the appropriate agency in government. Similarly, firms are expected to collect their employees' contributions to social insurance programs and to submit that money along with their own share of the contributions to the proper authorities (often different from the authority to which they submit withholding receipts). Finally, the businesses are required to report all this information to the employee so that he or she knows what taxes they have paid, especially in countries with self-assessment for income tax.

In some cases, firms are required to report to government the income of people who are not their employees. This is most obviously the case for banks, who must report to government the interest income earned by their depositors. In a few countries, banks must not only report the income earned by their depositors, but must withhold a portion of that income as tax for government, just as other firms must do for their employees. This information collection would be sufficiently complicated within a single country, but with the increasing financial integration of Western Europe, tax withholding is now being undertaken for governments other than the one of the country in which the bank is located (*Accountancy*, April, 1989). Governments have become willing to impose substantial administrative costs on private firms to ensure that they receive the revenue due to them, and they have the power to make those impositions effective.

The Costs of Compliance

There are a number of estimates (Vaillancourt, 1989) of the cost incurred by businesses and individuals in complying with tax law. The costs vary significantly depending upon the country and upon the particular tax involved. Both businesses and individuals have been found to be required to invest a considerable amount of time and energy in complying with the tax laws passed by their governments. These costs are especially high for the self-employed and for small businesses, but even the average employee will have to spend some time in most countries complying with tax laws unless he or she is in one of the few countries in which almost all the work is performed by government. In that case, however, the taxpayer will often wonder if he or she is being treated fairly.

One of the more thorough and interesting estimates of the cost of taxation was developed by Cedric Sandford and his colleagues at the Centre for Fiscal Studies of Bath University in the United Kingdom. Sandford and his colleagues (1989b) have estimaed the costs of compliance with all types of United Kingdom taxes, including personal taxes, but placed special emphasis on business taxes. A summary of their findings is presented in table 8.4. First, this research found that, in total, it cost almost £5 billion for governments at all levels in the United Kingdom to collect their taxes. Of that total, less than one-third was the direct cost to government, and over two-thirds was the costs imposed on individuals and firms by the tax laws. This finding is for a country that does not utilize self-assessment for individual income taxes, so that in other countries the costs of taxpayers would almost certainly be higher.

In addition to the total costs of compliance, different taxes were found to be more or less efficient to collect. In the United Kingdom, the value-added tax was the least efficient, with operating costs of

Table 8.4 Operating costs of taxes in the United Kingdom, 1986–1987 (million £)[a]

	Revenue	*Administrative costs*	*Compliance costs*	*Operating costs*	*Operating costs as % of revenue*
Income tax and national insurance	65,000	946	2,104	3,050	4.70
VAT	21,400	220	791	1,011	4.72
Corporation tax	13,500	70	300	370	2.74
Petroleum tax	1,200	1	5	6	0.56
Excise duties	16,500	42	33	75	0.45
Other	4,600	39	68	107	2.33
Total central government	122,200	1,318	3,301	4,620	3.78
Local rates	15,500	236	58	294	1.89
Total taxes	137,700	1,554	3,359	4,914	3.59

[a] Slight inconsistencies in some totals are the effect of rounding.
Source: Sandford, 1989b

almost 5 percent of the value of the tax collected. Excise duties, on the other hand, had operating costs equal to less than one-half of 1 percent of their revenue. Excise taxes were, however, the only central government tax for which the government's share of total collection costs were greater than the compliance costs of individuals and firms. The difference between direct government administrative costs and compliance costs varied substantially among taxes. The corporation tax, for example, had compliance costs for firms more than four times as great as direct administrative costs for government, with the VAT having almost the same imbalance. Local rates (now a thing of the past except for business), cost four times as much for government to collect as it did for citizens and businesses to comply.

Sandford does note, however, that the balance sheet for compliance with tax laws by firms is not all debits. Firms have experienced some benefits as a result of acting as agents for government in collecting revenue. One of the major benefits is that collecting tax revenues can ease cash flow problems for a firm. VAT receipts are paid to government only once every three months, so that on average the firm is holding 1.5 months of tax receipts. The firm is able to collect interest (or defer borrowing costs) with these funds. The VAT money represents something approaching an interest free loan for the business. Similarly, the payroll taxes a firm collects are retained for some time, so that the firm has use of those funds. Finally, the VAT was argued by some respondents to Sandford's surveys to force firms to keep better inventory records, and use better accounting techniques in general. These may be, however, relatively minor credits when compared with the major expenses of compliance with tax laws.

The costs of such compliance do not impact all firms of all individuals equally; in general, however, this aspect of the tax system is regressive. Sandford (1989b, 141) found, for example, that tax compliance costs amounted to 3.36 percent of the taxable turnover from small firms, but only 0.17 percent for large firms. Much of the bookkeeping required is the same regardless of the size of the firm, and larger firms can spread these overhead expenses over a larger volume of business and keep their costs down, while for small firms accounting may amount to a major expense. Similarly, more affluent individuals can afford the expensive tax advice that can save them a great deal on their tax bills, while the average citizen must be content with less skilled advice, or no help at all. Tax reform may yet make extensive tax advice somewhat less necessary, and working- and middle-class people appear to have fared reasonably from tax preferences that have been available under the unreformed system.

For example, in 1986 almost one-third of all deductions for mortgage interest, and almost one-quarter of all deductions against the personal income tax in the United States, went to taxpayers with incomes under $30,000 (Internal Revenue Service, 1988). Still, they might have done even better with access to more and better advice.

Administering Local Taxes

The above discussion has concentrated on administrative questions for national income taxes, such as the income tax and the value-added tax. Subnational governments may encounter many of the same problems discussed there when they impose the same types of taxes. Almost all states (44 of 50) in the United States, along with many local governments, impose their own income tax. The same is true of subnational governments in Scandinavia, Switzerland, Germany, and several other countries. Officials at this level of government have the same difficulties as do national governments in identifying income, identifying employers, and calculating the right amount of tax, and encounter some additional problems collecting taxes across jurisdictional borders. Also, firms and individuals encounter the same types of compliance costs for subnational taxes that they do for national taxes. In fact, given that the different levels of government may use different definitions of taxable income, allowable deductions and so on, the presence of multiple income taxes will only further complicate the lives of citizens and their accountants.

In general, however, subnational income taxes tend to be simpler than are national taxes; one early estimate is that the compliance costs of state taxes is about 11 percent of federal taxes (Wicks, 1965). In many instances the governments have decided to try to prevent the elaborate systems of deductions and exemptions which complicate national tax codes, and to charge a flat-rate percentage on all income earned by their citizens. This makes the tax system almost impossible to use for social or economic policy purposes, but it does make administration substantially easier. The administrative tasks of the subnational governments are also eased because they have access to national data, and have a way of checking the comprehensiveness of their coverage of citizens. In some cases, in fact, the state or local income tax is just a simple percentage of the national income tax. Either the state or local government levies that additional tax itself or, as in Germany, the taxes are collected together (by the *Länder* in the German case) and are then distributed among the levels of government according to an agreed formula (Reissert and Schaefer, 1985).

Although their job is in some ways easier, subnational governments also face some very difficult tasks in administering their own taxes. First, they have to decide who is liable to pay what taxes where. Many people live in one place and work in another, and arrangements must be made about where he or she is to pay income taxes. This is usually resolved in favor of paying taxes where the individual lives, which in turn may present central cities with the financial problems of providing services for a large work force with a smaller tax base. In addition, corporations and even individuals may have multiple addresses. For a large corporation, what percentage of their total income is allocated to which sites? Location can make a considerable difference in tax liabilities when there are substantial variations in tax rates. Not surprisingly, there has been a great deal of intergovernmental bargaining, and of litigation, over how to treat the multiple homes of both individuals and corporations for tax purposes. Some states in the United States have attempted to impose a "unitary tax" on all income of corporations doing business within their borders, but have found that the mobility of the corporations and possible constitutional threats make such a tax unworkable.

The final problem for subnational governments is that they are in competition with one another for business locations, and taxes are an important component of the competition. When a business wants to locate a major new plant or office, it will let this be known and will usually be contacted by a number of localities wanting the facility. The localities want more jobs, more business for existing retail stores, etc. The business is then in a position to have the localities "bid" for the new facility, with one portion of the bidding being the amount of reduction of local property and corporation taxes the locality is willing to offer. While there is some evidence that tax concessions are not the determinate factor in many decisions (Gray and Spina, 1980), they are a part of the bargain. In making these tax concessions, however, the local government may restrict its ability to provide the local services that are also important factors in business location decisions.

Administering The Property Tax

Many subnational governments are able to utilize income taxes and taxes on goods and services for a substantial share of their income. In the Anglo-American democracies and to a lesser extent in other countries, however, a local property tax constitutes a major source of local government revenue. This tax has the virtue of being, unlike income tax, a revenue source that is not shared among levels of government (41 states in the United States also have a property tax, although in most it is quite small). It also has the virtue that property is easily visible, while incomes are not, and does not move around as businesses and individuals may. Identifying what should be taxed is not difficult when using the property tax.

This tax is, however, somewhat more difficult to administer if government revenue is to stay closely in line with changes in prices. Further, if revenue keeps pace with changing prices (especially rapidly increasing property values), the property tax becomes highly visible, and can generate a great deal of political opposition. Even it if is not changed often, taxpayers tend to be aware of what they are paying in property tax, sometimes more so than for other types of taxes which are assumed to be more "visible" (Cmnd. 6453, 1976; Wagstaff, 1965). It should be noted, however, that the property tax may be easier to administer than some alternatives to it. The new community charge in Britain is estimated to cost several times as much to administer as the old property tax, or rates (Travers, 1989). Buildings are much easier to identify than are the individuals who constitute the taxing unit for the community charge, and buildings do not have multiple locations while individuals have multiple residences.

The property tax is calculated as a percentage of the value of a property. There are usually differences in the tax rate (called millages in the United States and poundages in the United Kingdom) charged for unimproved land, houses, and business property. Deciding whether a house is used primarily as a residence or for business purposes can present some difficulties, but most problems for tax administrators arise in determining the current value of the property. This is easy to do at the time of the sale of the property – it is what the market said its value was. Unless property is bought and sold often, however, it is difficult for local government officials to use the market as the basis of their assessments. Of course, if similar properties in the same neighborhood are purchased, then the assessors can gain an idea of what a particular house might be worth, and of how fast values are increasing, but it is at best informed guesswork to apply such a general formula to any individual piece of property. The assessment problem may be even more complicated if the means of taxing property is the "cadastral income," or imputed rent, of the property as it continues to be in Belgium or Italy, or was traditionally in the United Kingdom. How much is it worth to the owner to have the use of the property during the year is a very difficult question to answer.

These difficulties in valuation present the local tax officials with three options. One is to employ rules of thumb, such as the average increase in the prices of properties sold in the area during the year, and attempt to keep the tax rolls of the local government reasonably up to date. The other is to do nothing in most years about properties that do not change hands, and then have a major revaluation after a period of, say, ten years. The final option is to invest the time and energy to revalue property annually, or at least at very frequent intervals. Each of these three options presents some real difficulties for the local governments involved.

The first option is an easy way to attempt to keep local government revenues in line with general changes in the economic base, and to some extent therefore in line with the growing expenditure needs for a local government. On the other hand, this strategy runs the risk of producing some substantial inequities among homeowners or businesses in the community. Although the value of property may be increasing in general, some types of property may be losing value, or property values in some geographical areas may be going down in price. Other areas, such as those which are being gentrified, may be increasing in value very rapidly. This may be compounded by the difficulty that tax officials who do not monitor changes in properties will probably not know if some property owners are making improvements and increasing their market values. The right of citizens to appeal against increased tax assessments may help correct the first problem, but almost certainly will not help the second.

The second approach, that of only reassessing property infrequently, will be very acceptable except in those few awful years in which tax assessments increase. In most years this strategy keeps citizens reasonably content with no tax increases unless there is a measure to increase tax rates. It also keeps down the administrative expenses of government, so that the local administration appears rather efficient. Also, this option may please some citizens by slowing down the rate of increases in local expenditures. All these virtues are counterbalanced by the shock and upset which the periodic reassessments may produce. This type of sharp upward revaluation, fueled by rapid housing inflation, was one of the principal triggers for Proposition 13 in California; some homeowners had their assessments doubled or tripled, or more (Oakland, 1979). Other reassessments have produced real, but less dramatic, political repercussions for local governments. Furthermore, for the local governments in question infrequent revaluations make it difficult to keep up with increasing expenditure demands caused by inflation, much less those caused by new or increased demands for services.

The final option for governments is to invest the personnel, money, and effort in keeping property assessments up to date. This is an expensive process, as some attention, albeit fleeting, must be paid to every piece of property in the government area. Further, it makes local tax increases a chronic complaint, rather than the acute shock that periodic reassessments produce. This may be preferable, but it does place the property tax in the political spotlight regularly. On the positive side, however, frequent reassessment does prevent massive shocks to homeowners and businessmen, and also gives local governments a better chance of generating the type of revenue they need to provide services without the need for a very visible increase in the tax rate; prompt reassessments may be able to provide a revenue increase while perhaps even lowering the millage rate. What could be better for a politician than to say that he or she lowered a tax?

To some extent the shock of any increases in valuation, and the consequent increase in property taxes, will be mitigated by the use of mortgage companies and escrow accounts to pay an increasing share of property taxes. As a "service" (or a money-making device for themselves), banks and mortgage companies will include one-twelfth of the annual property tax in each month's mortgage bill, and then pay that to the government at the appropriate time. Rather than having one big check to write to local government each year, the taxpayer never sees the money actually go to the local government, and the pain is spread over twelve smaller payments made throughout the year. Just as using PAYE makes collecting income tax easier for government, so too does this plan facilitate collecting property tax. It is easier to pursue a bank for the money that it should have on account than to pursue hundreds of individual taxpayers who may not have saved enough during the year to pay the tax.

Protecting the Homeowner Although administering the property tax would appear to be a relatively straightforward affair of collecting a percentage of the value of a piece of property, this tax scheme can be used for other, social purposes just as are other forms of taxation. For example, several countries (especially Portugal) tax unoccupied houses more heavily than occupied ones in order to promote the market in rental property. A number of countries tax agricultural land at lower rate than other open land. Just as varying types of income can be treated differently, so too can alternative types of property.

The particular question involved here is protecting the right of homeowners, especially elderly homeowners, to live in their own home, even if they encounter difficulties in paying the property tax. As property values have risen dramatically in a number of cities in the United States and Canada, a number of the elderly have found that their current income does not correspond to the increased value of the property they own. Increased property values will eventually mean increased property taxes, and the elderly homeowners may be faced with losing their home in a sheriffs' sale for non-payment of the property tax. The political and ethical desire on the part of many local governments to assist these people in keeping their homes has produced a number of policy responses. One has been the so-called "circuit breaker" in which citizens (sometimes only the elderly) do not have to pay over a certain percentage of their income as property tax (Gold, 1981). In other cases, a citizen with rapidly appreciating property may be allowed to pay a reduced rate of tax, but must pay the difference between the amount actually paid and what the real tax would have been out of the proceeds of selling the property when the time comes. This approach has been used especially in areas where property has been "gentrified" and has become much more valuable than when the original owners bought it (*Pittsburgh PostGazette*, June 5, 1990). These provisions allow the property tax to collect the amount of revenue owed on a property while still meeting another important political and humane goal of helping people stay in their own homes.

In some states and localities in the United States, the right of homeownership and the potential threats to that virtue from government are important political issues. Some states have homeowner's exemptions that permit owner-occupied property to be granted a substantial exemption before it is taxed, sometimes up to as much as $100,000. Any homeowner with a house valued at less than the exemption figure does not have to pay any property tax at all. This exemption does help citizens buy and keep houses, but it imposes a substantial revenue deficit on many local governments. This may have to be made up with regressive taxes, such as the sales tax, or it may result in poorer quality services (Paul, 1975). The problem of revenue deficits is especially pronounced when property assessors are elected officials, and help to keep their offices by making assessments as close to the exemption figure as possible.

The difficulties in keeping up assessments and thereby keeping local government revenue equal to rising costs are affected by the type of assessors used even when there is not a homestead exemption. In some areas of the United States, tax assessors are elected, and often are powerful political actors. In most of the United States and in other areas of the world that use the property tax, assessors are merit system officials with training and experience in real estate valuation. Political assessors have a strong incentive to keep assessments low, especially for the more attentive and powerful members of the locality (Lowery, 1982; 1984). In some states the courts have intervened to mandate greater equality of assessment and some reduction of political favoritism. Some citizens may like the opportunities for influence afforded by elective assessors, but local governments and less influential citizens may desire greater impartiality and administrative competence. Also, the actions of political assessors may make the property tax more regressive by favoring individuals with political (and usually economic) influence with lower taxes.

Summary Administering the property tax is far from just the simple calculation of the value of the property multiplied by the appropriate tax rate. Rather, it involves a number of important political, administrative, and even ethical issues. The property tax is, in general, very visible, although the use of mortgage companies and their escrow accounts helps to make it less so in the United States. Therefore, any governments that depend upon this tax must do everything they can to maintain adequate revenues from it without unduly alarming their citizens. The crucial question is how often to reassess the value of property, how to set the tax rate charged on those assessments, and how to keep the inevitable changes in tax obligations from that process from creating political shock waves. The other side of that same question is how to generate sufficient revenue for government to pay for all the services demanded by the same citizens who complain about reassessments. Using politically selected assessors has been one mechanism to keep revenue and service balanced politically, but often this has turned to favoritism rather than equity and efficiency in revenue collection.

Amnesty: A New Approach to Administration

Tax administration is intended to reduce as much as possible the opportunities for tax fraud and tax evasion. It can never be 100 percent effective in doing this, just as social service agencies can never be in eliminating welfare fraud or defense agencies in eliminating contract fraud (Cook, 1989). Knowing that some evasion does inevitably take place, tax agencies would like to recover as much of the money lost through that illegal activity as possible, but do not have sufficient resources to track down every evader. Therefore, a number of European countries and several states in the United States have declared tax amnesties, and have permitted any citizen who may have evaded taxes to clear their consciences by amending their tax return for the year(s) in question, usually without penalty or interest. In return, the tax agencies will forego any possible civil or criminal proceedings against those taxpayers.

Amnesties were first used in the Netherlands four times between 1934 and 1955, and Switzerland implemented an amnesty in 1969 (OECD, 1990a). In the more contemporary period, perhaps because of its historic high levels of tax evasion, Italy was among the first countries to introduce a tax amnesty. In 1982 it allowed citizens to file amended returns for their taxes from the prior two years and if they paid the money due that was the end of the matter. Shortly thereafter, Austria introduced a very similar amnesty program for its taxpayers covering the prior five years. Since that time a number of countries have used amnesties. The results of these exercises have been variable. In some instances (Ireland, New Zealand, Switzerland) they brought forth a number of taxpayers who, because of conscience or fear of prosecution, wanted to settle their obligations to government but had been afraid to do so. Once freed from the threat of prosecution or high penalties, they were apparently very pleased to be able to pay up. In other countries (Austria, Belgium) the results were disappointing and citizens apparently did not want to take a chance on exposing their earlier wrongdoing.

A number of states in the United States, beginning with Massachusetts (Jackson, 1986), also have introduced tax amnesties. These programs all originated with the idea of collecting badly needed revenue and then keeping the new found taxpayers on the tax rolls (Leonard and Zeckhauser, 1987). The success of amnesties have been variable across the states. New York collected over $400 million, and California, Illinois, and Michigan all collected over $100 million, while Texas and some smaller states collected less than $1 million each (McKie and Beck, 1990). Most of the participants in the amnesties were small offenders, with over half of those coming forth in Illinois owing less than $100. In addition, only about a third of those participating in the amnesties have continued to pay taxes (Fisher, Goodeeris, and Young, 1989). If the purpose was to bring a number of new taxpayers onto the rolls, these programs are perhaps less useful than stringent enforcement of tax laws. Amnesties may actually reduce compliance with tax laws by making people believe that there will be other chances to pay up without penalty, and by alienating regular taxpayers who feel cheated by the breaks given to the less law abiding.

Summary

Making tax policy is not just passing laws about taxes. It also involves ensuring that those laws are put into effect and do produce the revenue that they were intended to. As with almost all other public policies, administration and implementation play a crucial role in the success or failure of tax policy. In fact, taxation depends perhaps more than most policies on administration. More details must be worked out concerning individual cases, and those cases may be more variable than for other types of policies, even social policies. In addition, tax policy brings government into direct contact with almost every citizen, and working out the details of their tax obligations is often a difficult and threatening relationship between the two parties. Therefore, it is important that tax administration be implemented efficiently and humanely.

Tax administration is not, however, something which is undertaken entirely by government employees. A great deal of the cost and bother of administering taxes is displaced onto the private sector. Individuals are required to keep records of their income and expenditures to justify any claims they may make for tax relief. Firms even more than individuals are required to keep records – of their own activities, of what they have paid their employees, and what amounts of tax they have withheld from the employees' pay. Banks must report interest earned by taxpayers, and firms may have to report the dividends paid to their stockholders. The work of government in collecting tax revenues is a great deal easier because it can require the assistance of organizations in the society, and the work of those organizations is easier because of advances in electronic record-keeping. Early governments may have had difficulty in finding tax handles to support themselves, but there is no shortage of those handles for governments in the late twentieth century. Depsite those advances, collecting taxes is a costly and time consuming process, but one essential for effective government.

9
Tax Reform

Taxation is always a political issue, but rarely has it been so central a political issue as it has been during the late 1980s and early 1990s. In almost all the OECD countries, there have been major proposals for reform of the tax system (Pechman, 1988; Hagemann, Jones, and Montador, 1988). There are several notable features in those proposals. The first is that they have come forward in so many countries at about the same time. Further, the proposals are themselves rather similar. Most have attempted to simplify the tax system, and have involved a reduction in the number of tax brackets, a reduction of the higher marginal tax rates, and the elimination of a large number of tax preferences for certain classes of income and expenditure. Finally, given the radical nature of these reforms (as compared to the tax systems existing when they were proposed) it is especially surprising that so many of the reform proposals have been successful. Although altering the then existing tax structures in any number of ways, and eliminating special privileges that had almost become rights, many of these proposals were adopted with a minimum of political difficulty, and with remarkable speed. A few proposed reforms have faltered politically (Haskel, 1987), but most have gone from concept to policy more quickly than should have been expected for comprehensive reforms of the tax system.

This almost unprecedented success of the tax reform proposals requires an explanation. Unfortunately, most of the models of tax politics available appear better suited to explaining why the reforms were impossible, than for explaining how and why they did succeed. This chapter, therefore, will need to undertake four tasks. The first is to describe the tax reforms which have occurred within the OECD countries. This discussion will concentrate attention on reform of the personal income tax, but some attention will be given to other taxes as well. The second task is to inquire as to just what assistance the available models of tax politics would provide to explain these reforms. Third, on the basis of those models and my own observations of the changes in tax laws, an attempt will be made to develop an explanation of the successes of tax reform. Such an explanation necessarily will be speculative, but should help us understand these rapid policy changes. Finally, the future of tax reform will be considered. This one round of reform produced some important results, but a number of tax issues remain to be resolved. The success of the reforms of the 1980s demonstrates to many politicians and analysts that additional reforms may be more possible than has been thought.

The Nature of Tax Reform

As noted, tax reform has been a worldwide phenomenon; even some Third World countries have undertaken it as one strategy for dealing with some of their pressing economic problems (Gillis, 1989). We are, however, interested primarily in the spate of tax reforms in the OECD world. There is a tendency to think of tax reform just as the events and issues occurring in the late 1980s and into the early 1990s, revising tax codes to make them at least appear simpler to citizens and reduce the administrative burdens of tax collection. These reforms, however, should be understood as to some extent the second wave of tax reforms, with the first wave occurring in the early 1980s with the election to office of a number of committed conservative leaders. These leaders – Ronald Reagan and Margaret Thatcher chief among them – undertook one round of rather simplistic tax reforms. These changes mostly involved just reducing taxes (Reagan: see Peterson and Rom, 1988), or shifting the burdens rather quickly and substantially between direct and indirect taxation (Thatcher: see Dilnot and Stark, 1988). These initial reforms then set the stage for the more comprehensive and more detailed reforms of taxes that have occurred approximately a decade later.

It is also important to understand tax reform as an exercise in symbolic politics as well as a set of real changes in the tax structures of these countries. Tax reform became a shibboleth that some political leaders wielded with great skill to produce the types of changes they wanted. Reform often has positive connotations – for all policies not just taxation – although the hopes of reformers are usually only partially realized at best. The discontent many citizens felt with the existing tax systems (see chapter 5), and their largely inadequate understanding of the nature of tax policy, made this policy area a very likely target for political manipulation. Some of the results produced by the reforms have been positive, but many have not produced the real benefits promised by their proponents, or expected by the public. In fairness, however, the reforms have not produced the disasters promised by their critics either.

Tax Reform: Round 1

Margaret Thatcher was elected Prime Minister in the United Kingdom on May 3, 1979, and Ronald Reagan was elected President of the United States on November 4, 1980. One of the most important items on each leader's agenda was the reduction of the income tax on individuals and corporations. Both had campaigned vigorously for the need to reduce the public sector "burden" on the economy, and stressed the economic and social benefits that this tax reduction would produce. Although they had the same common goal of reducing direct taxation, and especially taxation on incomes, they went about achieving that goal somewhat differently.

Ronald Reagan had accepted the ideas of "supply-side" economics and the "Laffer Curve" during the campaign for the presidency, and believed that if income tax rates were reduced sufficient income would be generated through increased economic activity to make up quickly for any short-term falls in federal revenues (Bartlett and Roth, 1983). Although this policy proposal had been called "voodoo economics" by his future Vice-President, George Bush, and was rejected by most of the conventional economics establishment, Reagan and his personal advisors persisted with the idea. They proceeded to have the supply-side "theory" (Roberts, 1984) enacted into law through the cleverly-named 1981 Economic Recovery Tax Act (ERTA). Although many people in and out of government were extremely skeptical about this approach to fiscal policy, the President had sufficient popularity, and a sufficient mandate from the public, to have this law passed by Congress during his "honeymoon period."

This tax act resulted in a reduction in federal revenues of over $700 billion during the first five years, mostly coming from personal and corporate income taxes. Unfortunately for the President (and the country) the expected rapid increases in economic activity did not take place, and this was the beginning of the most massive peacetime deficit spending in American history. In the eight years that Ronald Reagan was president, the federal deficit increased from $1 trillion to $2.87 trillion; when adjusted for inflation, the deficit increased by over 160 percent. Congress attempted to rectify the growing deficit problem somewhat by passing the (also cleverly-named) Tax Equity and Fiscal Responsibility Act (TEFRA) in 1982 and a subsequent Deficit Reduction Act. These acts restored some of the tax revenue eliminated earlier, but were only partially successful in reducing the federal budget deficit. In fairness, it should be said that the US economy did grow during most of the years that Reagan was in office (an average of almost 3.4 percent per annum real growth), but not at a rate sufficient to generate the needed and predicted revenue. The Reagan tax cut was popular with many citizens and businesses who saw their federal taxes go down, but has presented the federal government with a continuing fiscal problem. The deficit and the resulting debt may be one of the most enduring legacies of Ronald Reagan to the American people.

Mrs Thatcher, on the other hand, had much the same desire to reduce the income tax burden, but went about it in a more cautious manner. Instead of reducing the overall level of taxation, she shifted the distribution of taxes from direct onto indirect taxes (Howe, 1982). In particular, Mrs Thatcher's policies reduced the impact of the income tax by reducing the higher marginal rates and increasing a variety of allowances. At the same time, however, she increased the value-added tax and excise taxes substantially. These changes together were broadly "revenue neutral," but shifted some of the tax burden from the more affluent to the working classes and the unemployed. Even with the exclusion of food, rent, and some clothing from the VAT, the less affluent had to continue to buy things on which VAT was charged, and also to spend a larger proportion of their income on the items on which excises were charged (see, for example, Woolley and Le Grand, 1990). This shift in the incidence of taxation, of course, did serve the interests of the people who had elected Mrs Thatcher to office. Further, as with President Reagan, the Conservative economic policy was associated with a slightly improved economic growth rate.

It was not, however, just the United States and the United Kingdom which engaged in this first round of tax reform. A number of other governments participated, by reducing overall levels of tax and by beginning to shift some of the burden to indirect taxes. For example, Belgium undertook a significant shift in its tax structure and began to place greater reliance on indirect taxes in the early 1980s (Gysen, 1980). In Canada the MacEachen Budget of 1981 sought to broaden the tax base and reduce marginal tax rates. It encountered vigorous political opposition and a number of its provisions were not implemented (Doern, Maslove, and Prince, 1988, 65–6). Still, it represented an important effort at reform through the normal budgetary process.

In addition to the exercises in lowering rates, a number of other types of tax policy changes were introduced in the early 1980s. Several countries introduced indexation of income tax brackets during this time, and this served to limit the automatic increase of income tax revenue that would otherwise come through inflation or economic growth. The effects of an unindexed tax could be a considerable benefit for government; Pechman estimated that Americans paid 15 percent more than they would have with indexed taxes between 1975 and 1981 (Pechman, 1983). Eight countries introduced indexation between 1970 and 1980, with a few more adding it in the early 1980s. Further, with Spain and Portugal joining the European Community, they were required to begin to harmonize their tax structures with the other members, which involved greater use of the value-added tax. In short, Round I of tax reform did not produce the major headlines in most OECD countries that the second round has, but it still produced some significant changes in their tax structures. The odd country during the early 1980s in many ways was France, with its newly elected Socialist president and programs of increased income, corporation and capital taxation. This program did not last very long, however, and in the reversal of economic policies occurring in the mid-1980s (Hall, 1987; Lipietz, 1983), Mitterrand returned French economic policy to something closer to those of the other OECD countries.

It was not just ideology and partisan politics which were generating the changes in the tax policies of the OECD world. The economic downturns of the late 1970s, with high continuing unemployment (relative to the recent past) combined with high inflation, helped to generate changes in the tax structures. Governments were all looking for ways to stimulate economic growth – and particularly employment – and modifying the tax structure appeared to be a good way to achieve this goal (*European Taxation*, 1983). In most instances, whether the governments came from the political right or the political left, they believed that making it less expensive (in tax terms) to earn money or to pay workers might help ease the economic problems of the time. This belief then contributed to the shift away from income-based taxes onto consumption-based taxes.

The goals of this early round of tax reform were partially achieved by the mid-1980s. Economic growth did not return to the high and predictable levels of the 1950s and 1960s, but it improved on those of the late 1970s. Employment levels did not recover as much as economic growth in most European countries, but they fared better as well. Similarly, inflation rates returned to levels that were more accptable. It is not clear whether the tax changes introduced in the early 1980s were responsible for these changes, or if they were just a part of the general recovery from a trough in the business cycle. Certainly the political leaders of the time were willing to take credit for the positive changes. Further, they were willing to argue that the economic system had returned to "normalcy," and that there might be some room for even greater changes in the tax system.

Tax Reform: Round II

The earlier tax reforms then set the stage for the second, and more dramatic, round; more dramatic because the changes which have occurred in a number of OECD countries appear to defy the conventional wisdom about politics, and about tax politics in particular. The details differed among the OECD countries, but the general pattern was the same. Top rates for the income tax (corporate and personal) were lowered, the number of tax brackets was reduced, and the special treatment (tax expenditures or loopholes) for a large number of expenditures and income was reduced or eliminated. These changes were, in most cases, broadly revenue neutral because the elimination of so many special preferences broadened the tax base to which the lower rates were applied.

Income tax remained the largest single tax in most countries (18 of the 22 OECD countries for which we have clear data), but after reform it was very different in character, becoming much simpler, and closer to proportionality in its impacts across income classes. Therefore, this tax ceased to have as much of the redistributive effects usually associated with a tax on income. In fairness, however, the pre-reform income tax often did not have the progressive effect it was intended to have, because of the numerous "loopholes" built into the tax laws (Mathews, 1984). The difference with the post-reform tax is that the proportionality became more obvious than it had been when the complexity of tax laws masked the significant reduction of the tax base through special treatments. This change, in turn, made the issue of progressivity and proportionality easier to advance politically.

Some idea of the extent of the effects of tax reform can be gained from examining tables 9.1 to 9.3. These tables provide information on the changes in the minimum and maximum rates of personal income tax, maximum rates of corporation tax, and the number of brackets of the personal income tax. In all three cases there are significant differences in the pre- and post-reform tax structures among the OECD countries. The evidence on changes in exemptions and deductions is more difficult to quantify, but qualitiative evidence indicates that changes in those categories are, if anything, more dramatic than for these quantitative indicators.

In table 9.1, changes – both achieved and projected – in the top rates of personal income tax are reported. Where applicable these rates combine subnational as well as national income taxes, although most of the changes in rates have occurred at the national level. On average, these 12 countries have made commitments to reduce the top rate of income tax by 16.5 percent. The changes in a number of instances are dramatic, with the United States leading the way with a 53 percent reduction in the top rate (federal only), followed by the United Kingdom with a 52 percent reduction. Italy anticipates the least reduction in the tax rate, although income tax is a less important source of revenue for that country than for the others, and this does not have as much of an effect as it might in the other countries. Canada and Germany also have much lower than average rate reductions, although both had lower top rates than most of the other countries at the beginning of the reform period. In sum,

Table 9.1 Changes in tax rate, 1975–1989 (in percent)

	Maximum		*Minimum*	
	1975	*1989*	*1975*	*1989*
Australia	65	49	20	24
Canada	47	29	9	17
France	60	57	5	5
Germany	56	53	22	19
Ireland	72	56	26	32
Italy	72	50	10	10
Japan	75	50	10	10
Netherlands	71	60	27	35[a]
New Zealand	57	33	19	24
Sweden	56	42	7	5
United Kingdom	83	40	35	25
United States	70	33	14	15

[a] Not strictly comparable. 1989 figure includes social insurance tax.
Source: Kay, 1990

these reductions represent a major shift in the way these countries (representing almost two-thirds of total world GNP) plan to finance their public sectors in the future.

The figures reported in table 9.1 demonstrate that the bottom portions of the income distribution were not so fortunate. In five of the twelve countries with comparable data the lower bracket tax rate is expected to increase with reform, and in three others the rate will remain the same. The less affluent did the best in the United Kingdom, where the rate dropped by almost 29 percent, while in Canada the tax rate almost doubled in the lowest bracket. On average, the tax rate for the lowest income bracket increased by over 8 percent in these twelve countries. These figures are perhaps not as regressive as they may appear because the income level at which the income tax begins to be charged was also increased in most cases. In Canada, for example, the threshold for paying tax and some tax credits went up substantially at the same time that the tax rate was being doubled, so that most lower income taxpayers gained slightly (Maslove, 1989). In general, however, the effect of tax reform has been to impose a somewhat higher rate on lower and middle incomes.

The picture of reform is not so clear for corporation tax rates. Of the eleven countries included in table 9.2, two actually have increased the maximum corporation tax rate, and a third (Sweden) has not altered this rate, despite a number of proposals to do so. The two countries which did raise the rates (Denmark and Italy) had the two lowest rates of corporation tax at the beginning of the period, but ended the period with among the highest rates. Of the eight countries which did choose to reduce their top corporation tax rates, the average reduction was almost 17 percent; for all 12 the average reduction was almost 9 percent. Again the United States had the largest reduction of tax rates, with the United Kingdom and France close behind. Also, despite its image as the stronghold of state support for business, Japan had the lowest level of rate reduction among those countries that did reduce the maximum corporate rate, and is left with one of the highest corporate tax rates among these 11 countries.

Despite these lowering of the highest marginal tax rates, the net effect of tax reform in many countries has been to shift a larger share of the tax burden onto corporations. This apparent paradox is the result of dramatically reducing the tax expenditures available to them. The apparently easy life of corporations under the pre-reform tax system was one component of the politics of tax reform in many countries, and the projected larger corporate tax revenue

Table 9.2 Changes in corporate tax rates, 1984–1990

	1984	*1990*	*Percentage change*
Australia	46	39	−15
Canada	51	44	−14
Denmark	40	50	+25
France	50	39	−22
Germany	56	50	−11
Italy	36	46	+28
Japan	55	50	−9
Netherlands	43	35	−19
Sweden	52	52	0
United Kingdom	45	35	−22
United States	51	39	−23

Source: Pechman, 1989

Table 9.3 Changes in number of tax brackets, 1975–89

	1975	*1989*
Australia	7	5
Canada	13	3
France	13	13
Germany	[a]	[a]
Ireland	6	3
Italy	32	7
Japan	19	5
Netherlands	10	3
New Zealand	22	2
Sweden	11	3
United Kingdom	10	2
United States	25	3

[a] German tax schedule based on polynomial formula.
Source: Kay, 1990

helped to smooth passage of the reform legislation.[1] Some of the changes in the law, such as reduction of research and development credits, ultimately may be damaging to economic growth, but the political pressures for the changes were inescapable.

A third aspect of the tax reforms has been a radical reduction in the number of brackets in the income tax system. Table 9.3 shows these changes for twelve OECD countries. The average number of brackets prior to reform was over 15. After reform, the average number of brackets will be under 4.5. The most significant reforms here were Italy (dropping 25 brackets) and the United States (dropping 22), followed closely by New Zealand (20). On the other hand, France is not reducing the number of brackets it uses at all, perhaps becuase of the influence of the Socialist government and the ideological desire for greater progression in the tax structure. Without France, the average reduction in the number of brackets is even greater, going from 15.5 brackets before the reforms to 3.6 after. The income tax systems in these countries have obviously been made much simpler, if apparently also less progressive.

As noted, the evidence about the reduction of exemptions and deductions as ways of broadening the tax base is more difficult to quantify, but some specific changes occurring in this category of reforms are worthy of note. Perhaps the most important of these changes was the decision by the Canadian government to eliminate the exemption on fringe benefits provided to employees, and to begin to tax these as income. These benefits, such as pensions, life insurance, health insurance, and a host of other "goodies" traditionally have not been taxed – in Canada or anywhere. This was true even though almost everyone agreed that they are items of value provided to employees in lieu of higher salaries. Many employees, in fact, prefer fringe benefits to higher salaries because they can receive value but escape taxation. Few other countries have yet chosen to follow Canada's lead in full, although Finland has made some steps in that direction (Hagemann, Jones, and Montador, 1988). Further, Australia and New Zealand have begun to tax these benefits through the corporation providing them rather than as a part of the individual's taxable income (in the United States the amount of tax-free fringe benefits also is now limited). Also, some countries have begun to tax more luxurious benefits not offered to all employees, such as company cars in the United Kingdom and Sweden (Taylor, 1989). Taxing more general fringe benefits is still being discussed (Holberton, 1990), but little movement in that direction has yet taken place in most countries.

Another important special treatment of income in the tax laws is the treatment of capital gains. That is, if an asset (property, stocks, whatever) increases in value and the taxpayer sells it, how should the profit be treated for tax purposes? Is it ordinary income, or is it taxed at a lower rate, or perhaps not taxed at all in order to encourage investment? For much of continental Western Europe and in Japan, capital gains are not treated as income, and there is no apparent thought of making these gains fully taxable as such (Daly, Jung, Mercier, and Schweitzer, 1985; Ishi, 1989). The opportunity for any country to begin to tax capital gains is limited because the loosening of restrictions on the movement of capital internationally, and especially within Europe, would cause money to leave a country if it began to treat these gains differently from others (Giovanni, 1989). As one part of the tax reform of 1986, the United States became unique among the OECD countries in treating capital gains simply as ordinary income, although Canada, Australia, Sweden, France, and the United Kingdom do tax capital gains, but at a lower rate than ordinary income. The capital gains issue continues to resurface in the United States as President Bush has sought to reintroduce special treatment of capital gains as a part of his deficit reduction tax package. This special treatment was intended both to encourage investment and to encourage investors to sell stock, thereby receiving some tax revenues on the sale, albeit at a lower rate.

Impacts of Reform

All this shifting of taxation inevitably had effects on the distribution of the tax burden, and therefore on the distribution of income in societies. It might be expected that these changes would benefit the more affluent, and extract more revenue from the middle and working classes. After all, the upper tax brackets have been reduced substantially – an average of over 16 percent. That is not necessarily the case, however. At least in the United States the impact of tax reform has been progressive (Pechman, 1989, 84–5). The lowest decile now pays 44 percent less in income and corporation taxes than it did before the reform, and the upper classes pay somewhat more. Closing the loopholes and shifting more of the burden back onto corporations has tended to benefit the less affluent taxpayers at the expense of the more affluent (Murray, 1986a; 1986b), which demonstrates something about the importance of the tax preferences existing before reform.

The evidence about the impact of tax reform in other countries is less clear. For example, in Canada Maslove (1989) found that both the bottom 20 percent of income earners and the top 1 percent gained under tax reform, but that the latter were by far the biggest gainers. The exact gains and losses under the reformed tax system depended somewhat upon factors such as family composition, sources of income, and age. Somewhat similar results have been found for other tax reforms, including those in the Scandinavian countries, and in general the very affluent have profited through reform. This was especially true of some of the tax reforms adopted during the first stage, but was also somewhat true for later changes (Peterson and Rom, 1988). Thus, the Unites States has been the odd one out in having a tax reform which produced a more egalitarian result.[2] The tax reform, however, was only a part of a package of economic programs under the Reagan administration which together tended to make the rich richer and the poor poorer (Phillips, 1990).

These data demonstrate the magnitude of the tax reforms undertaken in the OECD countries. The tax base was widened substantially by eliminating a large number of "loopholes" in the tax laws, and escaping taxation became more difficult. Using this broader income base, however, permitted charging lower rates on the income taxed, so that average and marginal tax rates could be reduced. These changes were most pronounced for the personal income tax but similar types of changes also affected the corporation income tax. The system which emerged appeared to most people to be simpler and fairer than the pre-reform system. The overall distribution of the tax burden by income groups was not altered significantly, but perhaps most important politically was the perception that average taxpayers – rather than organized interests lobbying for tax concessions – were for once able to benefit from changes in the tax laws.

The Politics of Reform

The above description of changes represents a striking change in tax politics from the usual stereotypes of a process dominated by special interest groups seeking concessions and preferences for their members (Rabushka, 1988). Further, given that these reforms in many cases were occurring under the auspices of conservative governments, the positive redistributional effects are somewhat surprising. Finally, the simplification of the tax system, and the reduction in the number of brackets, appears to run counter to the experience and interests of tax professionals who had constructed the Byzantine system. That system had the advantage of appearing to be progressive because of the number of brackets and the very high marginal rates charged in the upper brackets, while masking the benefits available to the more affluent. These reforms then necessitate some serious thinking about tax politics, and about why they were successful during this period. Tax reform had been talked about for years in a number of countries but appeared suddenly to have occurred. What happened?

Interest Groups

The first place one would apparently not turn to for an explanation of what happened in tax reform would be the interest group literature. The success of tax reform appears to be a clear repudiation of the conventional wisdom that interest groups dominate tax policy and that the public at large is unable to generate sufficient power to eliminate the special preferences granted to groups through tax policies. Taken another way, however, this political result may point to changes in the pressure groups involved in politics rather than a clear diminution of their power. The politics of tax expenditures had been described as "client politics" in the framework proposed by James Q. Wilson (1980). The politics of tax expenditures had been those of concentrated benefits for the members of interest groups, with the costs being diffused (largely invisibly) among all taxpayers. Further, the decisions on granting tax preferences generally were made incrementally so that they did not attract much public notice (Witte, 1985, p. 247). This is clearly not a method of change suitable for comprehensive tax reform.

What appears to have happened in part, however, is that the power of a number of "public interest groups" that have been advocating greater fairness in the tax system increased during the 1970s and 1980s. Particularly important in the United States was the group entitled Citizens for Tax Justice. In addition, splits emerged within the business community and many powerful businessmen began to see the virtues for economic development of a "level playing field" that might be produced by tax reform (Mucciaroni, 1990, 12–13). A few business groups were in fact formed to lobby for tax reform, and these included representatives from some of the giants of American industry. This one result should not be taken to indicate that public interest groups have supplanted the more traditional interest groups as political powers, or that business is permanently divided. It may mean, however, that on certain issues and perhaps especially in the United States (Scholzman and Tierney, 1986) the public interest groups do have some real influence. There is less evidence of public interest groups being involved in other tax reforms, although labor groups and "Green" groups perform some of the same functions in other OECD countries (Taggart, 1990).

Party Government

On the other hand, a party government model of politics does appear to have greater relationship to the tax policy changes which were adopted. Tax reform was an important item on the political agenda of many parties, and of several individual political leaders elected during the late 1970s and early 1980s. President Reagan and Chancellor Kohl of West Germany placed a special emphasis on tax reform in their campaigns. These political leaders also had the capacity to push their reforms through the legislative process and have them implemented (but see Steinmo, 1989). Although this explanation is in some ways satisfying, it is not clear why there should have been the positive redistributive effects found in some of the cases. This hardly seems a likely outcome for political parties such as Republicans in the United States, Conservatives in the United Kingdom, or the Progressive Conservatives in Canada.

Despite the appearance, comprehensive tax reforms did indeed correspond to the political agendas of many conservative governments. The conservatives elected during the 1980s were often more ideologically conservative than had been their predecessors in the same party. Therefore, as well as being allied with business interests, they also had a belief in the virtues of an economically neutral tax system (Maslove, 1989). These governments wanted to help business, but did not want to help one business at the expense of another. The pre-reform tax system was premised upon helping individual business sectors, perhaps at the expense of business and economic growth as a whole. Thus, the simple and apparently fair policy ideals embodied in comprehensive tax reform did have substantial appeal to conservatives of the Thatcher, Reagan, and Mulroney variety.

Institutional Explanations

Tax reform can also be seen as the outcome of a complex institutional process. In this case, the tax agencies in the public bureaucracy may have had a special influence over the choice of policies. The tax systems constructed over the years in almost all industrialized democracies were extraordinarily complex, and were proving increasingly difficult to administer. The number of exemptions and deductions offered in the tax laws, and the relatively narrow base of income on which tax was levied, made collecting government revenue more difficult. Further, the tax systems appeared unfair to many people charged with administering them. There appeared to be the need for a significant change in the way in which Western democracies generated their revenues.

Even if the above characterization of the values and ideas of the public bureaucracies is accurate (which I believe it is) it begs one significant question: why in the late 1980s? That is, the same tax systems had been in place for a number of years, and many of the same administrators, as well as the same organizations, had been responsible for tax policy during those years. Why all of a sudden was there this mass movement toward tax reform? From an institutional perspective, it could be argued that this resulted from the interaction of the tax administrations with changes in other institutions. For example, the first round of tax policy changes described above (pp. 273–276) appeared to open the way for further changes in taxes. A policy area that had been kept out of the public eye (albeit being discussed frequently by expert policymakers) had become more visible, and appeared more amenable to change.

The institutional perspective also seems capable of offering an explanation of why tax reform did not occur in some cases, most notably France. Given the presence of a Socialist President in France, it might have been expected that the government would push through a large-scale, comprehensive reform of the largely regressive tax system, with the intention being to benefit the working- and middle-class supporters of the Socialist Party. That did not, however, happen and the French tax system is only slowly beginning to reduce its heavy reliance on indirect taxation. The Finance Ministry apparently continues to support the existing complex and regressive system of taxation, fearing the consequences of poor tax collection and inflationary wage pressures if the system is changed (Graham, 1990). Also, the Ministry may fear a loss of its power (and employment) if the tax system were simplified.

In addition to the above institutional factors, at least for the United States, it has been argued that the legislative institutions had changed sufficiently to permit tax reform (Oppenheimer, 1980). Oddly enough, the same institutional changes that led to a large-scale growth of tax expenditures in the late 1970s and early 1980s (Witte, 1985) appear to be related to the acceptance of reform. In particular, the collapse of the seniority system and the declining institutionalization of leadership made it easier for policy entrepreneurs – such as Senator Bill Bradley – to promote their goals of tax reform (Bradley, 1984). In addition, the opening of most Congressional committee sessions to the public has made it more difficult for Congressmen to escape responsibility for their votes, or to slip special tax provisions into the law during closed sessions. American institutions are unique, but the general opening of government in OECD countries for greater public scrutiny has made majoritarian policies (Wilson, 1980; 1989) easier to adopt.

Political Culture

There also could be a cultural explanation for tax reform. We have noted earlier the important of the "tax revolt" in many of the OECD countries (see pp. 178–85). Whether manifested through referendum voting on local taxes or through voting for anti-tax, anti-government political parties, public acquiescence to big government and high taxes appeared to have lessened. There was some sense that poilicy changes were needed, although the exact nature of the desirable changes was less clear. One thing which did appear rather clearly was that taxes had to be seen to be fairer, and that perhaps one way to make them appear so was to reduce the number of "loopholes" and to make everyone pay something closer to their fair share of taxes. With that feeling went the belief among some that consumption taxes and user fees might be better sources of public revenue income because a larger portion of the population would contribute than would be true for income taxes.

As we noted above, the cultural explanation for tax policy is compelling in some ways, but also has several important weaknesses. One of these is that the connection between mass cultural change and real tax policies is weak. A number of political actions are necessary to link cultural transformations with policy changes, so that the cultural explanation may need to be complemented by a political one. In addition, it may be difficult to argue that the cultural changes discussed so often concerning the Western democracies during the 1980s had much relationship to the types of reforms which were adopted. Many of the cultural changes appeared to be opposed to taxes in general, rather than seeking to fine tune them.

International Competitiveness

Another possible explanation for the changes in tax policy is the increasingly international character of markets and even of public policies (Krasner, 1978; Katzenstein, 1985). Once the process of tax reform began in one country, it became easier (or even necessary with corporate taxation) for other countries to adopt similar reforms. Some of this international effect was the result simply of the diffusion of a policy innovation (Collier and Messick, 1975; Klingman, 1980), while a portion of the change may also be a result of the need to maintain competitiveness. For example, Switzerland, which is not a member of the European Community, found it necessary to adopt a form of the value-added tax to replace an older consumption tax so that its industries could compete easier with EC firms (Schneider, 1989). The old tax was not especially inefficient or ineffective, it just was different. Likewise, part of the argument for tax reform in Canada in 1987–8 was that its tax system had to be compatible with the United States under the Free-Trade Agreement or capital (financial and human) quickly would migrate to America.

An interesting case of the impact of international markets on tax reforms in a single nation has occurred over a proposed stock transfer tax in the United States. This tax was intended to prevent speculation as much as to raise revenue. As it was considered, however, it became increasingly clear that the tax would simply cause a great deal of stock trading to move from New York to London or Tokyo. The development of international securities markets and efficient telecommunications means that a single country cannot independently determine the way in which it can control its own internal markets, even the market in stocks of its own firms.

Political Entrepreneurship

Finally, we can explain the positive outcome of the tax reform process through the influence of successful political entrepreneurs. This is easily seen in the first round of reforms when these were being pushed by effective and (then) popular chief executives in government. At the second round, the impetus for reform appeared to shift to other less visible reformers. For example, in the United States, political leaders such as Senators Bradley (Democrat, New Jersey) and Packwood (Republican, Ore) and Congressman Rostenkowski (Democrat, Illinois), and Secretary of the Treasury Regan invested substantially in the reform process and in specific types of reform. They did this in part because of a sincere commitment to the goals of reform, and in part because it could be used to achieve other political goals. In addition, some interest group leaders, such as Robert McIntyre of Citizens for Tax Justice, also provided substantial leadership in promoting reform. Thus, there is an argument to be made that tax reform resulted from the willingness of political leaders to champion the cause.

The politics of tax reform have been written about less for other countries, but again there is some sense that individual leadership has been a major factor. For example, in New Zealand, a major and comprehensive tax reform has been associated with the Finance Minister Roger Douglas, who combined this reform into a whole package of economic reforms he was introducing (Douglas, 1988). The tax reform adopted transformed New Zealand from a country with little or no taxation other than the income tax and excise taxes to one with a much lower income tax but a significant value-added tax and a corporation income tax fully integrated into the personal income tax (Preston, 1987). As has been so often the case, this reform ran counter to the ostensible political interests of the individual politicians in the Labour government responsible for adopting it. Perhaps only a Labour minister, however, could have been successful in implementing a reform package which appeared so regressive.

The Next Round of Reform

The tax reforms of the 1980s were primarily reforms of the personal and corporate income taxes. These reforms are now in place and are functioning in many ways as they were expected to. Almost certainly there will be more reforms of these taxes during the 1980s, as anomalies in the new systems are discovered and some of the interest groups are successful in having their special treatments restored. Beyond those predictable political reactions to the previous round of reforms, however, there almost certainly will be several new sets of targets for tax reform. The first of these will be the existing system of excise taxation and the value-added tax, either individually, or as the subject of an attempt to integrate and harmonize all the consumption taxes levied by government. The latter is a more ambitious, and perhaps impossible, goal but one which may be necessary if tax policy is to achieve some of the objectives which contemporary reformers have set for it.

A second set of reforms being discussed concerns the integration of the several existing forms of taxes on personal and corporate income. As was mentioned earlier, in many ways a social insurance tax, or "contribution," is nothing more than a tax on income. Because it is levied differently from what is called income tax, the two often have somewhat perverse interactions. For example, in the United States, the social security tax is not levied after the first $51,300 of income, so people earning more than that amount enjoy a drop in their marginal tax rate even though they are quite affluent. In fact, even the average tax rate now declines after the ceiling of social security taxation is passed. Likewise, in many countries, the social security tax is levied on the first dollar (or whatever) earned, while the income tax is not applied until a more substantial amount of money is earned. If these two types of taxes were better coordinated, and then coordinated with social benefits, some of the perversities of "poverty traps" (Piachaud, 1980; Dilnot and Stark, 1988) might be eliminated.

Reforming Value-Added Tax

The most general aim in the reform of indirect taxation is to reform the general consumption tax; in most countries this means the value-added tax. In countries such as Canada and the United States that do not have the VAT, there is some pressure to adopt it, or a general consumption tax somewhat like it (McKie, 1988; 1990). The VAT would either replace a seriously flawed tax (Canada, 1987) or provide government with a new source of income (the United States: see McClure, 1987). The experience of the Japanese government in introducing a sales tax in 1989 and then experiencing widespread defections of disgruntled voters in the subsequent election may give some politicians cause for concern, but there does appear to be some pressures toward the VAT in countries which do not now utilize such a tax (Pechman, 1980, 115–20).

Almost all European countries, and all members of the European Community (EC), use the value-added tax as a major source of revenue. There are, however, substantial differences in the manner in which the tax is administered, and in the rates at which it is charged in the different countries (Tait, 1988; Cnossen, 1987a). These differences become extremely important as the EC moves toward a single integrated market. Significant variations in the rate or administration of VAT could provide one country or another with a competitive advantage and thus could defeat much of the purpose of developing the internal single market. Therefore, there will be substantial political pressure from the European Commission to create a common regime for the implementation of the VAT.

Some of the variation in the rates of the VAT among EC countries are shown in table 9.4. One country (Denmark) levies the same rate of VAT on all products, while another (Belgium) has five different rates and France and Italy use four different rates depending upon the product. Two countries (Ireland and the United Kingdom) charge no VAT on a large number of items deemed to be necessities (food, children's clothing) or socially desirable (books), but most countries impose at least some VAT on all goods and services. Clearly as it exists now, the VAT within the EC is a hodgepodge and is in need of rationalization if the goals of a unified market by 1992 are to be met.

In addition to different numbers of rates and the confusion and competitive advantages that they might cause, there are significant differences in the rates themselves. For example, the same product might be charged at 2 percent VAT in Italy but at 22 percent in Denmark. It might make little sense for a Danish shopper to fly to Italy for this difference on anything except an extremely large purchase; on the other hand, it may be sensible for a Danish shopper living in Schleswig to go across the border to Germany to buy some products being taxed at only 7 percent, or 32 percent of the VAT rate in Denmark. Likewise, a Belgian shopper may find it very worthwhile to make the short trip to Luxembourg to buy a luxury

Table 9.4 VAT rate in European Community (percent)

	Reduced	*Standard*	*Increased*
Belgium	6–17	19	25 33
Denmark	–	22	–
France	5.5–7	18.6	33 33
Germany	7	14	–
Greece	6	18	36
Ireland	10	25	–
Italy	2.9	18	38
Luxembourg	3.6	12	–
Netherlands	6	20	–
Portugal	8	16	30
Spain	6	12	33
United Kingdom	–	15	–

item at 12 percent VAT as contrasted to the 33 percent charged in Belgium. The close proximity of many European countries makes eliminating these tax advantages crucial for the success of the EC's goal of fair competition among the members.[3]

The European Commission has made proposals for the reform of the VAT and for its uniform application in all EC countries. These proposals involve the use of only two tax rates across all twelve countries – a reduced rate on necessities and other socially desirable items in the neighborhood of 6 percent, and a basic rate charged on most items at approximately 16 percent. These rates would mean that consumers (and taxpayers) in some countries would be worse off, and in other countries they would be better off. The big losers would appear to be Spain and Luxembourg, while the big gainers would appear to be residents of Ireland and Denmark. Of course, where taxpayers win governments lose and will have to find other means to generate revenue.

Reforming Excise Taxation

Some of the same questions arise in Europe concerning excise taxation as arise concerning the VAT. There are substantial differences among the several member countries of the EC in the rate at which they tax alcohol, tobacco, gasoline, and diesel fuel. Again, if the purposes of the unified market are to be achieved, then there will have to be closer coordination of excise taxes among the member countries. This coordination may be especially important for gasoline and diesel fuel since it is an intermediate good for so many other industries, especially transportation, and therefore may have a particularly significant impact on the relative competitiveness of the member countries.

Some idea of the magnitude of variation of excise taxes is provided by the data in table 9.5. In this table the excise tax rates charged by the member countries have been converted to European Currency Units (ECUs) based upon the exchange rates at the time (Pearson and Smith, 1988). This conversion provides a common basis for measurement of the real rate of excise tax. With that common basis, we can see the immense differences that exist in excise taxation. The tax on beer in Ireland is over 37 times as great as in Spain or France. Five countries (all large producers of wine) have no tax on wine at all, while Denmark levies a tax that is almost 52 times as great as that of France, and a tax on spirits that is 75 times as great as that levied by Greece. The differences for taxes on petroleum products

Table 9.5 Variations in excise taxes in the European Community

	Beer[a]	*Wine*[a]	*Spirits*[b]	*Gasoline*[a]
Belgium	0.13	0.33	3.76	0.25
Denmark	0.71	1.57	10.50	0.46
France	0.03	0.03	3.45	0.39
Germany	0.07	0	3.52	0.24
Greece	0.10	0	0.14	0.42
Ireland	1.13	2.79	8.17	0.38
Italy	0.17	0	0.69	0.53
Luxembourg	0.06	0.13	2.53	0.20
Netherlands	0.23	0.34	3.89	0.29
Portugal	0.09	0	0.74	0.41
Spain	0.03	0	0.93	0.20
United Kingdom	0.68	1.54	7.45	0.31

[a] ECU/litre.
[b] ECU/bottle (750 ml).
Source: Pearson and Smith, 1988

are not as great, but still there are differences of 100 percent and more between countries – even neighboring countries. Again, the EC has proposed some common rates of excise taxation which will have to be adopted by the member countries (Pearson and Smith, 1988). These proposed rates will fall somewhere in the middle of the existing rates, but are well below the current average tax rates for beer and wine (both produced in large quantities by a number of EC countries). If these rates are adopted, therefore, they will impose differential burdens on families, and on governments, in the member countries.

As dramatic as the differences in excise taxation on everyday purchases may be, the tax differences on autombiles are even more significant (*The European*, 1990). The same automobiles may cost almost three times as much in one country in the European Community as it does in another (see table 9.6). It may make little sense for a consumer to go across a border to purchase just a pack of cigarettes, but it might to save thousands of drachmas or kroner on an automobile. The need to register automobiles may make it difficult for a citizen to actually take advantage of these potential benefits, but it does appear to be easier still to be a citizen of some countries

Table 9.6 Variations in car prices in the European Community (in ECUs)[a]

	Before taxes	*After taxes*
West Germany	10,919	12,448
Luxembourg	11,316	12,673
Belgium	10,397	12,996
France	11,032	14,172
Italy	12,283	14,617
Netherlands	10,554	15,930
United Kingdom	13,219	16,468
Portugal	12,989	19,474
Ireland	13,032	22,353
Denmark	8,926	28,230
Greece	9,549	34,397

[a] Prices for BMW 316i; no information for Spain although taxes approximately the same as France.
Source: *The European*, 1990

than of others, and citizens of the more expensive countries have very large incentives to find ways to reduce their tax costs.

If the proposed changes by the European Community in VAT and in excise taxation are taken together, there may be substantial redistribution of tax burdens among and within the member countries. One analysis for the United Kingdom (see table 9.7) estimated the spending behavior of citizens confronted with new tax rates, and therefore with new prices, for the entire range of goods and services. The average United Kingdom family would spend a great deal more on alcohol and somewhat more on cigarettes and clothes, but would spend less on most other goods and services. The United Kingdom government, on the other hand, would stand to gain approximately £0.8 bn in revenue. Leaving the potential health costs of more smoking and drinking to government aside, this one national government would profit from the proposed indirect tax reforms of the EC. Other countries, such as Ireland and Luxembourg, which have reduced VAT rates on most necessities would also probably have increases in government revenues. On the other hand, countries such as Belgium and Greece, which have used increased VAT rates extensively, might lose revenue under the harmonization plan. For all EC countries, however, this plan for unifying the tax structures has the advantage that if tax changes (especially increases) do occur,

Table 9.7 Effects of EEC tax proposals on tax rates, household spending, and government revenues in the UK, 1988

	Average rate of tax		*Change in household spending (volume) (%)*	*Change in government revenue (£ bn)*
	Existing (%)	*Proposed (%)*		
Food	4	7	−3	+1.5
Alcoholic drinks	71	38	+39	−1.9
Tobacco products	279	241	+4	−0.7
Fuel	0	4	−5	+0.6
Clothing	12	15	+4	+0.5
Petrol	179	213	−12	+0.4
Travel (excluding petrol)	10	12	−9	+0.1
Other goods	11	12	+9	+0.4
Services	10	10	−5	−0.1

Source: Symons and Walker, 1989

they are not directly the result of actions of national politicians, but rather the fault of the more remote government in Brussels.

Beyond integrating excise taxation in the EC, there are growing pressures to increase the rate of excise taxation on products, such as alcohol or tobacco, with known health risks, or at least to index excise taxation so that it does not constitute a declining deterrent to excessive consumption. For example, in the United States, until taxes on beer and wine were increased in 1990, they had not been changed since 1954. During that time, their real levy had decreased by approximately 75 percent. Taxes on spirits were increased in 1987 but still had only about 40 percent of the economic impact they had in 1954. Even with the increases in beer and wine, and spirits excise taxes in 1990, real tax rates are approximately half of what they were during the 1950s. Taxes on tobacco have kept closer pace with inflation, and were also increased in the 1990 budget compromise, but are still somewhat less in real terms than in the 1950s. In addition to producing additional revenue for the federal government which is desperately needed, this change in taxation may have an important health benefit by reducing consumption (see Cook, 1983; Fry and

Pashardes, 1988). The question of the role of excise taxation for health benefits is especially pronounced in the United States, but is also thought to exist in countries such as Sweden, Denmark, and Finland which use extremely high rates of excise taxation to attempt to restrict consumption of what are considered dangerous products.

The Social Security Tax

One of the fastest growing elements of taxation in most of the OECD world has been social insurance contributions – social security in most Anglo-American systems. This tax grew on average 24 percent (as a proportion of GDP) from 1975 to 1985, as compared to an average of 21 percent for all taxes, and a slight decline for the personal income tax (OECD, annual). In 1988, social insurance accounted for an average of almost 25 percent of all tax revenues in the OECD countries. Despite its importance, there has been relatively little discussion of needed reforms in social insurance. The direct linkage with benefits and the perceived absence of special loopholes (but see below) make this tax more palatable to most citizens than the income tax. Further, because it is extracted as a matter of course from the paycheck and no further filling of forms is required, it is a relatively invisible tax (Wilensky, 1976; but see Hanneman, 1982). Despite these positive features – at least politically – there are calls for reform of social insurance taxation. This is true for the social insurance taxes themselves, and perhaps especially for their lack of coordination with the personal income tax.

First, the social security tax itself does in practice have loopholes. The biggest one is that it is a tax on income from employment, but not a tax on all income (Sandford, 1989a). This means that in most countries a wealthy person earning income from stocks and bonds does not pay this tax, while the average working person does. This feature, combined with the tendency for the tax not to be charged above a certain income level, means that social insurance tends to be a regressive tax. Even with attempts to minimize that regressivity, such as the earned income credit in the United States and the elimination of tax below £41 per week in the United Kingdom, the tax remains regressive (Pechman, 1986; Kay and King, 1986). Further, the social security tax is a tax on employment and, when employers must also contribute heavily to the program for each worker, it may deter their hiring additional workers. As taxes go, social security has been popular, but appears to be living off its reputation rather than the reality.

As noted above, personal income taxes and social insurance contributions are usually discussed as very different sorts of tax instruments, but in many respects they function the same way. They are both taxes on the earnings of a citizen, and in most cases they are both extracted from the paycheck of the employee before he or she has an opportunity to spend the money. The two taxes differ in that one is a general tax while the other is earmarked for social purposes. Further, employers usually make some contribution to supplement their employees' social insurance contributions while they must make no such contributions for the personal income tax. Although they are directed at the same tax handle, these two taxes often are inadequately coordinated and the absence of coordination can create anomalies and difficulties for the taxpayer and for governments (Dilnot and Stark, 1989).

Even after being reformed the personal income tax remains a progressive tax. There may not be as many brackets as before, but ther are different rates for the tax depending upon income levels. Social insurance, on the other hand, tends to be flat-rate, or to have an extremely small degree of progression if any. Further, in some countries the social insurance tax is paid only on the first portion of earnings, e.g. up to $51,300 in the United States and £15,860 in the United Kingdom. If the taxpayer is making much more than an average wage, he or she will finish making the "contribution" for the year and will not have to pay any more social insurance taxes. This means that this tax is, in essence, regressive. Further, the social insurance contribution tends to be paid on the first dollar or pound of earnings, while income tax systems do not begin to extract any revenue until the citizen has begun to earn something at or above a minimal income (depending upon family size). Finally, if two members of a family are working they both pay the full amount of social insurance tax, while their earnings would be pooled for the income tax. These two taxes on personal income, levied on essentially the same tax handle, therefore can interact to produce some rather perverse outcomes for individual citizens, and many analysts believe there is a need to better integrate them.

The interactions between the two forms of taxation are further complicated by interactions with the social benefit system (Dixon and Foster, 1988). The eligibility for various benefits – public assistance, housing benefits, etc. – is withdrawn at different income levels in OECD countries, and taxes may be imposed on benefits above a certain level. Social benefits are rarely phased out across a range of income but tend to be either available or unavailable. This means that the individual who earns the marginal pound or franc may sometimes have less disposable income because of taxes beginning to be charged or benefits being withdrawn (Courchene, 1988). This is perhaps especially a problem in the United Kingdom, although changes after 1988 have prevented the marginal tax (including withdrawal of benefits) rates from being 100 percent or more on the working poor. Still, an individual who earns £200 per week is only £29.57 better off than the person who earns only £50 per week when taxes and benefits are taken into account (Kay and King, 1986, 67; Kandur and Keen, 1989). This small amount is perhaps not a sufficient incentive for an individual to work that much harder in the market economy.

At least one country – the Netherlands – has already undertaken a major reform of social security contributions and their linkage to income tax (Netherlands, 1986). There is now a single tax that rolls together the two former taxes. Further, the employer's share of contributions has been virtually eliminated and replaced by a tax on employees so that the true impact of the tax is now more visible to citizens. This also eliminates a disincentive for employers to add new employees, which appears to be the effect of a high social insurance contribution in other countries. The effects of this change in the Netherlands are not yet fully known, but this is one model for the reform of social insurance, and one that has been undertaken in a country with a very large social service sector.

Corporate and Personal Income Taxation

Another issue in tax reform, similar to integrating personal income taxes with social security taxes, is integrating personal income taxes with the corporation tax. The principal problem in this case is that the money that corporations distribute as dividends to their investors may be taxed twice, first as corporate profits, and then again as income for the individual investor. This double taxation means that, everything else being equal, the investor receives less net gain from his or her investments in industry and may try to find some other place to invest, or may simply spend the money. This, in turn, reduces the amount of capital available for industry and may therefore retard economic growth.

The double taxation of corporate profits is a particular problem in the United States, while the tax laws in many other countries exclude dividends from taxable income (McClure, 1979). The justification for taxing dividends as individual income is, like the justification for *not* taxing them, based on incentives for investment. If dividends are taxed twice, corporations may have more incentive to retain profits rather than distributing them to stockholders. At least stockholders would have less incentive to demand higher dividends. The corporation could then retain their profits to reinvest in the firm. The relative strength of the two arguments depends upon whether a lawmaker thinks either individuals or corporations are more likely to invest if they have greater incentives to do so.

Summary

When the tax reform packages were passed in the United States and other OECD countries in the late 1980s many tax policymakers breathed a sigh and thought that their job would be over for a long time. That does not appear to be the case, however, and there is apparently need to reform other parts of the tax system. Governments may have to take a breather to recover their strength (literally and figuratively) before they embark on this next reform exercise, but it does appear to be necessary. Having learned that comprehensive tax reform is possible, it may be difficult to resist public pressures to make the government financial system more efficient, and perhaps even more equitable. In many ways the prickliest nettle has already been grasped, and much of what remains will be less controversial and less dangerous for politicians.

Conclusion

Tax reform was a political call to arms during the 1980s, but to some extent the events of that decade are part of a continuing saga of changes in tax policies (and indeed all public policies). There have been numerous rounds of reform before this one, and some of those reform efforts produced policies that needed to be corrected in this more recent round of change. In fact, there does appear to be a cycle of reform, with comprehensive changes being followed by the accretion of numerous special benefits and then another comprehensive reform. There are still numerous changes needed if tax systems of most industrialized democracies are to fit anything like a characterization of rational financial policies. Tax reform in the 1980s has removed some of the worst anomalies, and some of the most glaring inequities, but there are still numerous problems in all tax systems.

Although really just one part of a continuing saga, the tax reforms of the 1980s are nonetheless remarkable. Rarely has there been such a sweeping set of reforms adopted in so many countries during one decade. Further, in a number of instances these reforms appeared to run counter to all the conventional wisdom about how tax politics, and politics more generally, is practiced. While politicians in the OECD countries did not become saints overnight, many appeared to be attempting to atone for some previous sins. Yet virtue alone will not account for the changes produced; some real political considerations went into them. Rather than the group pressures usually associated with tax politics, however, this appeared to have been more partisan, specifically involving the leadership of extremely influential and/or fortunate leaders such as Reagan, Kohl, Mulroney, and Douglas. Further, there is some sense that the average taxpayer was fed up with business as usual and wanted more equitable treatment in the tax system. The results of the tax reform processes often did not deliver those desirable outcomes, but changes which were marketed politically as providing those benefits to the average citizen did occur. The tax reforms of the 1980s may not mark the beginning of a new age of politics, but they may well signal the end of the old one.

NOTES

1 For example, in the United States, pressure groups for reform were circulating information about large corporations that had been able to escape taxation entirely. See AFSCME, 1988.

2 Some of this effect will probably be mitigated by clever use of the tax laws by the affluent and their advisors once the dynamics of the new law are understood fully. Further, the shifting of spending (and therefore taxing) responsibilities to the states with more regressive tax structures also will eliminate some of the redistributive effect.

3 It should be noted that different rates of sales and excise taxation do not appear to hamper commerce among the states in the United States. The differentials may not be as great as in the EC, but they are still significant. For example, Delaware with no sales tax borders Pennsylvania with a 6 percent sales tax, but the roads are rarely jammed with Pennsylvanians going to purchase goods in Delaware.

Bibliography

Aaron, H. J., and J. A. Pechman (1981). *How Taxes Affect Economic Behavior*. Washington, DC: The Brookings Institution.

Advisory Commission on Intergovernmental Relations (ACIR) (annual). *Changing Public Attitudes on Governments and Taxes*. Washington, DC: ACIR.

Ahlbrandt, R. (1973). Efficiency in the provision of fire services. *Public Choice*, 16, 1–16.

Aldenderfer, M. S., and R. K. Blashfield ((1984). *Cluster Analysis*. Beverly Hills, CA: Sage.

Alestalo, M., and H. Uusitalo (1986). Finland, In P. Flora (ed.), *Growth to Limits*, Vol. 1. Berlin: De Gruyter.

Allingham, M. G., and A. Sandmo (1972). Income tax evasion: A theoretical analysis. *Journal of Public Economics*, 1, 323–38.

Alt, J. E. (1983). The evolution of tax structures. *Public Choice*, 41, 181–222.

Alt, J. E., and J. Turner (1982). The case of the silk-stocking socialist and the calculating children of the middle class. *British Journal of Political Science*, 12, 239–48.

Alworth, J. S. (1987). Taxation and the cost of capital: A comparison of six EC countries. In S. Cnossen (ed.), *Tax Coordination in the European Community*. Boston, MA: Kluwer.

American Federation of State, County and Municipal Employees (AFSCME) (1988). *The Fairest of Them All*. Washington, DC: AFSCME (April).

Anastassopoulos, J.-P. (1985). State-owned enterprises between autonomy and dependency. *Journal of Public Policy*, 5, 521–39.

Andersen, J. G. (1984). Decline of class voting in class voting? Social classes and party choice in Denmark in the 1970s. *European Journal of Political Research*, 12, 243–59.

Anton, T. J. (1980). *Moving Money: An Empirical Examination of Federal Expenditure Patterns*. Cambridge, MA: Oelgeschlager, Gunn & Hain.

Ardant, G. (1971). *L'histoire de l'impôt*. Paris: Fayard.

Arnhem, J. C. M. van, and G. J. Schotsman (1982). Do parties affect the distribution of income?: The case of advanced capitalist democracies. In F. G. Castles (ed.), *The Impact of Parties*. London: Sage.

Arnold, R. D. (1979). *Congress and the Bureaucracy: A Theory of Influence*. New Haven, CT: Yale University Press.

Atkinson, A. B., and J. E. Stiglitz (1980). *Lectures on Public Economics*. New York: McGraw-Hill.

Baker, P., and S. McKay (1990). *The Structure of Alcohol Taxes: A Hangover from the Past?* London: Institute for Fiscal Studies.

Barthelemy, P. (1988). The macroeconomic estimates of the hidden economy: A critical analysis. *Review of Income and Wealth*, 34, 183–208.

Bartlett, B., and T. P. Roth (1983). *The Supply Side Solution*. Chatham, NJ: Chatham House.

Baumol, W. J. (1967). The macroeconomics of unbalanced growth. *American Economic Review*, 57, 415–26.

Beck, M. (1976). The expanding public sector: Some contrary evidence. *National Tax Journal*. 29, 15–21.

Beck, N. (1982). Parties, administrations and American macro-economic outcomes. *American Political Science Review*, 76, 83–93.

Beckerman, W. (1968). *Introduction to National Income Analysis*. London: Weidenfeld and Nicolson.

Beedle, P., and P. Taylor-Gooby (1983). Ambivalence and altruism: Public opinion about taxation and welfare. *Policy and Politics*, 11, 15–39.

Behn, R. D. (1981). The receding mirage of the balanced budget. *The Public Interest*, 67, 118–130.

Beichelt, B., *et al.* (1969). *Steurmentalität und Steurmoral in Grossbritannien, Frankreich, Italien und Spanien*. Cologne: Westdeutscher Verlag.

Beito, D. T. (1989). *Taxpayers in Revolt*. Chapel Hill, NC: University of North Carolina Press.

Bekke, A. J. G. M. (1985). Private organizations and the state: Mutual prisoners blocking de-bureaucratization. In I. T. M. Snellen (ed.) *Limits to Government: The Dutch Experience*. Amsterdam: Kobra.

Bell, D. (1973). *The Coming of Postindustrial Society*. New York: Basic Books.

Bennett, R. J. (1980). *The Geography of Public Finance*. London: Methuen.

Bergwik, S. (1985). The powers of the tax authorities. *European Taxation*, 25, 280–2.

Beyme, K. von (1981). Der liberale Körporatismus als Mittel gegen die Unregierbarkeit? In U. von Alemann (ed.), *Neokörporatismus*. Frankfurt: Campus.

Birnbaum, J. H., and A. S. Murray (1987). *Showdown at Gucci Gulch*. New York: Random House.

Blades, D. (1982). L'économie souterraine et les comptes nationaux. *Perspectives Economiques de l'OCDE*. Paris: OECD, June.

Blais, A., and S. Dion (1987). Les employés du secteur public: Sont-ils differents? *Revue Française de Science Politique*, 37, 76–97.

Blakey, R. G., and G. C. Blakey (1940). *The Federal Income Tax*. New York: Longmans, Green.

Blomquist, N. S., and U. Hansson-Brusewitz (1990). The effects of taxes on male and female labor supply in Sweden. *Journal of Human Resources*, 25, 317–57.

Board of Inland Revenue (annual). *Annual Report*. London: HMSO.

Bogason, P. (1987). Capacity for welfare: Local governments in Scandinavia and the United States. *Scandinavian Studies*, 59, 184–202.

Bornisher, V. (1978). Einkommensungleichheir innerhalb von Ländern in Komparativer Sicht. *Schweizerischer Zeitschrift für Soziologie*, 4, 3–45.

Bos, M., and H. Nelson (1988). Indirect taxation and the completion of the internal market. *Journal of Common Market Studies*, 27, 27–44.

Boskin, M. J. (1984). Federal government deficits: Some myths and realities. *American Economic Review*, Papers and Proceedings, 296–303.

Braak, H. van de (1983). Taxation and tax resistance. *Journal of Economic Psychology*, 3, 95–111.

Bradley, B. (1984). *The Fair Tax*. New York: Pocket Books.

Braun, R. (1975). Taxation, socio-political structure and state-building: Great Britain and Brandenburg-Prussia. In C. Tilly (ed.), *The Formation of Nation States in Western Europe*. Princeton, NJ: Princeton University Press.

Brittain, J. A. (1972). *The Payroll Tax for Social Security*. Washington, DC: The Brookings Institution.

Brittan, S. (1975). The economic consequences of democracy. *British Journal of Political Science*, 5, 129–59.

Brittan, S. (1990). Fiscal virtue under strain. *Financial Times*, July 12.

Broderson, C. (1987). Limits on the international exchange of tax information. *European Taxation*, 27, 171–7.

Brooks, S. (1981). A balanced budget, 1972–1978: What would

have happened? In A. R. Sanderson (ed.), *D. R. I. Readings in Macroeconomics*. New York: McGraw-Hill.

Browning, E. K., and W. R. Johnson (1979) *The Distribution of the Tax Burden*. Washington, DC: American Enterprise Institute.

Buchan, D. (1990). EC ministers to finalise removal of tax barriers. *Financial Times*, July 23.

Buchanan, J. M., and R. E. Wagner (1977). *Democracy in Deficit: The Political Legacy of Lord Keynes*. New York: Academic Press.

Buiter, W. H. (1983). Measurement of the public sector deficit and its implications for policy evaluation and design. *Staff Paper* (International Monetary Fund), 30, 2 (June).

Bunce, V. (1981). *Do New Leaders Make a Difference?*. Princeton, NJ: Princeton University Press.

Caballero, M. A. G. (1986). Portugal 1986 budget: Comprehensive developments affecting individual and corporate tax payers. *European Taxation*, 26, 247–55.

Cagan, P. (1958). The demand for currency relative to the money supply. *Journal of Political Economy*, 66, 303–28.

Cameron, D. (1978). The expansion of the public economy: A comparative perspective. *American Political Science Review*, 72, 1243–61.

Campbell, C. (1983). *Governments Under Stress*. Toronto: University of Toronto Press.

Campbell, C., and G. Szablowski (1979). *The Superbureaucrats: Structure and Behaviour in Central Agencies*. Toronto: Macmillan of Canada.

Canada (1987). *Tax Reform 1987: Sales Tax Reform*. Ottawa: Department of Finance.

Cassell, M. (1989). Poll tax cushion to cost over £1bn. *Financial Times*, October 12.

Castles, F. G. (1982). The impact of parties on public expenditure. In F. G. Castles (ed.), *The Impact of Parties*. London: Sage.

Catsambas, T. (1988). Budget deficits, inflation accounting, and macroeconomic policy: A skeptical note. *Journal of Public Policy*, 8, 49–60.

Cebula, R. (1987). *The Deficit Problem in Perspective*. Lexington, MA: D. C. Heath.

Central Statistical Office (annual). *Statistical Abstract of the United Kingdom*. London: HMSO.

Central Statistical Office (1988). The effects of taxes and benefits on household income. *Economic Trends*, 422, 89–98.

Centro de Investigaciones Sociologicas (1988). *Politica Fiscal, Gasto*

Publico e Impuestos. Estudio 1,752. Madrid: Centro de Investigaciones Sociologicas.

Chapman, B. (1955). *The Prefects and Provincial France*. London: George Allen and Unwin.

Chicoine, D. L., N. Walzer, and S. C. Deller (1989). Representative vs. direct democracy and government spending in the median voter model. *Public Finance*, 44, 225–36.

Citizens for Tax Justice (1988). *The Corporate Tax Comeback*. Washington, DC: Citizens for Tax Justice (September).

Clark, T. N., and L. C. Ferguson (1983). *City Money: Political Processes, Fiscal Strain and Retrenchment*. New York: Columbia University Press.

Cmnd. 6453 (1976). *Local Government Finance*. (The Layfield Report). London: HMSO.

Cnossen, S. (1987a). *Tax Coordination in the European Community*. Deventer: Kluwer.

Cnossen, S. (1987b). VAT and RST: A comparison. *Canadian Tax Journal*, 37, 573–615.

Cnossen, S., and R. M. Bird (1990). *The Personal Income Tax: Phoenix from the Ashes*. Amsterdam: North-Holland.

Collier, D., and R. E. Messick (1975). Prerequisites versus diffusion: Testing alternative models of social security diffusion. *American Political Science Review*, 69, 1299–315.

Comeau, R. L. (1979). Comparing direct spending and tax spending. *Canadian Taxation*, 1, 42–5.

Congressional Budget Office (1990). *The Federal Deficit: Does it Measure the Government's Effect on National Savings?* Washington, DC: CBO (March).

Contini, B. (1979). *Lo sviluppo di un'economia parallela*. Milan: Edizioni di Communita.

Cook, D. (1989). *Poor Law, Rich Law*. Milton Keynes: Open University.

Cook, P. J. (1983). The effect of liquor taxes on drinking, cirrhosis and auto fatalities. In R. J. Zeckhauser and D. Leebart (eds), *What Role for Government?* Durham, NC: Duke University Press.

Coombes, D. *et al.* (1976). *The Power of the Purse*. London: George Allen and Unwin.

Cooper, G. (1979). *A Voluntary Tax?: New Perspectives on Sophisticated Estate Tax Avoidance*. Washington, DC: The Brookings Institution.

Courchene, T. J. (1988). Tax reform: The impact on individuals. In E. A. Carmichael (ed.), *Tax Reform: Perspectives on the White*

Paper. Toronto: C. D. Howe Institute.

Collender, S. E. (1988). *The Guide to the Federal Budget, Fiscal 1989*. Washington D.C.: Urban Institute Press.

Cowart, A. T. (1978). The economic policies of European governments, part II: Fiscal policy. *British Journal of Political Science*, 8, 425–40.

Cronin, T. (1989). *Direct Democracy*. Cambridge, MA: Harvard University Press.

CSR, Inc. (1980). *A General Taxpayer Opinion Survey*. Washington, DC: Internal Revenue Service, Department of the Treasury.

Cullis, J., and A. Lewis (1985). Some hypotheses and evidence on tax knowledge and preferences. *Journal of Economic Psychology*, 6, 271–87.

Cuzan, A. G. (1981). Political profit: Taxing and spending in the hierarchical state. *American Journal of Economics and Sociology*, 40, 265–75.

Dahl, R. (1973). *Polyarchy: Participation and Opposition*. New Haven, CT: Yale University Press.

Dalton, R. J., S. C. Flanagan, and P. A. Beck (1984). *Electoral Change in Advanced Industrial Democracies*. Princeton, NJ: Princeton University Press.

Daly, M., J. Jung., P. Mercier, and T. Schweitzer (1985). The taxation of capital income in Canada: A comparison with Sweden, the United Kingdom, the U.S.A. and West Germany. *Economic Council of Canada Discussion Paper*, No. 289. Ottawa: Economic Council.

Davies, D. G. (1986). *United States Taxes and Tax Policy*. New York: Cambridge University Press.

Dean, P., T. Keenan, and F. Kenney (1980). "Taxpayers'" attitudes to income tax evasion: An empirical study. *British Tax Review*, 1, 28–44.

DeCanio, S. J. (1979). Proposition 13 and the failure of economic policies. *National Tax Journal*, 32, 55–66.

Deleeck, H. (1978). L'effet Mathieu: de la réparation inégale des biens collectifs. *Recherches Sociologiques*, 3, 301–26.

Deleeck, H., J. Huybrechs, and B. Cantillon (1983). *Het Matheuseffect: De ongelijke verdeling van de sociale overheidsuitgaven*. Antwerp: Kluwer.

Delley, J.-D. (1978). *L'initiative populaire en Suisse: Mythe et realité de la démocratie directe*. Lausanne: Edition l'age de l'homme.

De Swaan, A. (1988). *In Care of the State: Health Care, Education and Welfare in Europe and the USA in the Modern Era*. New York: Oxford University Press.

Diamond, J. (1977). The new orthodoxy in budgetary planning: A critical review of the Dutch experience. *Public Finance*, 32, 56–76.

Dilnot, A. and G. Stark (1988). The distributional consequences of Mrs. Thatcher. *Fiscal Studies*, 7, 25–30.

Dilnot, A., and G. Stark (1989). The poverty trap, tax cuts and reform of social security. In A. Dilnot and I. Walker (eds), *The Economics of Social Security*. Oxford: Oxford University Press.

Dixon, D., and C. Foster (1988). Social security constraints on tax reform. *Government and Policy*, 6, 21–40.

Doern, G. B., A. M. Maslove, and M. J. Prince (1988). *Budgeting in Canada*. Ottawa: Carleton University Press.

Donnelly, M. W., and A. Nakamura (1990). LDP bashing: The day Japan's ruling party was defeated. *The Pacific Review*, 3, 163–70.

Douglas, R. O. (1988). Budget 1988, Part I. New Zealand House of Representatives. July 28.

Downs, A. (1960). Why the public budget is always too small in a democracy. *World Politics*, 12, 541–63.

Einhorn, E., and J. Logue (1989). *Modern Welfare States: Politics and Policies in Social Democratic Scandinavia*. New York: Praeger.

Eisenstadt, S. N. (1963). *The Political System of Empires*. New York: The Free Press.

Eismer, T. (1979). Budgets and ballots: The political consequences of fiscal choice. In D. Rae and T. Eismer (eds), *Public Policy and Public Choices*. Beverly Hills, CA: Sage.

Eisner, R. (1985). Fact and fancy on debt and deficits. In H. W. Long (ed.), *Confronting the Budget and Trade Deficits*. Dover, MA: Auburn House.

Elvander, N. (1972a). *Svensk skattpolitik 1945–70*. Stockholm: Rabén & Sjogren.

Elvander, N. (1972b). The politics of taxation in Sweden, 1945–70; A study of the function of parties and organizations. *Scandinavian Political Studies*, 7, 63–82.

Erickson, B. (1983). Sweden's budget system in a changing world. *Public Budgeting and Finance*, 3, 64–80.

The European (1990). Tax gaps must close for fair trade in Europe. *The European*, July 13.

European Taxation (1983). Tax incentives to combat unemployment. *European Taxation* 23, 285–9.

European Taxation (1986). Denmark – political parties agree on tax reform for 1987. *European Taxation*, 26, 10–12.

European Taxation (1988). Results of tax examinations conducted in 1986. *European Taxation*, 28, 26–7.

Evans, P. (1985). Do large budget deficits produce high interest rates? *American Economic Review*, 75, 68–87.

Evans, R. (1990). Limiting the poll tax damage, *Financial Times*, April 20.

Feige, E. L. (1979). How big is the irregular economy? *Challenge*, 22 (Nov.–Dec.), 5–13.

Fessler, P. (1988). State revenue forecasting is no science, *Governing* (November), 64–6.

Fiorina, M. P. (1981). *Retrospective Voting in American National Elections*. New Haven, CT: Yale University Press.

Fiorina, M. P. (1989). *Congress: Keystone of the Washington Establishment*. 2nd ed. New Haven, CT: Yale University Press.

Fisher, R. C., J. H. Goodeeris and J. C. Young (1989). Participation in tax amnesties: The individual income tax. *National Tax Journal*, 42, 1527.

Flora, P. (ed.) (1986a). *Growth to Limits. Vol. I. Sweden, Norway, Finland, Denmark*. Berlin: De Gruyter.

Flora, P. (ed.) (1986b). *Growth to Limits. Vol. II. Germany, United Kingdom, Ireland, Italy*. Berlin: De Gruyter.

Flora, P. *et al.* (1983)., *State, Economy and Society in Western Europe, 1815–1975*. Chicago: St James Press.

Franklin, M. N., and T. T. Mackie (1984). Reassessing the importance of size and ideology in the formation of governing coalitions in parliamentary democracies. *American Journal of Political Science*, 28, 671–92.

Free, L. A., and H. Cantril (1968). *The Political Beliefs of Americans*. New York: Simon and Schuster.

Freeman, J. L. (1965). *The Political Process: Executive Bureau-Legislative Committee Relations*. Garden City, NY: Doubleday.

Freeman, J. L. and J. Stevens (1987). A theoretical and conceptual re-examination of sub-system politics. *Public Policy and Administration*, 2, 137–55.

Frey, B.S., and W. W. Pommerehne (1982). Measuring the hidden economy: Though this be madness, there is method in it. In V. Tanzi (ed.), *The Underground Economy in the United States and Abroad*. Lexington, MA: D.C. Heath.

Frey, B. S., and H. Weck (1983). Estimating the shadow economy: A "naive" approach. *Oxford Economic Papers*, 35, 23–44.

Friedman, B. (1978). Crowding out or crowding in? Economic consequences of financing government deficits. *Brookings Papers on Economic Activities*, 3, 593–654.

Fry, V., and P. Pashardes (1988). *Changing Patterns of Smoking: Are There Economic Causes?* London: Institute for Fiscal Studies.

Gale Research Co. (annual). *Encyclopedia of Associations.* Detroit: Gale Research Co.

Game, C. (1988). The underwhelming demand for the poll tax. *Public Money and Management*, 8 (winter), 55–8.

Garcia, G. (1978). The currency ratio and the subterranean economy. *Financial Analysts Journal*, (November/December), 34, 22–6.

Gaudin, J. and M. Schiray (1984). L'économie cachée en France: Etat du débat et bilan des travaux. *Revue Economique*, 35, 691–731.

Ghekiere, P. (1985). Belgium – 1986 tax law. *European Taxation*, 25, 136–40.

Gillis, M. (1989). *Tax Reform in Developing Countries.* Durham, NC: Duke University Press.

Giovanni, A. (1989). Capital taxation. *Economic Policy*, 9, 345–86.

Gold, S. D. (1981). Homeowner property taxes, inflation and property tax relief. *National Tax Journal*, 34, 167–84.

Good, D. (1980). *The Politics of Anticipation: Making Canadian Federal Tax Policy.* Ottawa: School of Public Administration, Carleton University.

Goode, R. (1984). *Options for Tax Reform: Papers.* Washington, DC: The Brookings Institution.

Gourevitch, P. A., *et al.* (1984). *Unions and the Economic Crisis: Britain, West Germany and Sweden.* Boston, MA: George Allen and Unwin.

Graham, G. (1990). "An Old Tax is a Good Tax." *Financial Times.* Insert on France, June 28.

Gravelle, J. G. (1981). Depreciation policy options. In *Studies in Taxation, Public Finance and Related Subjects. Vol. 5.* Washington, DC: Fund for Public Policy Research.

Gray, J. C., and D. A. Spina (1980). State and local industrial location incentives: A well-stocked candy store. *Journal of Corporation Law*, 5, 517–687.

Gremion, P. (1976). *Le Pouvoir Périphérique: Bureaucrats et Notables dans le Système Politique Français.* Paris: Sueil.

Gretschmann, K., and P. Kenis (1990). Political exchange: a theoretical reconsideration and some epirical evidence from taxation. In B. Marin, (ed.), *Governance and Generalized Exchange: Self-*

Organizing Policy Networks in Action. Amsterdam: North-Holland.

Grunow, D., F. Hagner, and F.-X. Kaufmann (1978). *Steuerzahler und Finanzamt*. Frankfurt: Campus.

Guess, G., and K. Koford (1984). Inflation, recession and the federal budget deficit (or, blaming economic problems on a statistical mirage). *Policy Sciences*, 17, 385–430.

Gutman, P. M. (1977). The subterranean economy. *Financial Analysts Journal*, 33, (November/December), 217–25.

Gysen, S. (1980). Program law, 1979–1980. *European Taxation*, 20, 350–64.

Hadenius, A. (1981). *Spelet om Skatten*. Stockholm: Norstedts.

Hadenius, A. (1985). Citizens strike a balance: Discontent with taxes, content with spending. *Journal of Public Policy*, 5, 349–63.

Hadenius, A. (1986). *A Crisis of the Welfare State?* Stockholm: Almqvist & Wiksell.

Hagemann, R. P., B. R. Jones, and R. B. Montador (1988). Tax reform in OECD countries: Motives, constraints and practice. *OECD Economic Studies*, 10, 185–226.

Hall, P. A. (1986). *Governing the Economy: The Politics of State Intervention in Britain and France*. New York: Oxford University Press.

Hall, P. A. (1987). The evolution of economic policy under Mitterrand. In G. Ross, S. Hoffman, and S. Malzacher (eds.), *The Mitterand Experiment*. New York: Oxford University Press.

Hanneman, R. A. (1982). Taxation and economic management in Western nations. *The Annals*, 459, 123–33.

Hansen, S. B. (1980). Taxes, benefits and public opinion. In B. S. Rundquist (ed.), *Political Benefits*. Lexington, MA: Lexington Books.

Hansen, S. B. (1983). *The Politics of Taxation: Revenue Without Representation*. New York: Praeger.

Haskel, B. (1987). Paying for the welfare state: Creating political durability. *Scandinavian Studies*, 59, 221–53.

Hastings, E. H., and P. K. Hastings (1984). *Index to International Public Opinion, 1982–1983*. Westport, CT: Greenwood Press.

Hastings, E. H. and P. K. Hastings (1988). *Index to International Public Opinion, 1986–1987*. Westport, CT: Greenwood Press.

Hausman, J. A. (1981). Labor supply. In H. J. Aaron and J. A. Pechman (eds.), *How Taxes Affect Economic Behavior*. Washington, DC: The Brookings Institution.

Haycraft, J. (1985). *Italian Labyrinth*. Harmondswoth: Penguin.

Headey, B. (1978). *Housing Policy in the Developed Economy*. London: Croom Helm.

Heidenheimer, A., H. Heclo, and C. T. Adams (1989). *Comparative Public Policy* 3rd. ed. New York: St Martin's.

Heller, W. W. (1966). *New Dimensions of Political Economy*. Cambridge, MA: Harvard University Press.

Heroverwegingen (1980–1). *Samenvattend eidnrapport: Rijksbegroting*. Tweede Kamer der Staten-General, 16625, 2–3.

Hesse, J. J. (1978). *Politikverflechtung im föderativen Staat*. Baden-Baden: Nomos.

Hibbs, D. and H. J. Madsen (1981). Public reactions to the growth of taxation government and government expenditure. *World Politics*, 33, 413–35.

Hills, J. (1984). What is the public sector worth? *Fiscal Studies*, 5, 26–39.

Hirschman, A. O. (1970). *Exit, Voice and Loyalty*. Cambridge, MA: Harvard University Press.

HMSO (1981). *The Government's Expenditure plans. 1981–2 to 1983–4*. (Cmd 8175). London: HMSO.

Hochstein, M. (1985). Tax ethics: Social values and noncompliance. *Public Opinion*, 7 (February/March), 11–14.

Hoffmann, S. (1956). *Le Mouvement Poujade*. Paris: A. Colin.

Hogwood, B. W. (1987). *From Crisis to Complacency: Shaping Public Policy in Britain*. Oxford: Oxford University Press.

Hogwood, B. W., and B. G. Peters (1983). *Policy Dynamics*. Brighton: Wheatsheaf.

Hogwood, B. W., and B. G. Peters (1985). *The Pathology of Public Policy*. Oxford: Oxford University Press.

Holberton, S. (1990). IoD proposes reform of taxes on benefits. *Financial Times*, February 5.

Howard, M. A. (1989). State tax and expenditure limitations: There is no story. *Public Budgeting and Finance*, 9, 83–90.

Howe, G. (1982). Tax policy in the United Kingdom. *European Taxation*, 22, 379–82.

Hulten, C. R. (1981). *Depreciation, Inflation and the Taxation of Income from Capital*. Washington, DC: The Urban Institute.

Institute for Fiscal Studies (1988). *Who Pays Indirect Taxes?* London: Institute for Fiscal Studies.

Internal Revenue Service (1984). *Taxpayer Attitudes Study*. Washington, DC: Internal Revenue Service.

Internal Revenue Service (1986). *Service Programs Are Not Effectively Promoting Taxpayer Compliance.* Washington, DC: Internal Revenue Service, Internal Audit Division.

Internal Revenue Service (1988). *Statistics of Income, 1987, Individual Income Tax Returns.* Washington, DC: Government Printing Office.

Internal Revenue Service (annual). *Annual Report of the Commissioner of Internal Revenue.* Washington, DC: Government Printing Office.

International Labour Office (1988). *Costs of Social Security.* Geneva: International Labour Office.

International Monetary Fund (1987). *Government Finances Yearbook.* Washington, DC: IMF.

International Monetary Fund (monthly). *International Financial Statistics.* Washington, DC: IMF.

International Monetary Fund (annual). *Government Finance Statistics Yearbook.* Washington, DC: International Monetary Fund.

Inter-Parliamentary Union (1986). *Legislatures of the World.* New York: Facts on File.

Ishi, H. (1989). *The Japanese Tax System.* Oxford: Clarendon Press.

Ishi, H. (1990). Taxation and public debt in a growing economy: The Japanese experience. *Hitosubashi Journal of Economics*, 31, 122.

Jackson, I. A. (1986). Amnesty and creative tax administration. *National Tax Journal*, 39, 317–24.

Jackson, J. H. (1990). *Restructuring the GATT System.* London: Chatham House Papers.

Jaffre, J. (1986). Front national: la relève protestaire. In E. Dupoirier and G. Grundberg (eds), *Mars 1986: La Drôle de Défaite de la Gauche.* Paris: Presses universitaires de France.

Jeffe, D., and S. B. Jeffe (1988). Proposition 13 Ten Years Later. *Public Opinion*, 11 (May/June) 18–19, 57–88.

Jenkins, R. (1968). *Mr. Balfour's Poodle.* New York: Chilmark Press.

Johnson, R. (1990). Report urges "Green" taxes in budget, *Financial Times*, January 26.

John, P. (1989). *Introduction of the Community Charge in Scotland.* London: Policy Studies Institute.

Johnston, M., and D. Wood (1986). Right and wrong in public and private life. In R. Jowell (ed.), *British Social Attitudes, 1986.* Aldershot: Gower.

Johnstone, D. (1975). *A Tax Shall be Charged.* London: Civil Service College.

Jones, C. O. (1986). *An Introduction to the Study of Public Policy*, 3rd. ed. Monterey, CA: Brooks/Cole.

Jones, C. O. (1989). *The Reagan Legacy*. Chatham, NJ: Chatham House.

Jordan, A. G. (1981). Iron triangles, woolly corporatism and elastic nets: Images of the policy process. *Journal of Public Policy*, 1, 95–123.

Kaldor, N. (1955). *An Expenditure Tax*. London: Allen & Unwin.

Kandur, R. and M. Keen (1989). Poverty, incentives and linear income tax. In A. Dilnot and I. Walker (eds), *The Economics of Social Security*. Oxford: Oxford University Press.

Katzenstein, P. E. (1985). *Small States in World Markets*. Ithaca, NY: Cornell University Press.

Kay, J. A. (1990). Tax Policy: A survey. *The Economic Journal*, 100, 18–75.

Kay, J. A., and M. A. King (1986). *The British Tax System*, 4th ed. Oxford: Oxford University Press.

Keating, M. (1988). Does regional government work?: The experience of Italy, France and Spain. *Governance*, 1, 184–209.

Keman, H. (1982). Securing the safety of the nation state. In F. G. Castles (ed.), *The Impact of Parties*. London: Sage.

Kesti, J. (1987). Norway: Tax reform under discussion. *European Taxation*, 27, 297–300.

Key, V. O. (1966). *The Responsible Electorate*. Cambridge, MA: Belknap Press.

Keynes, J. M. (1936). *The General Theory of Employment, Interest and Money*. New York: Harcourt, Brace.

Kinder, D. R., and D. R. Kiewit (1979). Economic discontent and political behavior: The role of personal grievances and collective economic judgment in congressional voting. *American Journal of Political Science*, 23, 495–527.

King, A. (1975). Ideas, institutions and the policies of governments: A comparative analysis, *British Journal of Political Science*, 5, 409–24.

King, J. A. (1990). Tax policy: A survey. *The Economic Journal*, 100, 18–75.

Kingdon, J. W. (1984). *Agendas, Alternatives and Public Policies*. Boston, MA: Little, Brown.

Klepper, S., and D. Nagin (1989). The role of tax preparers in tax compliance. *Policy Sciences*, 22, 167–94.

Klingman, D. (1980). Temporal and spatial diffusion in the comparative analysis of social change. *American Political Science Review*, 74, 123–37.

Köhler, P. A., F. Zacher, and M. Partington (1982). *The Evolution of Social Insurance*. London: Frances Pinter.

Kohut, A. and L. Hugick, (1989). Taxes and federal programs. *Gallup Report*, October, 4–6.

Kone, S. L., and R. F. Winters (1989). Taxes and voting: Electoral retribution in the American states. Mimeo, Hanover, NH, Dartmouth College.

Kosters, M. H., and M. N. Ross (1988). A shrinking middle class? *The Public Interest*, 90, 3–27.

Krasner, S. D. (1978). *Defending the National Interest: Raw Materials Investments and U.S. Foreign Policy*. Princeton, NJ: Princeton University Press.

Kristensen, O.P. (1982). Voter attitudes and public spending: Is there a relationship? *European Journal of Political Research*, 10, 35–52.

Kristensen, O. P. (1984). On the futility of the demand approach to public sector growth. *European Journal of Political Research*, 12, 309–24.

Kristensen, O. P. (1986). Tax structure and public spending – or how the electorate is deceived into paying for bigger public spnding than it really wants. *Scandinavian Political Studies*, 9 (new series), 317–36.

Ladd, H. F., and C. Tideman (1981). *Tax and Expenditure Limitations*. Washington, DC: Urban Institute Press.

Laegreid, P. (1988). *Oljebyråkrati: Om Statsadministrajonen i ein Oljealder*. Oslo: TANO.

Lafferty, W. M., and O. Knutsen (1984). Leftist and rightist ideology in social democratic states: An analysis of Norway in the midst of the conservative resurgence. *British Journal of Political Science*, 14, 345–67.

Landau, M. (1969). The rationality of redundancy. *Public Administration Review*, 29, 346–58.

Laney, L. O., and T. D. Willett (1983). Presidential politics, budget deficits, and monetary policy in the United States, 1960–76. *Public Choice*, 40, 53–70.

Laurin, U. (1986). *På Heder och samvete: Skattefuskets orsaker och utbredning*. Stockholm: Nordstets.

Leonard, H. B. and R. J. Zeckhauser (1987). Amnesty, enforcement and tax policy, in L. H. Summers (ed.), *Tax Policy and the Economy*. Cambridge, MA: MIT Press.

Lepelmeier, D. (1979). *Soziale Sicherung und Parafiscalität*. Frankfurt: Peter D. Lang.

Leu, R. E., R. L. Frey, and B. Buhmann (1985). Taxes, expenditures and income distribution in Switzerland. *Journal of Social Policy*, 14, 341–60.

Levi, M. (1988). *Of Rule and Revenue*. Berkeley, CA: University of California Press.

Levine, C. H. (1978). Organizational decline and cutback management. *Public Administration Review*, 38, 316–25.

Levine, C. H., and P. L. Posner (1981). The centralizing effects of austerity on intergovernmental relations. *Political Science Quarterly*, 96, 67–85.

Lewis, A. (1979). An empirical assessment of tax mentality. *Public Finance*, 2, 245–57.

Lewis, A. (1980). Public awareness of the fiscal connection. In C. T. Sandford (ed.), *Control of Public Expenditure*. Bath: Bath University Centre for Fiscal Studies, Occasional Paper no. 14.

Lewis, A. (1982). *The Psychology of Taxation*. Oxford: Martin Robertson.

Lewis, A. (1983). Public expenditure: Perceptions and preferences. *Journal of Economic Psychology*, 4, 159–67.

Lewis, A., and D. Jackson (1985). Voting preference and attitudes toward public expenditure. *Political Studies*, 33, 457–66.

Lewit, E. M., and D. Coate (1982). The potential for using excise taxes to reduce smoking. *Journal of Health Economics*, 1, 121–46.

Lieberman, M. (1989). *Privatization and educational choice*. New York: St Martin's.

Linder, S. H., and B. G. Peters (1989). Instruments of government: Perceptions and contexts. *Journal of Public Policy*, 9, 35–58.

Linklater, M., and D. Leigh (1986). *Not With Honour*. London: Sphere.

Lipietz, A. (1983). *La Crise*. Paris: Serios.

Lipsky, M. (1980). *Street-Level Bureaucracy: Dilemmas of the Individual in Public Services*. New York: Russell Sage Foundation.

Listhaug, O., and A. H. Miller (1985). Public support for tax evasion: Self-interest or symbolic politics. *European Journal of Political Research*, 13, 265–82.

Long, J. E., and J. B. Caudill (1987). The usage and benefits of paid tax return preparation. *National Tax Journal*, 40, 37–45.

Lord, G. (1973). *The French Budgetary Press*. Berkeley, CA: University of California Press.

Lowery, D. (1982). Public choice when services are costs: The divergent case of assessment administration. *American Journal of Political Science*, 26, 57–76.

Lowery, D. (1984). Tax equity under conditions of fiscal stress: The case of the property tax. *Publius*, 14, 55–65.

Lowery, D. (1985). The Keynesian and political determinants of unbalanced budgets: U.S. fiscal policy from Eisenhower to Reagan. *American Journal of Political Science*, 29, 428–60.

Lowery, D. and L. Sigelman (1981). Understanding the tax revolt: Eight explanations. *American Political Science Review*, 75, 963–74.

Lund, M. S. (1989). Between welfare and the market: Loan guarantees as a policy tool. In Lester M. Salamon (ed.), *Beyond Privatization: The Tools of Government Action*. Washington, DC: The Urban Institute Press.

Macafee, K. (1980). A glimpse of the hidden economy in national accounts. *Economic Trends*, 316, 81–7.

McCaffrey, J. (1984). Canada's envelope budget: A strategic management system. *Public Administration Review*, 44, 316–23.

McClure, C. (1979). *Must Corporate Income be Taxed Twice?* Washington, DC: The Brookings Institution.

McClure, C. E. (1987). *The Value-Added Tax: Key to Deficit Reduction?* Washington, DC: American Enterprise Institute.

McDaniel, P. R., and S. S. Surrey (1985). *International Aspects of Tax Expenditures: A Comparative Study*. Boston: Kluwer.

McKie, A. B. (1988). Sorry saga of Canadian sales taxation. *European Taxation*, 28 (June), 68–71.

McKie, A. B. (1990). Sales tax reform – continued. *European Taxation*, 30 (March), 72–4.

McKie, M., and W. Beck (1990). Amazing grace: Tax amnesties and compliance. *National Tax Journal*, 43, 2337.

McQuaig, L. (1987). *Behind Closed Doors*. Markham, Ont: Viking.

Maguire, M. (1986). Ireland. In P. Flora (ed.), *Growth to Limits*, Vol. 2. Berlin: De Gruyter.

Maier, C. S. (1975). *Recasting Bourgeois Europe: Stabilization in France, Germany and Italy*. Princeton, NJ: Princeton University Press.

Manley, I. F. (1970). *The Politics of Finance: The House Ways and Means Committee*. Boston, MA: Little, Brown.

March, J. G., and J. P. Olsen (1989). *Rediscovering Institutions*. New York: The Free Press.

Marlow, M. L., and D. Joulfaian (1989). The determinants of off-budget activity of state and local governments. *Public Choice*, 63, 113–23.

Maslove, A. M. (1979). The other side of public expenditure: Tax expenditures in Canada. In G. B. Doern and A. M. Maslove, *The Public Evaluation of Government Spending*. Montreal: Institute for Research on Public Policy.

Maslove, A. M. (1989). *Tax Reform in Canada: The Process and Impacts*. Halifax, NS: Institute for Research on Public Policy.

Mathews, J. T. (1990). Energy tax options. *Washington Post National Weekly Edition*, August 6–12.

Mathews, R. L. (1984). *The Mythology of Taxation*. Sydney: George Allen and Unwin.

Meltsner, A. J. (1971). *The Politics of City Revenue*. Berkley, CA: University of California Press.

Midwinter, A., and C. Mair (1987). *Rates Reform: Issues, Arguments and Evidence*. Edinburgh: Mainstream.

Mieszkowski, P. (1969). Tax incidence theory: The effects of taxes on the distribution of income. *Journal of Economic Literature*, 7, 1103–24.

Mills, G. B., and J. L. Palmer (1983). *The Deficit Dilemma: Budget Policy in the Reagan Era*. Washington, DC: The Urban Institute Press.

Mitchell, B. R. (1980). *European Historical Statistics, 1750–1975*. New York: Facts on File.

Modigliani, A., and F. Modigliani (1987). The growth of the federal deficit and the role of public attitudes. *Public Opinion Quarterly*, 51, 459–80.

Moore, W. S., and R. G. Penner (1980). *The Constitution and the Budget*. Washington, DC: American Enterprise Institute.

Morrissey, O. (1990). Scanning the alternatives before taxing with consensus: Lessons for policymaking from the Irish wealth tax. *Administration* (Dublin), 38, 24–40.

Morrissey, O., and S. Steinmo (1987). The influence of party competition on post-war UK tax rates. *Policy and Politics*, 15, 195–206.

Moyer, H. W., and T. E. Josling (1990). *Agricultural Policy Formation: Politics and Process in the EC and USA*. Ames, Iowa: Iowa State University Press.

Mucciaroni, G. (1990). Public choice and the politics of comprehensive tax reform. *Governnance*, 3, 1–32.

Muhl, W. (1986). Plans for a fundamental tax reform in the Federal Republic of Germany. *European Taxation*, 26, 203–15.

Murray, A. (1986a). Individuals' top rate would plunge to 28 percent: Curbs offset benefits to wealthy. *Wall Street Journal*, 18 August.

Murray, A. (1986b). Industry-by-industry review of tax bills shows loss of special deductions offsets rate cut. *Wall Street Journal*, 19 August.

Musgrave, R. A. (1969). *Fiscal Systems*. New Haven, CT: Yale University Press.

Musgrave, R. A. (1989). *Strengthening the Progressive Income Tax: The Responsible Answer to America's Budget Problem*. Washington, DC: Economic Policy Institute.

Musgrave, R. A., and P. B. Musgrave (1984). *Public Finance in Theory and Practice*. New York: McGraw-Hill.

National Tax Administration – Japan (1988). Report on costs of collecting taxes. Cited in Ishi, 1989.

Netherlands (1986). *A Step Toward Simplicity*. The Hague: Ministry of Finance.

Newton, K. (1980). *Balancing the Books: Financial Problems of Local Government in West Europe*. London: Sage.

Nielsen, H. J. (1976). The uncivic culture: Attitudes toward the political system in Denmark and vote for the Progress Party. *Scandinavian Political Studies*, 11 (old series), 147–56.

Niskanen, W. A. (1978). Deficits, government spending, and inflation. *Journal of Monetary Economics*, 4, 591–602.

Norway (annual). *Statistiska Årsbok*. Oslo: Statistisk Sentralbyrå.

Nozick, R. (1974). *Anarchy, the State and Utopia*. New York: Basic Books.

Oakland, W. H. (1979). Proposition 13: Genesis and consequences. *National Tax Journal*, 32, 387–407.

Oates, W. E. (1977). *The Political Economy of Fiscal Federalism*. Lexington, MA: Lexington Books.

OECD (1984). *Tax Expenditures: A Review of the Issues and Country Practices*. Paris: OECD.

OECD (1985) *Social Expenditures 1960–1990: Problems of Growth and Control*. Paris: OECD.

OECD (1986). *The Personal Income Tax Under Changing Economic Circumstances*. Paris: OECD.

OECD (1988a). *The Taxation of Fringe Benefits*. Paris: OECD.

OECD (1988b). *Ageing Populations: The Social Policy Implications*. Paris: OECD.

OECD (1989). *Revenue Statistics of Member Countries 1965–1988*. Paris: OECD.

OECD (1990a). *The Personal Income Tax Base*. Paris: OECD.

OECD (1990b). *Taxpayers' Rights and Obligations*. Paris: OECD.

OECD (1990c). Financing public expenditures through user charges.

OECD Occasional Papers in Public Management. Paris, OECD (May).

OECD (monthly). *OECD Economic Outlook*. Paris: OECD.

OECD (annual a). *Revenue Statistics of OECD Member Countries* Paris: OECD.

OECD (annual b). *National Accounts of OECD Member Countries*. Paris: OECD.

Office of Management and Budget (annual). *Budget of the United States Government*. Washington, DC: Government Printing Office.

O'Higgins, M. (1985). Inequality, redistribution and recession: The British experience, 1976–82. *Journal of Social Policy*, 14, 279–308.

O'Higgins, M., G. Schmaus, and G. Stephenson (1989). Income distribution and redistribution: A microdata analysis for seven countries. *Review of Income and Wealth*, 35, 107–31.

Olsen, J. P. (1983). *Organized Democracy*. Oslo: Universitetsforlaget.

Olson, M. (1965). *The Logic of Collective Action*. Cambridge, MA: Harvard University Press.

Olson, M. (1982). *The Rise and Decline of Nations: Economic Growth, Stagflation, and Social Rigidities*. New Haven, CT: Yale University Press.

Oppenheimer, B. I. (1980). Policy effects of US House reform: Decentralization and the capacity to resolve energy issues. *Legislative Studies Quarterly*, 5, 5–29.

Orvik, N. (1975). *Norway's No to Europe*. Pittsburgh, PA: International Studies Association.

Ott, D. J. and A. F. Ott (1977). *Federal Budget Policy*. 3rd. ed. Washington, DC: The Brookings Institution.

Owen, S. (1985). Publish and be praised. *European Taxation*, 25, 247–53.

Paddison, R. (1983). *The Fragmented State*. Oxford: Basil Blackwell.

Page, B. I. (1983). *Who Gets What From Government?* Berkeley, CA: University of California Press.

Paul, A. (1975). *The Politics of the Property Tax*. Lexington, MA: Lexington Books.

Peacock, A. T. and J. Wiseman (1961). *The Growth of Public Expenditure in the United Kingdom*. Princeton, NJ: National Bureau of Economic Research.

Pearson, M. and S. Smith (1988). 1992: Issues in indirect taxation. *Fiscal Studies*, 9(4), 26–35.

Pechman, J. E. (1980). *What Should be Taxed, Income or Expenditure?* Washington, DC: The Brookings Institution.

Pechman, J. (1983). U.S. Individual Income Tax. In S. Cnossen (ed.), *Comparative Tax Studies*. Amsterdam: North-Holland.

Pechman, J. A. (1986). *Who Paid the Taxes, 1966–85?* Washington, DC: The Brookings Institution.

Pechman, J. A. (1987a). Tax reform prospects in Europe and Canada. *Brookings Review*, 5, 11–19.

Pechman, J. A. (1987b). *Federal Tax Policy*, 5th ed. Washington, DC: The Brookings Institution.

Pechman, J. A. (1988). *World Tax Reform: A Progress Report*. Washington, DC: The Brookings Institution.

Pechman, J. A. (1989). *Tax Reform, The Rich and the Poor*. 2nd ed. Washington, DC: The Brookings Institution.

Pen, J. (1987). Expanding budgets in a stagnating economy: The experience of the 1970s. In C. S. Maier (ed.), *Changing Boundaries of the Political*. Cambridge: Cambridge University Press.

Penner, R. G. (1982). Forecasting budget totals: Why can't we get it right? In M. J. Boskin and A. Wildavsky (eds), *The Federal Budget: Economics and Politics*. San Francisco, CA: Institute for Contemporary Studies.

Penniman, C. (1980). *State Income Taxation*. Baltimore: Johns Hopkins University Press.

Perez-Diaz, V. (1987). Economic policies and social patterns in Spain during the transition. In I. Scholten (ed.), *Political Stability and Neo-Corporatism*. London: Sage.

Peters, B. G. (1972). Economic and politics effects on the development of social expenditures in France, Sweden and the United Kingdom. *Midwest Journal of Political Science*, 16, 225–39.

Peters, B. G. (1974). Income Redistribution in France, Sweden and the United Kingdom, *Political Studies*, 22, 311–23.

Peters, B. G. (1980). Choices in taxation policy. In T. R. Dye and V. Gray (eds), *The Determinants of Public Policy*. Lexington, MA: Lexington Books.

Peters, B. G. (1981). The problem of bureaucratic government. *Journal of Politics*, 43, 56–82.

Peters, B. G. (1989). *The Politics of Bureaucracy*. New York: Longmans.

Peters, B. G. (1990). *European Politics Reconsidered*. New York: Holmes and Meier.

Peters, B. G. (1991). The European bureaucrat. In A. Blais and S. Dion (eds), *The Budget-maximizing Bureaucrat*. Pittsburgh: University of Pittsburgh Press.

Peters, B. G., and M. O. Heisler (1983). Thinking about public sector growth. In C. L. Taylor (ed.), *Why Governments Grow: Measuring Public Sector Size*. Beverly Hills, CA: Sage.

Peters, B. G., and B. W. Hogwood (1985). In search of the issue-attention cycle. *Journal of Politics*, 47, 238–53.

Peters, B. G., and B. W. Hogwood (1988). Births, deaths and metamorphoses in the U.S. federal bureaucracy, 1933–83. *American Review of Public Administration*, 18, 119–34.

Peters, B. G., and C. D. Klingman (1980). Politics, economics and the development of public expenditures in Scandinavia. *Political Studies*, 28, 279–308.

Peterson, P. E., and M. Rom (1988). Lower taxes, more spending, and budget deficits. In C. O. Jones (ed.), *The Reagan Legacy: Promise and Performance*. Chatham, NJ: Chatham House.

Pettenati, P. (1979). *Le travail illegal et non declaré en Italie*. Paris: OECD.

Phillips, K. (1990). *The Politics of Rich and Poor*. New York: Random House.

Piachaud, D. (1980). Taxation and social security. In C. Sandford, C. Pond, and R. Walker (eds), *Taxation and Social Policy*. London: Heinemann.

Plesko, G. A. (1988). The accuracy of government forecasts and budget projections. *National Tax Journal*, 41, 483–502.

Pliatzky, L. (1989). *The Treasury Under the Tories*. Oxford: Blackwell.

Pommerehne, W. W. (1978). Institutional approaches to public expenditure, *Journal of Public Economics*, 9, 255–80.

Pommerehne, W. W., and F. Schneider (1978). Fiscal illusion, political institutions, and local public spending. *Kyklos*, 31, 381–408.

Portney, K. E. (1980). State tax preference-orderings and partisan control of government. In L. Wade and W. Samuels (eds), *Taxing and Spending Policy*. Lexington, MA: D. C. Heath.

Pressman, J. L., and A. Wildavsky (1973). *Implementation*. Berkeley: University of California Press.

Preston, D. A. (1987). Taxation and benefit reform 1985. *Public Sector*, 9(3), 29–32.

Public Opinion (1987). Opinion round-up. *Public Opinion*, 9, (March/April), 24–9.

Puchala, D. (1984). *Fiscal Harmonization in the European Community*. London: Frances Pinter.

Rabushka, A. (1988). The tax reform act of 1986: Concentrated costs, diffuse benefits – an inversion of public choice. *Contemporary Political Issues*, 6, 50–64.

Radian, A. (1980). *Resource Mobilization in Poor Countries*. New Brunswick, NJ: Transaction.

Ranney, A. (1978). The year of the referendum, *Public Opinion*, 1 (November/December), 26–7.

Ranney, A. (1981). Referendums and Initiatives, 1980. *Public Opinion*, 4 (April/May), 23–6.

Ranney, A. (1985) Referendums and initiatives 1984. *Public Opinion*, 7 (December/January), 15–17.

Ranney, A. (1987). Referendums and initiatives 1986. *Public Opinion*, 9 (January/February), 44–6.

Ranney, A. (1989). Referendums. *Public Opinion*, 11 (January/February), 15–18.

Ratner, S. (1942). *Taxation and Democracy in America*. New York: John Wiley & Sons.

Rawls, J. (1972). *A Theory of Justice*. Cambridge, MA: Harvard University Press.

Reese, T. J. (1980). *The Politics of Taxation*. Westport, CT: Quorum.

Reich, S. (1990). *The Fruits of Fascism: The Pre-War Roots of Prosperity*. Ithaca, NY: Cornell University Press.

Rein, M., and L. Rainwater (1986). *Public/Private Interplay in Social Protection*. Armonk, NY: M. E. Sharpe.

Reissert, B., and G. F. Schaefer (1985). Centre–periphery relations in the Federal Republic of Germany. In Y. Meny and V. Wright (eds), *Centre–Periphery Relations in Western Europe*. London: Allen & Unwin.

Rhinow, R. A. (1984). Grundprobleme der schweizerischen Demokratie. *Zeitschirift für Schweizerishes Recht*, 103, 117–271.

Ridley, N. (1990). Resource management in the UK customs and excise. *Optimum*, 20(3), 21–37.

Rizzo, I., and A. Peacock (1987). Government debt and growth in public spending. *Public Finance*, 42, 283–96.

Roberts, P. C. (1984). *The Supply-Side Revolution*. Cambridge, MA: Harvard University Press.

Robertson, J. D. (1989). Coalition leadership, government stability and macroeconomic policy in European democracies. In B. D. Jones (ed.), *Leadership and Politics*. Lawrence, KS: University of Kansas Press.

Robinson, A., and C. Sandford (1983). *Tax Policy-making in the United Kingdom*. London: Heinemann.

Rogaly, J. (1990). Not everyone is ready for Labour. *Financial Times*, May 5.

Roig, C. (1964). Theorie et realité de la décentralisation. *Revue française de science politique*, 14, 463–4.

Roley, V. V. (1981). The financing of federal deficits: An analysis of crowding out. *Economic Review* (Federal Reserve Bank of Kansas City), July–August, 16–29.

Romer, T. and H. Rosenthal (1979). The elusive median voter. *Journal of Public Economics*, 12, 143–70.

Romer, T. and H. Rosenthal (1982). Median voters or budget maximizers: Evidence from school expenditure referenda. *Economic Inquiry*, 26, 536–78.

Rose, R. (1976). The priorities of governments. *European Journal of Political Research*, 4, 247–89.

Rose, R. (1980). Misperceiving public expenditure: Feelings about "cuts". *Studies in Public Policy*, 67. Glasgow: Centre for the Study of Public Policy, University of Strathclyde.

Rose, R. (1985). Maximizing tax revenue while minimizing political costs. *Journal of Public Policy*, 5, 289–320.

Rose, R. (1989). The mysterious logic governing charges for public services. *The Independent*, September 13.

Rose, R. (1990). Inheritance before choice in public policy. *Journal of Theoretical Politics*, 2, 263–91.

Rose, R., and Karran, T. (1986). *Taxation by Political Inertia*. London: Macmillan.

Rose, R., and B. G. Peters (1978). *Can Government Go Bankrupt?* New York: Basic Books.

Rose, R. *et al.* (1985). *Public Employment in Western Nations*. Cambridge: Cambridge University Press.

Roseveare, H. (1969). *The Treasury*. New York: Columbia University Press.

Rytohonka, R. (1985). Finland-Tax Reform, *European Taxation*, 25, 196–8.

Samuelson, M. (1990). Carbon tax urged to cut pollution. *Financial Times*, February 1.

Sandford, C. (1986). The costs of paying tax. *Accountancy*, 97 (November), 108–11.

Sandford, C. (1988). Tax reform in the United Kingdom and Ireland. *Government and Policy*, 6, 53–70.

Sandford, C. (1989a). The next tax for reform. *Accountancy*, 103 (February), 20–1.

Sandford, C. (1989b). What it costs to pay taxes. *Accountancy*, 103 (February), 140–2.

Sandford, C. *et al.* (1981). *Costs and Benefits of VAT*. London: Heinemann.

Sandford, C., and A. Robinson (1988). Indirect taxation: Back to the drawing board. *Accountancy*, 102 (August), 84–6.

Santerre, R. (1986). Representative versus direct democracy: A Tiebout test of relative performance. *Public choice*, 48, 55–63.

Savage, J. D. (1988). *Balanced Budgets and American Politics*. Ithaca, NY: Cornell University Press.

Savas, E. S. (1987). *Privatization: The Key to Better Government* Chatham, NJ: Chatham House.

Sawyer, M. (1976). Income distribution in OECD countries. *OECD Economic Outlook, Occasional Studies* (July).

Sbragia, A. (1979). The politics of local borrowing: A comparative analysis. *Studies in Public Policy*, no. 37, Glasgow: Centre for the Study of Public Policy, University of Strathclyde.

Sbragia, A. (1986). Capital markets and central–local politics in Britain. *British Journal of Political Science*, 16, 311–40.

Scharpf, F. W. (1987). *The Political Calculus of Inflation and Unemployment in Western Europe*. Cambridge, MA: Center for European Studies, Harvard University.

Schick, A. (1986). Controlling nonconventional expenditures: Tax expenditures and loans. *Public Budgeting and Finance*, 6, 3–19.

Schick, A. (1988). Micro-budgetary adaptations to fiscal stress in industrialized countries. *Public Administration Review*, 48, 523–33.

Schmitter, P. C. (1974). Still the century of corporatism? *Review of Politics*, 36, 85–131.

Schmitter, P. C. (1981). Interest intermediation and regime governability in contemporary Western Europe and North America. In S. Berger (ed.), *Organized Interests in Western Europe*. Cambridge: Cambridge University Press.

Schmitter, P. C., and G. Lehmbruch (1979). *Trends Toward Corporatist Intermediation*. London: Sage.

Schmolders, G. (1969). *Steuernorm und Steuerwirklichkeit*. Cologne: Westdeutscher Verlag.

Schneider, F. (1984). Public attitudes toward economic conditions and their impact on government behavior. *Political Behavior*, 6, 211–27.

Schneider, F. (1987). Public attitudes toward economic conditions and their impact on government behavior. In H. Eulau and M. Lewis-Beck (eds), *Economic Conditions and Electoral Outcomes*. New York: Agathon.

Schneider, H. (1989). Schweizerische Steuerpolitik und EG 92. *Zeitschrift für Volkswirtschaft und Statistik*, 24, 421–39.

Scholzman, K. L., and J. L. Tierney (1986). *Organized Interests and American Democracy*. New York: Harper and Row.

Scott, G., P. Bushnell and N. Sallee (1990). Reform of the core public sector: New Zealand experience. *Governance*, 3, 138–67.

Sears, D. O., and J. Citrin (1985). *Tax revolt: Something for nothing in California*. Enlarged ed. Cambridge, MA: Harvard University Press.

Seldon, A., *et al.* (1979). *Tax Avoision: The Economic, Legal and Moral Interrelationships Between Avoidance and Evasion*. London: Institute of Economic Affairs.

Seldon, A. (1981). *Charge!* London: Temple Smith.

Seldon, A. (1986). *The Riddle of the Voucher*. London: Institute of Economic Affairs.

Shackleton, M. (1990). *Financing the European Community*. London: Frances Pinter.

Shibata, H., and Y. Kimura (1986). Are government deficits the cause of growth in government expenditures. In B. P. Herber, (ed.), *Public Finance and Public Debt*. Detroit: Wayne State University Press.

Slemrod, J. (1990). Optimal taxation and optimal tax systems. *Journal of Economic Perspectives*, 4, 157–78.

Slemrod, J., and N. Sorum (1984). The compliance costs of U.S. individual taxpayers. *National Tax Journal*, 37, 461–74.

Smeeding, T., M. O'Higgins and L. Rainwater (1989). *Poverty, Inequality and Income Distribution in Comparative Perspective*. Hemel Hempstead: Harvester.

Smith, A. (1990) Stakes are high in a popularity test for Thatcher and the poll tax. *Financial Times*, April 17.

Smith, R. S. (1990). Factors affecting savings, policy tools and tax reform: A review. *IMF Staff Papers*, 37, 1–70.

Smith, T. W. (1989). Inequality and Welfare. In R. Jowell, S. Witherspoon and L. Brook (eds), *British Social Attitudes: Special International Report*. Aldershot; Gower.

Södersten, B. (1989). The political economy of tax reform in Sweden. *Political Life in Sweden*. New York: Swedish Information Service, May.

Song, Y., and T. E. Yarborough (1978). Tax ethics and taxpayer attitudes. *Public Administration Review*, 38, 442–52.

Spicer, M. W., and S. B. Lundstet (1976). Understanding tax evasion. *Public Finance*, 31, 295–305.

Stathopoulos, G. N. (1982). 1982 Budget. *European Taxation*, 22, 129–31.

Steinmo, S. (1989). Political institutions and tax policy in the United States, Sweden and Britain. *World Politics*, 61, 500–35.

Steuerle, C. E. (1986). *Who Should Pay for Collecting Taxes?* Washington, DC: American Enterprise Institute.

Stewart, M. (1971). *Keynes and After*. Harmondswoth: Penguin.

Stiglitz, J. E. (1976). The corporation tax. *Journal of Public Economics*, 5, 303–12.

Strumpel, B. (1969). The contribution of survey research to public finance. In A. T. Peacock (ed.), *Quantitative Analysis in Public Finance*. New York: Praeger.

Surrey, S. S. (1957). The Congress and the tax lobbyist: How special tax provisions get enacted. *Harvard Law Review*, 70, 1145–82.

Surrey, S. S. (1973). *Pathways to Tax Reform*. Cambridge, MA: Harvard University Press.

Surrey, S. S. and P. R. McDaniel (1985). *Tax Expenditures*. Cambridge, MA: Harvard University Press.

Swedish Institute (1986). *The Swedish Tax System*. Stockholm: The Swedish Institute.

Symons, E. and I. Walker (1989). The revenue and welfare effects of fiscal harmonization for the UK. *Oxford Review of Economic Policy*, 5(2), 61–75.

Taggart, P. (1990). Green parties and the politics of ecologism: Green parties as new social movement organizations. Unpublished Paper, Department of Political Science, University of Pittsburgh.

Tait, A. A. (1988). *Value-Added Tax: International Practice and Problems*. Washington, DC: International Monetary Fund.

Tanzi, V. (1969). *The Individual Income Tax and Economic Growth: An International Comparison*. Baltimore: Johns Hopkins University Press.

Tarschys, D. (1983). The scissors crisis in public finance. *Policy Sciences*, 15, 205–24.

Tarschys, D. (1984). Good cuts, bad cuts: The need for expenditure analysis in decremental budgeting. *Scandinavian Political Studies*, 7 (new series), 241–59.

Tarschys, D. (1985). Curbing public expenditure: Current trends. *Journal of Public Policy*, 5, 23–67.

Tarschys, D. (1988). Tribute, tariffs, taxes and trade: Changing sources of government revenue. *British Journal of Political Science*, 18, 1–20.

Taylor, R. (1989). Swedes are vague on tax changes – but they're sure they don't like them. *Financial Times*, November 2.

Taylor, R. (1991). Sweden's tax shake-out. *Financial Times*, 4 January.

Taylor-Gooby, P. (1982). Two cheers for the welfare state. *Journal of Public Policy*, 2, 319–46.

Taylor-Gooby, P. (1985). *Public Opinion, Ideology and State Welfare*. London: Routledge and Kegan Paul.

Taylor-Gooby, P. (1989). The role of the State. In R. Jowell, S. Witherspoon, and L. Brook (eds), *British Social Attitudes: Special International Report*. Aldershot: Gower.

Theil, S. van (1988). Harmonisation of turnover taxes in the EC: Towards the internal market without frontiers. *European Taxation*, 28, 77–84.

Towe, C. M. (1991). The budgetary control and fiscal impact of government contingent liabilities. *IMF Staff Papers*, 38, 109–34.

US Bureau of the Census (1979). *Historical Statistics of the United States*. Washington, DC: Government Printing Office.

The Wall Street Journal (1991). Tax report. April 17.

Thirsk, W. R. (1987). The value-added tax in Canada: Saviour or siren song? *Canadian Public Policy*, 13, 259–83.

Tobin, J. (1984). A Keynesian view of the budget deficit. *California Management Review*, 26, 7–14.

Travers, T. (1989). The community charge and other financial charges. In J. Stewart and G. Stoker (eds), *The Future of Local Government*. London: Macmillan.

Trettner, B. (1974). *Die Steuermentalität: Ein internationaler Vergleich*. Berlin: Duncker and Humblot.

Tufte, E. R. (1978). *Political Control of the Economy*. Princeton, NJ: Princeton University Press.

UNESCO (1988). *Statistical Yearbook*. Paris: Unesco.

USGAO (1989). *Accessibility, Timeliness and Accuracy of IRS' Telephone Assistance Program*. Washington, DC: US General Accounting Office, Feb. 2 (GAO/GGD–89–30).

USGAO (1990). *Monitoring the Accuracy and Administration of IRS' 1989 Test Call Survey*. Washington, DC: US General Accounting Office, Jan. 4. (GAO/GGD–90–36).

Vaillancourt, F. (1989). The compliance costs of taxes on business and individuals: A review of the evidence. *Public Finance*, 42, 395–414.

Veljanovski, C. (1987). *Selling the State: Privatisation in Britain*. London: Weidenfeld and Nicolson.

Verdier, J. M. (1988). The President, Congress and tax reform: Patterns over three decades. *The Annals*, 499, 114–23.

Verney, D. (1957). *Parliamentary Reform in Sweden, 1866–1921*. Oxford: Clarendon Press.

Virmani, A. (1988). Tax reform in developing countries: Issues, policies and information gaps. *Public Finance*, 43, 19–38.

Vogel, J. (1974). Taxation and public opinion in Sweden: An interpretation of recent survey data. *National Tax Journal*, 27, 499–514.

Wagner, M. (1982). Einkommenshierarchien. In M. Fischer-Kowalski and J. Bucek (eds), *Lebensverhaltnisse in Österreich*. Frankfurt: Campus Verlag.

Wagner, R. E. (1976). Revenue structure, fiscal illusion and budgetary choice. *Public Choice*, 31, 45–61.

Wagner, R. E., R. D. Tollinson, A. Rabushka, and J. T. Noonan (1982). *Balanced Budgets, Fiscal Responsibility and the Constitution*. Washington, DC: Cato Institute.

Wagstaff, J. V. (1965). Income tax consciousness under withholding. *Southern Economic Journal*, 32, 73–80.

Warren, A. (1980). Would a consumption tax be fairer than an income tax? *Yale Law Journal*, 89, 1081–124.

Weaver, R. K. (1988). *Automatic Government: The Politics of Indexation*. Washington, DC: The Brookings Institution.

Webb, E. J., D. T. Campbell, R. D. Schwartz, and L. Saechrest (1966). *Unobtrusive Measures: Nonreactive Research in the Social Sciences*. Chicago: Rand McNally.

Webber, C., and A. Wildavsky (1986). *A History of Taxation and Expenditure in the Western World*. New York: Simon and Schuster.

Wheeler, J. C. (1982). Tax Reform Proposals, *European Taxation*, 22, 389–93.

Wickman, J. (1977). *Fremskridtspartiet: Hvem og Hvorfor?* Copenhagen: Akademisk Forlag.

Wicks, J. H. (1965). Taxpayer compliance costs from the Montana personal income tax. *Montana Business Quarterly*, 1, 37–42.

Wildavsky, A. (1977). Doing better and feeling worse: The political pathology of health policy. In J. H. Knowles (ed.), *Doing Better and Feeling Worse*. New York: Norton.

Wildavsky, A. (1980). *How to Limit Government Spending*. Berkeley, CA: University of California Press.

Wildavsky, A. (1985). Keeping kosher: The epistemology of tax expenditures. *Journal of Public Policy*, 5, 413–31.

Wildavsky, A. (1986). *Budgeting: A Comparative Theory of Budgetary Processes*. Rev. ed. New Brunswick, NJ: Transaction.

Wildavsky, A. (1987). *Budgeting: A Comparative Theory of the Budgetary Process*. 2nd. ed. New Brunswick, NJ: Transaction Books.

Wilensky, H. L. (1976). *The "New Corporatism", Centralization and the Welfare State*. Beverly Hills: Sage.

Wilkes, J. (1980). *The Politics of Taxation*. Sydney: Hodder and Stoughton.

Wilkinson, M. (1986). Tax expenditure and public expenditure in the UK. *Journal of Social Policy*, 15, 23–49.

Willis, J. R. M., and P. J. W. Hardwick (1978). *Tax Expenditures in the United Kingdom*. London: Institute for Fiscal Studies.

Wilson, J. Q. (1980). The politics of regulation. In J. Q. Wilson (ed.), *The Politics of Regulation*. New York: Basic Books.

Wilson, J. Q. (1989). *Bureaucracy*. New York: Basic Books.

Winer, S. L. (1983). Some evidence on the effect of the separation of spending and taxing decisions. *Journal of Political Economy*, 91, 126–40.

Witte, J. F. (1985). *The Politics and Development of the Federal Income Tax*. Madison, WI: University of Wisconsin Press.

Woolley, F. and J. Le Grand (1990). The Ackroyds, the Osbornes and the Welfare State. *Policy and Politics*, 18, 17–30.

Index